Research Methods and Analysis

RESEARCH METHODS AND ANALYSIS
SEARCHING FOR RELATIONSHIPS

Michael H. Walizer
University of Illinois

Paul L. Wienir
Western Michigan University

Harper & Row, Publishers
New York Hagerstown San Francisco London

Sponsoring editor: Dale Tharp
Project editor: Penelope Schmukler
Designer: Gayle Jaeger
Production supervisor: Stefania J. Taflinska
Compositor: P & M Typesetting, Incorporated
Printer and binder: Halliday Lithograph Corporation
Art studio: Danmark & Michaels, Inc.

RESEARCH METHODS AND ANALYSIS: Searching for Relationships
Copyright © 1978 by Michael H. Walizer and Paul L. Wienir

LIBRARY OF CONGRESS CATALOGING IN PUBLICATION DATA
Walizer, Michael H
    Research methods and analysis.

    Includes index.
    1. Research—Methodology. 2. Research—Statistical methods. I. Wienir, Paul L., joint author. II. Title.
Q180.55.M4W34   001.4'2   78-1541
ISBN 0-06-046879-3

CONTENTS IN BRIEF

CONTENTS

/ next semester

As teachers of research methodology and statistics to both under-graduate and graduate students, we have become increasingly con-vinced that the common practice of presenting separate courses in "methods" and in "stat" does a disservice to students. We have found that many of the methodological considerations in the con-duct of research on human subjects rest on the statistical founda-tions used for the analysis of data. Likewise, many of the statistical procedures available have been developed because of the nature of research on human subjects, and unless seen in this light, seem rather meaningless. We have also observed that the common prac-tice of offering such courses late in an undergraduate's career also does a disservice to students. In virtually all college departments, the content of most courses after an introductory sequence relies heavily on research that has been produced in the respective fields. Students who are not equipped with a basic understanding of re-search procedures and analysis cannot critically and intelligently confront the required readings in such courses. Rather, students must rely solely on the interpretation of these works by teachers who then serve as the "ministers" of knowledge. Historically, texts in separate courses have not integrated scientific research method-ology and techniques of analysis. In addition, they have been written in rather formal terms, with technical examples that do not relate to the students' own experiences and aptitudes. The language in such texts tends to put students off, or even frighten them.

With these convictions in mind, we have attempted to write a text which not only integrates methodological considerations with statis-tical processes, but is written in such a way that beginning under-graduate students can appreciate how the elements of scientific re-search fit together. This text is written as though two friends were having a discussion on the folkways, customs, practices, and tech-nologies of the researcher—albeit that one friend is more knowl-edgable than the other. The vocabulary and sentence structure is purposely simple. This is done not only to suit the needs of early un-dergraduate students, but because many of the principles of method-ology and statistics can functionally be understood better if pre-sented in simple English.

In the area of research, most texts contain the same basic materi-als. Presentation, organization, and articulation separate good texts from poor texts. Some texts are written more for the elite student and/or the teachers of such courses, and some texts are written in such a simplistic manner and with such brevity that only superficial understanding is possible. In this text we have tried to write in a style that appeals to all students. Additionally, we have tried to in-clude sufficient detail, depth, and description of actual research practices and considerations to interest all students from the wea-kest to the strongest. The material is organized so that one chapter flows to the next. Each chapter is preceded by a list of terms, along with their meaning, which may be new to the students. Specific objectives are also provided for students to guide reading and to serve as a basis for evaluation. At the end of each chapter a summary section reviews the major ideas in the chapter and places the various topics in perspective. Each chapter is followed by a set of exercises and problems that not only covers the material in the chapter but provides an opportunity for students to integrate material from various chapters. The exercises are also designed to spur the students' creativity and imagination by going beyond the obvious material in the chapter. In addition to the problems and exercises a "project" assignment is provided at the end of each chapter. Students and instructors who desire to supplement the learning experience can use these assignments to carry on a small-scale study. Project assignments are coordinated with the content of each chapter.

Manuscripts of this text have been extensively class tested. With the help of student comments, many refinements which probably could have resulted only from classroom experience have been made. These refinements have encompassed the problems and exercises as well as the body of the text. While care has been taken to use informal language, this has not been at the sacrifice of thoroughness. Students who master the material in this book will not only have a sound preparation for graduate studies but, more importantly, they will be able to be informed citizens and consumers. People are increasingly being presented with research findings and statistical analyses. Newspapers, magazines, and even television are presenting research findings to a public that may or may not be trained in the skills necessary to interpret such information wisely. As more of society is being guided by research results, the consumer of information must become more knowledgable about the procedures used to conduct such research and the techniques used to present such findings. Becoming an informed consumer of scientifically produced information may make the difference between having to trust the experts to make all the decisions in our life versus our being able to actively take a part in the determination of our future.

We are grateful to the Literary Executor of the late Sir Ronald A. Fisher, F.R.S., to Dr. Frank Yates, F.R.S. and to Longman Group Ltd., London, for permission to reprint Table IV from their book *Statistical Tables for Biological, Agricultural and Medical Research.* (6th edition, 1974.).

As authors, we take full responsibility and credit for the strengths and weaknesses of this text. However, we must acknowledge those who have had an impact on our thinking and our writing. We thank those authors who have preceded us and whose thoughts and orientations have guided us. Although we have not always made page-by-page citations, we know that certain of our presentations and examples have been heavily influenced by other texts. We also thank our teachers for their effort in imparting a love for research. Most of all we thank our students who have helped us to shape the form of our presentation. While many of these people go nameless, there are some that must be mentioned by name. Robert Herriott and Hubert M. Blalock, respectively, were the teachers who stand out in our minds. Subhash Sonnad and Milt Brawer are colleagues who have co-taught courses with us from which some of the materials in this book have been refined. Barbara McFadden has been our typist extraordinaire. Finally, our wives, Nancy and Linda, have put up with us while we have toiled. We sincerely hope that they all share our pride in this text.

Michael H. Walizer, *Chicago*
Paul L. Wienir, *Kalamazoo*

CHAPTER 1
THE QUEST FOR UNDERSTANDING

After studying this chapter, students should be able to:

1. Cite examples and explain all the various ways of knowing.

2. Discuss how science is a unique way of knowing when compared to the alternative ways.

3. Give examples and participate in the process of conceptualizing phenomena.

4. Define and identify concepts that are variables.

5. Define, identify, and construct simple theories.

6. Determine when a condition is a necessary one versus a sufficient one.

7. Give a simple definition of association.

8. Enumerate and discuss the importance of each of the conditions necessary for causation.

9. Discuss why science can neither "prove" nor "disprove."

10. Provide a simple definition of the term "generalization."

11. Say why replication is important to the scientific way of knowing.

12. List and discuss the four major reasons why science is a tentative way of knowing.

13. Feel comfortable with the assumptions of science and the discussion of the methods of science.

Association Mutual patterned change between two variables; that is, a systematic change in one variable can be observed to be related to a systematic change in another variable.

Authority Knowing gained by referring to another person or source.

Common sense Using memory, culture, and personal experience to gain knowledge.

Conceptualization The process of discovering, inventing, or constructing meaningful ways to interpret and classify what is observed.

Generalization The process of going beyond observations made at one point in time to making more general statements.

Intuition Using unconscious connection to gain knowledge.

Necessary condition A condition that must be present for a subsequent event to occur.

Reciprocal cause Two variables supposedly causing each other at the same time.

Replication Repeating research in another time and place under similar circumstances.

Revelation A way of knowing through personal experience, often transcendental in nature.

Science Making probability statements on the basis of systematic observations.

Sufficient condition A condition that, if present, will always result in a subsequent event.

Theories Sets of cause-and-effect statements that show how concepts are related to one another. (Technically, sets of interrelated propositions.)

Variable A concept for which the values, states, or types may differ from time to time, place to place, person to person, or unit to unit.

1. INTRODUCTION

We hold several beliefs about students of research methods and analysis that have affected the organization of this text. By sharing them with you we hope to enhance your ability to do well in courses that make use of this text. We believe that many students who read this book will never become researchers. Most students who have heard about courses in research methodology and/or statistics approach such courses with some apprehension about their perceived weaknesses in or dislike of "math," and nearly all students enter these courses trusting "science" and valuing many of the products and consequences of scientific research. Rather than just having to *accept* teachers' interpretations of research typically presented in most classes, students would prefer to become knowledgeable enough to become "informed consumers" of research results.

This is a rather complex set of circumstances to deal with in writing a textbook on the research process, but we have attempted to deal with them in an informative and pleasant manner. Our goal has been to provide the framework in which learning about the research process can take place. Not so much so that students can *become* researchers, but rather so that students will be able to *understand* researchers and the products they produce. Although the materials presented will provide basic training for those students who may wish to pursue research careers in social science, education, business, or behavioral science, the major purpose is to help produce informed consumers of research. The stress is on *becoming* expert enough in the research process to make some independent judgments. This would include the ability to assess the usefulness of scientific research.

Becoming expert necessitates a certain amount of exposure to the major areas of research, including the analysis of data. The premise of this text is that teaching research methodology without teaching analysis of data is misleading and possibly confusing. It is for this reason that we have attempted to incorporate basic understandings of statistics and analysis along with the other aspects of research methodology. With the advent of the computer age, we are increasingly being exposed to statistical analyses—not only scientific research, but analyses presented in newspapers, magazines, and on television. Many economic, political, and social policies and practices are based on data; and, like it or not, if we do not have some understanding of these techniques, we are somewhat at the mercy of those who purportedly do. We feel very strongly that simple statistics can be presented in a way that even those students who do not "like" math can grow to understand, even enjoy, statistics. The types of analyses presented in this text require only simple arithmetic to compute, and any problems with "numbers" will seem small when compared to the satisfaction that goes with becoming expert in this area.

There is one problem that seems to go along with acquiring the technical sophistication associated with becoming expert. Perhaps an analogy might prove helpful. For a moment imagine what it would be like to accompany some first-semester architecture students on an assigned tour of some houses. The first house seems to have a roof that does not drain well. Another house has siding which does not insulate well or fit in with the surrounding terrain. One student notices that one dwelling would be expensive to keep up. The point is that everything they see would be criticized on some basis or another. Foundations, landscaping, floor plans, use of windows, and even things we might not have thought about will come under the same harsh scrutiny. What *we* would see as beautiful houses and lovely neighborhoods are rejected time after time by these students for some "architectural" flaws. It soon becomes obvious that these students, while appearing to be sophisticated in architecture, have lost their perspective. Good, livable, relatively efficient dwellings all seem to be treated negatively.

However, suppose that these same students have been asked by an instructor to assist in shopping for a new home to live in. Although the teacher and students will still see the same type of flaws as in the previous tour, houses will be viewed in a relative context. They will be seen in terms of social tradition, relative economic conditions, the materials available at the time the building was constructed, what the fashions of the times are, and a host of other considerations which result in compromising theoretically strict architectural excellence for a reasonable place to call home.

In the process of becoming expert, it is fairly easy to lose perspective. The ability to use relative judgment and to be technically sophisticated at the same time requires much more than just being able to criticize at will.

Just as the architecture students first went on a tour, we will take you on a "tour" of social research methods and analysis. We hope that as a result of this tour you will gain the necessary knowledge to be able to criticize all of the aspects of planning and conducting scientific research. But we hope that because of the way the material is presented, along with your class work, you can maintain perspective. Researchers are limited by the social conditions, economic circumstances, the procedures and techniques presently available, and other factors which lead to compromises with perfection. Researchers often have to settle for a product that is less perfect than they are satisfied with or that they are capable of doing themselves. But just as architects must sometimes go on living and designing dwellings that remain just satisfactory until they are able to find or do better, so too social scientists feel that they must "live with" some pieces of research even though they are imperfect. And just as architects could not destroy all buildings that are in some way imperfect, researchers do not totally discount all scientific findings that have some identifiable limitation. A relative perspective must be gained and maintained as a part of the human condition.

While stating this, we must hasten to point out that we want you to recognize good scientific research and to appreciate it—and perhaps even to make decisions with it. However, we also want to introduce you to the role of the scientist. Science demands that researchers never be satisfied, always find flaws, criticize, and never permanently accept anything. This is the paradox of the working social scientist – to be continuously questioning and criticizing research and yet to respect and use it as effectively as possible.

2. WAYS OF KNOWING

Staying with the analogy of architecture students helping an instructor shop for a home, we might suspect that these students will use several techniques to evaluate a house. There are many techniques other than science that are used to reach conclusions. First, we will take a brief look at these other processes and then focus on the scientific way of knowing. Each of the alternative ways of knowing explored below are legitimate observation–decision-making processes that may lead to conclusions about or knowledge of the world we experience. Although they may overlap somewhat, we feel that each may be posed as an alternative to the scientific way of knowing. It is important to note that there is no way any of the various techniques presented can be discredited or supported by an alternate technique. Each is a different kind of approach to knowledge with different customs for deciding what is correct or true. This means that there is no way to "test" which technique is "right." Each technique, including science, must start with basic premises and assumptions that are "given" as opposed to "proved." Indeed, none of these assumptions are "provable," and that is what is meant by "given." We will attempt to sketch a brief picture of each of these ways of knowing without bias, but this is difficult when one is steeped in a scientific tradition. Of course, we shall then raise questions about each perspective from a scientific point of view.

Revelation

Revelation is coming to know through some sort of personal experience. One way our student friends might choose a house is to simply "know" which one is the best. Conclusions drawn by revelation have the quality of "aha!" or instant wisdom gained all at once.
Revelation may occur as a result of divine experiences, prayer, spiritual encounters, written words, mystical experiences, magic, and other such immediate occurrences. Such knowledge or information usually has a sacred, absolute character, and is often held as unchallengable. Of course such revelations might be true or they might be false. But how are we to externally determine the accuracy of such knowledge? Using revelation to pick a home might result in

choosing one with extensive termite damage, an inadequate heating system or a perfectly good home. It is also possible that one student may choose one house by revelation and another might choose a different house by the same technique. Which revelation should be followed? Very often knowledge gained through revelation is associated with types of religious phenomena. Since the processes of revelation are internal to individuals, there is no way for a third party to observe the process of decision making *or* to question the outcome of revelation.

Authority

Other students may take a different approach to deciding on an appropriate house. These students may consult a copy of *Better Homes and Gardens* as the ultimate word in residential design or some students may have faith in their mother's opinion about houses.

As external observers, we can question the basis of this trust and faith. An authority is designated as such because of some kind of experience in the field. However, the qualifications of authorities are seldom questioned. That is, we seldom investigate the source of an authority's expertise or examine the information that the authority may have used to reach conclusions. Indeed, the central aspect of authority is that it is unquestioned. Knowledge is given *from* the authority *to* the novice or lay person, and there is often the implicit idea that the novice does not have the ability to adequately examine the knowledge or decision of the authority. This is the reason to rely on authority in the first place.

Tradition, training, certification, and reputation all may enter into the identification of authority. Wise persons of a tribe may be authorities by tradition. Nationally known scholars may be authorities via their reputations. Medical specialists may be given the status of authorities because of their advanced training and degrees. The interplay between authority and science is an interesting one to explore. Science has its authorities in many various fields. What they say is often taken at face value and one often sees researchers citing authority for their theories, methods, or conclusions. The key difference between citing authority in science and using authority as a way of knowing is that supposedly other scientists have the ability and desire to question the basis of scientific authority. In general, however, knowledge gained by authority is vested more in the authority itself as opposed to the way in which the authority became an authority. Using scientific authority will be discussed further in Chapter 5.

Intuition

A third way of knowing is often call intuition. Architecture students using this form of knowing may simply drive around a neighborhood until some house catches their eye – until they see a house that they "feel" is the right one. We presume that what this really means is that without spelling it out explicitly, the students notice some things about the house and/or neighborhood which indicate that the house is probably a good one. Although they may not have consciously worked it through, they may make these connections simply by "feeling" them. Intuitive feelings seem to be internally generated as a result of these "connections." These feelings are different from the feelings produced by revelation because revelations are thought to be, at least in part, externally produced.

Thus, intuition may be nothing more than unconscious connections which give the observers a feeling about what they see or experience. We must emphasize again that knowledge gained from intuition may be accurate. The familiar observation of the presumed effectiveness of women's intuition is a reflection of this fact. The problem with this type of knowing is similar to the previous two types. How are we to know whether it is right? Since one who makes decisions based on intuition is not aware of how connections are made to arrive at knowledge, how can we examine those connections or observe the process of coming to know? The problem with intuition is that the unconscious connections that are made may be inaccurate or inappropriate and there is no way to externally evaluate them.

Everyday experience – common sense

One way of knowing, which is often said to be very desirable and is held up as a very accurate path to knowledge, is called common sense. If our architectural students attempt to make a decision on a home based on common sense, they would consult their own memory for factors they have experienced in the past to be good indicators of desirable housing. They may have lived in a brick house and found that this type of house is more airtight than wood frame houses, or they may have read that six inches of insulation saves heating costs. Using common sense may involve intuition and authority as well as experience. Common sense often gives us sayings to go by; such as "all politicians are crooked." Even more often, common sense gives us contradictory sayings, such as "birds of a feather flock together," and "opposites attract." Such sayings may be useful to explain or justify events that occur, but they are often only useful *after* the events occur. If two people who have similar habits and characteristics get married, we may use the first saying. However, if two people who seem to be different in many ways get married, we might use the second saying to explain their marriage. Because common sense is sometimes good only after the fact, it may not be useful for decision making. As in the case of revelation, authority, and intuition, we must ask, "How can we trust what we tentatively conclude?" In the case of common sense, the problem is that what to one person seems very obvious and a matter of "common sense" may seem ridiculous to another person. The question often becomes—"Whose common sense should we believe?"

Science

The process of gaining knowledge through science differs from the previous ways of knowing on several important dimensions. Although each of the previous ways may have led the architecture students to a conclusion about which house to purchase, students using science will be unable to tell the instructor which house to buy. They may be willing to make specific statements about particular houses, but *these statements will always be probabilistic in nature*. That is, none of the statements will be firm and absolute. They will be tentative in nature, such as copper tubing plumbing will *probably* give better service than galvanized pipe. They will likely be in the form of predictions based on similar observations in other settings.

A scientist first conceptualizes what features of the problem should be examined. *Conceptualization* involves the process of discovering, inventing, or constructing meaningful ways to define, describe, and interpret what is observed. For example, rather than seeing a set of tubes with connections and valves filled with a liquid, we would refer to the concept of "plumbing." In the case of selecting a home, we might consider and examine such concepts as foundations, floor plans, maintenance features, neighborhood, and so on. Note that each of these features or concepts can be different in different houses. That is, they are variable. Not all houses have the same type of foundation or siding or neighborhood. Concepts that may have different values, scores, types, or conditions are called *variables*. These differences may occur at different times, in different places, or between different people. (Variables will be discussed at length in Chapter 2.) Scientists would say that "the variables to be examined are selected" instead of saying that "the features or characteristics to be considered are determined." After selecting the important variables, the scientist must then determine how to assess, observe, examine, or measure each. If the scientist cannot determine how to observe or measure the variable in question, the scientist cannot make researchable statements about the concept. Scientists go out of their way to make rules to minimize subjectivity and personal bias. Finally, the scientist is never content with any conclusion—conclusions are always tentative. This is because the scientist is always open to the possibility that, with further observation, conclusions previously drawn might be changed. Throughout the remainder of this chapter we shall spell out the reasons why scientists believe that all their conclusions must be tentative.

There are three crucial assumptions underlying the scientific approach to knowing. First, reality is knowable. This implies that there is an order to things that occur in our environment and that, with study, we can comprehend them. Second, our senses can give us accurate and reliable information about what goes on around us. Through our senses of touch, sight, smell, hearing, and vision we can meaningfully experience (observe) our environment. Sometimes phenomena are only observable indirectly, with the aid of measuring instruments or devices. Such aids may be necessary to magnify or clarify our sensory perceptions. Finally, information gained through our senses is the best, perhaps only, way to achieve objectivity. The stress on objectivity goes hand in hand with the assumption that gaining information through our senses offers the best chance of being objective.

An important part of the assumption that the world is knowable, and that through our senses we can know it, is the idea of cause and effect. Scientists do not believe that things "just happen," or that events occur in isolation. They confront the observable world with the idea that one thing *causes* another. A central part of searching for relationships is searching for *causal* relationships. While we might want to know what "causes" delinquency or divorce or war or mental illness or motivation, in each case we are essentially interested in "cause and effect."

Any of the basic assumptions of each of the ways of knowing can be questioned. Some people feel that the assumptions of science are faulty or limited. Science can be seen as limited particularly if people want certainty; if they want answers without any reservation; if they seek a set of absolutes. Science can also be seen as limited if people feel that the five senses are not very reliable, or if they believe that other types of experiences are just as accurate as those obtained through the senses.

We will not question the basic assumptions of science in this text. However, we will examine the consequences of the assumptions of science, particularly the types of procedures that have been developed to be faithful to them. We shall also explore how scientists may go beyond the realm of science in order to make certain decisions. (For a good review of the philosophy of science, consult

Kuhn, 1962.) These perceived limitations are not without foundation. There are four sets of circumstances which the scientist must confront and which present problems for the scientist in searching for relationships. They are:

1. unseens and unknowns
2. representativeness of observations
3. distorted observations
4. ambiguity of information processing (data analysis)

Each of these problem areas will be discussed at length later on in this chapter.

The architecture analogy has served as a vehicle to discuss some different ways of knowing. In the following sections we will further explore the notion of cause and effect; the four problem areas confronting the scientist; and the organization of this text.

3. THE MEANING OF CAUSE AND EFFECT

A major goal of the scientific research process is to make tentative statements about cause–effect relationships among specific units (variables) in our environment. These conclusions should be as useful as possible for understanding the variables and should fit together into sets that form coherent wholes. Sets of statements that fit together to make sense out of some phenomena are often called *theories*. Another goal of science is to make these theories as parsimonious as possible, that is, as simple as possible. When we say that one event "causes" another, we mean that there is a crucial link between the events. In the case of variables, we mean that a change in the cause variable will directly produce a change in the effect variable. The change in the cause variable can be used to *explain* and *understand* the change in the effect variable. For example, when we say that a decrease in temperature (below 0°C) *causes* water to freeze, we mean that the temperature change and not some other event is "responsible" for the water freezing.

Before moving on to a formal discussion of causation, it is useful to explore the issue of what it means to assert that one event is responsible for causing another.

Sometimes cause-and-effect relationships are explored using the idea that some conditions are necessary for others to follow and that some conditions are sufficient for others to follow. A *necessary condition* is one that must be present for a subsequent event to occur, but such a condition does not guarantee that the subsequent event will always occur. For example, in most situations a high school diploma is a necessary condition for being admitted to college. That is, one must have a high school diploma (a necessary condition) in order to be admitted to college (the subsequent event). However, having a high school diploma does not guarantee that one will be admitted to college.

A *sufficient condition,* on the other hand, is one which, if present, will always result in a subsequent event occurring. Examples of sufficient conditions are much more difficult to construct because sufficient conditions are absolute; there can be no exceptions. Suppose we had a weight suspended on a string above the floor. Cutting the string with a pair of scissors would be a sufficient condition for having the weight fall to the floor. That is, cutting the string (a sufficient condition) will always result in the weight falling to the floor (the subsequent event).

Notice that causation is not demonstrated merely by determining that an event or condition is a necessary or sufficient one. Just because a high school diploma is a necessary condition for college admission does not mean that getting a high school diploma "causes" college admission. Likewise, show that cutting the string is a sufficient condition for having a suspended weight fall to the floor does not automatically lead to the conclusion that cutting the string "caused" the weight to fall. We could conceive that gravity was the "real" cause of the weight falling.

In addition, it is common for us to use probability statements when discussing causation. For example, we could agree that children who run between parked cars are more likely to get hit by an auto than are children who do not. That is, there is a higher likelihood (probability) of children getting hit when they cross the street between parked cars. In this sense, running between parked cars could be seen as a "cause" of getting hit for a child involved in an accident even though not all children who run between parked cars get hit. Similarly, people who are exposed to a patient who has a contagious disease have a higher probability of contracting that disease than do people who are not exposed. We could say that such exposure "causes" someone to contract the disease even though not all people who are exposed to the patient will contract the disease. In this type of situation, exposure to the diseased patient is neither a necessary nor a sufficient condition for contracting the disease.

We can see that determining whether or not one event or circumstance is responsible for causing another is not a simple question. Scientists have developed a formalized system for demonstrating causation that does not completely satisfy all of the issues involved, but it is based on the topics just discussed.

There are three conditions that must be met before we can formally demonstrate cause and effect:

1. time order
2. mutual patterned change (association)
3. no other plausible explanation

A fourth condition is not necessary in terms of the formal require-ments of science, but seems to be equally crucial in terms of the way researchers operate. It is:

4. _belief_ in a true link

Time order

To talk about cause we must make time order observations and/or assumptions. The type of logic we usually use in everyday life (there are other kinds) dictates that a cause must happen _before_ an effect, and that an effect cannot cause a cause! For example, if we want to know what causes people to open umbrellas they are carrying, we might look at the variable of rain. From observation we know that when rain starts people put up their umbrellas. Rain comes prior to opening umbrellas, not the other way around. This is one reason we know that rain causes umbrella opening instead of umbrella open-ing causing rain.

Before proceeding, we need to make an aside about the notion of cause and time order. There are events that occur prior to the rain, such as the movement of weather fronts, and events that occur af-ter rain, such as muscle tension in the arm, which are in the chain of events that result in opening the umbrellas. There are no rules to aid the scientist in deciding which variable to focus on when talking about what causes umbrella opening. In this example, talking about weather fronts may be too remote from the act of opening umbrel-las, and talking about muscle tension may diminish our understand-ing of the meaning of umbrella opening. The choice of where to focus in the causal chain is important for many reasons, but the choice is not made as a result of scientific methods. It will be made on the basis of values, usefulness, theory, practical concerns, or other nonscientific grounds.

There are many cause–effect relationships that are not as straight-forward as the previous one because we recognize the possibility that events may cause each other. These cases are called _reciprocal causation_. For example, we may expect that broken homes may lead to delinquency, but also the presence of delinquency may lead to broken homes. Some researchers use the term _transaction_ in these situations rather than reciprocal causation. The idea of trans-action is that both variables _simultaneously_ lead to changes in the other. We expect that this may appear to be true only if the time measuring is so imprecise that what looks like the same time is re-ally alternating events. For example, when focusing on any two transactional variables, A and B, what may be really happening is that A has an effect on B which has an effect on A which has an ef-fect on B, and so on. What appears to be simultaneous transaction may really be reciprocal causation. Thus time order is only one condition which must be met, and it is only a necessary condition — not a sufficient one.

Mutual patterned change (association)

A second factor considered in determining cause and effect is mutual patterned change in two variables. This means that when one variable changes in a certain way another variable also changes in a predictable way. For example, when the weather changes from clear to rain, people will predictably open their umbrellas. However, if the second variable changes without changes in the first variable, cause and effect would be questioned. If people opened their umbrellas when it became cloudy, even if it did not rain, then we might think something besides rain causes people to raise their umbrellas. When two things do change together in patterned ways we say they are associated. When we say two variables are associated we mean that when the first variable changes, the second variable also changes, in a predictable, anticipated, patterned way.

Not all associated variables are related in a cause–effect fashion. For example, when people are angry a part of the brain called the hypothalamus usually stimulates their heart beats and increases their blood pressure. Heart rate and blood pressure are associated but one does not "cause" the other. Anger causes both. It is important to remember that just because two things are associated does not mean they are causally related. However, if variables are causally related, a change in the first will result in patterned change in the second.

No other plausible explanation

A third necessary condition that must be met to infer causation is that we can not find a reasonable alternative explanation for the association we observe. There is a classic example which serves to illustrate this point very graphically. If you are accustomed to following firefighters you will observe that as the number of firefighters at a fire increases (change in the first variable), the amount of damage reported increases (change in the second variable). It might be concluded that firefighters cause damage because the more firefighters, the more damage. This may not seem very reasonable to most of us because we have not mentioned one very important factor — the size of the fire. It is more plausible to most of us that the size of the fire causes both the number of firefighters to change and the amount of damage to change. We would not accept the idea that firefighters cause damage because the size of the fire is a more plausible explanation. Causal relationships can be questioned if it is possible to find another causal variable which is more appealing or which makes more sense. If no such alternative plausible explanation can be found, then we can have more confidence that the relationship in question is really causal.

Belief in a true link

Many of the decisions about cause-and-effect relationships rely on value choices or assumptions that go beyond the scientific method of doing research. One of the consequences of having a number of different ways of knowing is that sometimes conclusions reached by different paths are contradictory. We may be led to believe one thing by our intuition and another by some authority (such as our parents), and perhaps another by science. Even if we can objectively establish time order association, and eliminate many plausible alternative explanations, we may be unwilling to grant that two variables are causally related. This may be because it just does not make sense or because knowledge gained by another technique may conflict with that conclusion. Decisions about causation must fit in with our conceptions of reality to be accepted. We will be very reluctant to accept a cause–effect assertion if it goes against the way we see the world. Thus scientists have often been very reluctant to accept new views, theories, or breakthroughs even on the basis of scientific evidence.

A final note on causation

One of the necessary conditions for determining causation produces an interesting situation for scientists. The fact that other plausible explanations might exist raises the question of how we know whether we have considered all of the competing explanations that might exist. Scientists are continual skeptics in as much as they always leave open the possibility that other plausible explanations may be found. In this sense, nothing is ever *proved* or *disproved* to the scientist. Statements are either supported by observations or not supported by observations. Scientists usually avoid using the term "proof," but some researchers proceed as if they can "disprove" what has been tentatively supported by observation. We think it is important to note that it is no more possible to "disprove" than to "prove" in science. The same conditions which make proof impossible also make disproof impossible. The next section explores further the tentative nature of scientific statements.

While we have stressed in this chapter the notion of examining cause-and-effect relationships (causal research), not all studies proceed in this manner. For a variety of reasons scientists may simply wish to describe a single variable or uncover mutual patterned change without making causal inferences. This usually occurs in the initial phases of researching an issue or question (exploratory research). We believe that even if a study does not specifically address itself to causation, the general aim of science is to *eventually* provide causal explanations.

4. THE TENTATIVE NATURE OF SCIENCE

Knowing through science results in several limitations, many of which we have discussed above. Perhaps the most striking paradox in science is that as a way of knowing, science does not produce certainty. We are never *certain* of what we know when using the scientific process. The continuous questioning, lack of absolute statements, and tentative nature of statements are the result of four "problems." These problems prevent the scientist from making "for sure," "absolute," and "for always" statements. Each problem below must be confronted in the scientific way of knowing.

Unseens and unknowns

We have previously given examples showing how important it is that there is always a possibility of alternative explanations for phenomena. The single greatest difficulty with causation is eliminating alternative causal variables. The basic problem is that no matter how many other variables we are able to consider as possibly making any causal statement inaccurate, we still find that it is always (theoretically) possible to find one more. It is always possible that we have omitted some variable that may have explained why the two original variables look like one caused the other when in reality they did not. Likewise, it is always possible (theoretically) to find a variable that may result in showing that two original variables we thought were not related are, in fact, causally related.

The earlier examples of the hypothalamus changing heart rate and blood pressure and the size of the fire causing the increased number of firefighters and the extent of damage serve to illustrate this problem. Another often quoted example is that the rum prices in Jamaica are associated with the average salary of clergy in Boston. Is it plausible to suggest that higher rum prices "cause" clergy salaries to go up? Rum prices do go up prior to clergy salaries; they are associated, but can we find a plausible alternative explanation and can we believe that changes in rum prices cause changes in clergy salaries? This situation may be a result of the fact that all prices and wages are responsive to general world economic conditions, and that rum prices are more responsive to such conditions than clergy salaries. The recurrent problem in research is that for any observed relationship, it is always possible that some unseen or unknown is involved, and we must be ever vigilant for such alternative causal explanations (variables). The general procedure for such vigilance involves attempting to deal explicitly with such possible unseen or unknown variables by seeking them out, that is, trying to discover them.

Representativeness of observations

Scientists cannot see (observe) all things at all places at all times, past and present. Because of this, there is the possibility that at some other time in some other place the scientist might observe something different than has been observed in a particular piece of research. However, the scientist is interested in forming general causal statements that will hold for all time in all places. All of our observations are samplings. We sample in time and in place every time we make scientific observations. *Sampling* involves the selection of times, cases, subjects, measures, events, and variables for the purposes of describing causal links. The problem of going beyond observations made at one point in time to making more general statements is called the process of *generalization*. Scientists have developed various techniques to aid in their decisions about generalizing, but it is a mandate of science that we always be open to new observations and thus always open to changing our general statements as a result of different observations in different time or space.

Distorted observations

An assumption of science is that our senses are accurate, but we have much anecdotal evidence to the contrary. We know that when a group of people witness a crime it is likely we will get various descriptions of the suspects involved. We know that when we watch a movie with friends we pick up some things in the movie that they did not and vice versa. This is evidenced by the fact that every time we see a movie again, we usually observe something that we did not see in previous viewings. All of our observations pass through a filtering process. Each of us has a set of filters resulting from training, previous experiences, past socialization, our physiology, and other conditions that may exist. Much of scientific training is designed to eliminate such filters; to become objective. However, many people think that this is not possible; we can never eliminate our personal bias in observation. To aid the researcher, various procedures have been developed to remove the possible disturbance in observations caused by individual bias. We have increased faith in the objectivity of observations when they are done by trained researchers and are done more than once in more than one place at more than one time. Repeating research of the same sort is referred to as *replication,* but even with replication we must continually be aware of the possibility of distorted observations.

Ambiguity of data analysis

You may have heard the cliche that "one can say anything with statistics." Although we strongly disagree with this statement, it is possible that one who is knowledgeable in statistics can manipulate data so that another person who is not sophisticated will not know what the data say. Also, it is probably true that many researchers are not familiar with all of the available ways to process information and that both human and mechanical errors sometimes occur in the process of analysis. Of course no piece of research is complete until some sense has been made from scientific observations; until the information has been processed; the data analyzed. Training, continuous checking and rechecking, and consultations with others help to insure that ambiguity and errors do not occur in this phase of the research act. In addition to errors, it is incumbent on the researcher to present observations so that they will be clearly interpretable by consumers of the research.

5. THE PLAN OF THE BOOK

The remainder of this text deals extensively with the four "problems" of relying upon science as a way of knowing. It is often not possible to isolate each problem and deal with it independently. Therefore many chapters deal with more than one of them at a time. In addition, care has been taken not to artificially segment the various topics. Specifically, a stress is placed on integrating topics that have been traditionally called "research methods," with topics often found in statistics courses. We follow the philosophy that one cannot really understand one without the other.

After an initial introductory section, Part II specifically deals with defining and understanding what a relationship between variables is, and what tools are used to describe relationships. Part III contains chapters which explore the initial steps in searching for relationships, including a chapter on computer use, a necessity for modern research. Following these beginning stages, Part IV shows that there are many alternative ways to structure research observations and to analyze relationships. Part V reminds us that not all observations and conclusions will lead to accurate understanding of relationships. Chapters in this part of the text offer detailed procedures used by scientists to question their conclusions. Finally, Part VI shows how to use all the information presented in this text to critique published research articles, and a final chapter places the search for relationships in a general perspective.

Although we may have emphasized the "problems" of scientific research, all of the different ways of knowing have their own set of problems. As we said in the beginning of this chapter, most of us have a great deal of faith in the products and processes of science, and this faith is not lessened by admitting the limitations of the method. Indeed, it is our belief that by explicitly dealing with the difficulties associated with knowing through science, we strengthen our position. In our opinion, science *is* the best, most objective way to know the world around us, and the better we understand science, the more useful it becomes.

6. SUMMARY

Five different ways of knowing were introduced and described in this chapter. Revelation as a means of knowing is characterized by its "transcendental" nature. When knowledge is dependent on referral to some person or object, authority is said to be the source of knowledge. We pointed out that while scientists often refer to authority, this process is different than knowing by authority because scientists often question the wisdom and source of the authority. Intuitive knowledge is gained by unconsciously making connections. As a result the observer has a feeling and "knows" because of that feeling. Knowing because of common sense is seen as a product of generalizing past experience often combined with intuition and authority. This usually results in explanations for events "after the fact" and creates a problem in terms of its usefulness for understanding future events. One major comment about all these ways of knowing is that there is little basis for an outsider to question the accuracy or appropriateness of knowledge gained by these techniques. On the other hand, the scientific way of knowing is unique in several ways. First, the process of conceptualization makes what is being discussed very explicit. This is accomplished by specifying variables. Second, there are some specific assumptions made in science. Reality is seen as knowable; the senses are believed to be accurate; and objectivity supposedly can be gained by using the senses. Third, science provides only probability statements instead of certain knowledge.

Several problems with the scientific way of knowing can be identified. These include: unseens and unknowns, representativeness of

cf. natural science — controlled exp.

observations, distorted observations, and ambiguity of information processing. These problems are discussed in terms of how they affect the process of determining cause-and-effect relationships. In order to demonstrate cause and effect, four conditions have to be determined. Cause must precede effect. There must be mutual patterned change between the cause and effect. No other plausible explanations should exist, and finally the cause-and-effect statement must "fit in" with our picture of reality. Because there is always the possibility that another plausible explanation can be found, scientific conclusions are tentative. Science often proceeds by showing that one or more of the four conditions for determining cause are not met. In conclusion, the plan of the book is presented in terms of dealing with the four problems confronted in the scientific way of knowing.

EXERCISES

1. Our peer group has a definite impact on what we feel, do, and know. Try to recall an instance when your peer group attempted to influence you by using each "way of knowing."

2. Many decisions are made on the basis of knowledge (sometimes unconsciously obtained). In small groups discuss which "way of knowing" (there may be more than one) most of us have used to obtain information necessary to make decisions about:
   a. which courses to take
   b. which religion to believe in
   c. which person of the opposite sex to go out with
   d. what the weather will be tomorrow
   e. what is right and wrong
   f. which clothes to buy
   g. which car to buy
   h. what medicine to take

3. Make a list of three bits of knowledge you have gained through the scientific way of knowing and comment on how thoroughly you could question or examine the process used to obtain this knowledge.

4. There are many areas of life in which scientifically derived information is available. For those areas listed below discuss the extent to which you have been, or would be, influenced by the scientific way of knowing. Be specific and also consider possible conflicting knowledge available from other "ways of knowing."
   a. child-rearing practices
   b. your position on the death penalty
   c. how to study effectively

5. Discuss whether or not the event or condition in column A is a necessary or sufficient condition for the corresponding event in column B.

A	B
flipping the switch	having the lights go on
being born	having a birthday
being born	having a birthday party
being rich	going to college
age	being elected President of the United States
getting a haircut	having your picture taken
being attractive	getting married
having your heart stop	dying
watering	plants growing

6. There are many beliefs about cause-and-effect relationships that are common in our culture. Listed below are several of these causal statements. Examine each of them according to the four aspects necessary for demonstrating causation presented in this chapter and discuss whether or not you believe there is a sufficient amount of information available to determine the causal relationship as stated.

a. smoking marijuana causes people to use harder drugs.

b. giving a child almost everything causes the child to become spoiled.

c. poor family life causes a deterioration in morals.

d. going to college causes people to become smarter.

PROJECT

At the end of each set of exercises throughout most chapters of the book will be a section entitled *Project*. Many instructors feel that for students to understand the research process they must be involved with the entire research process. The chapters are organized in a way that with appropriate supervision you should be able to complete a few small research projects throughout a one- or two-semester course. Appropriate supervision is necessary for two reasons. First, some of the research topics you may be interested in cannot be handled practically in your university/college community given the resources available to you. Second, some projects may be feasible for you to accomplish but may violate certain research ethics. Discussing each problem with your instructor should be a good safeguard of your time and of the rights of others. If you wish to think through some of the ethical problems, you may wish to consult Chapter 6.

As you read through Chapter 2, try to be thinking of social science questions you wish to study. At the end of Chapter 2, we will suggest that you pick a topic (concept) on which to focus.

REFERENCES

24

AGNEW, N., AND PYKE, S. *The Science Game.* Englewood Cliffs, N.J.: Prentice-Hall, 1969.

GIBBS, J. *Sociological Theory Construction.* Hinsdale, Ill.: Dryden Press, 1972.

KAPLAN, A. *The Conduct of Inquiry.* San Francisco: Chandler Publishing Company, 1964.

KUHN, T. *The Structure of Scientific Revolutions.* Chicago: University of Chicago Press, 1962.

LASTRUCCI, C. *The Scientific Approach.* Cambridge, Mass.: Schenkman, 1967.

(*Note:* The following are other general research methods texts that would be valuable sources throughout the rest of your course.)

BABBIE, E. *The Practice of Social Research.* Belmont, Calif.: Wadsworth, 1975.

KERLINGER, F. *Foundations of Behavioral Research,* 2d ed. New York: Holt, Rinehart and Winston, 1973.

NACHMIAS, D., AND NACHMIAS C. *Research Methods in the Social Sciences.* New York: St. Martin's Press, 1976.

PHILLIPS, B. *Social Research: Strategy and Tactics,* 2d ed. New York: Macmillan, 1971.

SELLTIZ, C., WRIGHTSMAN, L., AND COOK, S. *Research Methods in Social Relations,* 3d ed. New York: Holt, Rinehart and Winston, 1976.

SIMON, J. *Basic Research Methods in Social Science.* New York: Random House, 1969.

WALLACE, W. *The Logic of Science in Sociology.* Chicago: Aldine Atherton, 1971.

WILLIAMSON, J., KARP, D., AND DOLPHIN, J. *The Research Craft: An Introduction to Social Science Methods.* Boston: Little, Brown, 1977.

CHAPTER 2
SEEING OUR ENVIRONMENT WITH
CONCEPTS AND VARIABLES

After studying this chapter, students should be able to:

1. Effectively participate in the conceptualization of simple phenomena to arrive at useful concepts.

2. Discuss the strengths and weaknesses of the discovery view.

3. Discuss the strengths and weaknesses of the creative view.

4. Identify various dimensions of familiar concepts.

5. Identify concepts that are being used as variables.

6. Engage in the explication of concepts, including the construction of conceptual definitions; the identification of indicators; and the writing of operational definitions.

7. Identify potential indicators of familiar concepts and variables.

8. Evaluate the adequacy of particular operational definitions.

9. Define reliability of indicators.

10. Define validity of indicators.

11. Construct categories of variables that are both mutually inclusive and mutually exclusive and be able to evaluate sets of categories according to these criteria.

12. Identify and give examples of nominal variables.

13. Identify and give examples of ordinal variables.

14. Identify and give examples of interval variables.

15. Identify and give examples of ratio variables.

16. Discuss the issues and importance of being able to identify the level of measurement of variables.

17. Define what the limits of a category are and why they are important.

18. Locate and/or compute the upper and lower limits of the categories of variables.

19. Determine when variables are using discrete units and when variables are using continuous units.

20. Discuss the importance of the conceptualization process in the various ways of knowing, particularly the scientific way of knowing.

21. Describe the differences between an index and a scale.

22. Describe Likert scaling procedures.

Concept   The end product of conceptualization; both the label (word) and the complex set of events or ideas that form the whole referred to by the word.

Conceptualization   The mental process of organizing one's observations and experiences into meaningful and coherent wholes.

Continuous variables   Variables that have been conceptualized and measured in such a way that they can be meaningfully broken into smaller and smaller subparts or subcategories.

Creative view   A perspective held by those who claim that one's linguistic and cultural framework are not limiting and that problem solving promotes flexibility, creativity, and new ways of observing and classifying data.

Dimension   One aspect, area, or part of the concept that can be discovered and potentially measured.

Discovery view   A perspective held by those who claim that people are limited by their culture and language in terms of what they are capable of perceiving and observing.

Discrete variables   Variables that have been conceptualized and measured in such a way that they cannot be meaningfully subdivided (broken into subparts or subcategories).

Explication   The process of moving from definition to measurement and back to definition.

Indicator   A class, set, or group of potentially observable phenomena which stands for or represents a conceptual definition for purposes of measuring a variable.

Interval variable   A variable in which the categories are unique, can be ordered, and have a known distance between them.

Limits   The boundaries of a category of a variable and the description of what is inside and what is outside a particular category.

Lower limit   The lowest possible value included in a category.

Mutually exclusive   Each unit can be assigned to only one of the available categories of a variable.

Mutually inclusive (exhaustive)   At least one value or category available for every unit measured; the set of categories "exhausts" all possible values.

Nominal variable   A variable in which the categories are unique.

Operational definition   A complete set of instructions for what to observe and how to measure a variable (concept) so that one can classify phenomena in one's environment into the various categories of the variable.

Ordinal variable   A variable in which categories are unique and can be ordered.

Ratio variable   A variable in which categories are unique, can be ordered, have a known distance between them, and can be described by proportional statements. (Technically, an interval level variable with a "true" zero point.)

Reliability   Consistency of obtaining the same relative answer when measuring phenomena that have not changed.

Upper limit   The highest possible value included in a category.

Validity   The degree of match between the conceptual definition of a variable and the operational definition of that variable; that is, measuring what you intend to measure.

Variable   A concept that has more than one value, state, category, score, or condition.

1. INTRODUCTION

Perhaps the most basic distinction between scientists and others seeking information is the manner in which they experience their environment. It might be said that a scientist is "oversensitive" to what goes on in the environment. This oversensitization is reflected in the fact that scientists use a great many concepts, techniques, theories, beliefs, and practices not commonly used by most people. The most fundamental process of science is abstract conceptualization, the process of making sense out of one's experiences and/or observations. More precisely, *conceptualization* is the mental process of organizing one's observations and experiences into meaningful and coherent wholes. For example, we would think it very unusual to hear this type of statement from one of our friends: "I went to a restaurant for lunch and there were very attractive people walking around the restaurant with interesting clothes on. Another person was talking into a microphone about the clothes these people were wearing. It was strange that most of the diners stopped eating and applauded—right in the middle of their lunch!" It would be much more typical for our friend to say something like, "Wow, there was a really nice fashion show at the restaurant where I just had lunch!" The difference between these two statements is that the second reveals that your friend had *conceptualized* a rather complicated and involved set of experiences into one meaningful whole, and has labeled (categorized) it a "fashion show."

The term *concept* refers to the end product of conceptualization, both the label (word) and the complex set of events or ideas that form the whole referred to by the word. One can see from this example that we all have the ability to abstractly conceptualize and we all use many concepts to understand our environment and to communicate with other people. Of course, for good communication it is important that when we use a word representing a concept, we have the same imagery in our mind that others who are listening to us have in theirs. Because a concept is a word or symbol used to represent a meaningful whole, we must take the idea behind the concept and describe it. Once this is done, we can use the word to represent the idea we have described. However, the words we use to form the description of a concept are also concepts. Thus in our fashion show example we talked about a restaurant, lunch, attractive, and so on. All these terms are also concepts. The concept "fashion show" was formed from other ideas, observations, and the like and allowed us to organize much of what went on in the restaurant. To fully understand the description of a given concept, each concept in that definition must also be understood.

In addition to organizing our observations into meaningful wholes, concepts also *separate* phenomena. The concept of fashion show separates one set of events from other similar and dissimilar events. How much organizing and separating a concept does depends on two things: (1) the nature of the phenomena under study, and (2) the purpose of the scientific study. Take a simple example like the concept of apples and the concept of oranges. You may have heard the expression, "You can't add apples and oranges." In some cases it is certainly true that they are not the same. For example, we cannot get vitamin C from an apple or cider from an orange. Yet in other ways we may want to treat them as the same—they are both fruit. Because we can combine or separate concepts, our environment becomes more understandable.

When we introduced the importance of objectivity in scientific observations in Chapter 1, we pointed out that scientists do not just go out and "gather the facts." The data-gathering process is a complex interplay between the conceptualization process and the actual observation or measurement process. Of course there are physical, psychological, cultural, and technological limitations to conceptualization and measurement (observation). Facts do not just speak for themselves or stand out. They are limited by the creation of conceptual and perceptual frameworks and by measurement techniques. Some philosophers go so far as to say that these limitations are the major factor in creating and furthering knowledge. Concepts are not completely arbitrary; they must have some match with a "reality" with which most of us are in touch. Of course there are disagreements about whether reality is always there and we merely *discover* it, or whether we actually *create* reality by using concepts.

The scientific way of knowing has some perplexing but apparently very productive and useful rules for conceptualization and measurement. Scientists agree that "truth" is never actually obtained in terms of "proving" something. Therefore, at any one point in time, they treat every piece of information and every observation (measurement) as problematic. They continually question the reality of what they see; its form, shape, size, substance, composition, dimensions, scope, and so on. Good scientists challenge observations and conceptualizations; they probe, examine, and reexamine everything that has been found before. However, in another way they use their research results to make assumptions about reality and to make "factual" statements about reality and the relationships between concepts. In this chapter we shall discuss the framework by which conceptualization and observation (measurement) is tentatively created. In Chapter 14 we shall discuss how the reality created by scientific conceptualization and measurement may be challenged and probed.

2. THE CONCEPTUALIZATION PROCESS

There are two different views of how people psychologically operate in the process of data collection (making observations) and each has a counterpart for interpreting how scientific observation works: the creative view and the discovery view. The *discovery view* assumes that people are limited in what they are capable of perceiving and observing by their culture and language (previously learned concepts). The *creative view* assumes that one's linguistic and cultural framework are not limiting and that problem solving promotes flexibility, creativity, and new ways of observing and classifying data (information).

As an example of the discovery view, some have pointed out that Alaskan Eskimos are capable of distinguishing among eleven different kinds of snow because they have eleven different words (concepts) to make such distinctions. The average skier in the United States may have learned to distinguish among corn snow, powder, hard-packed, and slow snow; nonskiers only distinguish between snow, slush, and no snow. These facts seem to indicate that if your language has the framework (concepts), you may observe distinctions; if your language is limited, you may not really distinguish various phenomena. Observations, then, may be culturally and linguistically bound or limited (Whorf, 1956). Because scientists are members of a society with its culture, it follows that scientists are, or might be, limited in their fact gathering by the framework their culture provides. Accepting this view would lead us to the conclusion that scientists cannot really be "objective" in their data collection and interpretation because objectivity is limited and defined by their culture. Since culture is somewhat arbitrary, science must also be arbitrary. Those who accept the discovery view would not be likely to place much emphasis on the objectivity of science; they would emphasize the usefulness of the results of science.

On the other hand, the creative view stresses the fact that culture is not so limiting. Otherwise how would new discoveries creep into an existing society? Although most people in our culture "see" only a few different types of snow and Eskimos "see" eleven, this does not mean that most of us are incapable of "seeing" more kinds of snow. The fact that skiers see more varieties of snow illustrates the possibility for people living in the United States to see other types of snow as experience promotes it. This view acknowledges the potential limitations that culture may impose, but points out that exposure to new environments, culture, concepts, or experiences may modify such limitations.

One viewpoint concludes that what is seen by the scientist is determined by what is being looked for, that is, reality is created. The other suggests that out of experience scientists discover what is there. We favor neither view. Rather, we see research observations as being the product of going through stages which influence each other—as the result of a process. Although the stages of this process, listed below, will be presented as if each one were a separate phenomenon, they often overlap and may occur in an order different from the way shown. The stages are: (1) conceptualization, (2) definition, (3) indicator selection, (4) operationalization, (5) observation (measurement), and (6) conceptualization. The sixth step of conceptualization indicates the process nature of experiencing our environment. Very often our observations will modify previous, or create new, definitions or world views, making the process circular.

3. THE DEFINING PROCESS

As we pointed out, concepts are ways of perceiving and organizing our environment. The process of definition is a sometimes complicated task of deciding what parts of our environment are encompassed (the organizing role of concepts) by a given concept and what parts of the environment are outside (the separating role of concepts) particular concepts. One everyday example of definition that most of us have encountered is what shades of colors are within particular color groups. The color blue is often a troublesome color. We all have had disagreements with friends about whether some object was colored blue, or green, or turquoise. Definitions of concepts in our everyday vocabulary are often loose ideas including more or less a set of similar things. The major problem produced by "loose" definitions is the potential miscommunication or lack of communication in conversations or writing. Without *clear criteria* for deciding what shades fit into the blue category, the definition of the concept of blue would be a "loose" definition.

Scientists differ from other people in the extent to which they will accept loose definitions. They go overboard to specify definitions to the point where they can be assured that if others know their definitions, there will be no question as to what is included in the concept and what is excluded. This is necessary for science but it may not be as necessary for everyday life. This ideal of constructing "tight" definitions may be difficult to come by, but that is the goal of the scientist. Students often have a tough time getting used to using only "tight" definitions supplied by the scientist. If you want to infuriate your friends during a conversation, keep asking that person to define the words they are using. Such common words as "nice," "bad," "good looking," "exciting," and "right" can have many definitions, and if these definitions are not shared in the conversation, miscommunication is likely.

Another important aspect of the defining process is that scientists are not interested in single events, unique entities, or individual phenomenon. The task of defining is to discover the *general* rules about classes of phenomena which we are willing to treat as the same. The concept of "ball" can serve as an illustration. Depending on the season of the year and your interests, you may include in your concept of ball, roundness and identification as a play object. However, you might realize that one very common ball used in the fall sports season is not round but oblong with pointed ends. Without clearly detailing what the definition of "ball" is, observation and communication using the term may be difficult. This is why scientists stress the communication and standardization of definitions. Are all round objects balls? If so, are cherries and grapefruits balls? Are all things that are thrown or hit in sports balls? Are frisbees or badminton birdies balls? Whether or not you say yes or no to these questions depends on what does and does not fit your concept of ball. The definitions scientists develop must allow us to categorize our observations as definitely within the concept or definitely outside the concept. Definitions are basically sets of criteria for deciding which conceptual categories our observations fall into. *In one sense, any criteria chosen for a definition will be correct because all conceptual definitions are arbitrary.* However, it is essential that consensus be developed in the definition of concepts, for there are certain reality limitations upon the concepts and definitions with which scientists work. In order to remain in a scientific system, concepts must be observable either directly or indirectly. For example, if we were all color-blind to blue, it would not do us much good to have a concept of blue unless we could find a machine or other sensing device we could trust to discriminate blue from other colors. That is, in a sense we may create any conceptual definition for a concept, but unless we can observe (measure) what we create, we tentatively assume the concept is unreal. If the concept is not real in the sense of being observable, either directly or indirectly through our senses, then scientists do not work with it in scientific systems. Of course the possibility is always kept open that an "unreal" concept may at some point in time become observable. In this sense definitions of concepts are not entirely arbitrary nor entirely created. Although those concepts that are retained in science must be grounded in the reality of observation, this does not mean that reality totally wins out in speaking for itself.

Within the limitations discussed above, the process of determining criteria for a formal definition is often started by identifying the dimensions of a concept. This is often the process used to arrive at a "tight" definition. A dimension of a concept is one aspect, one area, one part of the phenomena which can be discerned and potentially measured. To refine a definition for scientific use, we might specify the dimensions of a concept. Again using the example of a "ball," we might specify at least three dimensions. The first dimension might be *shape*. Some part of the object must be round to be a ball. The second dimension might be what the object is used for, its *function*. We could decide that the major function of a ball must be either recreational or sports related. A third dimension which might be specified for this concept could be the construction of the object, its *composition*. In order to be a ball, the object must be made out of wood, leather, plastic, or rubber. To test the completeness of a definition, we would attempt to classify various items. If any confusion resulted from classifying items as being a ball or not being a ball, the definition of a ball would not be complete. A definition is *complete* if no disagreements occur in classifying phenomena as being encompassed or not encompassed by the definition.

Let us try to clarify this rule of completeness by offering a sociological example. A nonconformist could be defined as one who deviates from norms. In order to test the completeness of this definition, we can examine whether confusion might arise under certain circumstances. Would a person who goes to church every week be a nonconformist? Statistically speaking, most Americans do not go to church this often, and yet we would probably not like to use the term "nonconformist" in describing someone who goes to church this often. Of course if a person were a monk, this type of church-going behavior might be considered nonconforming because we would expect a monk to attend church more often. The problem is that the definition of nonconformist has not specified which set of norms we are supposed to examine. Formal norms may differ from informal norms, and some subcultural norms may differ from other subcultural norms. Thus a person might be deviating from one set of norms, but be in conformity to another. We would need a more complete definition of nonconformist in order to use this conceptual definition in scientific research.

One final consideration must be raised when discussing the definition of concepts in the scientific process: the question of *usefulness*. Conceptualizations are more or less valued in science to the extent to which they aid the scientist in discovering, explaining, or predicting. For example, the concept of inertia has been most useful to physicists in understanding the laws of motion. The definition of social class has been important in many sociological theories, and the concept of motivation has proved useful in studies of educational achievement. Not all concepts which have been "invented" or "discovered" have been equally useful in furthering science.

In summary, conceptual definitions may vary in several ways: clarity, observability, completeness, and usefulness. Definitions can be easy or difficult to understand (clarity). There may or may not be methods, techniques, machines, or devices to measure or observe the phenomena being defined. In specifying the dimensions of a concept, there may or may not be problems deciding whether or not phenomena are encompassed within the definitions (completeness). Finally, concepts may be more or less useful in developing and/or refining science. The goal of the defining process is to develop clearly worded conceptual definitions which carefully specify dimensions of a concept so that classification of observable and theoretically useful phenomena is possible.

4. FROM DEFINITION TO MEASUREMENT AND BACK AGAIN

There is an old expression that goes, "If there isn't any difference, it doesn't make any difference." The basic activity of science is to attempt to explain differences. Why do some children achieve more in school than others (differences in achievement)? Why do some people act more aggressive than others (differences in aggression)? Why are some people Democrats and others Republicans (differences in political preference)? Why do some people suffer from mental illness when others do not (differences in mental health)? When a concept has more than one state, value, or condition, that concept is called a variable. A *variable* is a concept that has more than one value, state, category, or condition. Scientists tend to focus almost all of their energies on variables since they are attempting to examine and explain differences. This is done by analyzing variables and determining how they are related to one another. For example, scientists might attempt to understand differences in achievement level by referring to differences in measured intelligence. In this case, achievement level would be a variable and measured intelligence would be a variable. In both concepts there are multiple states, values, or categories (differences in people's scores). Measured intelligence might be very low, low, average, above average, genius, and so on, and achievement level might vary in terms of grade-point average.

The language used when talking about variables can sometimes be confusing. For example, a "chair" is not a variable even though there are different kinds of chairs. However, "chair shape" can be a variable. There are categories of chair shape; that is, there are different states of chair shape. A chair can be straight backed, square, round, bucket shaped, and so on. "Social norms" could not be a variable even though there are many different rules which govern behavior. However, the "importance of a norm" could be a variable. It would be possible to categorize norms as having different degrees of importance to society. The norm prohibiting murder would certainly be more important than the norm requiring that the color of both shoes in a pair be the same. Similarly, "marriage" would not be called a variable, but "marital status" would be. Objects are never variables but some characteristic of the same objects could be variable. When speaking of social or behavioral phenomena, the phenomenon itself is often not a variable but a "thing." However, if the dimensions of the phenomena or concept can be specified, the dimensions often form the bases for different variables. For example, the concept of "values" would not be considered a variable. Some dimensions of the concept of values might be universality, centrality, and rigidity. One variable could be the degree to which values are universally held. The *variable* in this case would be the "universality of the value." Another variable could be the "centrality of the value." This could refer to the idea that some values are more central to a person's existence than are others. The "rigidity of values" could also be a variable which would indicate the degree to which a value was open to change. You can easily see that it is very important to use precise language when talking about variables.

One of the most controversial parts of the research process revolves around developing measurement techniques to be used in observing variables.

The process of moving from definition to measurement and back to definition is sometimes called *explication*. This process can be exemplified by using the variable of intelligence. Conceptually, intelligence can be defined as the highest potential a person has for cognitive activities. In attempting to observe intelligence, psychologists have developed paper and pencil tests that allow for the assignment of an IQ score. Although IQ (the observation (measurement) of the variable intelligence) has historically come to mean intelligence, recently many psychologists and educators have re-emphasized that IQ tests represent only a narrow part of "intelligence," and that it would be incorrect to assume that a person's total potential is measured by an IQ score. The fact that scientists have found IQ tests (the measurement device) to be unrepresentative of the concept of intelligence will likely result in either a modification of the definition of intelligence, the invention of a new concept to correspond to whatever IQ tests actually measure, or the abandonment of IQ tests to measure (observe) intelligence. The discussion about the lack of match between IQ scores and general intelligence has resulted in re-thinking some of our conceptual ideas about intelligence. Historically, many psychologists thought that the various dimensions of the concept of intelligence were related. That is, if a person was superior in a particular area of cognitive functioning, this would hold for other dimensions of intelligence as well. Currently, the generalized nature of intelligence is being questioned. It is possible that the IQ controversy may lead to more careful specification of the dimensions of intelligence. The crucial thing for this discussion is that one does not always start with a clear, observable, complete, and useful conceptual definition and then attempt to observe (measure) that variable. Indeed the process of explication indicates that final conceptualization and measurement results from an interplay of these two activities.

Several parts of the explication process have been identified. We have already discussed one important part, the conceptual definition. Another part of the process is the specification of a class of indicators which will represent or stand for the conceptual definition. An *indicator* is a class, set, or group of potentially observable phenomena which stands for or represents a conceptual definition.

For example, one indicator of intelligence might be the quality of school performance. Another indicator might be the ability to solve very difficult problems. Another indicator might be the frequency with which someone obtains unique solutions to everyday problems. One can quickly see that there may be many indicators for any given variable. As more dimensions of a concept are found, the number of possible indicators also increases. Out of this set or "universe of indicators" a researcher must select a specific one to focus on in the next phase of the explication process.

The scientist must develop an operational definition for the variable under study. An *operational definition* is a complete set of instructions for what to observe and how to measure a variable (concept). It allows one to classify phenomena in one's environment into specific categories of the variable. The indicators previously selected serve as the bases for the development of operational definitions. For example, an IQ test specifies which questions to ask subjects, in what order, in what kind of a setting, and in what time frame. In addition, it specifies how to summarize the answers to these questions to arrive at an IQ score. The scores are defined as categories within the variable of intelligence. An operational definition specifies the categories of a variable and tells the researcher how to assign units (subjects) to particular categories of the variable. Another way to put it is that operational definitions define the boundaries or limits of each category of a variable so that phenomena may be classified as being in or out of a particular category of a variable. (The notion of boundaries and limits will be discussed further in Section 7.) Figure 2.1 shows the process of explication.

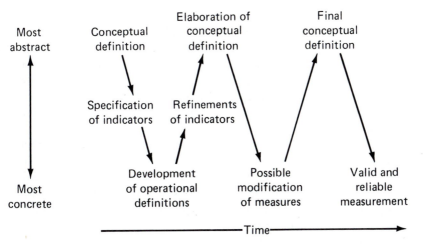

FIGURE 2.1
Diagram representing the explication process

Once an operational definition is developed, scientists may actually observe their environment and measure research variables. Measuring research variables is another way of saying that we classify phenomena into categories of a variable. Putting an operational definition into practice is called *measurement,* and the operational definition is often referred to as the measurement instrument or device. There are many types of operational definitions devised for the large number of research variables that scientists use. Because many variables have more than one dimension, that is, they are *multidimensional,* operational definitions often incorporate more than one observation. When operational definitions use more than one observation (question) to categorize a variable, they are often called indexes or scales.

5. SCALES AND INDEXES

Both indexes and scales are designed to assign individual cases (people, formal organizations, cities, or other units of measurement) to categories of a variable. That is, they both result in a score of a variable being associated or assigned to the unit being measured. The difference lies in the formality of the procedures used. The construction of scales proceeds according to a set of rules which determine how multiple indicators are developed, tested, and assembled into a composite value. This value allows a score of the variable to be assigned. The construction of an index has no such systematic set of instructions, but there are some common steps. Both indexes and scales combine a number of questions or observations into one "score." Unless strict procedures of scaling are employed, some researchers feel that a set of items could not be considered a scale. Other researchers, however, are less strict in their use of the term "scale." Scales and indexes are usually used in either questionnaires or interviews, but the procedures can be used in most any type of research. Perhaps the most widely used scaling procedure is called *Likert scaling.*

In the Likert procedure a number of questions are designed which take a position with respect to some attitudes or some dimension of a variable. The respondent then can either agree, strongly agree, disagree, strongly disagree, or take a neutral stance with the position stated in the item. A Likert scale is sometimes called a "summated rating" scale because the answers are weighted and added to produce a sum. This weighting process is represented in Table 2.1. From the table one can see that weights are assigned according to how the item is worded. The Likert procedure then scales the individuals responding by adding up the weights of the responses chosen.

TABLE 2.1
Likert scale responses and weights

Responses	Weight	Positively worded item Abortions should be free on demand			Negatively worded item Abortions take a life and should not be permitted Weight
Strongly disagree	1	Con		Pro	5
Disagree	2	↑	Attitude	↑	4
Neutral	3		on		3
Agree	4	↓	Legalized	↓	2
Strongly agree	5	Pro	Abortion	Con	1

No such set of formal rules exist to construct an index. However, just as in scaling, multiple indicators of a variable are used to construct an index. When values of more than one indicator of a variable are combined in some fashion to produce one summary value or score for a particular subject (unit) being measured, the result is called an *index.* Usually the construction of an index involves some type of summing of more than one indicator. Perhaps the best-known example of an index in sociology would be an index of socioeconomic status (SES). SES indexes are often obtained by summing scores on income, occupational prestige, and level of educational attainment. Any process which involves combining indicators of a variable to come up with one value, score, or category would result in an index of a variable.

There are many collections such as Bonjean (1967), Miller (1964), Robinson (1969), and Shaw and Wright (1967) which have published many scales and indexes that have proved to be useful in past research. These sources can be consulted to obtain indicators as opposed to creating new ones. No matter whether research measures are established or newly created, two major difficulties arise—determining their reliability and validity, the topic of the next section.

6. GENERAL IDEAS OF VALIDITY AND RELIABILITY

In order to be considered adequate measures, operational definitions must be deemed both reliable and valid. The different types of reliability and validity will be discussed in Chapter 14, but the general ideas are quite simple to understand. A measure is *reliable* if we can consistently get the same answer at different points in time when measuring phenomena that have not changed. For example, an operational definition of intelligence would be considered reliable if the same person received the same IQ score at different points in time (assuming intelligence did not change). In another use of the term, one IQ test would be reliable if an individual received the same relative score on different parts of the IQ test. A measure would be considered *valid* if the operational definition actually measures, or corresponds to, the conceptual definition. In other words, *validity* refers to the degree of match between the conceptual definition of a variable and the operational definition of that variable. For example, an IQ test would be a valid operationalization of intelligence if it actually measured potential of cognitive functioning (assuming that was your conceptual definition).

Because there is an additional step in the measurement of a variable—that of going from the operational definition to mechanically carrying out the instructions of the definition—there is another way in which a final measure of a variable may not be valid. Validity also rests on performing the actual measurement that the operational definition describes. Since there is potential for error at this point, there is another type of invalidity that must be considered. Examples of such possible invalidity caused by the operationalization process might involve such things as: improperly recording a response from a subject; turning a wrong dial on a piece of experimental apparatus; a research assistant not carrying out instructions; and so on. If any of these types of things occur, then, even if the op-

40

erational definition might have been valid, the way it was carried out resulted in an invalid measure which does not accurately reflect the conceptual definition of the variable being measured.

An archery analogy is helpful in understanding validity and reliability. Shooting arrows consistently into the bull's-eye of a target would be parallel to a reliable and valid measure. If arrows were to be inconsistently shot into the target, even sometimes missing it altogether, we would have an unreliable and invalid situation. If arrows were consistently shot into the target at the same place, but not the bull's-eye we would have a reliable indicator but not a valid one. You should note that reliable (consistent) shots are a necessary condition to valid (bull's-eye) shots. Without reliability, one can never achieve validity. Validity, however, is a sufficient condition for reliability. That is, if a measure is valid, it must be reliable by definition. Figure 2.2 represents this analogy.

7. THE NATURE OF CATEGORIES AND INTERVALS

The goal of any measurement process—the careful construction of a conceptual definition, selection of an indicator, development of an operational definition, and collection of data—is to assign subjects (either people or some other unit) to a category (value) of a variable. Each unit is to be independently measured and assigned to only one category and there must be a category for every unit. In other words, the total set of categories (values) of any variable must be mutually inclusive and mutually exclusive (exhaustive). To be *mutually inclusive* there must be at least one value or category available for every unit measured. That is, all appropriate categories of the variable must be included. To be *mutually exclusive* each unit can be assigned to only one of the available categories of a variable.

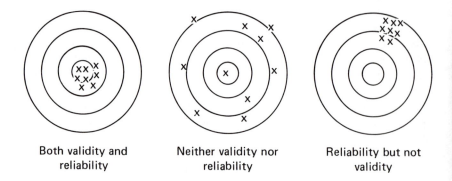

| Both validity and reliability | Neither validity nor reliability | Reliability but not validity |

FIGURE 2.2
Archery analogy for validity and reliability of measures

The following are some examples that illustrate these two require-ments of variable categories (values).

Example of categories that are not mutually inclusive:

Religious Affiliation of Subjects: Catholic
                                     Protestant
                                     Jew
                                     None

What category would you assign to a Hindu subject? There is no cat-egory into which a Hindu would fit. Therefore this set of categories is not mutually inclusive. Let us try another set of categories.

Example of categories that are not mutually exclusive:

Religious Affiliation of Subjects: Catholic
                                     Protestant
                                     Lutheran
                                     Jew
                                     Other
                                     None

Now there would be a category for a Hindu subject—"other"—but to which category would a Lutheran subject be assigned? Either "Prot-estant" or "Lutheran" would fit such a subject. Thus this set of cat-egories is not mutually exclusive. There is more than one category for a Lutheran subject. To make this set of categories mutually ex-clusive, we could omit the category "Lutheran."

Example of categories that are both mutually inclusive and ex-clusive:

Religious Affiliation of Subjects: Catholic
                                     Protestant
                                     Jew
                                     Other
                                     None

To make a set of values of a variable mutually inclusive, a common practice is to add an "other" category and a "none" category so that any subjects not fitting into specific categories could be placed in one of these "residual" categories. Of course, if too many subjects fit into the "other" or "none" categories, we would want to revise the list of categories so we could specifically identify as many sub-jects as possible. Once we are certain that the operational definition used to represent a variable specifies mutually inclusive and exclusive categories, it is possible to further examine the ways in which the categories of a variable can be different.

Because of the power, flexibility, and usefulness of mathematics and statistics, it is important to differentiate the categories of variables to ascertain which characteristics of numbers that the categories of a variable possess. There are four characteristics of numbers that categories of a variable might possess: uniqueness, order (relative size), distance between them, and a zero point which enables one to make proportional statements. Depending on which of these characteristics the categories have, they are labeled either nominal, ordinal, interval, or ratio level variables. Table 2.2 shows which characteristics of numbers each type of variable possesses.

TABLE 2.2

Levels of measurement according to characteristics of numbers possessed by categories of a variable

Characteristics of numbers	Levels of measurement			
	Nominal	Ordinal	Interval	Ratio
Uniqueness	yes	yes	yes	yes
Order	no	yes	yes	yes
Known distance between	no	no	yes	yes
Zero point (proportions)	no	no	no	yes

A *nominal level* variable has categories which are *only* mutually exclusive and mutually inclusive; that is, they are unique. For example, the variable "race of a subject" often has nominal level of measurement. If the categories are Caucasian, Negroid, and Mongoloid, there is no way to order these categories, to subtract them, to add them, or to perform any mathematical operations with them.

An *ordinal level* variable has categories that are not only mutually exclusive and inclusive, but that can be ordered or ranked. Ordinal level variables have categories that can be *meaningfully* arranged along some dimension from more to less, or smaller to greater, or on some other unidimensional feature. If the variable of "place of residence" had the categories of large city, small city, town, and rural, these could be arranged in a meaningful way along the dimension of rural-urban residence, with the large city being the "most" urban and the farm being the "least" urban (or the most rural). Since these categories are not only mutually exclusive and inclusive but can be ordered along some dimension, they would be ordinal level of measurement and the variable would be called an ordinal level variable.

If a variable has categories that are not only mutually inclusive and exclusive and can be ordered, but also have a known distance between their scores (midpoints), the variable would be an *interval level* variable. Some attitude researchers feel that their measures may be scaled at the interval level. Therefore, the score of one subject on such an attitude scale could be compared to another score, and these scores could be subtracted to determine how far apart the scores would be on the "scale." Since it is difficult to imagine someone with *no* attitude (this is different than someone with a neutral attitude), no true zero point exists for most attitude scales. We should note that there is some controversy about whether some attitude scales which are supposed to be interval are actually interval.

A final characteristic of numbers which can be considered is the idea that they have a zero point. When categories have a zero point, it is possible to make proportional types of statements. If categories of a variable are mutually exclusive and inclusive, can be ordered, have a determinable distance between them, and proportional statements can describe them, then they are a *ratio level* of measurement. For example, weight is one example of a ratio level of measurement if the categories are kilograms (kg). An example of a proportional statement would be that 100 kg is twice as much weight as 50 kg or that 5 kg is to 25 kg as 10 kg is to 50 kg.

Notice that each successive level of measurement subsumes the characteristics of numbers which the preceding level possesses. Ordinal variables have all the features of nominal variables; interval variables have all the features of ordinal variables; and ratio level variables have all the features of interval level variables. The fact that different sets of categories have different characteristics of numbers means that there are some mathematical operations that cannot be performed on some level variables. These differences will be fully explored in the next chapter, but an example at this point can demonstrate the point. If we were to use the categories of Protestant, Catholic, Jew, other, and none for the variable of religious affiliation, these would be nominal categories. Therefore, it would not be possible to add these categories or subtract them. It would not make any sense to add a "Jew" and "Protestant" to get a "Catholic," or to subtract an "other" from "Catholic" and get a "none" (no pun intended). To attempt to average scores of the variable of religious affiliation would not make sense because to average you must first add together. In this context an extremely important *caution* is necessary. *In order to determine the level of measurement of a variable, it is necessary to carefully examine the meaning of the categories of the variable—not merely the numerical labels used to stand for the categories.* For example, again using religion, suppose a researcher were to assign numbers to represent the categories in the following manner:

Protestant = 1
Catholic   = 2
Jew   = 3
Other   = 4
None   = 5

If we were not alert and failed to recognize that the numbers were just labels, we might think that these categories were ratio level (numbers themselves are always ratio level). We could subtract 4 from 5 and get a 1. This obviously does not make any sense if we translate back from the number labels to the *meaning* of the categories. It is not meaningful to subtract "other" from "none" and get a "Protestant." Remember, when determining the level of measurement of a variable, the *nature* of the categories must be determined—not just the labels of the categories! Another feature about the categories of variables that can be explored has to do with the limits of categories.

Labels of categories almost always refer to some group of phenomena instead of just one single phenomenon. (Remember, concepts organize our observations.) For example, the category "Protestant" includes not only Lutherans but Methodists, Presbyterians, Christian Reformed, Baptists, and an array of other denominations. Thus the label "Protestant" refers to a range of values or a range of phenomena that fit under or within that label. The category "Caucasian" includes English people, French people, German people, and a host of other nationalities. All categories have width or size to them. The category of "fifteen years old" for the variable of *age* includes all those people who have been alive from fifteen years, no days to fifteen years, 364 days. All people between such boundaries would be placed into the "fifteen" category (value). The idea that all categories of a variable have width, size, or boundaries is often phrased in terms of the limits of the categories of a variable. The *limits* of a category are established by the rules governing the decision of which units are included in the category and which units are excluded from the category. In other words, the limits of a category determine what is inside and what is outside a category.

Variables that have nominal, ordinal, interval, or ratio categories could be discussed in terms of the limits which define the boundaries of various categories. However, limits are most useful and important in discussing interval and ratio level variables because the categories of interval and ratio variables have many of the properties of numbers. The limits of the categories of these types of variables can be defined with numbers (mathematically). Since interval and ratio level categories are often labeled with numbers, the limits of such categories are understood in terms of "real (true) limits." *Real limits* of a category (value) are defined by the highest possible value included in the category—*the upper limit*—and the lowest possible value found within that category—*the lower limit*. The general rules for calculating the true limits of interval and ratio categories represented by numbers are:

Upper True Limit: Add a 5 to the decimal place to the right of the last number appearing in the *highest* value specified by the category.

Lower True Limit: Subtract a 5 from the decimal place to the right of the last number appearing in the *lowest* value specified by the category.

If the categories of a variable are defined by whole numbers, to find the upper limit we add .5 to the highest value specified by the category, and to find the lower limit we subtract .5 from the lowest value specified by the category. The limits of other numbers could be similarly determined. Table 2.3 provides some illustrations.

We can now use the idea of real limits to assign observations to categories. Table 2.4 could define categories in an attitude scale.

TABLE 2.3
Examples of true (real) limits

Numbers	Lower limit	Upper limit
5	5 − .5 = 4.5	5 + .5 = 5.5
7	7 − .5 = 6.5	7 + .5 = 7.5
25	25 − .5 = 24.5	25 + .5 = 25.5
2.3	2.3 − .05 = 2.25	2.3 + .05 = 2.35
162.13	162.13 − .005 = 162.125	162.13 + .005 = 162.135

TABLE 2.4
Hypothetical attitude scale

Attitude scale scores	Upper limit	Lower limit
5	5.0 + .5 = 5.5	5.0 − .5 = 4.5
4	4.0 + .5 = 4.5	4.0 − .5 = 3.5
3	3.0 + .5 = 3.5	3.0 − .5 = 2.5
2	2.0 + .5 = 2.5	2.0 − .5 = 1.5
1	1.0 + .5 = 1.5	1.0 − .5 = .5
0	0.0 + .5 = .5	0.0 − .5 = −.5

Now suppose our attitude test was so precise that a person could receive a value of 3.5; into which category would you classify this person? In the situation where a score is exactly at the boundary of the limits of two categories, the procedure is to use some rule of rounding. There are many different sets of rules for how to round a number. The rule we shall adopt is to round to the nearest number in the desired place. If we want to round to the units place, 3.0–3.4 would be rounded to 3 and 3.6–3.9 would be rounded to 4. Because 3.5 is halfway between 3 and 4, an additional rule must be employed. This rule is to round to the nearest *even* number. Using this rule 3.5 would be rounded to 4 and numbers such as 2.5 would be rounded to 2. The logic of this convention is to make the sum (and hence the average) of a group of numbers (scores) the same whether or not rounding is used. For example, the sum of $2.5 + 3.5 = 6$. Rounding these numbers to the units place would result in adding $2 + 4$ which also equals 6. Table 2.5 gives some examples of rounding different types of numbers to different places. True limits and rounding rules constitute a set of decision rules for placing particular observations (cases or subjects) into categories of interval and ratio level research variables.

TABLE 2.5
Examples of rounding numbers

Original number		Rounded numbers		
Number	to tenths	to hundredths	to tens	to hundreds
514.503	514.5	514.50	510	500
2.56	2.6	[a]	0	0
25.278	25.3	25.28	20	0
3.2	[a]	[a]	0	0
8.500	8.5	8.50	10	0

[a] Rounding can only occur if there are measured numbers to the right of where you are rounding.

A final important characteristic of categories is whether they are continuous or discrete. *Discrete variables* are those that have been conceptualized and measured in such a way that they cannot be meaningfully broken into subparts or subcategories. For example, the population of a country is a discrete variable because although societies can be different sizes, population is determined by counting discrete units, that is, the number of people. It would not be very meaningful to talk about the population of the United States as being 30,000,000.67 people because .67 people is not a meaningful unit for this variable. *Continuous variables* are those that have been conceptualized and measured in such a way that they can be meaningfully broken into smaller and smaller subsections, subparts, or subcategories. The average number of children in a family is often reported in decimal form, such as 2.6 children per family. Average family size is a continuous variable. With this variable it may be perfectly meaningful to talk about parts of a person. This kind of confusion makes it somewhat difficult to determine if a variable is discrete or continuous just by looking at the unit being observed. You must also take into account the *meaning* of the categories in the context of the definition of the variable. Money is another example of a continuous variable. When speaking of hourly wages as a variable, one can meaningfully talk about smaller and smaller parts of a dollar. An hourly wage of $4.2553 is just as meaningful as an hourly wage of $3.50. In this variable, a smaller and smaller part of a dollar can be denoted without destroying the essential idea of money. Another interesting situation that sometimes arises is that variables which appear to be discrete may actually be continuous. One example of this type of variable is the gender of a respondent. Gender is often labeled as either male or female, certainly a discrete variable. However, the idea behind the importance of gender is often continuous. That is, we often use gender to denote certain personality characteristics or socialization history or some complex interplay between biology, psychology, and sociology. We have all known females who are very feminine and females who tend to be more masculine. Similarly, we have met males who are more or less masculine. Although ideally a scientist might wish to conceptualize gender along a continuum of categories from the most stereotypical "female" to the most stereotypical "male," this procedure would be much more costly and time consuming than merely asking a subject to check a box on a questionnaire indicating either male or female. Often this type of economy leads to using discrete variables as opposed to continuous ones. The distinction between discrete and continuous variables is one of those esoteric types of distinctions that are often taught to methodology and statistics students, but are seldom discussed or even considered in the actual research world.

8. SUMMARY

The four major areas of concern in this chapter are the conceptualization of phenomena, the defining process, the explication of variables, and the characteristics of categories of a variable. Our conceptualization stressed the notion that concepts help us to organize and to separate our observations. In order to communicate the idea behind a concept, it is necessary to construct a definition that others can understand. We pointed out that although "loose" definitions are very common in everyday experience, scientists go to great lengths to arrive at "tight" conceptual definitions. Conceptual definitions can be assessed on several levels: they may have different degrees of clarity; they may be more or less directly observable; they may be complete or incomplete; and they may have different degrees of usefulness in understanding our environment. Concepts that have more than one value are said to be variables. The development of definitions of variables may be viewed from two perspectives—the discovery view and the creative view. In either case, in order to be used by researchers, concepts must be made observable through explication.

The process of explication begins with specifying a set of indicators which could represent a given conceptual definition. From these indicators operational definitions must be developed. Operational definitions provide complete directions for what to observe and how to categorize our observations. Operational definitions may include more than one observation or bit of information. Because of this, it is often helpful to use scales and/or indexes for operational definitions of some concepts. The Likert procedure is one very common type of scaling. No matter how variables are operationalized, it is possible to examine the categories resulting from an operational definition.

The last part of this chapter discusses several ways in which categories of variables can be described. The first characteristic deals with whether an operational definition validly and reliably reflects the conceptual definition. Validity refers to the closeness of match achieved between the operational definition and the conceptual definition of a variable. Reliability basically refers to the consistency of measurement of an operational definition. Second, in addition to being reliable and valid, categories of a variable must be mutually inclusive and exclusive. There must be one and only one category for every observation. Third, categories can be examined to see what characteristics of numbers they possess. Such an examination will result in determining the level of measurement of the variable. Categories will either be a nominal, ordinal, interval, or ratio level of measurement. Fourth, all categories have a certain size or dimension. For interval and ratio level variables, the size of the categories can be mathematically described with true limits. True limits are used to determine which observations are in each category. At the boundary of two true limits, rules of rounding must be used to determine to which category an observation belongs. The last characteristic of categories of a variable deals with whether variables are discrete or continuous. Even if the unit being observed is a discrete entity, variables using such entities can be considered continuous.

1. The following list is comprised of a series of discussions in the literature concerning various concepts. Select one of these discussions and read it. Then generate a possible operational definition for the particular concept under consideration and discuss the operational definition's strengths and weaknesses in light of the conceptual discussion.

Concept	Reference for conceptual discussion
Aggression	Kaufman (1970), chapter I, pp. 1–12.
Achievement Motivation	Travers (1977), pp. 359–372.
Conformity	Wrightsman (1977), pp. 607–628.

2. Many concepts have more than one dimension. For each of the commonly used concepts listed, specify as many dimensions as seem appropriate.

    happiness *a feeling of wellbeing laughing, hugging, singing*
    mental illness
    attitude

3. Focusing on the dimensions you have provided in Exercise 2, ✓ develop a conceptual definition for *one* of the concepts.

4. For the concept you have conceptually defined in Exercise 3 suggest at least three possible indicators for each dimension.

5. For three of the indicators specified in response to Exercise 4, describe a possible operational definition.

6. Assess how well you feel each operational definition in Exercise 5 reflects your conceptual definition developed in Exercise 3.

7. The following is a list of concepts:

    power*ful*   conservative
    ✓female   hyperactive
    argument*ative* love   *See p. 35*
    achievement*oriented* good communication
    lower class

    a. Which of these is more likely to be treated as a constant than as a variable?
    b. State what must be done to change each concept to a variable (e.g., identify the variable of which this constant is a part or redefine the concept in such a way that it is a variable).
    c. Define each concept in such a way that it can be treated as a variable.

8. The following is a list of concepts that various social scientists use which appear to be difficult to conceptualize and/or

operationalize. Break into small groups (2–5) and try to go
through the explication process together. As you do so, try to
identify why you are or are not satisfied with each other's task.
(Is one person taking the creative view while the other is taking
the discovery view? Is the conceptualization too broad/narrow,
vague/precise, abstract/concrete? Is the conceptualization too
difficult to operationalize? Does the operational definition
match the conceptual one? Is the sample of indicators
adequate?)

crime	personality
norm	personality adjustment
aggression	neurotic
creativity	social institution
marital adjustment	intelligence

9. For each concept:
   a. Tell what level of measurement would be most appropriate to
   use.
   b. Explain all of the qualities of that level of measurement.

race	class status
IQ scores	client categories
weight	number of clients

10. For the given categories, identify a variable for which the
    following categories are used, and identify the apparent level of
    measurement used based on the labels.
    a. (1) Freshman   (2) Sophomore   (3) Junior   (4) Senior
    b. (1) Polish   (2) Russian   (3) Indian   (4) Korean
    c. (1) enabler   (2) broker   (3) activist (4) advocate
           role   role   role   role
    d. (1) 0–50   (2) 51–100   (3) 101–150
    e. (1) low   (2) medium   (3) high

11. What are the upper and lower limits of the following intervals?
    a. .0001–.0005
    b. 530–534
    c. 3245–3355
    d. 4.1–5.9
    e. .025–.045

12. Identify which of the following descriptions of categories are
    discrete and which are continuous:

    number of people in a sociology class
    average number of people in a sociology class
    birth rate
    length of sentences
    number of books purchased per semester
    number of books read per semester

At this point you should begin to think of at least three or four concepts (variables) that you may wish to study for various projects throughout the rest of the course. You may have some familiarity with some of the tasks in the future chapters, so we may be able to help you to make a selection of possible variables by anticipating some of the tasks.

One social science technique to gather data is the experiment (Chapter 9). Experiments are usually conducted on campus, but there is no reason why they may not be conducted elsewhere (in the "field"). You may wish to consider topics that have often been explored experimentally in the past and that you would enjoy conducting. These include aspects of leadership, conformity, social attraction, hostility or aggression, attitude change, ways to improve learning, cheating, and many other social processes.

A much more common technique in sociology is the survey. In surveys we typically gather data by administering questionnaires. Note that although different indicators are used, the same concepts that we mentioned for experiments could be studied in surveys. You may be interested in pursuing one of those. Alternately, you may remember a concept investigated in a survey that would be interesting to explore experimentally.

We shall also suggest that you explore different data-gathering techniques such as participant observation (where you are "on the scene" in which the activities you are studying are occurring), content analysis (where you use the mass media and documents as sources of data), simulation (in which you may consider asking people to role-play), and unobtrusive measures (where typically you observe without the person's awareness or you find later "evidence" of previous events).

We suggest that you postpone making your final decision until you go to the library (Chapter 5) to explore previous research on the concepts you are considering.

Keep in mind that the overall purpose of this project is to enable you to design your own study(ies), and to collect and analyze your own data.

Below is a list of concepts students have enjoyed studying on their own campus. We intend this list only as a means of stimulating your thinking of possibilities. As you consider alternatives, try to think of potential indicators.

drug/alcohol use	voting behavior	prejudice/ discrimination
cheating	aggression/violence	liberation movements
gambling	educational goals or values	crime
reactions to death	current fads	personality structure
political attitudes	alternative lifestyles	

REFERENCES

BLALOCK, H. JR. *Social statistics,* 2d ed. New York: McGraw-Hill, 1972.

BONJEAN, C., HILL, R., AND MCLEMORE, S. *Sociological Measurement.* San Francisco: Chandler, 1967.

CARROLL, J., AND CASAGRANDE, J. *The Function of Language Classification in Behavior.* In Maccoby, E., Newcomb, T., and Hartley, E. (eds.). *Readings in Social Psychology,* 3d ed. New York: Holt, Rinehart and Winston, 1958, 18–31.

EDWARDS, A. *Techniques of Attitude Scale Construction.* New York: Appleton-Century-Crofts, 1957.

KAUFMANN, H. *A Definition of "Aggression" and Agression-related Terms.* In *Aggression and Altruism.* New York: Holt, Rinehart and Winston, 1970, 1–13.

MILLER, D. *Handbook of Research Design and Social Measurement.* New York: David McKay, 1970.

ROBINSON, J., ATHANASIOU, R., AND HEAD, K. *Measures of Occupational Attitudes and Occupational Characteristics.* Ann Arbor, Mich.: Institute for Social Research, 1969.

ROBINSON, J., RUSK, J., AND HEAD, K. *Measures of Political Attitudes.* Ann Arbor, Mich.: Institute for Social Research, 1968.

ROBINSON, J., AND SHAVER, P. *Measures of Social Psychological Attitudes.* Ann Arbor, Mich.: Institute for Social Research, 1969.

SHAW, M., AND WRIGHT, J. *Scales for the Measurement of Attitudes.* New York: McGraw-Hill, 1967.

TRAVERS, R. *Essentials of Learning,* 4th ed. New York: Macmillan, 1977.

WHORF, B. *Language Thought and Reality.* New York: Wiley, 1956.

WRIGHTSMAN, L. *Social Psychology,* 2d ed. Monterey, Calif.: Brooks Cole, 1977.

II WHAT ARE WE SEARCHING FOR?

CHAPTER 3
RELATIONSHIPS

After studying this chapter, students should be able to:

1. Describe what is meant by a system of variables and tell its importance in the research enterprise.

2. Discuss the importance of the boundary of a system of variables.

3. Define and discuss the meaning of a bivariate relationship.

4. Discuss simple notions of a multivariate analysis.

5. Define and determine independent and dependent variables.

6. Define and discuss what relationships are.

7. Define, describe, construct, and interpret simple scatterplots.

8. Determine and describe whether scatterplots are representing direct, inverse, linear, and nonlinear relationships.

9. Draw the best fitting line in scatterplots.

10. Describe and discuss the meaning of the form, extent, and precision of relationships.

11. Define what is meant by the strength of a relationship.

12. Discuss the role of theory, propositions, and hypotheses in the research process.

Best fitting line   An estimation of the linear least squares line which "fits" the dots of a scatterplot.

Bivariate relationship   A relationship between two variables.

Boundary   The border of a system decided by the researcher.

Dependent variable   The presumed effect or variable that happens second.

Direct relationship   When X increases, Y increases.

Extent of a relationship   The degree of change in the dependent variable for a given change in the independent variable.

Form of a relationship   Refers to whether a relationship is direct, inverse, curvilinear, or no relationship.

Hypotheses   Propositions that are to be tested by research.

Independent variable   The presumed cause or variable that happens first.

Inverse relationship   When X increases, Y decreases.

Linear relationship   Straight line relationships.

Multivariate analysis   Considering a system with at least three variables.

Nonlinear relationships (curvilinear relationship)   When X increases, Y increases and decreases in a patterned way.

Precision of a relationship   The distance that the dots in a scatterplot are away from the best fitting line.

Propositions   Statements about the assumed or demonstrated relationship between concepts.

Relationship   Patterned mutual change between two variables.

Scatterplot (scattergram)   A graphic technique used to determine and describe a relationship between two interval or ratio level variables which utilizes a coordinate system.

Slope   A precise measure of extent in terms of the number of units Y changes for a unit change in X.

Strength of a relationship   A combination of the extent of a relationship and the precision of a relationship.

System   A number of variables that are interrelated and are of theoretical importance.

Theories   Sets of interrelated propositions.

X   A conventional symbol for an independent variable.

Y   A conventional symbol for a dependent variable.

1. VIEWING SYSTEMS OF VARIABLES

The importance of conceptualizing our environment by using variables cannot be stressed too much at this point. All sciences use variables to try to understand different phenomena. In order to reach understanding, however, scientists do not stop with conceptualizing single, isolated variables. A basic premise of science is that our environment can be understood by understanding how different variables are connected or related to one another. Sets of variables that are thought to be interconnected, that is, related to one another, are called *systems of variables*. Only by understanding interrelated systems of variables can we begin to understand the nature of our environment, to understand the world around us. It must be remembered that variables are not "real things," they cannot be touched or seen. They are abstractions. Variables are developed as a result of mental gymnastics. They are intellectual tools which we hope will help us to understand and master phenomena occurring around us.

You may recall an example from high school chemistry or physics concerning the relationship between the temperature (one variable), pressure (another variable), and volume (a final variable) of a gas. The combination of Boyle's and Charles' law allows us to understand this system of three variables with respect to the behavior of gases. Figure 3.1 shows this system of variables in a graphic way.

Notice that whenever a system of variables is considered, a boundary is implied by the selection of variables to be considered. Those variables or conditions not considered are not in the system. The dotted line represents the boundary of the system. The solid lines in the diagram represent relationships between variables.

Using a social science example will further illustrate the idea of a system of variables. Focusing on school achievement level as a vari-

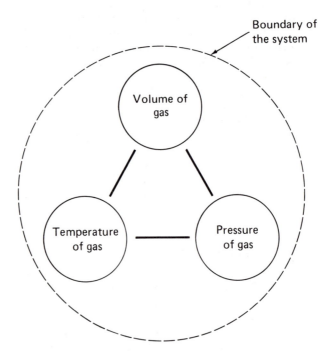

FIGURE 3.1
System of variables of the behavior of gases

able, we might also want to consider pupil intelligence, quality of instruction, pupil social class, degree of education of faculty, and type of school organization as other variables in a system. Notice that there may be other variables that could be related to variables within this system which we have not enumerated. For example, pupil motivation is often considered important for school achievement. Figure 3.2 represents this system of variables. Notice that even though pupil motivation might be related to school achievement, since it is not explicitly included in that system it is outside the system of variables. If motivation were to be included in the system, there would be six new relationships possible in that new system.

The goal of science is to investigate an entire system of variables. These systems can be quite complex, as Figure 3.2 illustrates.

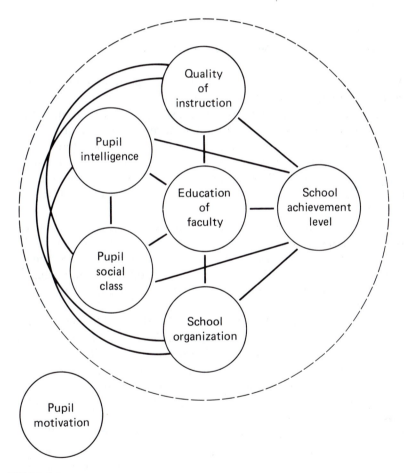

FIGURE 3.2
System of school achievement variables

Therefore, we will first focus on one relationship, one of the solid lines in the diagram. In this chapter the discussion will be limited to the consideration of the relationship between two variables—a *bivariate relationship*. When *more than two* variables are considered, the investigation would be called a *multivariate analysis*. (Chapter 11 specifically deals with multivariate analysis.) Although it is necessary to fully understand how bivariate relationships are defined, described, and determined, it is probably safe to say that almost always the researcher would prefer to do a multivariate analysis. This is especially the case if the consideration of additional variables might modify the nature of the bivariate relationship viewed in isolation. That is, sometimes by enlarging the system of variables considered, the nature of relationships within the system are modified. Keep this fact in mind as we continue to focus on one bivariate relationship.

2. THE ROLE OF RELATIONSHIPS IN CAUSATION

When discussing a system of variables, it is perhaps more common to talk about the system in terms of cause and effect than it is to just talk about "relationships." For example, rather than talking about the relationship between temperature and volume of a gas, we would probably say something like: "Does a higher temperature *cause* the volume of gas to change?" Instead of saying that school achievement and pupil intelligence are related, we would like to find out if high intelligence is one of the causes of good achievement.

We said in Chapter 1 that there are four conditions which must be demonstrated before causation can be claimed: (1) temporal order, (2) mutual patterned change, (3) the elimination of alternative explanations, and (4) belief in a "true link." As an indication of time order, the two variables in a bivariate relationship are given two different labels. One is to denote the presumed cause and the other is to indicate the presumed effect. The variable that occurs first in time, the presumed cause, is called the *independent variable*. The variable that occurs second in time, the presumed effect, is called the *dependent variable*. In this text and in many others the independent variable is represented by X and the dependent variable is denoted by Y. These terms and symbols can be used interchangeably: first variable = presumed cause = independent variable = X; the second variable = presumed effect = dependent variable = Y.

A *relationship* is defined as patterned mutual change between variables. That is, as X changes, Y changes in a patterned way. Demonstrating a relationship between variables is a necessary part of ascertaining causation, but it is only one part of causation. Simply because a scientist observes a relationship does not automatically mean that causation is present. There are many techniques that scientists use to determine whether relationships exist and for describing the nature of a relationship. The following section introduces one such technique, the scatterplot.

3. FINDING PATTERNED, MUTUAL CHANGE—THE SCATTERPLOT

A *scatterplot* is a graphic technique used to determine and describe a relationship between two interval or ratio level variables. This technique cannot accurately be used for variables that are either nominal or ordinal, but the logic of the scatterplot carries over to these two lower levels of measurement. One way of determining patterned mutual change is to ask the following question: "As values of the independent variable (X) increase, what kind of changes occur in the values of the dependent variable (Y)?" There are two kinds of "change" in X that are implied by this question. The first situation that is conceptualized as "change" in X is straightforward. Subjects' category on X may be observed at different points in time. For those subjects whose score (category or value) is different over that period of time, we say there is a change in X for that subject. Therefore the independent variable is said to change.

The second situation that is conceptualized as change in X is not quite so straightforward. Different subjects may be observed at the same point in time and have different values of the independent variable; that is, subjects are in various categories of the X variable at the same point in time. "Change" is seen as existing in the independent variable because different values are held by different units. Comparing these values between units can be conceptualized as *change*. To view this type of change we need paired observations of X and Y for different subjects at one point in time. To observe the former type of change we need observations for X and Y over time for the same subjects. In either case, since we want to know about patterned *mutual* change, we need paired raw data (observations) on both the independent and dependent variables.

To graphically represent paired raw data, a coordinate system of graphing can be used. Many of you have already been exposed to coordinate graphing systems in high school, but we will review this technique.

A coordinate system is composed of perpendicular intersecting lines, one horizontal and one vertical. The point at which these lines (*axes*) intersect is called the *origin*. Starting from the origin, arbitrary sized lengths represent various values. Values along the horizontal axis to the right of the origin are positive and values to the left of the origin are negative. Values along the vertical axis above

62

the origin are positive and values below the origin are negative. Figure 3.3 is a general coordinate system.

For most research involving people the norm is to use only positive values of variables. Since this is the case, one usually only uses the first quadrant of the system. Most often, the horizontal axis represents values or categories of the independent variable (X) and the marks on the vertical axis represent or correspond to categories or values of the dependent variable (Y).

Figure 3.4 is the general form of the most common type of scatterplot for representing a bivariate relationship. In order to explore the different possible general types of scatterplots, the type of labeling present in Figure 3.4 will be referred to as standard labeling. Anytime scatterplots in this text are not otherwise labeled, you can assume standard labeling. To construct a scatterplot the matched pairs of values of X and Y are plotted on the coordinate system. Note that in area *a* of Figure 3.4 all paired values would have a relatively low value of X and a relatively high value of Y. In area *b* the paired values would still have relatively high values of Y but now they would also have relatively high values of X. In area *c* both X and Y values for each pair would both be relatively low. Finally, in area *d*,

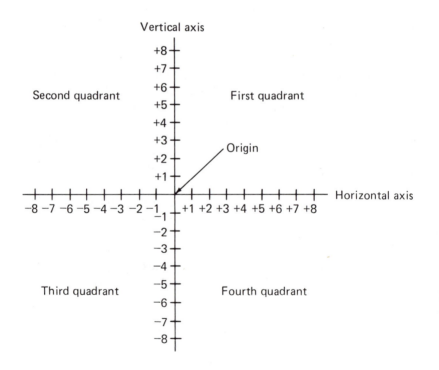

FIGURE 3.3
General coordinate system

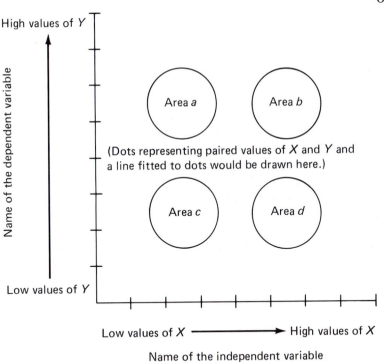

High values of *Y*

Name of the dependent variable

Area *a*   Area *b*

(Dots representing paired values of *X* and *Y* and a line fitted to dots would be drawn here.)

Area *c*   Area *d*

Low values of *Y*

Low values of *X* ⟶ High values of *X*

Name of the independent variable

FIGURE 3.4
General form of bivariate scatterplot

Y values would be relatively low but X values would be relatively high. After the matched paired values are appropriately plotted, a line which best describes (fits) the dots is drawn. Moving from raw data to a scatterplot is fully explored in the next section, but for the moment let us look at some models of scatterplots.

There are five possible answers to the question, "As X increases, what kind of change occurs in Y?" They are: (1) Y also increases, (2) Y decreases, (3) Y increases *and* decreases in a patterned way, (4) Y changes but not in a patterned way, and (5) Y does not change at all. The way that scatterplots are constructed helps us determine which of these answers is found in our data. Values of X (the independent variable) are arranged from low to high as we go from left to right on the graph. As we move our eyes from left to right we will see "increases" in X because of this feature. As we move our eyes the pattern of the line on the scatterplot will tell us which answer we have for changes in Y. If the line only goes up as we scan from left to right, Y is also increasing. If the line only goes down, Y is decreasing. If the line goes up and down in a patterned way, Y is changing in a patterned way (decreasing = down; increasing = up).

64

If no simple line can be drawn, then Y is changing but not in a patterned way. If the line is horizontal, then Y is not changing at all. (Of course, if the line is vertical, X is not changing.)

When the answer to the question is "Y also increases," there is a relationship between X and Y. In this case the relationship is called a *direct relationship* (sometimes called a positive relationship). The *form of the relationship* is direct. Different types of direct relationships are represented by the lines in Model I scatterplots displayed in Figure 3.5. The exact manner of fitting this line to an actual scatterplot will be discussed in the next section.

When the answer to the question is "Y decreases," the form of the relationship between X and Y is said to be *inverse* (or negative). Various types of inverse relationships are represented by the Model II scatterplots in Figure 3.6.

Both Model I and Model II scatterplots show one straight line which "fits" the dots representing paired values of X and Y. In both

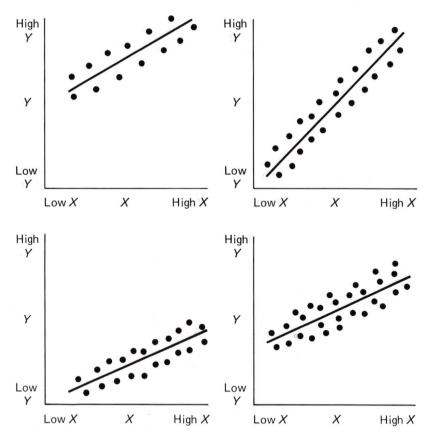

FIGURE 3.5
Model I scatterplots — direct relationships

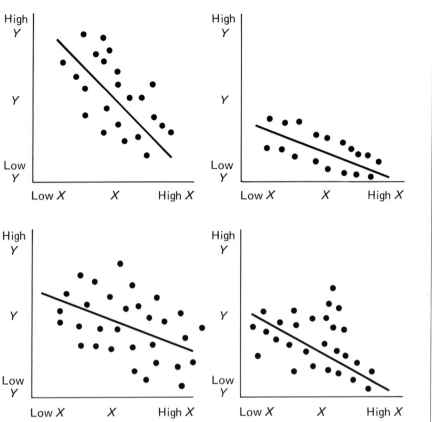

FIGURE 3.6
Model II scatterplots—inverse relationships

of these cases the relationships are called *linear relationships*. Linear means straight line. When a straight line (but one which is neither horizontal nor vertical) best fits the dots on a scatterplot, a linear relationship exists.

When the answer to the question posed above is "Y increases and decreases in a patterned way," there is also a relationship called *nonlinear* or *curvilinear* because the patterned change cannot be described with a straight line. Figure 3.7 shows a series of curvilinear-type scatterplots.

Although the Model III scatterplots show series of connected straight lines, it is also possible to smooth these series of lines out into a curve, thus the name *curvi*linear.

A fourth type of model scatterplot results when the answer to the question is "Y changes but not in a patterned way." Figure 3.8 is one such type of plot. The haphazard arrangement of the dots in such a model makes it impossible to detect any pattern. In this case

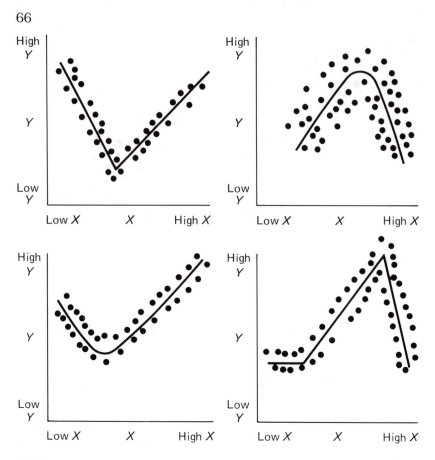

FIGURE 3.7
Model III scatterplots — curvilinear relationships

the conclusion would be that there is no relationship between X and Y.

Figure 3.9 also demonstrates the case where there is no relationship between X and Y. Since there is no change in the dependent variable, mutual pattern change cannot exist.

A final type of scatterplot exhausts all the possible types of models, but it does not result from answering the same question which has been posed to create the first five models. Model VI scatterplots show that if both variables do not simultaneously change in a patterned way, then a relationship cannot exist. The remaining possibility is that Y changes but the independent variable (X) does not change. Figure 3.10 shows such types of scatterplots. Because X is not changing, no relationship exists between X and Y.

Now that we have presented the six possible types of scatterplots which could result from plotting a bivariate relationship, we can

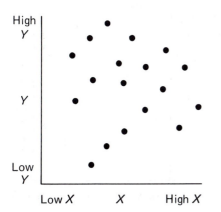

FIGURE 3.8
Model IV scatterplots — no relationships

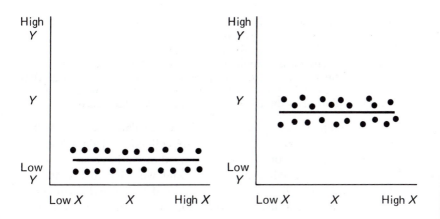

FIGURE 3.9
Model V scatterplots — no relationships

turn to the task of taking actual observations (raw data) and plotting them on a scatterplot. Then we can come to a conclusion about the relationship (or lack of relationship) that exists in the data.

4. MOVING FROM OBSERVATIONS TO SCATTERPLOTS

There are seven distinct steps in analyzing a bivariate relationship between interval or ratio level variables by using a scatterplot. They are as follows:

1. Collect paired bivariate data.
2. Label axes of plot with names of variables.

68

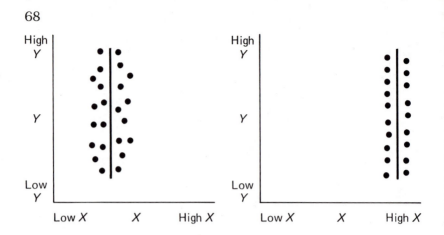

FIGURE 3.10
Model VI scatterplots — no relationships

3. Mark units of both variables on respective axes.
4. Plot data with dots or numbers.
5. Draw an envelope around the plotted data.
6. Draw a best fitting line to describe the envelope of dots.
7. Describe the form, extent, and precision of the relationship that exists, or conclude that there is no relationship between the two variables plotted as depicted by the particular data used.

The first step is to collect paired bivariate data. Several of the chapters that follow are addressed to the collection of data (making observations). At this point let us assume that we have successfully collected a set of paired bivariate data and we wish to discuss the relationship or lack of relationship portrayed in the data. However, remember that a great deal of careful planning and work goes on in the research process prior to the time of the actual analysis. The ideal research project will have an analysis plan prior to the collection of data. This is one of the reasons for understanding something about analysis prior to discussing data collection. Remember that there are two types of changes that may be examined in searching for mutual patterned change: different values of a variable for many subjects at one point in time, or different values in the same subjects (units) over a period of time. The second type of change is represented in the following illustration of the construction of a scatterplot. The "subjects" (Table 3.1) are 15 leading universities and 15 leading corporations. The observations are made over a period of years, from 1963 to 1976. Although these data are hypothetical, they are similar to actual data that could be considered.

For the 15 universities, the number of federal research grants is listed. If these data were presented in a research article, the authors would likely argue that this could be an indicator of "progress of

TABLE 3.1

Observations of progress of knowledge and economic health for the years 1963–1976

Year of observation	Progress of knowledge[a]	Economic health[b]
1963	7	7
1964	19	14
1965	19	11
1966	29	18
1967	25	18
1968	15	9
1969	8	4
1970	5	11
1971	15	12
1972	25	17
1973	12	11
1974	10	9
1975	28	19
1976	11	11

[a] Number of research projects in 15 leading universities
[b] Average profit margin in 15 leading corporations

knowledge" or some other such variable. For the 15 leading companies, the average profit margin is given. It could be argued that this could be an indicator of "economic health" of a society. While these data could be conceptualized in many ways, if the data are conceptualized this way we actually have one observation of the concept of "progress of knowledge" and one observation of "economic health" for each year from 1963 to 1976. Since we have the data for these two variables for the same year, the data are *paired.* For plotting we would then have 14 sets of paired data. Since there are 14 years or 14 "points in time" when each unit is measured, these data represent one type of change in X. Each unit is measured on the same variables at different points in time.

The second and third steps involve setting up a blank scatterplot with the variables labeled and the units marked on the axes. Figure 3.11 shows the "blank" scatterplot for the data in Table 3.1. Note that a decision must be made as to which variable is independent and which is dependent. For this illustration, we assume that Progress of Knowledge logically precedes Economic Health. Hence, if there is a relationship between these variables, Progress of Knowledge leads to Economic Health (or lack of it). With this decision made, the axes can be labeled with the names of the variables. Now the axes must be marked off with the units of the variables. Assuming that the data are at least interval level, the units should be equally spaced along the axes. Usually the axes are both nearly

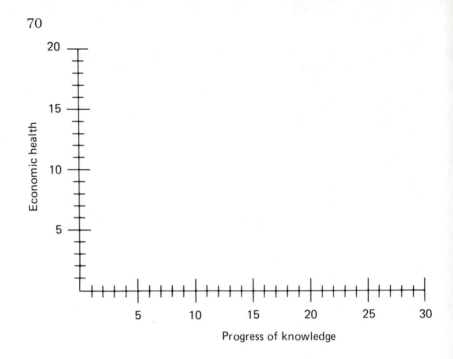

FIGURE 3.11
Blank scatterplot for analyzing the relationship between progress of knowledge and economic growth

the same length. The units usually start with zero at the origin and continue along the axes until just a few more units than exist in the data are marked on the axes. Note that for the variable of Progress of Knowledge the highest value is 29, so if we mark 30 units on the axis there will be enough units for the plot. On the other hand, the variable of Economic Health has a maximum value of 19. Therefore 20 units marked on the Y axis is sufficient. Notice, also, that a heading is provided for each figure. This heading should give enough information so the reader can determine the exact content of the figure.

The fourth step is to actually plot the data on the blank form of the scatterplot. Figure 3.12 shows the progress of plotting the data on the graph. The first plot shows the dot representing the first matched pair of values for the two variables. In 1963 the X value is 7 so we find the unit marked 7 on the horizontal axis and mentally we draw a vertical line extending up from the 7 mark. The Y value is also 7 for 1963 so we find the 7 mark on the vertical axis and mentally draw a horizontal line to the right of that mark. Where these two imaginary lines cross, a dot is placed. This dot shows both the value of the dependent and independent variable for the 1963 set of paired observations. The second plot shows adding the second

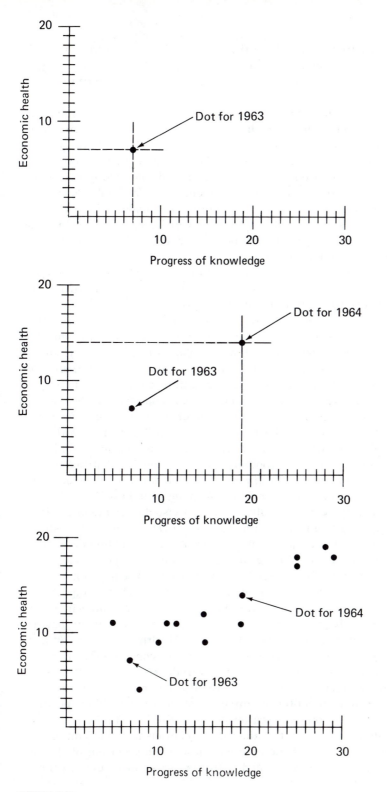

FIGURE 3.12
Graphing the illustrative data on a blank scatterplot

paired set from 1964 where the value of X is 19 and the value of Y is 14. The final plot shows a completed graphing of all the sets. As an exercise, focus on any one of the dots and try to determine which year the dot represents.

When there are relatively few data cases, as in this example, there is usually no matched pair that is like any other matched pair. However, when there are more than one pair of observations with the same values, it would not be possible to put more than one dot in the same location on the scatterplot and still be able to distinguish each observation. To solve this problem, either a number or letter is placed on the plot to signify that more than one dot is located at that place. Because we will deal with relatively simple plots in this chapter, no numbers or letters will be used. There will be no overlapping dots in the examples used.

Once all of the cases have been plotted, it is possible to attempt to detect a pattern. The first step in this process, and the fifth in the total procedure, is to draw an envelope around most of the dots. If there are a few dots that are apart from most of the dots, the envelope would not encompass them. Figure 3.13 shows the envelope that could be drawn around the dots plotted in the previous step. If the envelope is either in the form of a cigar or a snake, then a pattern exists. If this is not the case, a pattern does not exist. If a pattern does not exist, then a relationship does not exist in the data.

The sixth step is to draw a line which best fits the envelope. In doing this, of course, the line will also "fit" or represent the dots themselves. Figure 3.14 shows the best fitting line for the envelope drawn in Figure 3.13 Another name for the best fitting line for linear relationships is the *linear least squares line,* also sometimes referred to as the *regression line*. Although the best fitting line can be calculated mathematically, for now a visual estimate of the linear least squares line is adequate. The *best fitting line* is the estimate of the linear least squares line for either direct or inverse relationships. Once the best fitting line has been drawn, the envelope is no longer useful and is not retained in the finished scatterplot.

The last step is to interpret the form of the relationship. We can now refer to the model scatterplots previously presented in Section 3 of this chapter. The data showing the relationship between Progress of Knowledge and Economic Health is like the Model I plots found in the Figure 3.5. Therefore we conclude that there is a direct relationship between the two variables; that is, as Progress of Knowledge increases, Economic Health increases. The *form* of the relationship is direct (or the direction of the relationship is positive).

If we have a complete scatterplot as in Figure 3.14, then there are two additional characteristics of a relationship that can be discussed: the extent of the relationship and the precision of the relationship. Extent is concerned with the degree of change in the de-

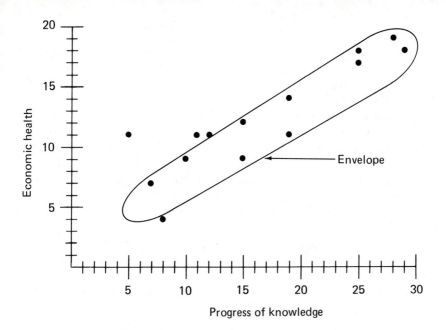

FIGURE 3.13
Drawing an envelope around the dots

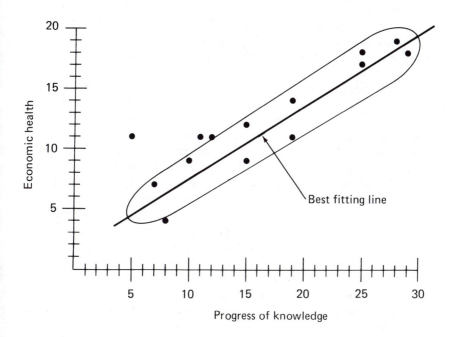

FIGURE 3.14
Best fitting line for envelope around the dots

pendent variable for a given change in the independent variable. The extent of the change in a relationship is often called the *slope* of the best fitting line. If Y changes a lot for a given change in X, then the extent is "high." If Y changes a little for a given change in X, then the extent is "low." (Extent can be referred to in rough terms such as low, medium, or high.) A more precise measure of extent can be computed by calculating the slope of the best fitting line. *Slope* is defined as the number of units that Y changes for a unit change in X. It is calculated by dividing the change in Y associated with a given change in X. If we use the symbol Δ (delta) to stand for change, a formula for extent (slope) would be

$$\text{Extent} \approx \text{Slope} = \frac{\text{Change in dependent variable}}{\text{Change in independent variable}} = \frac{\Delta Y}{\Delta X}$$

The best fitting line can be used to determine slope in the following way. Referring to Figure 3.15, first take an arbitrary distance along the X-axis and mark it off. Draw lines straight up from the ends of the marked-off region until they reach the best fitting line. At the points where they reach the best fitting line, draw two lines directly to the left (horizontally) until they reach the Y-axis. The distance between these two points on the Y-axis is delta (Δ)Y. The distance between the two points originally marked on the X-axis is delta X. Dividing these numbers gives the slope, which is the number of units that Y changes for every unit change in X. *Extent is used in this text as an estimate of the slope.*

When dealing with linear relationships, the greater the tilt of the best fitting line, the greater the extent (i.e., the greater the quotient of $\Delta Y / \Delta X$, the greater the extent). Of course, if the linear relationship is inverse, the slope will be negative. Thus, a minus sign would precede the slope of an inverse relationship. However, even in the inverse case, the greater the tilt of the best fitting line, the greater the extent of the relationship between the variables presented on the scatterplot. If there is a curvilinear (nonlinear) pattern in the scatterplot, extent is not a meaningful way to describe the relationship, because slope is constantly changing on a curved line. Of course, if there is no patterned mutual change, extent of a relationship is not a meaningful concept.

The third characteristic of a relationship to be described by a scatterplot is the *precision* of the relationship, sometimes called the *goodness of fit*. *Precision* refers to how exactly the best fitting line describes the dots. If the dots are close to the line, precision of the relationship is high. If the dots are not close to the line, precision is low. Precision is relevant for a curvilinear relationship as well as for linear relationships because there is a best fit-

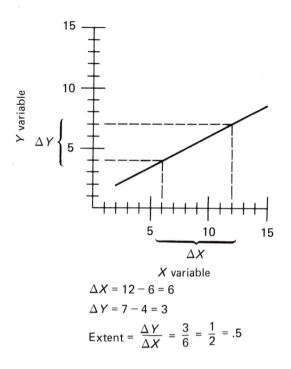

$$\Delta X = 12 - 6 = 6$$

$$\Delta Y = 7 - 4 = 3$$

$$\text{Extent} = \frac{\Delta Y}{\Delta X} = \frac{3}{6} = \frac{1}{2} = .5$$

FIGURE 3.15
Determining slope (extent) of a direct relationship

ting line that describes the pattern of dots in both cases. Although the sum of the vertical distance between the dots and the best fitting line can be mathematically determined, it will be adequate for this book to estimate the sum of these distances by using such terms as "high," "medium," or "low." Precision is a term we use to denote the estimate of this mathematical computation.

In summary, after any scatterplot is constructed, it is possible, and desirable, to discuss the nature of a relationship in terms of the *form, extent,* and *precision* of the relationship graphed. *Form* refers to patterned change and is sometimes called direction. If there is a patterned change, then a relationship exists. If no pattern exists in the scatterplot, then there is no relationship. Therefore the presence of form is one way to test for the *existence* of a relationship. Form can be direct (positive), inverse (indirect or negative), or curvilinear (nonlinear). *Extent* is the estimate of the slope of the best fitting line for linear relationships, and is positive for direct relationships and negative for inverse relationships. Extent is not meaningful for curvilinear bivariate relationships. Extent can be described either by terms ranging from very high to very low, or by actually computing a mathematical slope of the best fitting line. *Pre-*

cision (goodness of fit) of a bivariate relationship estimates how near the dots of a scatterplot are to the best fitting line. Precision can be described by using terms ranging from very good to very poor; or the actual distance that the dots are from the best fitting

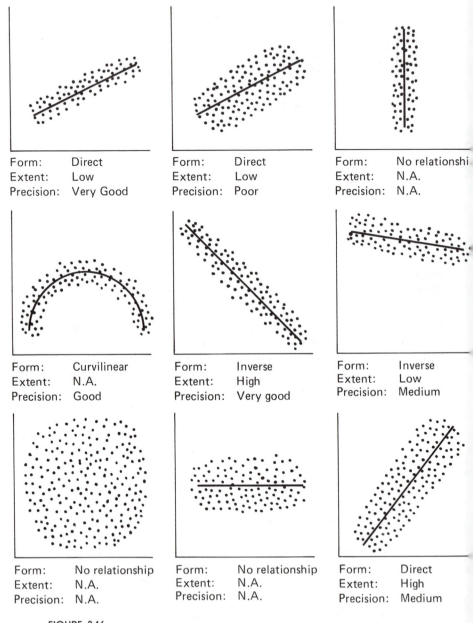

Form:	Direct
Extent:	Low
Precision:	Very Good

Form:	Direct
Extent:	Low
Precision:	Poor

Form:	No relationshi
Extent:	N.A.
Precision:	N.A.

Form:	Curvilinear
Extent:	N.A.
Precision:	Good

Form:	Inverse
Extent:	High
Precision:	Very good

Form:	Inverse
Extent:	Low
Precision:	Medium

Form:	No relationship
Extent:	N.A.
Precision:	N.A.

Form:	No relationship
Extent:	N.A.
Precision:	N.A.

Form:	Direct
Extent:	High
Precision:	Medium

FIGURE 3.16
Form, extent, and precision of illustrative scatterplots

line can be mathematically computed. Sometimes the term *strength* of a relationship is used to refer to a combination of extent and precision. When describing the nature of a relationship, all three features should be discussed. It should be noted that the most common terms for describing the nature of a relationship are direction, slope, and goodness of fit. We believe that the notions of form, extent, and precision are useful ways to approximate these more formal terms.

The description of extent and precision is somewhat arbitrary. Formal standards for what is high extent or good precision do not exist. However, consensus in this judgment can be developed if enough experience is gained. Figure 3.16 shows a series of scatterplots using standard labeling, and below each plot is given our decision concerning the form, extent, and precision of the bivariate relationship described by each graph.

5. NONGRAPHIC WAYS TO DETERMINE RELATIONSHIPS

The scatterplot is a graphic technique used for describing relationships for interval and ratio level variables. There are two other types of procedures for describing bivariate relationships: percentage tables and statistical measures of association. Chapter 4 is devoted to describing relationships with percentage methods and Chapter 13 is devoted to measures of association.

Strictly speaking, there are no graphic techniques for describing the nature of a relationship for nominal or ordinal level variables. However, if we are willing to assume that the distance between ordinal categories of a variable are equal (which cannot really be determined), then the scatterplot technique could be used in an analogous fashion. This is the case since it would still be meaningful to discuss ordinal variables in terms of "as X increases, how does Y change?" Such a question has no meaning when dealing with nominal variables because the categories cannot be arranged in any type of order from low to high. Therefore the form of a relationship between nominal variables has no parallel meaning. Extent of a relationship between ordinal variables is directly analogous to interval and ratio level variables, but for nominal variables the closest we can get is to talk about the size of percentage differences. The procedures for such techniques are covered in Chapter 4. Precision for ordinal variables and nominal variables can only be discussed in terms of the ability to predict the degree to which only one particular level of Y is associated with particular values of X. There are measures of association for ordinal level variables that describe form, extent, and precision. In addition, there are measures of association for nominal variables that have as their basis the strength of the relationship. Such measures of association are covered in Chapter 13.

Once an understanding of how to describe the nature of a bivariate relationship is reached, we can again remind ourselves that this analysis is often near the "end" of the research act. Now that we have a glimpse of the end product of research (describing relationships), we can begin to deal with the processes that result in finding relationships.

6. THEORY, PROPOSITIONS, AND HYPOTHESES IN RESEARCH

Theories are often defined as sets of interrelated propositions; *propositions* are statements about the relationship between concepts; and *hypotheses* are considered propositions that are to be tested by research. There is much discussion concerning the interplay of theory and research. Some of these considerations were introduced in Chapter 1. One polar perspective is that theory guides research and then research builds theory. The other polar view is that one can be misled by theories. In the latter view, it is felt that important facts are often not uncovered because theories do not indicate that they should be "looked for." In addition, those that are uncovered supposedly are used in a manner that does not lead to a better understanding of our environment. On the other hand, the first view believes in the "building block" model of science in which new science enlarges, refines, and expands previous science. The second view holds that previous science puts blinders on present science and only by throwing off the intellectual shackles of the past can a creative science emerge that will enable increased understanding. The first view is the more traditional and the one most closely followed in this text. We hope that scientists are continually alert to the possibility of new and creative ideas, theories, propositions, and hypotheses, and that our society will always provide the talent and resources necessary to pursue unorthodox investigations and lines of reasoning. Chapter 12 introduces some of the alternative research strategies that will hopefully serve this purpose.

One use of theory in research is to provide propositions that can be empirically tested. That is, very often the hypotheses tested in science stem from theory, which is often bolstered by some previous research. Again, an *hypothesis* is defined as a statement about the nature of the relationship between variables that can be empirically tested. Very often an hypothesis being researched is referred to as a working hypothesis or research hypothesis. If the research hypothesis is to be tested, it can be translated into a statistical hypothesis. Chapter 13 discusses how statistical hypotheses are derived from research hypothesis and how they can be tested.

Research hypotheses usually specify which variable is independent, which variable is dependent, and what the anticipated form of the relationship is. An hypothesis seldom provides predictions about the extent and precision of a relationship in the social sciences. It is left to the research analyst to conclude if the form of the relationship is as predicted by the research hypothesis. The analyst should also provide information about the extent and precision of the relationship which will expand understanding of the theoretical and practical usefulness of the relationship found in the data.

We have talked about theory as though it exists and that somehow it is just there when you need it. This is not the case. Depending on the phenomena or problem under investigation, the completeness and quality of theory may vary quite a bit. There is extensive theory concerning social class but much less concerned with extrasensory perception. Theory exists in the minds of scientists, in notes and logs of researchers, in published theoretical treatises, in research journals, in government reports, in master's and doctoral theses, in the popular press and media, and in the culture of society. The most available theory, and usually the most complete, is that which is published. Therefore most researchers rely heavily on published materials as sources of theoretical wisdom and hypotheses. In addition, publication of research and theory is seen as the most useful mechanism for fulfilling the building block model of science. It is therefore important to understand the manner in which publications are organized and the techniques for obtaining access to published research and theory. The process of gaining access to and reaching conclusions about published materials is discussed in Chapter 5. However, prior to this, Chapter 4 presents a very popular technique for describing bivariate relationships—percentage table analysis.

7. SUMMARY

Scientists want to describe systems of variables because it is thought that by understanding the relationship between variables in a system, we can better understand our environment. We can begin to explore systems by focusing on bivariate relationships (relationships between two variables). Scatterplots can be used to graphically represent different types of relationships between two variables. By answering the question, "As X changes what kind of changes take place in Y?" we can determine the form of a relationship. If Y also increases, a direct relationship exists. If Y decreases, an inverse relationship is found. If Y changes in a patterned way but not simply by increasing or decreasing, a curvilinear relationship is described. If either X or Y does not change, or if there is no patterned change between X and Y, no relationship exists. Although demonstrating a relationship between variables is a necessary part of causation, not all variables that are associated are causally related.

In addition to determining the form of a relationship, it is possible to describe the extent and precision of a scatterplot. Extent is an estimate of the slope of the linear least squares lines. Precision is an estimate of the goodness of fit of a scatterplot. Although it is possible to actually calculate slope and goodness of fit, estimates can serve our purpose at this point. The form, extent, and precision of scatterplots adequately describe relationships between interval and ratio level variables, but describing relationships between nominal and ordinal variables is not possible with scatterplots. Nevertheless, the concept of relationships applies in all cases.

Theory often serves as the basis for the investigation of relationships. In particular, hypotheses generated from theories are often stated prior to research and tested by observations. Hypotheses very often only predict the expected form of relationships being investigated. By testing hypotheses with the use of scatterplots, the scientist comes closer to understanding systems of variables. In this way analyzing the nature of relationships with scatterplots serves as a very important tool in the search for relationships.

EXERCISES

1. For the hypotheses mentioned below, discuss how clearly each spells out the nature of the relationship (including the identification of the independent and dependent variable).
   a. Complex variegated stimuli attract more attention than do simple ones.
   b. Broken homes cause delinquency.
   c. Status is related to church attendance.
   d. People's attitudes and behavior toward ethnic groups typically conform to the norms of the community and of the groups with which they live.
   e. The farther apart the classes, the fewer the personal relations as "equals."
   f. Sexual behavior differs by social class, especially for men.
   g. Intellectual ability increases up to age 18 after which it starts decreasing very rapidly.
   h. Between generations, the weaker the parents' feelings on a matter, the less influence they exert on their children.

2. Construct at least four *good* hypotheses from the following list of variables. You do not have to use all of them but use each variable only once.

a. anomie	g. divorce
b. female	h. socioeconomic status
c. birthrate	i. economic prosperity
d. suicidal tendency	j. bureaucratization
e. age	k. marital harmony
f. dissent	l. conditioning

3. Make up an hypothesis for each concept listed in Exercises 2, 7, and 8 in Chapter 2.

4. For the following sets of bivariate data:
a. Construct scatterplots.
b. Interpret the data in terms of the nature of the relationship (form, extent, precision).

Yearly income of parents based on $1,000	Years of formal education
7	7
19	14
19	11
29	18
25	18
15	9
8	11
4	4
15	12
25	17
12	11
10	9
28	19
11	11

Amount of land in acres per farmer in a preindustrial farming community	Number of children per farm family
15	3
75	4
120	6
35	2
10	2
115	5
240	4
180	7
160	6
135	5
95	4
40	3
85	5
60	4
25	2
170	9
185	11
220	5
210	4
175	6

Subject	Number of turns taken speaking within group	Leadership rating by other members[a]
1	20	3
2	30	4
3	65	5
4	15	1
5	40	3
6	70	6
7	45	4
8	35	2
9	60	6
10	25	1

[a] Ratings from 1 to 6, 1 being low

5. Your instructor will provide you with, or refer you to, social science articles such as those indicated below:

Latane, B., and Dabbs, J. M., Jr. "Sex, Group Size and Helping in Three Cities." *Sociometry*, 1975, 38, 2, 180–194.

Spanier, G. B. "Perceived Sex Knowledge, Exposure to Eroticism, and Premarital Sexual Behavior: The Impact of Dating." *The Sociological Quarterly*, 17, Spring 1976, 247–261.

a. State the major hypothesis.

b. Examine to what degree form, extent, and precision are spelled out in each hypothesis.

6. Construct hypothetical scatterplots according to the following criteria:

a. Two scatterplots with different extent (slope) but the same precision (goodness of fit).

b. Two scatterplots with the same extent but different precision.

PROJECT

For each of the variables you began to ponder in Chapter 2:

1. List an hypothesis you would find interesting to study.

2. Identify whether the concept you are considering is the independent or dependent variable.

3. For each dependent variable in your hypotheses, write at least two more hypotheses. That is, think of at least two other independent variables.

4. For each new variable in all your hypotheses, try to list two indicators.

5. Review your list of hypotheses. With your knowledge at this point, indicate which of these you would be able to research on your campus or in your community.

REFERENCES

ANDERSON, T., AND ZELDITCH, M., JR. *A Basic Course in Statistics.* New York: Holt, Rinehart and Winston, 1968.

BLALOCK, H., JR. *Social Statistics*, 2d ed. New York: McGraw-Hill, 1972.

MUELLER, J., SCHUESSLER, K., AND COSTNER, H. *Statistical Reasoning in Sociology*, 2d ed. Boston: Houghton Mifflin, 1970.

CHAPTER 4
DETECTING RELATIONSHIPS
WITH PERCENTAGES

After studying this chapter, students should be able to:

1. Discuss the initial ideas about how percentage tables can be viewed as estimates of scatterplots.

2. Discuss, explain, recognize, give examples of, and construct groups of units in a way that shows change in the independent variable for data that has been collected using any research design.

3. Discuss the wisdom of organizing observations to aid in understanding what we have observed.

4. Construct tallies from raw data.

5. Construct simple frequency distributions from tallies.

6. Discuss simple examples of coding and be able to employ simple coding instructions.

7. Discuss the importance of using percentages to compare distributions.

8. Translate frequency distributions into percentage distributions.

9. Discuss, explain, recognize, give examples of, and construct distributions which show change in the dependent variable for data that has been collected using any research design.

10. Determine cutting points and construct percentage tables given a set of data.

11. Discuss the issues surrounding the question of cutting points and give examples of how and why cutting points are important.

12. Determine the form and relative strength of relationships from percentage tables for all levels of variables.

13. Approximate scatterplots from percentage tables and construct percentage tables from scatterplots.

14. Discuss the problems associated with the interpretation of percentage table analysis.

Cell   One section of a percentage table.

Coding   Relabeling raw data in some manner. (The process of changing observations into usable data).

Contingency table analysis   Synonym for percentage table analysis.

Cross-sectional survey   Survey in which units are measured at one point in time.

Cross-tabs   Synonym for percentage table analysis.

Cumulative survey   Surveys where data are collected at different points in time but all the data are put together in one group.

Cutting points   The values that border particular categories of a variable and determine how many categories of a variable there are going to be.

Longitudinal panel survey   Survey in which the same units are measured at different points in time on the same variables.

Percentage distributions   Distributions where frequencies have been converted into percentages.

Percentage table analysis   Using percentages to determine mutual patterned change (a relationship) between two or more variables.

Raw data   Types of observations as originally recorded. (There is no such thing as cooked data.)

Scan (scanning)   Moving the eyes from left to right in order to "see" change.

Simple frequency distribution   A two-column table in which the categories of the variable are placed in the left-hand column and the sum of the tallies (frequency) is placed in the right-hand column.

Strength of a relationship   Combination of the extent and precision of relationships used in percentage table analysis and computed by determining percentage differences from column to column.

Tabular analysis   Synonym for percentage table analysis.

Tally   Counting how many cases one observes in each category of variable.

1. INTRODUCTION

Almost everyone knows what percentages mean. They are quite common in our everyday experience and involve only very simple math. Perhaps because of this, percentages are the most often used *and* most abused and misunderstood technique for determining and analyzing relationships. Percentage analysis is very imprecise – not nearly as exact as scatterplots. However, percentages can easily be used for nominal and ordinal level variables. This is one of the major reasons percentages are so widely used. (Remember, discussing the form, extent, and precision of relationships between nominal variables makes no sense in terms of our discussion in Chapter 3.) For beginning students, percentage table analysis is one of the most difficult to interpret even though it is the easiest method used for coming up with the "numbers." In other words, percentage analysis involves some of the most simple calculations but relationships are difficult to interpret once the calculations are complete. Percentage table analysis is called *cross-tabular analysis, cross-tabs, contingency table analysis,* or simply *tabular analysis.* The following sections show step-by-step procedures for determining relationships from percentages. Once these procedures have been mastered, constructing and interpreting percentage tables will become quite simple.

2. REVIEWING THE TYPES OF RELATIONSHIPS AND CHANGE

Remember that relationships between variables are defined as mutual patterned change. There is no relationship between variables if there is no change, and there is no relationship between variables unless that change is mutual and in a patterned fashion.

Change in variables can be conceptualized in two ways. The first is that the same units are viewed over time. Change occurs as a result of natural occurrences or because of some research design. The second is that different units can be viewed at one point in time. By categorizing and comparing units at one point in time, change can be seen. If we view this patterned mutual change in terms of causation, changes in the independent variable (first variable, presumed cause) "cause" changes in the dependent variable (second variable, presumed effect).

Relationships can be described in terms of their form (direction), extent (slope), and precision (goodness of fit). Before describing a relationship in these terms we must determine that the relationship exists. For purposes of this chapter we will assume that a relationship does exist in the data and we will assume that some "test" of existence has already been conducted.

To determine the *form* of a relationship we must answer the question, "As the independent variable (X) increases, what kind of change occurs in the dependent variable (Y)?" Table 4.1 reviews the possible answers to this question along with the name used to describe the form of the relationship. Simply stated, if one or both variables does not change, there is no relationship, and if change is not patterned, there is no relationship. If both variables change in the same direction, the relationship is direct. If the two variables change in the opposite direction, the relationship is inverse. If the best fitting line is not straight but change is patterned, the relationship is curvilinear.

TABLE 4.1
Typology of the form of a relationship

Changes in X	Changes in Y	Form of the Relationship
Increases	Increases	Direct (positive, +)
Increases	Decreases	Inverse (indirect, negative, −)
Increases	Increases and decreases in a patterned way	Curvilinear (nonlinear)
Increases	No change	No relationship
Increases	Changes but in a nonpatterned way	No relationship
No change	Any or no change	No relationship

In addition to determining the form of a relationship, it is also desirable to describe the extent and precision of a relationship. With scatterplots this is accomplished by examining the best fitting line. Extent is determined by the degree of tilt of the best fitting line and precision is determined by assessing how close the dots are to the best fitting line. Unfortunately, percentage tables do not have a best fitting line. Therefore there is no exact parallel to extent and precision in a percentage table. However, even without a best fitting line the idea of extent and precision are similar. Extent refers to the degree of change in Y for a unit change in X. Precision refers to how exactly the score on the dependent variable (Y) can be predicted if we know a unit's score on the independent variable (X).

3. PERCENTAGE TABLES AS ESTIMATES OF SCATTERPLOTS

The general idea of a percentage table analysis can be easily seen if thought of as an estimate of a scatterplot. It is an "estimate" because a percentage table does not provide as much detailed information about observations as does a scatterplot. This is often because percentage tables contain information about nominal or ordinal variables as opposed to interval variables. With interval variables there tend to be many values or categories of a variable. However, for nominal and ordinal variables there tend to be relatively fewer categories for each variable. One way to think of this is that a percentage table results from breaking up a scatterplot by means of a grid with a number of cells in the grid. Figure 4.1(a) shows a scatterplot between two variables. The top scatterplot could be analyzed in terms of the form, extent, and precision of the relationship. The bottom plot shows a grid placed over the scatterplot. This particular grid has four cells or four sections.

We could obtain an estimate of the scatterplot in Figure 4.1(a) by simply counting the number of dots in each cell of the grid. Figure 4.1(b) shows a four-cell grid with the number representing the number of dots within each cell. This table shows that there are 4 dots in the upper left of the scatterplot, 9 dots in the lower left, 13 dots in the upper right, and 5 dots in the lower right of the scatterplot. It is easy to see that just knowing which grid a dot is in does not give you as much information as knowing the exact location of a dot on the scatterplot.

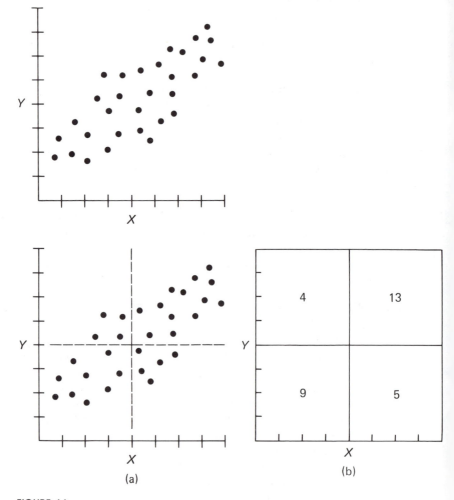

FIGURE 4.1

(a) Scatterplot with and without superimposed grid

(b) Number of dots in each cell of the scatterplot grid in (a)

Further evidence that the information in Figure 4.1(b) is only an estimate of the scatterplot can be seen by trying to construct the scatterplot in Figure 4.1(a) using only the information provided in (b). The task is virtually impossible. Figure 4.2 shows two possible scatterplots which could result in the same number of dots in each cell of the grid. Each of them is, of course, quite different from the other, and both are different from the scatterplot in Figure 4.1(a).

In practice, if one had a scatterplot of data it would not be desirable to change the scatterplot into a grid-type arrangement. As we said before, this practice of making a table from a scatterplot forms the basis for understanding what a percentage table is all about.

FIGURE 4.2
Reconstructing scatterplots from the information in Figure 4.1 (b)

However, in most cases there would be no reason for transforming a scatterplot into a table and then going on to conduct tabular analysis. Percentage tables are usually generated either because the variables are nominal or ordinal or because the researcher feels people would understand a percentage table easier than a scatterplot analysis. Constructing a grid over a scatterplot and counting the number of dots in each cell is equivalent to constructing a *cross-tabular frequency table*. Such a table forms the basis for a percentage analysis of relationships. A thorough presentation of how to construct frequency tables depends on understanding that observations (measurement) of variables are made in many different ways. Without fully discussing surveys and experiments at this time, it is possible to explore how different types of data must be viewed somewhat differently. Section 4 deals with the fact that in order to "see" change in the independent variable observations must be arranged depending on the type of research being conducted. Seeing change in the independent variable is, of course, the first step in determining the form of a relationship between two variables.

4. SHOWING CHANGE IN THE INDEPENDENT VARIABLE

Remember that in the case of scatterplots the first step in describing the form of a relationship was to scan the plot from left to right in order to "see" the independent variable increasing. The same type of scanning is required with percentage table analysis. Viewing change always involves a comparison. It is only through a comparison that change can be experienced. When scanning a scatterplot the comparisons were continuous because the plot was all one figure. When scanning a percentage table we are viewing a grid-type arrangement similar to the one in Figure 4.1(b). In the scatterplot there were a large number of possible values of X, but in a percentage table there are usually a small number of possible values for X. Each column of the grid (each vertical or up and down section) represents one value of the independent variable. In order to see change in the independent variable the units being observed must be arranged so that scanning from left to right will have the effect of seeing an increase in X.

Because data for cross-tabs come from many different research designs and procedures, it is not always in the same form. The two major designs for collecting data in social and behavioral research are the survey and the experiment. Surveys are fully discussed in Chapter 10 and experiments are presented in Chapter 9. However, even at this point most students have a general idea about these two procedures. The following sections discuss how to arrange data that have been gathered from surveys and experiments in such a way that change in X can be seen. Data from nearly all other designs can be fit into one of the following discussions.

Surveys

In Chapter 10, surveys are defined as designs that rely on people's responses to questions. Although this is the major definition of surveys, many studies rely on information collected from units other than people. The definition of survey can be extended to include any data that has been collected by asking questions of some unit or group of units. For example, a university could be "surveyed" to determine how many students were enrolled. In effect, we would be "asking" the university a question. Also the five major oil companies could be surveyed to determine the total amount of Federal subsidies they receive. In this example the effect would be that of asking the five oil companies about their subsidies. Increases in the independent variable would be viewed differently depending on the type of survey, under this expanded idea of surveys. (Of course, people are answering in each of these examples, but they are responding as representatives, not as individuals.)

Cross-sectional surveys
A cross-sectional survey is one in which units are only measured at one point in time. In order to view change in X with these types of data, we must separate the units depending on their value on the independent variable. At this point it does not matter what their value of any other variable is. We are only focusing on the value of X. Figure 4.3 shows how the units in a cross-sectional survey would be

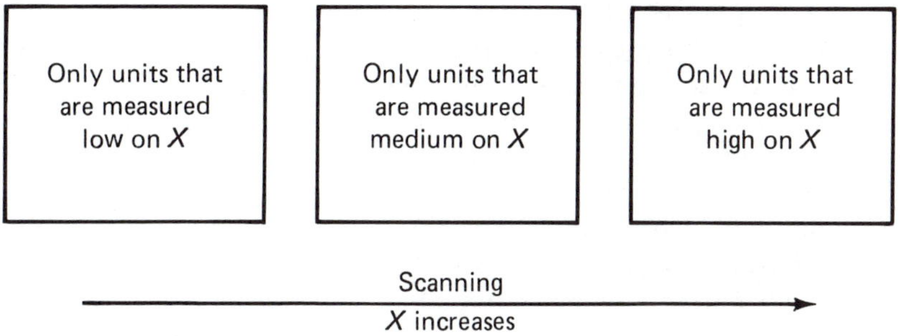

Only units that are measured low on X	Only units that are measured medium on X	Only units that are measured high on X

Scanning
——————————————————————————————▶
X increases

FIGURE 4.3
Changes in the independent variable in a cross-sectional survey

separated. If separated in this way, scanning from left to right would have the effect of "seeing" X increase.

An example of these types of data would be if respondents were asked in a mailed survey to give their age along with other other information. If age were an independent variable in some hypothesis, we could separate the subjects according to their age. We could categorize them into "young" people, "middle-aged" people, or "older" people. By scanning from young units to middle-aged units to older units, *age* would in effect be "increasing."

Longitudinal panel surveys
In longitudinal panel surveys the same units are measured on the independent variable at different points in time. In this type of design the independent variable is changing over time for all of the units either naturally or as a consequence of the research being conducted. For example, we might want to find out the consequences of military training on recruits. Therefore we would survey the recruits when they first enter training, during training, and at the end of training. You will note that in this type of research it is not really the subjects that are used as an index of change, but the conditions of the environment. As time continues for these recruits, training is increasing. Training becomes the independent variable. It is assumed that the change in the recruits' environment (training) is being experienced by the subjects. Figure 4.4 shows how scanning all the subjects over the time period the independent variable is changing results in "seeing" X increase.

Cumulative surveys
Cumulative surveys collect data at different points in time, then all the data are put together in one group. In this way the data accumulate over some period of time. Because each unit surveyed may be measured more than once during the study period, each may appear more than once in the analysis. However each time a unit is measured it may have only one value of the independent variable. So each time a unit is measured (observed) it is put into one of the categories of X. Each unit may be counted more than once in each category of X since measurements are made at more than one point in time.

Figure 4.5 shows how change is "seen" in cumulative surveys. An example of this type of study would be if industrial productivity was the independent variable and six selected factories were the units being studied over a period of five years. Focusing on one of the factory's productivity, it might be low in the first year of the study. Therefore it would be placed in the left-hand category of Figure 4.5. However, in the second year of the study that same factory's productivity might have been high. If this were the case, that factory

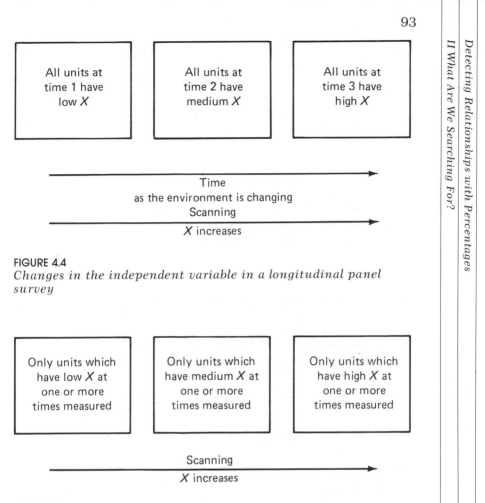

FIGURE 4.4
Changes in the independent variable in a longitudinal panel survey

FIGURE 4.5
Changes in the independent variable in a cumulative survey

would then be counted in the right-hand category for that year. If each of the *six* factories were measured on productivity for each of the *five* years, the result would be thirty (6 × 5 = 30) measures of productivity. Therefore there would be 30 units in such a cumulative analysis. The number of units then is determined by how many measurements were made, not by how many factories or years were involved.

Experiments

In one way experimental data are much "neater" for use in percentage table analysis. Subjects are already arranged in groups by

94

virtue of experimental designs. Each group of subjects has a value of the independent variable due to manipulation. Therefore the job of arranging the data to see change is simpler than in the case of surveys. Two of the most common experimental designs are reviewed below, but the other designs can easily be interpreted once these have been mastered. Experimental designs are fully presented in Chapter 9.

Classical (simple) design
In the classical design there are two groups of subjects: the control group and the experimental group. The subjects in the control group have a relatively low value on the independent variable since no manipulation is conducted on this group. The "no" value is interpreted

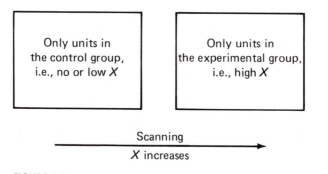

Only units in
the control group,
i.e., no or low X

Only units in
the experimental group,
i.e., high X

Scanning
→
X increases

FIGURE 4.6
Changes in the independent variable in a classical (simple) experimental design

Only units in
the control
group where
$X = 0$

Only units in
the first
experimental
group where
$X = low$

Only units in
the second
experimental
group where
$X = medium$

Only units in
the third
experimental
group where
$X = high$

Scanning
→
X increases

FIGURE 4.7
Changes in the independent variable in a multiple X experimental design

as a very low value on *X*. On the other hand, subjects in the experimental group have a higher value of *X* which has resulted from some experimental manipulation. By scanning from the control group to the experimental group, *X* can be seen as increasing. Figure 4.6 represents this type of arrangement.

Multiple-X designs

The multiple-*X* design "adds on" more experimental groups. The independent variable is manipulated in such a way that each group has a different value of *X*. By doing this, a more detailed picture of changes in *X* can be gained. The more values of *X* that can be scanned, the greater the degree of detail that can be seen in the change. Figure 4.7 displays the multiple-*X* design. Scanning from left to right in a fashion similar to the simple experiment results in being able to see an increase in the independent variable.

Summary for showing change in the independent variable

It is important to remember that units must be arranged in groups. Scanning from left to right will have the effect of "seeing" an increase in *X*. The purpose of this arrangement is to always create the effect of "as *X* increases" when scanning from left to right. You will recall that a relationship can be determined by answering the question, "as *X* increases, what kind of changes occur in *Y*?" With arrangements similar to those described above, we have achieved the first half of the question – the *X* part. Each of these respective groups could eventually constitute the columns of a percentage table.

Before we go on, we must determine what we are looking for as we scan from left to right. We are looking for a patterned change in the dependent variable. In other words, as we scan from left to right we are "seeing" increases in *X*. We now have to set things up in such a way that we will be able to see a change in *Y* as we scan the groups of units from left to right.

5. SHOWING CHANGE IN THE DEPENDENT VARIABLE

In the case of scatterplots we could "see" changes in the dependent variable by looking at the best fitting line. The location of the best fitting line determined whether *Y* was increasing, decreasing, or staying the same. In effect the best fitting line was a summary of all the dots. The location of the line summarized the whole distribution of dots on the scatterplot. When the location of the best fitting line changed this was a result of the fact that the distribution of Y scores was changing. In the case of percentage table analysis we also need a way to determine if the distribution of Y scores is changing as we scan from left to right. The scanning motion shows changes in X and the inspection of the relative distribution of Y scores shows whether Y is changing, and if so in what direction.

Before exploring how we determine if the Y distribution is or is not changing in cross-tabular analysis, we need to be able to construct a "distribution" of Y scores in a format that can be used in percentage tables. First we show how to construct simple frequency distributions and simple percentage distributions. Then we go on to explain how these simple distributions can be used to "see" change in the dependent variable within cross-tabs.

Constructing simple frequency distributions

To construct simple distributions we start with the notion that once concepts (variables) have been chosen and our observations have been made, they must be presented in a way that will allow us to understand what has been observed. Another way of saying this is that we need a way to determine the distribution of our observations.

For example, if a political scientist were taking a survey in a small town to predict whether or not voters would support an increase in taxes to finance a new swimming pool, the observations might be recorded on interview reports such as the one illustrated below.

INTERVIEW REPORT

Voter's name: *Elma Voter*

Answer to: Will you support the proposed increase in taxes to build a new swimming pool?

1. _____ yes   2. ___✓___ no   3. _____ undecided

The researcher would then have to "make sense" out of all the completed forms. This would be a difficult task if there were very many forms to look at. Even in a town of a few thousand people, the stack of paper would be many inches thick. The information on these forms must be organized so that conclusions can be reached.

Answers to questions, such as on the interview report, and other types of observations as originally recorded are often called *raw data*. The first step often employed in organizing raw data is the construction of a tally. A *tally* is the product of counting how many responses (observations) one observes for each possible answer to a question or category of a variable. To make a tally, a list of all the possible answers (or categories of a variable) is constructed. This list is called the *tally sheet*.

TALLY SHEET

3. "undecided":

2. "no":

1. "yes":

After the tally sheet is prepared, the raw data are examined and a mark is made on the tally sheet opposite the appropriate category of the variable. In our example, the tally would correspond to the voter's response to the question. A tally sheet representing 12 voters saying "yes," 8 voters saying "no," and 4 voters saying "undecided" would look similar to the example below.

TALLY SHEET

3. "undecided": ////

2. "no": TTHL ///

1. "yes": TTHL TTHL //

At this point, the tallies would be put into a table called a frequency distribution. A *simple frequency distribution* is a two-column table in which the categories of the variable are placed in the left-hand column and the sum of the tallies is placed in the right-hand column. In other words, the *frequency* of each respective category is listed on the right. The term frequency is often ab-

TABLE 4.2
Simple frequency distribution of voter choice

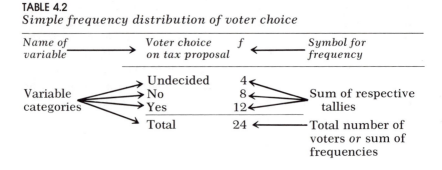

Name of variable →	Voter choice on tax proposal	f ←	Symbol for frequency
Variable categories	Undecided	4	Sum of respective tallies
	No	8	
	Yes	12	
	Total	24	Total number of voters *or* sum of frequencies

breviated with an *f*. Table 4.2 shows the distribution of responses of how many people answered within each possible category of the variable in our sample survey.

Sometimes researchers do not completely spell out the name of the variable in a table or give the names of the variable categories. By relabeling the above table, a "short-hand" procedure for presenting a frequency distribution will result. Instead of "voter choice," we can use an *X* to stand for any specific variable. Instead of the "yes" response, we could use the number 1; for a "no," we could substitute the number 2; and for "undecided," we could use a 3. Instead of "Total," we could use the letter *N*. This procedure of substituting numbers for verbal answers is done in order to analyze data with a computer. This is one example of *coding* data. Coding refers to any modification of data from the way it was originally recorded. Making these changes, the frequency distribution would be:

X	*f*
3	4
2	8
1	12
N	24

This is an obvious example of how different labels may mislead us as to the categories of the variable. The variable in this case remains a nominal one of voter choice despite the possibilities of using numbers as labels for these categories.

Constructing simple percentage distributions

All the distributions we have examined thus far have dealt only with the *number* of observations in each category of a variable.

However, very often we are not interested primarily in the actual number of observations in a category, but in the *proportional* or *relative* number of frequencies in particular categories. Also we are quite often interested in *comparing* two or more frequency distributions. In either of these cases, it is necessary to change frequency distributions to percentage distributions. *Percentage distributions* are distributions where frequencies have been converted into percentages.

The first step in constructing a percentage distribution is to divide the number of observations in each category of the variable (f) by the sum of the frequencies (N). After the division is carried out, the quotient is multiplied by 100, resulting in percentages. The political poll presented earlier serves as the example in Table 4.3. Note that in a simple distribution the total (T) of the percentages should equal 100 percent. However, if there is rounding, the total may be slightly different.

Percentages also take on special importance when comparing the distribution of a variable in two or more different groups, particularly when the groups are of different size. To illustrate how difficult it is to make comparisons with frequencies, we will examine two frequency distributions of employee involvement in decision making. These distributions are shown separately in part a of Table 4.4. Part b of the table shows a typical way of combining two distributions into a single table. Notice that all frequencies refer to the number of corporations, not the number of employees or decisions.

Comparing distributions such as these is quite difficult, but by converting to percentages, comparisons become simpler. Converting to percentages standardizes the size of each group of corporations as though there were 100 small corporations and 100 large corporations. In this way, direct comparisons can easily be made between

TABLE 4.3

Converting simple frequency distributions into percentage distributions

Frequency distribution		*Changing frequencies to fractions*	*Dividing to create proportions*	*Multiplying by 100*	Percentage distribution	
Voter Choice	f				Voter Choice	%
3	12⟶12/24	.50	50		3	50
2	8⟶ 8/24	.33	33		2	33
1	4⟶ 4/24	.17	17		1	17
N	24⟶				T	100

TABLE 4.4 (a)
Comparing frequency distributions

Small corporations		Large corporations	
Employee involvement in decisions	*f*	Employee involvement in decisions	*f*
High	3,240	High	23
Medium	9,356	Medium	72
Low	1,113	Low	17
N	13,709	N	112

TABLE 4.4 (b)
Combining two distributions into one table

	Corporation size	
Employee involvement in decisions	Small *f*	Large *f*
High	3,240	23
Medium	9,356	72
Low	1.113	17
N	13,709	112

groups as to the *relative* distribution of a variable. By converting to percentages, we can determine the relative part of each group of corporations within each category of employee involvement.

To interpret the percentage distributions in Table 4.5 one would say that if there were 100 small companies, 23.6 of them would have high involvement in decision making. If there were 100 large companies, 20.5 of them would have high involvement. We can conclude therefore that *relatively speaking* a greater proportion of small companies have high employee involvement than do large companies. However, there is only a small relative difference; to be exact 23.6 − 20.5 percent, or 3.1 percent difference. Similarly, small and large companies have fairly close involvement in the medium score (68.2 percent versus 64.3 percent). However, in the low category, large corporations are 7.1 percent (15.2 percent − 8.1 percent) higher than small companies.

The overall conclusion that we reach by standardizing frequencies with percentages is that small companies have relatively greater involvement of workers in decision making than do large companies. This kind of conclusion was not possible to discover simply by using

TABLE 4.5 (a)
Comparing percentage distributions

Small corporations		Large corporations	
Employee involvement in decisions	%	Employee involvement in decisions	%
High	23.6	High	20.5
Medium	68.2	Medium	64.3
Low	8.1	Low	15.2
T	99.9	T	100.0

TABLE 4.5 (b)
Combining two percentage distributions into one table

	Corporation size	
Employee involvement in decisions	Small %	Large %
High	23.6	20.5
Medium	68.2	64.3
Low	8.1	15.2
T	99.9	100.0

frequency distributions, and this is the main advantage of percentages.

Using percentages for cross-tabular analysis

In percentage table analysis seeing changes in Y requires that at least two distributions of the dependent variable be compared. The first percentage distribution of Y is examined and then a second distribution is examined and compared to the first. The decision that must be made is whether or not a change in Y has occurred. Second, we must decide whether the change has been an increase in Y or a decrease in Y. As a matter of convention in this book the categories of the distributions of Y will always be arranged with lower scores of Y on the bottom of the distribution and higher scores of Y toward the top of the distribution. The major reason for this convention is so that scores of Y will be in the same order as those in a scatterplot. By doing this, parallels to the scatterplot can be seen and inter-

TABLE 4.6

Comparing two percentage distributions of the dependent variable

Example	Values of Y	% Distribution I		% Distribution II
A	High	20		22
	Medium	35		34
	Low	45		44
		100	- No change -	100
B	High	20		50
	Medium	35		30
	Low	45		20
		100	Increase	100
C	High	20		30
	Medium	35		35
	Low	45		35
		100	Increase	100
D	High	20		15
	Medium	35		30
	Low	45		55
		100	Decrease	100
E	High	20		5
	Medium	35		20
	Low	45		75
		100	Decrease	100

pretation of percentage tables becomes easier (assuming inter-pretation of scatterplots has already been mastered).

You will recall that percentage distributions will always total 100 percent because all the cases in that distribution are there. This assumes no rounding errors. Table 4.6 provides some examples of comparing two percentage distributions of Y to determine if there has been a "change" in Y and in what direction that change is in. To make the examples a little easier, the first percentage distribution is the same in all the comparisons. Again, because "seeing" change requires a comparison, seeing changes in Y will require comparing distribution I with distribution II. Because the categories of Y are arranged in ascending order, a change up will be equivalent to an "increase in Y" and a change down will be equivalent to a "decrease in Y."

An analogy which might prove helpful is that of a high rise building with a bank of elevators. To use this analogy you would imagine that each category of Y is one floor of the building, and each of the percentages represents a number of people waiting on that floor for an elevator. The first distribution of Y is how many people are standing before the elevators come. The second distribution represents the number after the movement of people from one floor to another. The first question is, "have the people used the elevators in such a way that the number of people on each floor has changed?" The second question is, "have more people moved to a higher floor or to a lower floor after the elevators have operated?" If the answer is that more people moved up than down, there has been an increase in Y. If the answer is that more people moved down than up, there has been a decrease in Y. Using some examples should make this clear.

In example A, distribution I, of Table 4.6 we start with 20 percent of the units having high Y, 35 percent of the units with medium Y, and 45 percent with low Y. Comparing this to distribution II there are 22 percent with high Y, 34 percent with medium, and 44 percent with low. Is this a change? In one sense there has been a change between these distributions since they are not identical. However, you can see that in no comparison is there a difference of more than 2 percent. One rule of thumb is that *if there is no change in the distribution of more than 5 percent the distribution will be considered identical.* In other words, even though distributions I and II are different in example A, the rule of thumb dictates that we conclude there is no change in the distribution of Y. This rule is followed by many researchers.

Using the elevator analogy, we see that there is one person (one person = 1 percent) less on the "low" floor after the elevators came. There is also one less person on the "medium" floor but two more people on the "high" floor. In none of the cases is there a net change of more than five people. Therefore by the rule of thumb there is no change in the distribution from I to II. We have no way of knowing that the same 20 people who were originally on the high floor remained on the high floor or whether some of them went to another floor and others came to the high floor to replace them. The important point is that from the distributions we have no way of identifying particular people (units), only the net effect. It is the total distribution that is of concern to us, not the movement of particular cases.

There is a change between distributions I and II in example B since the percentages of at least one of the values of Y changes by 5 percent or more. Therefore the question of the direction of the change can be asked. By comparing the two distributions we see that more people took the elevators *up* than took them down. Therefore the shift is in an upward direction. In other words, there has been an increase in Y when the two distributions are compared.

Similarly in example C there is also an upward shift or an increase in Y. In order to obtain 30 people on the high floor, 35 people on the medium floor, and 35 people on the low floor after the elevators operated, more people had to go up than came down. Therefore

Y is said to "increase" when comparing distribution II to distribution I in example C. The degree of change in examples B and C is different and this difference will be important when relationships are analyzed using percentage tables. A later section will explore this in greater detail.

Focusing on example D and E, it can be seen that in both cases there is a change between distribution I and distribution II. The change is in a downward direction. In both examples, Y has "decreased" between the two distributions. In other words, more people took the elevators down than took the elevators up to achieve the changes in the distributions of Y. Again the degree of shift, that is, the number of people changing floors, is different in the two examples. There is a larger shift in example E. In summary, Y is not changing in example A; Y is increasing in examples B and C; and Y is decreasing in examples D and E.

This type of analysis can be extended to more than two distributions of Y as can be seen from Table 4.7. The change between distributions I and II represents an increase in Y. The change between distributions II and III represents an increase in Y, and the change between distributions III and IV represents a decrease in Y. Take a few moments to examine Table 4.7 using the elevator analogy to convince yourself of this.

Summary for the dependent variable

Remember, you have to look at the *total distribution,* not just one value. For example, in Table 4.7 you will notice that there is an increase in the total distribution of Y between distributions I and II. However, if you look only at the low value of Y, there is a decrease from 45 to 43 percent. If you do not look at the total distributions for making a comparison, errors may result. Once the technique of determining changes between two distributions of Y has been mastered, we can put it all together to construct and analyze percentage tables in search of relationships.

TABLE 4.7
Analyzing changes in Y using many distributions

Values of Y	% Distribution I	% Distribution II	% Distribution III	% Distribution IV
High	20	27	40	32
Medium	35	30	30	43
Low	45	43	30	25
	100	100	100	100
		Increase	Increase	Decrease

6. PUTTING IT TOGETHER: PERCENTAGE TABLES

A cross-tabular percentage table is constructed by placing the categories of the independent variable along the top of a table, ranging from low categories to the left and high categories to the right. Categories of the dependent variable are placed at the side of the table, with lower values of Y at the bottom and higher values at the top. This procedure results in a grid-type arrangement made up of some number of cells.*

Figure 4.8 shows a blank percentage table with three categories of X and four categories of Y resulting in twelve empty cells. The num-

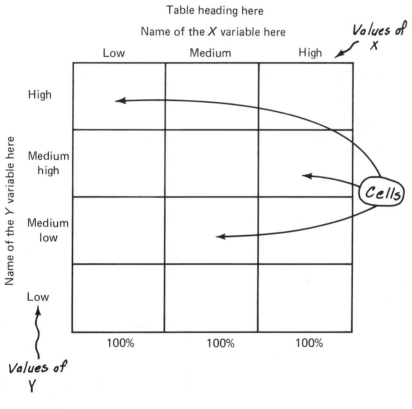

FIGURE 4.8
Blank percentage cross-tabulation table

---

*While this procedure will be used consistently in this text, some writers reverse the location of the independent and dependent variables. Also, some tables are constructed so that the lower values of the variable at the side of the table are at the top rather than at the bottom. Because of these differences, you should pay special attention to the labels of percentage tables and be able to interpret tables regardless of how they are arranged.

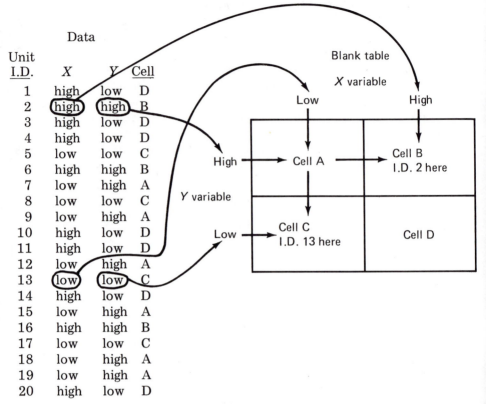

Data

Unit I.D.	X	Y	Cell
1	high	low	D
2	high	high	B
3	high	low	D
4	high	low	D
5	low	low	C
6	high	high	B
7	low	high	A
8	low	low	C
9	low	high	A
10	high	low	D
11	high	low	D
12	low	high	A
13	low	low	C
14	high	low	D
15	low	high	A
16	high	high	B
17	low	low	C
18	low	high	A
19	low	high	A
20	high	low	D

Blank table

X variable

	Low	High
High	Cell A	Cell B I.D. 2 here
Low	Cell C I.D. 13 here	Cell D

[a]Arrows show illustrations. All units would be placed in the cells in a similar manner.

Step 1: Tally all cells.

X

Y	Low	High
High	JHT I	|||
Low	||||	JHT I

Step 2: Add all columns.

X

Y	Low	High
High	6	3
Low	4	7
	10	10

Step 3: Compute percentages
on all columns.

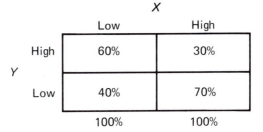

Step 4: The final table.

		X	
		Low	High
Y	High	60%	30%
	Low	40%	70%
		100%	100%

FIGURE 4.9
Constructing a percentage table[a]

ber of categories of X and Y is somewhat arbitrary. In some cases
the number of categories of X is determined by the design of the research. However, in other situations, such as the cross-sectional survey, the number of categories is determined by the "cutting points"
that the researcher decides. For example, using age as an independent variable, the cutting points would refer to how age would be
coded into three categories. Is young 18–25 or 18–30 or 18–40? Anytime original observations can be coded into different categories the
question of cutting points must be answered.

The general rule to follow in deciding cutting points is to determine them on the basis of some theory. If a theory cannot be found
on which to base the decision, common practice or custom could be
used. For example it would probably make little sense to include
people who are 50 years old in the young age category. If neither
theory, common custom, nor reasonable procedure can be found,
there are two methods often used. The first would be to *split the
range of the values* of the variable into equal parts. The second
would be to *split the frequencies* of the distribution into equal parts
and use the resulting set of values. For example, if a variable
ranged from 1 to 100 and you desired four categories, one appropriate way to decide the cutting points would be to divide the range
evenly. This would result in categories of 1–24, 26–50, 51–75, and
76–100. If you had 500 observations of a variable and desired 5 categories, the categories could be structured so that there were 100
units in each of five categories.

The question of cutting points is important because they could affect the interpretation of a given set of data. This will be more fully explained in the next section.

Once cutting points have been decided, the next step is to count the units measured and determine which cell they are in. It is a good idea to start with a blank table, similar to the one in Figure 4.8, labeled with the research variables. After this has been done, each unit will have to be examined simultaneously as to its score on X and its score on Y. Remember, in searching for a relationship we are after *mutual* patterned change. The values of both variables must always be measured for each unit and the unit then placed into the table according to both values. Figure 4.9 shows a simple example of how a table is constructed once the paired values of the coded independent and dependent variables are available.

The first step is to construct tallies within each of the cells of the table using the paired values of X and Y. In the illustration cell A contains all the units with low X and high Y; cell B contains all the units with high X and high Y; cell C contains all the units with low X and low Y; and cell D contains all the units with high X and low Y. The second step is to add the frequencies in each column. This is done in order to obtain a distribution of Y for each category of the independent variable. Adding across would not achieve this. The third step is to compute the percentage distributions of Y for each column. This results in the final form of the table. Once the final form has been completed, it can be interpreted.

7. VIEWING BIVARIATE RELATIONSHIPS WITH PERCENTAGES

The form of a relationship

Bivariate analysis with percentage tables usually involves examining one table in which the independent and dependent variable are represented. The task of bivariate analysis is to categorize the table as representing either no relationship, or, if there is a relationship, a direct, inverse, or curvilinear relationship. If a percentage table shows no change in the comparisons of the distribution of Y expressed in all of the columns, there is no relationship between the two variables. If *every* adjacent two-column comparison concludes that Y is increasing as X increases, the relationship between X and Y is direct. If *every* adjacent two-column comparison concludes that Y is decreasing, the relationship is inverse. However, if some comparisons show Y increasing and some show Y decreasing and/or some show Y remaining the same, the relationship is said to be nonlinear in form. In other words, if Y is always increasing as you scan from left to right, the form of the relationship is direct; if Y is always decreasing as you scan from left to right, the form of the rela-

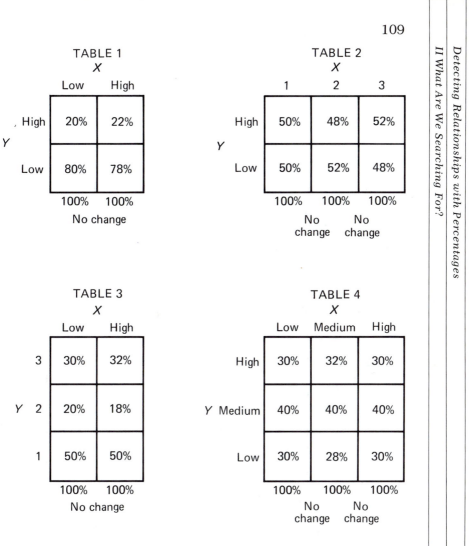

FIGURE 4.10
Examples of percentage tables with no relationship

tionship is inverse; and if Y sometimes increases and sometimes decreases or remains the same, the form of the relationship is curvilinear.

Figure 4.10 provides some examples of percentage tables in which there is no relationship between the independent and dependent variables. In all the tables, when the distributions of Y are compared, the comparison yields a conclusion of "no change." Since mutual patterned change is mandatory for a relationship to exist, no relationship is shown in any of these data. Note that the names of the categories of the variables in the tables may be different but they are always ordered from low to high if possible. The labels used in the examples signify ordinal and interval level variables.

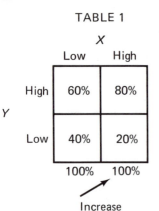

TABLE 1

	X	
	Low	High
High	60%	80%
Low	40%	20%
	100%	100%

(Y on left axis)

Increase

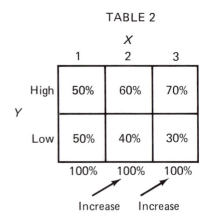

TABLE 2

	X		
	1	2	3
High	50%	60%	70%
Low	50%	40%	30%
	100%	100%	100%

(Y on left axis)

Increase   Increase

TABLE 3

	X	
	Low	High
3	60%	75%
2	30%	20%
1	10%	5%
	100%	100%

(Y on left axis)

Increase

TABLE 4

	X		
	Low	Medium	High
High	20%	20%	30%
Medium	20%	30%	30%
Low	60%	50%	40%
	100%	100%	100%

(Y on left axis)

Increase   Increase

FIGURE 4.11
Examples of percentage tables with direct relationships

Figure 4.11 shows similar types of tables. The data in the tables represent different direct relationships. Notice that within each table, the change in the distribution of Y is in the up direction, that is, an increase in Y. Whenever this is the case the relationship described by the data is direct.

In a similar fashion, Figure 4.12 shows four different inverse relationships. Consistency of the decrease is necessary in order to have an inverse relationship.

Figure 4.13 shows some examples of relationships which are inconsistent in the way that Y changes as X increases. Table 1 shows

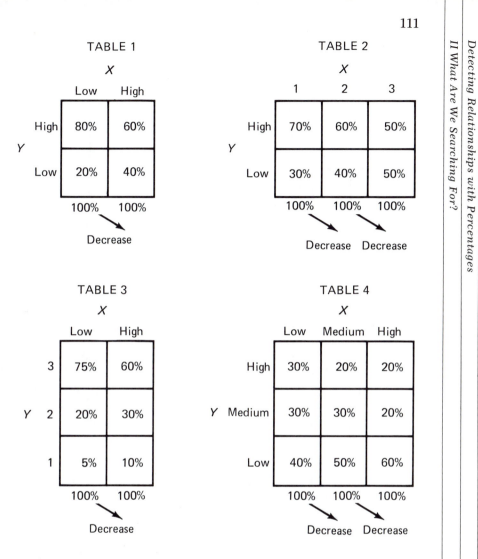

FIGURE 4.12
Examples of percentage tables with inverse relationships

Y first increasing and then decreasing. Table 2 shows Y first decreasing and then increasing. Table 3, on the other hand, shows an increase and then no change, and Table 4 shows a simultaneous decrease and increase in the distribution of Y as X increases. Note that at least three categories of X are necessary in order to determine a curve. At least two comparisons are required to be able to "see" a curvilinear relationship. While we would assume that the relationships in Figure 4.13 are curvilinear, the possibility exists that the changes in Y are not patterned and that there really is no relationship between the two variables. Because percentage tables are not

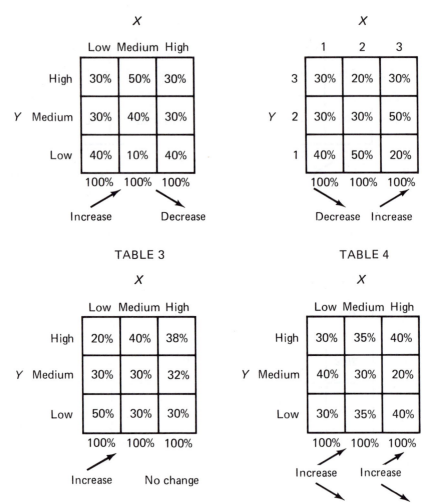

FIGURE 4.13
Examples of percentage tables with curvilinear relationships

as clear on this matter as are scatterplots, there really is no way to tell whether the changes in Y are really patterned. This would be revealed by more precise modes of analysis, such as scatterplots.

Extent and precision (strength) of a relationship

Once the *form* of the bivariate relationship has been established, it is also desirable to establish the *extent* and *precision* of the relationship. Unlike scatterplots, percentage table analysis does not allow one to differentiate between extent and precision. Therefore the combination of these two characteristics is referred to as the *strength* of the relationship.

The strength of the relationship can be determined by computing the percentage difference between the various categories in the distributions of the dependent variable. If the percentage differences tend to be large, the strength of the relationship is said to be strong. If the percentage differences tend to be small, the strength is said to be weak. Figure 4.14 shows some illustrations of relationships which have the same form but different strength. The top of the illustration shows two direct relationships. In the left-hand table the percentage difference in Y between those units in low X and those units in high X is 6 percent (30 and 36 percent) for those in high Y, 25 percent (20 and 45 percent) for those in medium Y, and 31 percent (50 and 19 percent) for those in low Y. These would not be considered to be a high percentage difference. However, the same differences in the right-hand table are 50, 10, and 40 percent, respectively. These percentage differences probably would be considered large enough to show a strong strength of relationship. It is largely a matter of judgment as to when the strength of a relationship is weak, medium, or strong. As you explore different research tables in various courses you take, the norms should become clearer. Similar differences in strength can be seen for inverse and curvilinear relationships in the remainder of Figure 4.14.

In Chapter 13 we will refer to one possible index of strength other than percent difference. This index is a measure of a relationship called association. Association scores usually vary between 0 and 1.0, or −1.0 and +1.0. The stronger the relationship, the closer an association score would be to 1.0 (or −1.0); the weaker it is, the closer to zero. Like the norms for percentages, the norms for determining the strength of relationships by measures of association become clearer with experience.

Estimating scatterplots and "reading the numbers"

Now that we have thoroughly dissected just how percentage tables are constructed and interpreted, it may seem to be much more complicated than it really is. In this section we will try to step back and remember just what we are trying to do with percentages and what percentage tables mean.

Let us start by looking at a percentage table and remembering what the numbers mean. Figure 14.15 shows a table that is a crosstab between annual family income in thousands of dollars as the independent variable, and the average number of leisure hours spent per week as the dependent variable. In other words, we would like to know: "What is the relationship between income and amount of leisure time?" The data could have come from a survey of 2,278

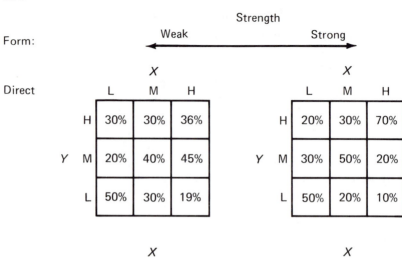

Strength

Form: Weak ←————————————→ Strong

Direct

Weak — X

Y \ X	L	M	H
H	30%	30%	36%
M	20%	40%	45%
L	50%	30%	19%

Strong — X

Y \ X	L	M	H
H	20%	30%	70%
M	30%	50%	20%
L	50%	20%	10%

Inverse

Weak — X

Y \ X	L	M	H
H	30%	20%	14%
M	30%	30%	36%
L	40%	50%	50%

Strong — X

Y \ X	L	M	H
H	30%	10%	0%
M	30%	30%	10%
L	40%	60%	90%

Curvilinear

Weak — X

Y \ X	L	M	H
H	20%	28%	21%
M	30%	32%	29%
L	50%	40%	50%

Strong — X

Y \ X	L	M	H
H	20%	90%	10%
M	30%	10%	10%
L	50%	0%	80%

FIGURE 4.14
Examples of different strengths of relationships in percentage tables

people about their income and leisure time. The first table is a frequency table out of which the percentage table has been calculated. *It is always necessary to change a frequency table into a percentage table before interpreting the relationship between the two variables* because we are interested in the *relative* distribution

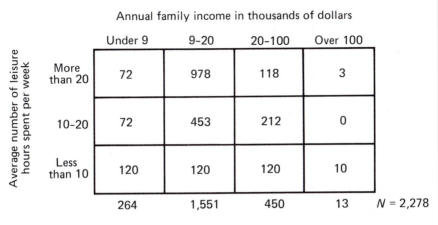

Annual family income in thousands of dollars

	Under 9	9–20	20–100	Over 100	
More than 20	72	978	118	3	
10–20	72	453	212	0	
Less than 10	120	120	120	10	
	264	1,551	450	13	N = 2,278

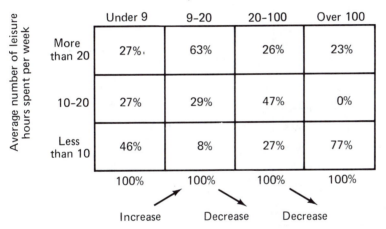

Annual family income in thousands of dollars

	Under 9	9–20	20–100	Over 100
More than 20	27%,	63%	26%	23%
10–20	27%	29%	47%	0%
Less than 10	46%	8%	27%	77%
	100%	100%	100%	100%

Increase   Decrease   Decrease

FIGURE 4.15
Interpreting the numbers in a percentage table

of the dependent variable. Computing percentages gives the effect of standardizing the table in such a way that it appears that there are 100 units in each category of X. By standardizing with 100 percentage units in each distribution, relative comparisons can be made.

The percentage table shows that 27 percent of the people in the survey who had income of under $9,000 spend more than 20 hours of leisure a week, on the average. In addition, 27 percent of those in that same income category spend between 10 and 20 hours, while 46 percent spend less than 10 hours per week on leisure activities. Focusing on those people who had over $100,000 income (the last

PERCENTAGE TABLES   SCATTERPLOT APPROXIMATIONS

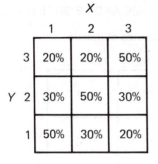

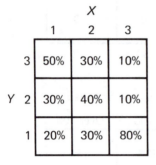

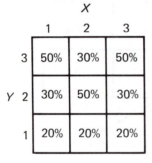

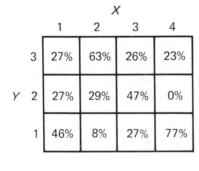

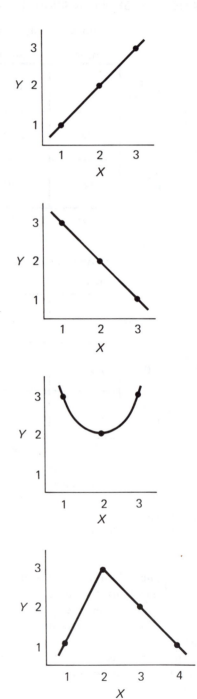

FIGURE 4.16
Translating percentage tables into scatterplot approximations

column), we see that 77 percent of them spend less than 10 hours a week on leisure, while 23 percent spend more than 20 hours. This gives a relative picture about the distribution of leisure time for those individuals. If we had looked at the frequency table, no such relative picture could have been obtained so easily. The remaining columns can be similarly interpreted.

By examining the changes in the distribution of Y between the first and second column we can see a shift up; between the second and third, a shift down; and between the third and fourth, another shift down. This of course is characteristic of a curvilinear relationship between income and amount of leisure.

With practice it is possible to estimate what a scatterplot-like figure could look like based on a percentage table. Figure 4.16 provides various examples of how percentage tables can be "translated" into approximations of scatterplots. It is more difficult to estimate the exact location of the dots in such a procedure so only the best fitting line is shown.

Of course, as we stated at the beginning of this chapter, the procedure could work in the reverse direction. That is, we could go from a scatterplot to a percentage table. Figure 4.17 shows a scatterplot which has two different grids imposed on it. Each grid represents a different percentage table with different cutting points for the values of the Y variable. Below the scatterplot are the percentage tables that result from such a procedure. Notice that they differ considerably, depending on which cutting points create the grid.

If the scatterplot were used to determine the form of the relationship between X and Y, it would clearly be a direct relationship. However, when the grid of longer dashes is used for cutting points on Y and the dots within each cell are counted, the relationship appears to be curvilinear in the percentage table. When the grid of smaller dashes is used the same procedures yield an interpretation of a direct relationship. In one case the cutting points resulted in a "false" interpretation of the data in the scatterplot. In the other, the interpretation was correct. In both cases, of course, the strength of the relationship in the percentage tables is more difficult to determine than if we were interpreting the extent and precision in the scatterplot.

8. SPECIAL NOTE ON NOMINAL LEVEL VARIABLES

Although form, extent, and precision do not constitute meaningful ways to describe relationships between nominal level variables, percentages can be used to analyze relationships between two nominal level variables or one nominal variable and one higher level variable. Instead of describing the form, extent, and precision of such relationships, we can only describe the distribution of the dependent

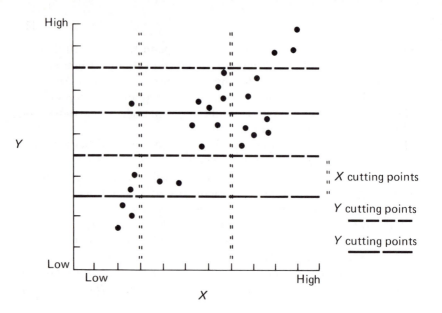

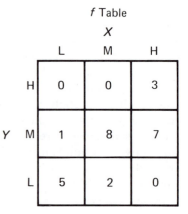

X cutting points

Y cutting points

Y cutting points

f Table

X

	L	M	H
H	1	5	5
M	2	5	5
L	3	0	0

Y

f Table

X

	L	M	H
H	0	0	3
M	1	8	7
L	5	2	0

Y

% Table

X

	L	M	H
H	17%	50%	50%
M	33%	50%	50%
L	50%	0%	0%

Y

% Table

X

	L	M	H
H	0%	0%	30%
M	17%	80%	70%
L	83%	20%	0%

Y

FIGURE 4.17
Translating scatterplots into percentage tables

variable separately for each category of the independent variable. Scanning from left to right is not done because the scanning does not have the effect of seeing an increase in X. Nominal categories cannot be arranged from low to high. Figure 4.18 shows a cross-tab table of two nominal level variables, state of residence and political identification. The only appropriate type of analysis would be to examine the distribution of political identification for each state and to comment on their similarities and/or differences. Assuming that state of residence is the independent variable, distributions of political identification would be examined. If for some reason it made more sense to view political identification as the independent variable, distributions of the states would be examined. This would necessitate reconstructing the table with the variables changed around and the percentages recomputed.

The example analysis shows that New York has the highest concentration of Democrats. New Jersey residents tend to be Republican. On the other hand, the sample of Pennsylvania residents is evenly distributed among the three major identity groups. The general conclusion from such an analysis would be that the distribution of political identification varies among the three states examined. Such a fact could lead to many hypotheses, but the present analysis would be largely descriptive. There is always the possibility that the nominal categories of one or more of the variables could be arranged in some meaningful way. For example, the states might be

	State of residence		
	New York	Pennsylvania	New Jersey
Democrat	40%	30%	20%
Republican	30%	30%	60%
Independent	25%	30%	18%
Other	5%	10%	2%
	100%	100%	100%

Political identification

FIGURE 4.18
Exploring nominal variable relationships with percentages

arranged in terms of the degree of their industrialization, and the political groups might be arranged to indicate their degree of political conservatism. If these arrangements could be defended, then another analysis between degree of industrialization and political conservativeness could be done using the same data as in Figure 4.18. The burden of proof for conceptualizing the variables in such a fashion would rest on the researcher. It would have to be defended and documented in order to be accepted.

9. A FINAL CAUTION

There are three major places where error, misunderstanding, misrepresentation, and misinterpretation can take place in percentage analysis. Each of these considerations must be dealt with every time a percentage table is either constructed or interpreted. The first has to do with the arrangement and labeling of the table; the second concerns the cutting points of the variables; and the last concerns the direction of percentaging.

The importance of labeling

In this text we have always been consistent in the labeling and arranging of each percentage table. The independent variable has been placed on the top of the table comprising the columns of the table with low values to the left. Similarly, the dependent variable has been placed on the side of the table comprising the rows of the table with low values at the bottom. This is only a convention and not all tables you will come across will be arranged in this way. Once you become familiar with reading tables, any legitimate table can be read with ease. In the meantime we would suggest that when you come across a percentage table, you mentally (or on a sheet of paper) rearrange it to correspond with the convention of this text. In this way you can avoid confusion. Most importantly, read the labels of any table *before* you attempt to interpret it and make sure you understand how it has been arranged.

Cutting points

Part of the labeling should include a clear definition of how the cutting points of the categories have been determined. Either in the table itself or in an accompanying text researchers must be explicit about how categories are developed. Without a clear stipulation of the cutting points of each variable, the possibilities of misinterpretation, either accidental or purposeful, are great. In addition, there should be some way for the consumer of research to determine that the cutting points used have not distorted the analysis. This could be in the form of a simple frequency distribution of each variable involved or a scatterplot of all the data.

Direction of percentaging

We have always percentaged down within each category of the independent variable. In order to interpret the relationship between two temporally ordered variables (an independent and dependent variable), it is always necessary to percentage within the categories of the variable that occurs first in time. No matter how a percentage table is labeled and arranged, the percentages must be in that direction. However, if X is on the side of a table and Y is on the top, percentages should go across instead of up and down. Sometimes if temporal order is not known or a study is not causal research, percentaging may be done in both directions. This allows the reader to interpret the table in the manner desired. Be aware of how the percentaging is done, especially since tables are not always labeled with the 100 percent printed either at the bottom or side. Sometimes tables are presented with an incorrect direction of percentaging, but if you keep in mind conventions presented in this chapter and remember the cautions of this last section, percentage table analysis will prove to be a valuable addition to your ability to analyze and interpret the search for relationships.

10. SUMMARY

Determining the form of a relationship with percentage table analysis presents certain problems. In order to answer the question, "as X increases how does Y change," units must be ordered so that scanning from left to right will enable you to "see" X increasing. For some research designs this may mean that observations made at different times are arranged according to the value of X at the time of observation. For other designs observations made at the same time will have to be grouped by their value on X. In order to see change in Y, a separate percentage distribution of Y must be constructed within each category of X. Comparing adjacent distributions will allow us to determine if Y is increasing, decreasing, or staying about the same. If all of these comparisons show Y increasing, the relationship is direct. If all of these comparisons show Y decreasing, the relationship is inverse. If there is no change in these comparisons, Y is not changing. If there is a mixture of increasing, decreasing, and remaining the same, the relationship is curvilinear. Since there is no analogy for the best fitting line in percentage tables, the determination of extent and precision is not possible. Because of this, the strength of the relationship is a combination of extent and precision and depends upon the degree of change in Y. When there are large percentage differences, strength is high. When the differences are smaller, the strength of the relationship is weaker. One way to interpret percentage tables is to convert them to scatterplot-like figures.

It is not appropriate to talk about the form of the relationship when nominal variables are involved. The only reasonable way to discuss such relationships is by describing the distributions of Y for each category of X. The descriptions can then be compared and contrasted.

If one pays careful attention to the labels on percentage tables, determines the cutting points are not misrepresenting the data, and finds the direction of percentaging is appropriate for the causal reasoning, percentage table analysis can be a very useful tool in the search for bivariate relationships.

1. For the scatterplots in Chapter 3, Exercise 4, make 2 by 2 and 3 by 3 tables, and compare the tables with the scatterplots.

2. Describe the nature of the relationship between the two variables represented by each of the tables below. Show how you arrived at your conclusions.

a.

College attendance

	Social class		
	Low	Medium	High
Yes	200	120	80
No	800	280	120

b.

Average hours of leisure per week

	Annual income (in thousands)			
	5–9	9–20	20–100	100+
10–20	72	453	212	0
Greater than 20	72	978	118	3
Less than 10	120	120	120	10

c.

Quality of performance

	Degree of centrality of communication		
	Low	Medium	High
High	53	197	429
Medium	106	197	257
Low	373	262	172

d.

Feeling of security

		L	M	H
	H	71	20	10
Wearing red	M	40	51	20
	L	20	30	40

e.

Amount of self-examination in
religious groups

		L	M	H
	H	10	50	10
Degree of crisis (Number of problems)	M	24	50	24
	L	75	50	75

f.

X
Rank

		4	3	2	1
	H	5	80	50	0
Y	M	25	30	20	5
	L	170	10	0	30

g.

X

		L	M	H
	H	80	20	60
Y	M	80	20	60
	L	80	20	60

h.

X

		L	ML	MH	H
Y	H	10	20	30	40
	L	40	40	40	40

i.

X

		L	M	H
Y	H	40	50	60
	L	20	90	120

3. Interpret the following percentage tables.

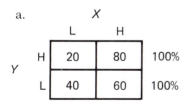

a.

X

		L	H	
Y	H	20	80	100%
	L	40	60	100%

b.

X

		L	M	H
	H	30	20	40
Y	M	30	60	20
	L	40	20	40

c.

	L	M	H
H	40	10	50
M	20	30	50
L	10	40	50

Y

d.

	X		
	50	50	50
Y	30	40	50
	20	10	0

4. Using the data below, construct a bivariate table and interpret the relationship between religious background and authoritarianism.

Religious background: F MR R MMF F R F F R MF F MR R MMF R F R M

Authoritarianism: H H L L L L L H H L L L L L H H L L L L L H L L

Code	Meaning
F	Fundamental
M	Moderate
R	Radical
L	Low
H	High

5. A sociologist is interested in the relationship between a father's occupation and his son's occupation. The following are the data obtained. What is the relationship, if any?

Father's occupation	Son's occupation	Father's occupation	Son's occupation

Key: B = Blue collar   W = White collar   P = Professional

Father's occupation	Son's occupation	Father's occupation	Son's occupation
P	P	P	P
P	P	W	P
B	W	B	B
B	W	W	W
W	W	B	B
W	W	W	W
P	W	B	B
P	P	W	W
W	P	P	P
B	B	B	W
B	W	W	W
W	W	B	B
W	B	W	P
P	P	W	W
P	W	B	B

1. Re-examine your project. If your hypothesis of main interest is actually the one you selected for analysis in the project, continue with it. If not, select any independent variable of your choice and a dependent variable.

   For all your variables, describe the cutting points you will use to place the data in bivariate tables, and the rationale for the cutting points you employ. (The size of your tables and the number of control tables you make will depend on the number of cutting points selected.)

CHAPTER 5
THE FIRST STEP IN EXPLORING
A RELATIONSHIP

After studying this chapter, students should be able to:

1. Identify the names of, find in the library, and use for simple literature reviews the most important abstracts, indexes, and periodicals of their field of interest.

2. Prepare proper citations of research references.

3. Find original sources in the library when given proper bibliographic citations.

4. Construct key word lists for appropriate research questions.

5. Say how reviews of the literature are conducted and what types of information might be gained by such reviews.

6. Discuss the role of literature reviews in the research process.

Abstract   A short summary of research.

Abstracts   Periodicals which contain subject and author lists of research published in particular journals that refer the reader to abstracts contained in separate sections.

Citation   A reference to published material which provides a complete bibliographic description of the source.

Indexes   Periodicals which contain subject and author lists of research published in particular journals.

Monograph   A book length report of research.

Periodicals   Published materials issued on a regular basis.

1. INTRODUCTION

Traditionally, one of the first steps a scientist takes is to become immersed in the problem that is about to be researched. That is, the scientist would read all possible information of a theoretical, methodological, or practical nature that has been written about the subject. In addition, if there are groups of professionals who are focusing on the area of research, it would be appropriate to consult, or possibly join, such a group and become acquainted with other people's thoughts and intuition. Finally, one would engage in a great deal of thought and reflection to try to "get it together" prior to actually beginning the work of the research. All of these efforts have one objective – becoming an expert. Maybe we do not get there sometimes, but that is what it is all about. Doing research has become a very esoteric specialty that is almost exclusively done by highly educated "experts," and just as dentists today have become much more reluctant to attempt oral surgery without becoming somewhat of an expert, neither would a researcher attempt research without becoming somewhat of an expert. For those students who will not likely be employed in the research field, this chapter is most meaningful in terms of the insights it may give as to what steps one usually undertakes to become expert. With this insight, one may better judge the adequacy of the expertise portrayed in written research. In addition it will be possible to "check" the source of the researcher's expertise. These judgments will determine to some extent the credibility of the research in question. For those students who may become employed in research, who may write term papers, or who may become research assistants in graduate school, this chapter provides a step-by-step description of the process of becoming an "expert" on a subject via the use of published materials. This step is often called a "review of the literature."

Becoming knowledgeable about published materials has many purposes and may proceed along various paths. However, the basic questions surrounding the pursuit of published materials are: what?, why?, where?, and how?

2. WHAT ARE WE LOOKING FOR?

It is reasonable to ask, "exactly what are we looking for in published materials?" The overall objective of reviewing previous science is to become expert so that better research can be achieved. However, it is also possible to enumerate specific types of things that can be obtained from such a search. The most common things are: research traditions, theoretical developments, hypotheses, definitions, specific findings, paraphrases, and quotations.

Research traditions

Very often a particular research project does not stand in isolation. That is, there have been previous studies which concern the same topic or somehow "fit" together into a research tradition. It is helpful to the researcher and to the reader of research reports to see a particular study in the context of previous work. The provision of the context of a particular study allows the reader to integrate the study in question with other information. This will better enable one to form an overall conclusion. In addition, particular types of methodology or procedures might have been developed in the past that a researcher may wish to continue or to build upon. By describing the way in which previous science has been done, research traditions can be continued.

Theoretical development

In addition to the discovery of research traditions, most researchers feel it is desirable for research to contribute to theoretical development. That is, studies should further our systematic understanding of the phenomena under investigation. In the search for relationships, one of the goals is to construct sound theories to explain whatever is being studied. In sociology, it might be a theory which explains criminal behavior. In education, attempts may be made to understand dropouts. In psychology, extreme depression may be the focus of attempts to gain understanding. As we have previously stated, theories are sets of interrelated propositions. Propositions are statements about the nature of the relationship between variables. In this vein a review of previous science may attempt to identify theoretical trends in previous research which can be enhanced by the study in question. It is very desirable for research to contribute to theoretical development.

Source of hypotheses

In addition to these general goals, there are several very specific uses of previous science. For example, previous science often provides the foundation or starting point for particular studies. We have spoken of the "building block" idea of science, and it is in reference to this idea that a review of previous studies can form the basis for new research. By becoming expert, a scientist may be able to determine the nature of the next "block" that is needed. Specifically, a researcher may be led to a particular hypothesis which needs to be tested in order to come to a more complete understanding of what is being studied. It may be that previous research leaves a question about whether a particular hypothesis is supported, or it may be that previous studies refine understanding in such a way that a new hypothesis is suggested. In any case, previous science often serves to suggest that specific hypotheses be tested.

Definitions

Previous science is often used as a source of *conceptual* definitions. Consistency in the definition of variables leads to findings that are more easily compared and findings that can be combined directly to arrive at a coherent conclusion. Without consistency in definition, the search for relationships becomes problematic. This is particularly the case if the same word is used to mean different things. By relying on previous definitions, consistency in conceptualization can be maintained.

The measurement of variables is always difficult in science, and previous research can be used to aid the researcher in developing *operational* definitions. A scientist may use the same directions for measuring a variable that have been used before. By doing this, conclusions will likely be more easily interpreted than if new measurements are attempted. The idea of consistency and comparability are the main concerns when utilizing previous science to operationalize variables.

Even if conceptual and operational definitions are not used exactly as in previous research, knowledge of previous definitions can be invaluable in developing definitions which are clearer, more complete, and useful.

Specific findings

Research findings are often compared to the conclusions of previous science. If current findings are similar to past findings, then there can be increased confidence in research results. If current findings are different from previous ones, new questions can be raised about either the methodologies employed or the theories being tested. Advances in scientific understanding are often the consequence of differences in research findings. If current results are not compared to specific previous research results, this progress may be impeded. In addition, present findings can be integrated with previous results to obtain a more complete picture of the phenomena under study. Research results that stand in isolation from other scientific research outcomes have less utility than those presented in the context of previous science.

Paraphrases

When preparing written reports of research, it may be helpful to refer to entire sections of some previous scientific writings. Perhaps a previous author was particularly creative in constructing a theory, or was innovative in constructing some operational definition, or in some other way, wrote something of particular note. In a case such as this, it might be useful to *paraphrase* a particular section from a previous research report. A *paraphrase* is a statement that attempts to capture the essence or sense of a section authored by another person. Paraphrases serve to emphasize, highlight, give credibility to, or to integrate present writing with previous research efforts.

Quotations

Sometimes an author will write something in a particularly clear way or in a manner which makes a point in such a way that a direct, word-for-word quote is appropriate. Also, some scientists are so well known in a particular field that quoting them may lend more credibility to research. In either case, the writing of research results may be enhanced by furnishing quotes from previous science. If quotations would enhance a research report in terms of style, or give credibility to research, or integrate findings and results, it is perfectly appropriate to seek such quotations from previous research findings. In all of the cases listed above, or if for any other reason previous research is directly utilized to write a research report, appropriate credit must be given to the author whose work is used.

In general, the answer to the question, "what are we looking for?" is citations of previous scientists' work as reflected in published materials. The rationale behind citing previous research is explored in the following section.

3. WHY DO WE WANT THEM?

One of the cornerstones of science is *replication* of research, that is, repeating similar studies at a different time and place. In order for one researcher to add to and build upon previous work, the results of science must be communicated to other scientists. Replication is also crucial because of the tentative nature of science. In these days of increasing sophistication of knowledge and specialization of skills, it becomes even more important to be able to communicate with others before and after the research act. Scientists are professionals who have special interest organizations and special interest publications. Virtually every university discipline has a set of professional journals which record the work of those producing research relevant to their occupation. The written word in publications has become the primary way in which scientists communicate to one another. Since this is the case, a review of published materials provides the most efficient way of becoming informed. Unfortunately, *becoming* an expert seems to be much less fun than *being* an expert. Learning and studying published materials is sometimes viewed as tedious and uninteresting. In addition, it takes time, effort, and sometimes money. The basic techniques that are used to find appropriate previous research are sometimes arduous. Much of the time spent does not result in anything of great use. We will explore these techniques in a following section and enumerate the problems and benefits associated with each procedure.

At this point we can specify at least three major answers to the question of *why* we explore previous research via publications. The first major reason for reviewing published materials is to enhance the likelihood of producing scientific findings that are considered to be of some value. By gaining an awareness of what other scientists are doing, one can obtain some awareness of what sorts of topics are currently being focused on. This does not necessarily mean that one can only do research others are interested in, but it does have implications for what type of work is valued, published, controversial, funded, and popular. By reviewing previous scientific research, it would be possible to determine (1) how theoretical considerations could be refined, (2) whether previous contradictions in the literature could be clarified, and (3) which studies should be replicated. Such research is valued because of the belief that science is cumulative. New research should be integrated with past research so that a more accurate picture of reality results.

A second reason for being aware of previous research efforts is to do research that is of superior quality. By becoming an expert, one can avoid pursuing techniques or questions which others have found to be unsuccessful.

There is, of course, a possibility that a researcher may produce useful results by going down the same path that others have unsuccessfully gone down, but the likelihood of success seems less. There has probably never been a study conducted wherein the scientists could not look back and think of something that they could have done better.

In general, hindsight is extremely wise and in research this is also true. One of the most helpful aspects of a review of published materials is that a researcher may benefit from the hindsight of others. Just as a child does not necessarily have to get burned to learn the idea of fire, a researcher does not have to start from ground zero as though nothing were known about the subject under investigation.

A final reason for being able to cite previous research findings is that, in science, authority is almost sacred. The name of the game in publication of research results is the "name game." In other words, since communication of findings is a cornerstone of science, the scientist must understand the standards and practices of those who control information. In this case, the controllers are the publishers, editors, and reviewers of professional media. The most closely held standard for publication of scientific work is the citation of previous scientific theory and research. Therefore it is important to incorporate previous ideas, theories, and findings in the interpretation of one's work. As students, most of us have a dislike for having to remember "names" and for being required to associate a name with particular research findings. At this time it may appear to be empty memorization without any particular purpose. However, as one continues to read, continues to work, and continues along the path to becoming expert, the names, findings, theories, and recommendations of scientists who have done previous work start to become meaningful.

It is perhaps only after one has become somewhat of an expert that it makes much sense to try to place previous science in an overall perspective.

There are some good reasons for knowing about and being familiar with published materials; there are some practical reasons, and some cultural reasons. All of which boils down to the fact that in order to do science, one must master previous research as portrayed in published works. In consuming scientific findings, one will have to put up with citations of previous science. Hopefully, these citations will allow a reader to become more of an expert than would be possible without them. The next logical question to ask is, "where do I pursue previous published science?" The simple answer is—*in the library.*

4. WHERE DO WE LOOK?

The library

Although the major purpose of this section is to acquaint you with just how to use library reference materials, an important point must be stressed: There are professionals that all libraries pay to organize and handle the reference section of the library—reference librarians. These librarians can be invaluable in your search for previous science. They are much more familiar with sources, floor plans, recent innovations, and technological advances in information retrieval than most researchers can ever hope to be. If you plan to do science, our advice is to get to know the reference librarians very well. With their help, your task of doing a thorough review of published materials will be greatly aided. If you will not be using the library on a steady basis, then it may be even more important for you to rely on the skill and assistance of the reference librarian.

There are five basic ways in which previous science is recorded and stored. Therefore there are five distinct types of searches that the scientist can engage in to become an expert. First, all sciences have *professional journals* (periodicals) that are published a certain number of times every year. Second, major research efforts often appear in book form, sometimes called *monographs*. Third, a significant number of research findings can be found in *official government documents*. Fourth, some specialized types of research are recorded in *special information systems* that can be used if particular types of information are desired. Finally, computers are being used more and more to store scientific information. In such cases, *computerized information retrieval mechanisms* can be employed to gain access to such stored information. Although these five types of sources for finding previous science sometimes overlap, it is useful to discuss each of them individually.

Periodicals
There are likely thousands of professional journals in all fields of study. Some are very limited in the scope of research reported and others are more general in nature. Typically, a scientist will personally subscribe to those journals of most interest, and rely upon the library to purchase others which may be useful from time to time. With the great number of available periodicals to choose from, it is becoming increasingly difficult for a scientist to "keep up" with periodical literature. In response to the need for scientists to be able to locate and read research findings, indexes and abstracts have been developed. The essential nature of both indexes and abstracts is that they select specific journals and periodicals and then create lists of the research reported in them. Two types of lists are constructed: an alphabetical list of authors of articles and an alphabetical list of subject matter. Subject matter is determined from the title or content of particular articles. In order to use these lists, one may look up the name of scientists that usually do work in a particular area, or one may devise a set of key terms and consult the list of subject matter. The process of devising a set of key terms is discussed in a following section. Using these lists is similar to using a dictionary or ency-

138

FIGURE 5.1
Typical author list

CUMULATIVE AUTHOR INDEX

Dodge, Philip R., 2113, 3600
Dodson, W. E., 2471
Doesburg, W. H., 3428, 3430
Doherty, Edward, 1576
Doherty, R. L., 2842
Dohn, Donald F., 401
Dolan, Margaret, 2715
Dolley, Diane Greenough, 469
Dolman, Clarisse L., 1247
Domingue, Gerald, 1854
Domino, George, 3534
Donald, Ian, 464, 3184
Donaldson, Milton H., 1187
Donhoff, Eric, 751
Doniach, D., 865
Donnell, G. N., 473, 3040, 3052, 3353
Donnelly, Edward F., 1535
Donnelly, William H., Jr., 2808
Donner, M., 2261
Donoghue, Elaine, 3402
Donohoe, W. T. A., 174
Dontanville, Virginia K., 2143
Dooling, Elizabeth C., 1265
Doolittle, Walter M., 2317
Dorau, Terrance A., 2134
Doray, Bernard, 3236
Dore, A., 2787
Dorfman, Albert, 1148, 2194
Dorfman, Leslie J., 2904
Dorman, D. C., 135
Dormandy, T. L., 2108, 2854
Dorn, G., 2252
Dorsch, N. W. C., 2281
Dorst, John P., 1256
Doty, Stephen B., 3065
Douglas, Carolyn, 3073
Douglas, Virginia, 239, 241, 1108
Douglass, Joseph H., 766
Doutsch, Cynthia P., 218
Dow, Ruth, 1290
Dowdle, Walter R., 1814, 1815, 2902
Downs, M., 1272
Doyle, P., 2526
Doyne, Emanuel O., 837, 839
Draghici, L., 246
Draper, David A., 167
Draper, G. J., 2890, 3349
Draycott, V., 3278
Dreger, Ralph M., 1479
Dreifuss, Fritz E., 2368, 3008
Drennan, J., 445
Drenzner, Marc, 3125
Dresser, Astha C., 3012

Drew, Clifford J., 526, 2585, 3475
Dreyfus, J., 256
Drillien, C. M., 352, 1260, 1294, 1299, 3279
Drouet, J., 1793
Drouhet, Victoria, 2804
Dryden, K. G., 1684
Drylie, David M., 2050
Dubach, U. C., 3093
Dubin, Elyse, 1713
Dubois, Reuben S., 270, 1983
Dubowitz, B., 789
Dubowitz, V., 304, 453, 789
Duc, Gabriel V., 2403

Duc, Tran Van, 1058
Ducasse, G. Clement, 1417
Ducharme, J. R., 2539
Duchin, Sybil, 1039, 2091
Duchting, M., 3201
Dudgeon, J. A., 927, 1059
Dudley, F. J., 865, 917, 1770
Duenas, D., 985, 1838, 1866, 2031
Duff, Raymond S., 2708
Duffy, Philip E., 2835, 2836
Duffy, Robert J., 599
Dufresne, Jean-Jacques, 1798
Dulaney, John T., 2188
Dumermuth, G., 258
Dumon, Jan E., 2410
Dumont, M., 1727
Dunbar, J. Scott, 1312
Duncan, Caroline, 3219
Duncan, Denise, 3082
Duncombe, David C., 2740
Dunham, Angela, 3176
Dunlap, Dickson B., 2556
Dunn, G. F. Newton, 2791
Dunn, Henry G., 1778, 2146
Dunn, Leo J., 2895
Dupree, Elton, 2779
Dupuis, C., 1455
Durand, P., 250, 324
Durant, Joseph L., 2192
Duravetz, J., 2773
Durrant, D., 1171
Dutton, G., 3261
Dweck, Harry S., 1047
Dybkjaer, Esben, 1784
Dybwad, Gunnar, 1621, 3563, 3587
Dyck, Peter J., 2110
Dyer, Geraldine Y., 196
Dyer, Jane S., 3150

Source: Mental Retardation Abstracts 10, 4, Oct.–Dec. 1973, 1105.

clopedia, but beside each author or subject entry is a complete bibliographic reference to some article in a particular issue of a particular journal. Once the reviewer has discovered a reference to an article that appears to be relevant, the original journal article can be found and read. The major difference between indexes and abstracts is the amount of information given about the original research report. Generally an index contains very little information. Abstracts contain short summaries of the findings, usually within a separate section. These summaries are also called *abstracts*.

The practice of creating lists of authors and subject matter from large numbers of journals is well established and has been going on for many years. Indexes and abstracts have become so extensive and numerous that they themselves have become periodicals. Issues of various indexes and abstracts are published on a regular basis and their lists cover particular calendar periods. Some indexes and abstracts also publish cumulative issues that cover many years. Because of this practice, a researcher can examine research from particular periods of time, for example for the last five years, or from 1950 to 1955.

Figure 5.1 represents a page from a typical author list. After each author's name appears a list of articles, indicated by number(s), by that individual.

Figure 5.2 shows a page from the subject list of the *Education Index*. Under each key word appears a list of articles concerned with the topic. Abstracts contain similar lists but, in addition, also contain a section that provides summaries.

Figure 5.3 is a page from a medical abstract and shows a series of abstracts of articles from various publications. The abstract for a particular reference can be found by referring to the code number appearing in the subject and author lists. If, after reading the abstract, it appears that the article is important enough for further consideration, a complete version of the original material can be consulted.

Some of the more important indexes for the social and behavioral sciences and education are: *Book Review Digest, British Humanities Index, Education Index, Reader's Guide to Periodical Literature, Social Science and Humanities Index,* and *Social Sciences Citation Index.*

Some of the more important abstracts for the social and behavioral sciences and education are: *Abstracts in Anthropology, Crime and Delinquency Abstracts, Dissertation Abstracts, Education Abstracts, Historical Abstracts, Psychological Abstracts,* and *Sociological Abstracts.*

Once the researcher becomes familiar with the indexes and abstracts, the task of finding previous science becomes quite simplified. Expertise in using these types of aides will greatly speed the

FIGURE 5.2
Typical subject list

EDUCATION INDEX

EMPLOYEES—Training—*Continued*
Modular learning in business. L. R. Hess and L. Sperry. bibliog il Education 93:322-8 Ap '73
Teaching partnership for technical staff; Union carbide and University of Tennessee. D. V. Brown. Com & Jun Col J 44:35-6 N '73
See also
Apprentices
Manpower development and training programs

Great Britain

Industrial appreciation course: an initial assessment. N. J. Adnett and J. J. Lawton. Voc Aspect Educ 25:61-5 Ag '73

EMPLOYEES, Government. See Government officials and employees

EMPLOYEES, Selection of. See Employment systems

EMPLOYEES representation in management participative decision making: an experimental study in a hospital. J. E. Bragg and I. R. Andrews. J App Behav Sci 9:727-35 N '73

EMPLOYMENT
Phenomenarchy: a suggestion for social redesign. W. McWhinney. J App Behav Sci 9:163-80 Mr '73
See also
Americans in foreign countries—Employment
Deaf—Employment
Handicapped—Employment
Mentally handicapped—Employment
Mentally ill—Employment
Negroes—Employment
Veterans—Employment
Vocational rehabilitation
Women—Employment
Work
Youth—Employment

Employability rating

Intelligence and vocational adjustment. L. K. Daniels. bibliog Train Sch Bull 70:135-9 N '73
Speech characteristics and employ-ability. R. Hopper and F. Williams. Speech Mon 40:296-302 N '72

Curacao (island)

Social intervention in Curacao: a case study. D. E. Berlew and W. E. LeClere. J App Behav Sci 10:29-52; Discussion. 53-61 Ja '74

United States

Reflections on manpower. R. W. Fleming. Voc Guid Q 22:224-9 Mr '74

EMPLOYMENT, Agricultural. See Agricultural employment

EMPLOYMENT agencies
Challenging decade for employment counselors. A. Fantaci. il Personnel & Guid J 52:160-6 N '73

EMPLOYMENT discrimination. See Discrimination in employment

EMPLOYMENT interviews. See interviews

EMPLOYMENT management
Business and industry look out for their own; employee counseling programs. K. R. Kunze. il Personnel & Guid J 52:145-9 N '73
Calculating staff affirmative action goals and timetables. P. R. Loggins. il J Col & Univ Personnel Assn 24:64-77 S '73
Structural approach to organizational change. R. A. Luke, jr. and others. il J App Behav Sci 9:611-35: Discussion. 636-41 S '73
See also
Communication in management
Employment systems
Job satisfaction
Time keeping

EMPLOYMENT of children. See Child labor

EMPLOYMENT of students. See Cooperative education; Student employment; Work experience

EMPLOYMENT of teachers. See Teacher employment in business and industry

FIGURE 5.3
Typical page from an abstract

MEDICAL ASPECTS   3193–3196

3193   COHEN, M. MICHAEL, JR.; HALL, BRYAN D.; SMITH, DAVID W.; GRAHAM, C. BENJAMIN; & LAMPERT, KENNETH J. A new syndrome with hypotonia, obesity, mental deficiency, and facial, oral, ocular, and limb anomalies. *Journal of Pediatrics,* 83(2):280-284, 1973.

A number of abnormalities shared by 3 patients of whom 2 were siblings are described as constituting a new syndrome. All 3 patients were white and all were products of full-term gestations during which decreased fetal activity was evident. Both sets of parents were apparently normal with no history of consanguinity. Poor weight gain characterized the early life period of all 3; other features in common—MR, abnormal craniofacies, micrognathia, narrow palate with crowded teeth, limb abnormalities, and spine abnormalities—were common in all 3. The patients differed in the ocular findings and in the presence of mild cutaneous syndactyly (in one case). The syndrome may follow an autosomal recessive mode of inheritance. (2 refs.) - *A. C. Schenker.*

School of Dentistry
University of Washington
Seattle, Washington 98105

3194   JONES, D. E. DARNELL; PRITCHARD, KATHLEEN I.; GIOANNINI, CAROL A.; MOORE, DONALD T.; & BRADFORD, WILLIAM D. Hydrops fetalis associated with idiopathic arterial calcification. *Obstetrics and Gynecology,* 39(3):435-440, 1972.

An unusual case of generalized arterial calcification associated with massive hydrops resulted in death for a 3,800g female Negro infant 21 hrs after full-term delivery by cesarean section. Throughout the newborn period, the infant was grossly hydropic, apneic, and bradycardic. Post-mortem findings included diffuse arterial calcification, myocardial infarction, and extensive periovarian psammoma bodies. Considering the infrequency of idiopathic generalization and its disproportionately high occurrence in siblings, a relationship between fibrinoid degeneration of maternal decidual vessels (present in this case) and altered ionic dynamics resulting in calcium deposition is a distinct etiologic possibility. (9 refs.) - *N. Mize.*

Duke University Medical Center
Durham, North Carolina 27706

3195   ADEMOWORE, ADEBAYO S.; *COUREY, NORMAN G.; & KIVE, JAMES S. Relationships of maternal nutrition and weight gain to newborn birth-weight. *Obstetrics and Gynecology,* 39(3):460-464, 1972.

Findings of an investigation into the relationships between maternal nutrition and weight gain and subsequent newborn birthweight in a well-characterized study population of 345 nulliparous women suggest, in particular, that the tendency toward smallness in nonwhite babies is probably more attributable to malnutrition of the mother than to genetic reasons. Generally, the data confirm a linear relationship between maternal weight gain in pregnancy and newborn birthweight, particularly for the nonwhite group. A particularly striking correlation between larger infant size and higher socioeconomic classification in the out-patient group was noted, a feature reflected again in marked differences observed between resident (living in the hospital for 9 or more weeks prior to delivery where an adequate diet was provided) and out-patient birthweights in the poverty level group. Resident birthweights were almost uniformly higher. For out-patients, a pattern of lower socioeconomic class associated with smaller babies prevailed. (16 refs.)-*I,N. Mize.*

researcher on the way to becoming expert. In addition to these two types of reference materials, the reader might want to become familiar with using encyclopedias, bibliographies, and guides. Consultation with the reference librarian will be helpful in finding and using appropriate materials of this sort.

Books in print

Very often published research in periodicals is limited to reports of specific research projects which are relatively limited in scope and purpose. If there is extensive theoretical work or large scale research to be reported, books or monographs are often produced. A *monograph* is a book length report of research that may or may not involve a great deal of theoretical development. Many of the most significant theoretical works are in the form of books, and a great deal of research which is reported in book length form is also among the most important. In addition, there are many books that are collections of articles or original chapters that focus upon particular subject matter. When trying to find books or monographs on particular subjects, there are three lists that can be helpful. These lists are contained in the *card catalogs* available in all libraries. One card catalog contains an alphabetic list of authors, another contains an alphabetic list according to the subject matter of library holdings of books, and another contains a list of titles. Use of the author catalog requires some familiarity with scientists doing work in the area of interest, but use of the subject catalog only requires the ability to construct key word lists. As stated previously, this technique will be covered in a later part of this chapter.

Documents

Each year the Government Printing Office (GPO) publishes masses of reports and findings for all government agencies and their contractors. The U.S. Department of Labor; Health, Education and Welfare; and Defense are among the most prolific producers of information which can be useful for scientific analysis. In addition, they sponsor many research projects every year which are often printed by the GPO. Most large university libraries contain a collection of government documents. However, unless one uses the document section of the library on a very regular basis, it is difficult to keep track of how to find particular documents. Whenever such a section is available in a library, there will be a special librarian(s) assigned to this section. *Relying on the documents librarian is a must* in order to utilize the information contained in this massive information storage system. We would make the generalization that without the help of a good documents librarian, this source of information for becoming expert will be of little use. However, with perseverance, a tremendous volume of information is available. A monthly publication, *U.S. Government Research Reports,* issued by the Department of Commerce can be obtained which contains an index of government publications.

Information systems

There are several systematic collections of research findings in special areas of interest that are available to the scientist. These specialized collections offer the advantage of having selected those studies most pertinent to a particular subject(s) and cataloging them in some fashion. One of the most familiar examples of such a system is the ERIC (Educational Resources Information Center) system which focuses on educational research materials. ERIC has almost 20 different centers where specific topics (such as information on junior colleges or early childhood education) are concentrated.

Another example of such a system is the National Clearinghouse for Mental Health Information (NCMHI) which, as the name implies, focuses on the areas of mental health and mental illness. There is also a Human Relations Area File (HRAF) which has served many scholars in the area of cross-cultural research and study of particular foreign areas. These are but three examples illustrating that when a significant number of scientists are studying particular phenomena, there are often specialized sources of information that should be explored prior to a general search of the literature. Again, the reference librarian can be extremely helpful in determining whether or not some specialized information system exists for reviewing pertinent published materials for a particular research effort.

Computer services

It is no secret that we are in the midst of an information explosion. Hundreds of serious scientific journals are currently published every year; dozens of private book publishers are producing untold thousands of books every year; and the government at all levels continues to fund and publish many hundreds of research projects every year. One response to the problems of becoming expert in the face of such a volume of information is to try to enlist the aid of the computer.

There has been some success with computerization. Some examples include computerization of library holdings and usage, computerized storage of abstracts, machines that can read and store information from printed sources, computerized abstracting of printed materials, translation of written material by computer, and so on. We are now just beginning to see the tip of the computerized iceberg with respect to information storage, retrieval, and communication. There is even a computerized machine that is being developed especially for use by blind people. This machine "reads" written material aloud for those who have vision problems.

Where these technological developments and others will take us is unknown at this time, but we can say for certain that computerized services are more and more prevalent and more and more useful.

Many libraries are currently subscribers to different types of computer services. Many of these systems rely on key words for their services, and some utilize computer teletypes to interact directly with the user so that maximum utility is derived. Although all of the types of sources discussed thus far are usually available without charge, most of the computer-assisted services do charge a fee for their use. It is likely therefore that only the active researcher would employ such aids. Examples of some of these types of services include: SSIE, The Smithsonian Scientific Information Exchange; NTIS, National Technical Information Service (U.S. Department of Commerce, Springfield, Va. 22161); and Lockheed Retrieval Service Information Systems Laboratory (Lockheed Systems Development Corp). For a fee, often a nominal one, these and other such services will retrieve information which they have stored in large computer memory systems. Based on key words, the systems search their files and match titles or subjects of entries. Entries may be simple titles with references; complete abstracts; or complete works. These services can be utilized with the aid of most reference librarians.

Personal contacts

Although no attempt to become expert would be complete without a thorough review of published materials, there is a potential for much added depth through personal contact with others doing similar types of research. Whereas spending many hours in the library may sometimes be rewarding, it is often quite laborious. In order to supplement this "impersonal" mode of becoming an expert, it is often advisable to make contact with other scientists. One's colleagues can be found through joining professional associations, attending various seminars, meetings or conventions, by walking down the hall, or by picking up the telephone. For professional scientists, this type of contact is often necessary to obtain financial support for one's work, or to gain the kind of constructive criticisms that can be obtained only from experienced researchers. For the student or consumer of research results, this means asking friends if they have ever come across similar research, or whether they have heard of the researcher who produced the study, or whether they know of other information that would be helpful. Many a term paper, for example, has been developed as a consequence of students "dropping in" to chat with professors from whom the student may not have even taken classes. Thus people are sources of information too. This source of information is sometimes more pleasant to utilize than published materials.

Commercial enterprises

In this age of specialization, information processing is becoming increasingly specialized. Also, automation and computerization of information systems creates conditions which require expertise not held by most scientists. These conditions are contributing to the growth of a new industry which processes information for research purposes. Many firms now specialize in information handling for businesses. Recent developments indicate that such activities will soon be commonplace in the research process. Researchers of the future will likely employ such firms as partners in the research process of becoming expert.

5. HOW DO WE GO ABOUT IT?

We have thus far considered *what* it is that we are seeking in the examination of printed matter; *why* we pursue published materials; and *where* to look for publications. The final consideration is *how* to go about utilizing the sources listed for the desired purposes. The first part of the answer is found in discussing the process of finding a list of key words to use when consulting the various subject lists discussed previously in this chapter. The second part of the answer is found in briefly discussing how citations to previous science are constructed when writing a research report.

Constructing key word lists

In order to use abstracts, indexes, encyclopedias, guides, and many of the automated and computerized services, you need to know either the author(s) who wrote research reports in a particular area, the title, or the subject heading under which such research would appear. Use of author lists requires more knowledge than researchers sometimes have and certainly more knowledge than most students about to write a paper have.

There are two basic strategies to follow when attempting to construct a key word list. The first is to identify the dependent variables of interest, and the second is to enumerate general areas of interest in which a particular type of study might appear. Both of these may be supplemented as one learns more about the subject matter. Once a key word list is constructed, the researcher can use the subject lists of most reference materials. Some examples of constructing such lists might prove helpful.

Suppose you are interested in doing a study or writing a research paper on why some students get good grades in school while others get poor grades. First of all, begin to construct a key word list by thinking about the names of the dependent variable under which such studies might be found. The question itself defines "grades" as the dependent variable. The question is, "are there any other terms that are synonymous with grades?" The following might result:

Grades
Marks
Achievement
Academic performance
School progress

To complete the list, one needs to think of general areas where research on grades might be found. Adding to the above list:

Schools:
  Grading
  Marks
  Students

Students:
  Marks
  Grades
  Achievement
  Performance

Achievement:
  Students
  Academic
  Affective

Armed with such a key word list, a researcher will likely be able to find most of the research on the area by using the subject lists of the major reference sources. In fact, if all of these terms are researched, one will likely find many articles or research reports listed under more than one subject entry.

After a key word list is constructed and/or the names of major researchers in the area have been discovered, the scientist would go to the types of reference sources discussed in Section 4. A supply of index cards should be acquired before going to the library. As you find potentially useful published materials by using the various author and/or subject lists, write the complete bibliographic reference of each of the original works on one of the cards. Each reference should contain the following information:

1. Name of the author(s).
2. Title of work, article, book, etc.

3. The name of the periodical, if the work appears in a periodical.
4. If particular pages of a book or periodical are involved, the page numbers should be included.
5. If the work is in a periodical, the volume and issue number of the periodical.
6. The year in which the work was published.
7. The publisher of the work, if it is a book or government publication.
8. The city in which the publisher is located, if appropriate.

Once the researcher has enough references that seem possibly helpful, it is time to go to the periodical or stack section of the library and find the original sources. The index cards can be used to make notes, record definitions, findings, quotes, and so on, which might be used when writing a report. If more complete information is needed, copies of particular pages may be made and stapled to the index card. Such a system will be most efficient for recording a lot of information from a large number of sources. It will also allow the writer of a research report to cite those sources that might be useful. Although this is only one way to organize the search of previous science, this system has proven helpful to many people in the past.

Follow-up on citations in previous works

The use of key word lists should result in finding some useful published research. When it does, the research will contain citations of other works. It is often profitable to go back to the original works that others have cited. This may produce valuable information including more citations.

Form of citations when writing

Anytime information from previously published materials is used when writing the results of your research, a citation of the original work should be made. This is particularly crucial when findings, paraphrases, or quotations are used. It is only fair to give the scientist who did the work the appropriate amount of credit. In fact, in some circumstances, if such citations do not appear in your writing, heavy penalties might result, including the possibility of law suits.

There are many conventions which determine how citations in research reports are made. The particular convention used will depend on where the research report is to be published. All government agencies, periodicals, and book publishers have well established systems of citations that must be learned when writing for them. One widely used system is that constructed by the American Psychological Association (APA). The APA citation manual may be purchased in most bookstores. This system discourages the use of footnotes.

Also, when a citation is to be made in the text, the author's name appears along with the date of publication of the material cited. An alphabetically arranged list of authors is placed at the end of the writing. Under each name full bibliographic references for the work cited are arranged by date of publication with the most recent being first. The norms of various citation systems will become second nature to those who write research reports or to those who make it a practice to read such reports on a regular basis.

6. SUMMARY

The first step in the research process is concerned with the attempt to become expert by studying previous scientific research as it appears in published materials. Specific goals of reviewing previous research include the discovery of research traditions, theoretical development, hypotheses, definitions, specific findings, paraphrases, and quotations. Knowledge of this sort is necessary in order to determine what type of information is valued, published, controversial, funded, and popular. Reviewing the literature should enable the researcher to refine theoretical considerations and clarify contradictions. In so doing, the need for replication should become clear. The general purpose in becoming expert in a given field is to produce research of superior quality which benefits from the knowledge of others, and to place such research findings in a proper perspective. The major repository of previous knowledge is the library. By using periodicals, books, documents, information systems, and computer services we can, with the help of the librarian, begin the process of becoming expert. Personal contacts and commercial enterprises can, of course, further the process. In order to utilize most sources of information for a review of the literature, it is necessary to construct key word lists. This is usually done by listing important concepts and their synonyms. Another important procedure for discovering previous science is to follow up citations in published works. This is one major reason why it is important to know how to construct and read citations systems.

Once the researcher feels that it is appropriate to begin work on the research project at hand, it is time to decide exactly how observations will be made to search for relationships. The following chapters present and discuss the major ways of making observations. Sometimes ways of making observations are called "research designs." This boils down to the idea that scientists make systematic observations of phenomena in order to come to conclusions. How these systematic observations are made is the topic of the next three chapters.

Select two concepts from Chapter 2, Exercises 2, 7, or 8. For each concept:

1. Construct a list of a few alternate subject headings (key words) under which each of your concepts may be located.

2. Locate at least three books from the subject list in the card catalog.

3. Locate at least two articles on the subject from important abstracts.

4. Check to see if your selection may be related to concerns in the various information systems available in your library (e.g., ERIC, NCMHI, HRAF). If so, locate at least two articles or summaries from each.

5. Find out if your library has a computer service and if it is available to you. If so, ask for a listing of material available for one of the concepts.

6. For each book or article located in Exercises 1 to 4, try to locate the book or complete article (rather than just the abstract).
   a. What are the major hypotheses concerning the concept?
   b. Is the concept the independent or dependent variable?
   c. How does (do) the author(s) relate their hypotheses to previous research?
   d. When the concept is the dependent variable, are there any suggested hypotheses that contradict one another?

7. Government documents are often a rich, however overlooked, source of information. Take one of your concepts and have the documents librarian show you what information is available. (In large classes your instructor may simply have the librarian provide lists on selected topics to avoid overloading the librarian with individual requests.)

Consult with your instructor about three possible dependent variables you may wish to study.

Before going to the library:

Construct a list of key words for each concept (dependent variable). Remember to consider dimensions, indicators, related concepts, and/or similar concepts.
Go to the library to find the following:
Alternative definitions for each concept (dependent variable).
At least three indicators for each concept.
At least two operational definitions for each concept (which you feel reflect the conceptual definitions).
At least three hypotheses from previous research (if any exist) in which the concept is the dependent variable.
At this point you and your instructor should conclude a tentative

150

agreement about which dependent variable(s) you will study in the data collection sections (experiment, survey, participant observation, content analysis, evaluation research, unobtrusive measures).

You should also indicate a set of at least three hypotheses you will examine. (To make your projects more interesting, when you get to the analysis section we will recommend that you gather data on more than the three independent variables you indicate at this point. Thus, if you have found three hypotheses in your library search, or if you can think of others, make a larger list.)

REFERENCES

HELMSTADTER, G. *Research Concepts in Human Behavior*. New York: Appleton-Century-Crofts, 1970, Chapter 5.

RUNCIE, J. *Experiencing Social Research*. Homewood, Ill.: The Dorsey Press, 1976, Chapter 2.

CHAPTER 6
THE ETHICS OF RESEARCH
ON HUMAN SUBJECTS

After studying this chapter, students should be able to:

1. Discuss the basic dilemma between the value of knowledge and protecting research subjects.

2. Discuss why the question of research ethics is important.

3. List, give examples of, and discuss the various issues raised concerning the subject as a person, including: the right of self-determination, voluntarism, informed consent, equal opportunity, delivery of promises, maintaining self-respect, and protecting privacy.

4. List and discuss the importance of avoiding the fabrication of data, plagiarism, and the exploitation of assistants and/or subjects.

5. List one source for a formal statement of ethics involving research on human subjects and discuss the use of review boards to decide about the ethical issues of research on human subjects.

Fabrication of data   Making up or altering data.

Informed consent   Principle that states subjects should be fully informed about the content and/or dangers of research before they volunteer to be subjects.

Plagiarism   Copying the previous writing or ideas of a researcher or writer without giving credit to that person.

Stooge   A confederate of the researcher who responds on the basis of instructions from the researcher.

1. THE IMPORTANCE OF ETHICS IN RESEARCH ON HUMAN SUBJECTS

In the last ten years researchers in the social/behavioral sciences and education have become increasingly concerned with ethical standards about research conducted on human subjects. This may be partially due to the fact that certain government agencies like the U.S. Department of Health, Education and Welfare began to formalize their standards when they granted research funds. It may be partially due to the general disenchantment of the 1960s and/or "Watergate." Or it may be partially due to the notoriety which some research projects have gotten in the recent past. A study such as the one that allowed syphilis victims to go untreated and the famous research of Stanley Milgram (1963) involving aggression are perhaps among the most notable influences that have led to this increased emphasis.

Whatever the reasons, this situation has importance for both the producers of research and the consumers of research information. For the producers, ethical considerations may prohibit certain kinds of studies, require design modification in research, or create circumstances in which sound scientific procedures may be difficult or impossible to carry out. For the consumers, the imposition of ethical considerations into the research process may have an influence on the type of information available to consume, and may therefore limit the degree to which certain phenomena can be understood.

2. THE BASIC DILEMMA

The question of ethics in research involving human subjects is not merely a simple matter of identifying the guys with the white hats and the guys with the black hats. The considerations are many and the problem complex. The basic dilemma concerns the possible conflict between a value that holds knowledge to be important and considers the free access to knowledge among the most important aspects of human existence, and the value that holds that harm to research subjects must be avoided and that humanity must be protected against potential harm in the future which might stem from research findings. The possible conflict is between the value of knowledge and the potential harm to people both now and in the future.

There has been a long-standing assumption in the scientific community that knowledge is "good" for its own sake. The presumption is that information produced by scientific procedures is more valuable to us than folklore, common sense, intuition, or custom. The logic is that we never know when a bit of scientific information may prove useful. Even information that has no apparent value in the present may eventually become important and central to our understanding. Therefore science must operate in a community of free inquiry and it must support all scientific inquiry no matter what the topic. If ethical considerations result in curtailing certain types of investigations, then in effect scientific information will have been censored. One possibility in this type of situation is that science might then become the tool of those imposing the so-called ethical standards. Perhaps only information supporting a particular religious or political persuasion would be allowed. Scientists have therefore maintained that information must be free to all, and that no questions should be prohibited or censored.

On the other hand, there are some serious problems with allowing the search for scientific knowledge to go on totally uncontrolled. The major problems are the possible harm to particular subjects and the potential harm that the uses of some knowledge may hold for the whole of humanity. For example, a recent article in the *New York Times Magazine* (August 25, 1976) discusses the controversy of genetic research. The question was raised that even allowing the research to continue could possibly result in some human error which could allow a dangerous cancerous agent to escape into the atmosphere and permeate our ecosystem. Of course, such knowledge could also lead to the prevention or cure of certain strains of cancer.

Although the question of harm to humanity has become an important question in the physical and natural sciences, this area of concern has not held the same importance for the social/behavioral sciences or education. We suspect that this is for two reasons. The first is that the technological sophistication and resources in the social sciences are not developed to the point where most people see a problem. For example, it is not now possible for sociologists to start a war just for the study of international conflict. Nor is this type of technology or influence within the foreseeable future. Second, social systems seem to be outside of most people's perceptions of what causes harm to humanity. That is, sociological harm to human systems is not yet seen as a likely result of research on human subjects in the social/behavioral sciences and education. Although we argue that this may very well be a potential problem, the reality of the situation is that ethical considerations in these areas have not focused on this aspect of free scientific inquiry. However, since these disciplines do conduct research on particular subjects, many questions have been raised as to how to treat human subjects.

Important research may carry a risk of some sort of harm to the people involved in the research. Because of this situation, there has been considerable effort and discussion expended to try to pinpoint certain areas where subjects should and could be protected. The simple solution would be to not do any research on human subjects where any possible harm could result. In this way no harmful effects would accrue to research subjects. In so doing, we might lose valuable information about how we could avoid delivering similar types of harm to others who are not subjects. Thus not doing research is not a very satisfactory answer. Another solution sometimes offered is that all such research should be conducted on animals. This presents two problems. The first is that there is some objection to exposing animals to possible harm. Second, it is unfortunately a fact that there is a limited ability to generalize animal studies to human beings.

There may be some circumstances in which scientists feel that it is acceptable to "violate" or ignore certain ethical principles without acutally violating the spirit of the rationale for these ethics. In the following sections we will try to explore some of the major areas that have been identified as important in research on human subjects. In addition, we will try to show how researchers deal with these areas and sometimes disregard them because they perceive that the knowledge being sought is valuable, and that such practices do not actually "harm" the subjects.

3. THE SUBJECT AS A PERSON

Two major areas of harm to subjects which are of concern are the possibility of physical harm and the possibility of psychological or emotional harm. It is generally felt that the first concern is not too central to the social/behavioral sciences or education. Research conducted in these areas seldom has the potential to induce physical harm to the subjects. There is, however, a general prohibition against doing research that will in any way physically harm subjects.

It seems much more likely that research in these areas might have the potential for psychological and/or emotional harm to subjects. Many of the concerns cited below focus on this possibility. However, they also apply equally to those studies that may involve potential physical harm.

Several considerations should be made concerning treating the subject as a person, treating the person with dignity, and conducting research with fairness. Even if there are no serious long-term effects of experimentation or observation, the research process itself may involve inconsideration, degradation, or lack of fairness. Although there is no "bill of rights" for subjects in social science research, there are many issues of common concern. These include the right of: (1) self-determination, (2) equal opportunity for treatment, (3) having direct or implied promises kept, (4) self-respect, and (5) privacy. Each issue implies a certain tension between the right of people to gain access to knowledge for the good of society and the rights of the human subject to be protected against harm.

The right of self-determination

Whether potential risk is involved or not, the final decision about participation as a research subject should belong to the subject. In this way the responsibility for the welfare of the subject is jointly held by the researcher and the subject. For subjects to have this determination, they should be volunteers who have full knowledge about the nature of the research in which they will be involved.

Voluntarism

The notion that subjects should be volunteers sounds straightforward. However, there may be several ways in which research using volunteers may be problematic. Subjects may volunteer because they have a different perspective or reaction to the content or procedures of the research. Volunteers may respond differently than in normal circumstances in order to please the researcher. Data gathered on volunteers may not be generalizable to other people. Whenever there seems to be little risk of harm to subjects, researchers may decide that it is fair to experiment or observe without subjects' permission. Of course, such research should not result in embarrassment to the subject or the invasion of the subjects' privacy. (See the succeeding sections for an expanded discussion of these concerns.) For instance, school children are often exposed to different educational programs and/or procedures without their permission or the permission of their parents.

Another issue of voluntarism concerns the idea that subjects who seem to be volunteers may not really have a free choice in the matter. The classic cartoon about volunteers in the army where the sergeant says, "I want volunteers for this dangerous mission ... you, you, and you," is an example of this type of situation. How much choice do prisoners have when their volunteering for a research project may be induced by earlier parole, privileged status, or other benefits? Is this self-determination, or is it coercion? Using college students as volunteers is somewhat similar in nature. Students are often required to "volunteer" to be subjects as part of some class requirements.

Informed consent

Many argue that the nature of the research involved should be fully disclosed to the subject. This procedure again places some of the responsibility for accepting risk with the subject. When there is known risk, most researchers agree with this practice. One major problem with this practice is that disclosure of what a study is about may change the nature of the responses of the subjects. This problem is similar to the testing effect in experiments. When researchers feel that there is very low risk to subjects, or that the risk is of simply enduring slight stress only during the study, they frequently feel that informed consent may be avoided.

Many social psychologists have felt that it is fair to deceive the subject about the true nature of a study (provide them with false information) so that subjects do not try to distort their "true" or "natural" responses to the real research purpose. For example, subjects may be told that they are involved in an experiment on learning or perception when they are really being studied for their conformity or willingness to be aggressive. Subjects may also think that they are participating with another subject when the other subject is really a confederate of the experimenter (often called a stooge). The *stooge* is not really responding to the subject or to the apparent experimental manipulation. Instead, the stooge is instructed to respond as part of the study.

One of the most controversial series of studies which combined some of these limitations to self-determination are the Milgram studies we mentioned earlier. These studies involved the use of stooges and deception about the true nature of the experiment. Many have objected to the procedures involved in these studies partly because they feel that some subjects were really harmed, and that subjects did not have self-determination or informed consent. We suspect that if subjects had not been harmed, no objections about the violation of the principle of self-determination would have been raised.

Milgram asked people to participate in an experiment on learning. This was not what the research was about. The true nature of the inquiry was whether the subjects would cooperate with the experimenters' request to ostensibly harm another subject by means of delivering severe amounts of electric shock. This was a second ruse because the second subject was really a stooge and did not really receive the severe amount of shock. In some studies the stooge protested as if a shock were really being received. This protestation, plus the thought that the subject may be harming the stooge, created displays of distress, discomfort, and embarrassment in the real subjects. Some subjects thought they did real injury to the "other subject" (stooge). This is part of the "harm" caused by the experiment. The subjects were debriefed at the end of the experiments and told that they had been fooled for scientific purposes, but nevertheless fooled. This revelation is also reputed to have harmed some of the subjects. The more serious supposed harm concerned the subjects' knowledge that they were capable of doing severe harm to another human being just because they were told to do so by a researcher. Over 60 percent of the subjects complied with experimental instructions to deliver (fake) severe electric shocks to fellow subjects. This awareness has been reputed to have caused permanent psychological damage for some subjects. This, of course, goes beyond enduring short-term stress during a study. It involves possible injury to the subjects' self-respect (an issue we will mention later). Since this injury was not something about which the subjects were forewarned, many feel that the study "harmed" subjects without their prior informed consent. These practices have been objected to as a violation of appropriate research ethics. As we mentioned at the outset of this chapter, we feel that the repugnance over what occurred in the Milgram studies was one strong impetus toward placing more emphasis on research ethics and tightening the control over research involving human subjects.

The type of harm we have considered thus far is harm that has resulted from researchers doing something to subjects, harm by commission. There is another type of harm that has become increasingly important, especially to those involved in public service programs. This is harm to subjects due to omission—harm caused by withholding services.

Equal opportunity

This second issue involves the "rights" of subjects in settings where the subject (client) comes for services, but where research may be connected with such services. Such research is often conducted in hospitals, schools, social agencies, or rehabilitation settings. As accountability in such agencies becomes more important, both basic research and evaluation research will become more frequent. Since people, students, clients, patients, and the like, come or are sent to such settings for service, rather than for research, many feel that the rights of the client-subject must be protected. Some feel that all who come are entitled to the best available services and/or treatment. The potential problem is that when certain types of research is conducted, some individuals or groups may possibly be either denied services or exposed to some "newfangled experimental" approach which is designed to replace or improve traditional ones. The assumption is made that traditional treatment is sound and better than no treatment at all, and that any "new" procedure could jeopardize the clients' welfare.

One problem with saying that all perspective clients should receive the best services is that unless research is conducted, how will we know which service is best, or even if a "service" has any effect. Objections may not be raised about research in general, but to the use of experimental designs in settings where important services are to be delivered. If this is the case, there are alternative arrangements that would more adequately meet the ethical objections to the classical experimental design. One alternative is to let all groups get "experimental" and traditional treatments. For example, students could receive some instruction in open classrooms and some in more traditional, formal ones. Delinquent youths could receive different types of supervision at different times. One group might get low supervision for the first half of a program and closer supervision for the other half. A similar group may initially get close supervision followed by looser supervision. In this way each group is a control for the other and each group gets the benefit of both types of programs.

Many designs in research settings let subjects serve as their own control. Sometimes this is not possible. For example, a dying patient may not be able to try one cure first and the second later. There may not be a later. For medical and similar research, the first approach is to do research on animals, to learn all we can before subjecting people to risk. However, ultimately in all such research, to know which approach is best we must experiment on humans. Since this is so, the issue becomes not one of equal treatment. The issue becomes one of informed consent. Subjects should be given some knowledge of the nature of the research in which they are involved. While parents may object to their children being included in a new classroom experiment, a cancer patient may object to *not* receiving a new experimental drug.

This issue is an extremely important one for agencies offering services to clients. While on the one hand there is a strong desire to provide all clients with the best possible services known, there is often a need for experimental research to determine just which procedure or service is the best or whether any are effective. There is no magic solution to this dilemma. When experimentation of some sort is necessary it probably is even more important to consider the issues raised in this chapter concerning the subject as a person. When the issues are considered and the appropriate precautions taken, perhaps both objectives can eventually be met with minimal risk to subjects.

Delivery of promises

The third issue involves the delivery of implied or direct promises to subjects. Research involving human subjects is a kind of social exchange. The scientist asks for volunteers, asks for paid participants, or takes a "captive audience" such as students and asks permission to do the research. We would argue that in each case there is sort of an *implicit* contract wherein each party expects to be obligated to do certain things. Each also expects to get certain things in exchange. The subject is expected to show up, to follow instructions, to be honest, to try hard where appropriate, and (typically) to not divulge the nature of the research to others until the research is completed. There are also expectations and implied obligations for the researchers.

Researchers are expected to show up for the study. This may seem like a trite point, but sometimes researchers get so busy that they cannot meet a subject and they may neglect to cancel appointments. Researchers should explain as much about the research as possible, without giving away hypotheses or otherwise distorting subjects' performance. The principle of explaining things to subjects becomes even more important after the study is completed. Subjects are entitled to full debriefing and reports on the results of the study when completed. These pieces of information should be presented in language which is fully comprehensible to the subjects. Researchers should be cautious about presentations that are too technical.

In addition to implied obligations, researchers often make direct promises to recruit subjects. Such promises are often made about the benefits of a study. The range from recruiting "come-ons," like the benefit of greater self-understanding, to promises of winning prizes or being paid. Subjects should not be promised such things if there is no intention to make good on the promises. If subjects are supposedly eligible for a prize, a drawing should be held. If subjects were promised that they would learn something about themselves, such knowledge should be discussed in the debriefing.

In short, care should be taken so that the implied and direct promises and responsibilities of the researcher are carried out. The keeping of direct promises is relatively easy to check. However, many of the implied promises may not be explicitly known to subjects. The subjects may only be left with a feeling that "something's wrong" after their participation in a study. All of the issues covered in this chapter can be seen as implicit promises of ethical researchers. Among the important implicit promises is that the subjects' self-respect will be protected.

Maintaining self-respect

There is a growing consensus among researchers that we should be more explicit about allowing subjects to maintain self-respect. As researchers get involved in gaining important information for the good of people in general, it may be easy to forget about maintaining the dignity of each individual subject. There are lots of ways in which the researcher may inadvertently contribute to a loss of self-respect of a subject. One of the most clear-cut examples may again be the Milgram experiments. Remember, the subjects thought that they may have been injuring other subjects by administering large doses of electric shock. The experimenter detachedly urged the subjects to continue and 60 percent did.

In the course of the experiment, or soon after, these subjects realized that they were capable of following instructions that could inflict injury or death to another person. This knowledge may have been very injurious to many subjects' self-concepts. The subjects were debriefed in an attempt to explain the true nature of the experiment and to eliminate any long-term effects of their realizations about what they could have done. They met the confederate and were assured that the confederate was all right. They were allowed to discuss and reflect upon their behavior. Presumably the subjects suffered during the experiment, but left feeling satisfied with themselves after the debriefing. However, some feel that the debriefing may have been inadequate to fully remove the scars of self-realization of what the subjects had done, and that some subjects should have received additional psychological care. Some feel that the possible harm to self-respect in such studies is not a fair cost for the knowledge gained.

Another possible source of the loss of self-respect in deception studies may be the feelings that emerge when subjects realize that they have been fooled. To be shown up as an "easy mark" may be very embarrassing. Sometimes, after the subject has been fooled by the presence of a confederate, the subject does not even believe the debriefing. After all, if the experimenters lied once, what is to stop them from lying again? The grapevine of research reports the story of subjects leaving a study where they were ostensibly involved in taking an intelligence test. They were informed that they had not done well. In debriefing they were told that this was a deception and that they had not taken an intelligence test. Some subjects were later overheard to say that they did not realize they were that stupid. The story may not be true, but it illustrates what may happen in research involving deception.

Subjects also may lose their self-respect when asked sensitive questions. Such questions may alert subjects to things about themselves or others that they had previously been able to suppress. For example, when people are asked about their death or the death of loved ones, it is possible that feelings of remorse or depression might occur. In our culture such topics are seldom open to discussion. If a study "forces" subjects to have such self-knowledge, it may be too high a price to pay for their cooperation. The potential for the loss of self-respect, and the risk that the loss may be more than short-lived, are unknown factors in most research. Because of this, it is difficult to know if such costs are reasonable for purposes of discovering research information. Closely associated with the idea of self-respect is the notion that, in our society, privacy is of paramount importance.

Protecting privacy

A long-standing tradition of the free world is that people have the right of privacy. The rationale for the right of privacy seems to be that privacy enables one to behave without interference. This prevents information about a person from being used against that person. If the proper precautions are taken to protect the identity of those being studied, then it is unlikely that information will be available to outsiders to be used against any subjects. However, it is always possible that research reports or documents may cause embarrassment or other undesirable consequence. This situation is perhaps most crucial in participant observation studies. Since many participant observation studies do not anticipate such negative consequences, many researchers using such designs are often willing to break the norm of protecting privacy. Typically participant observers disclose the general nature of their research to some subjects and thus it may appear that they are gaining permission to observe. However, many participant observers do not gain such permissions of all participants (see Chapter 12) and are therefore invading the subjects' privacy. In such instances many feel that disguised participant observation is unethical.

Even when informed consent is used and subjects are aware that private data are being collected, there is a possibility that subjects' privacy will be invaded beyond the obvious. Since data and records may be subpoenaed by certain government agencies, data gathered with the subjects' permission may fall into the hands of people other than the researchers. Social scientists do not have the same protection in the courts as other professionals such as doctors or attorneys. Even if the researcher promises the protection of confidentiality, this may not be assured if there are stored records and if these records can in any way be identified with subjects. Such records could also be stolen or used maliciously by some staff member.

The strategy which totally protects subjects is the anonymity of subjects. However, providing anonymity has some drawbacks. First, follow-up or longitudinal studies could not compare records from study to study. Second, it is harder to find or study nonrespondents since their identity is unknown. Third, it is not possible to match research data with other records. Therefore confidentiality is often preferred to anonymity.

Partial safeguards can at least maximize confidentiality. For example, surveys could use numbered questionnaires and other records and keep the name of the respondents associated with the numbers in a separate file. Both files should be under lock and key. When the names of the subjects are no longer necessary, they can be destroyed while the valuable research data remain intact. We have mentioned a number of the more traditional practices in various sections of this text. One newer strategy has been developed which allows for confidentiality while protecting the subject. The researcher hands a card to the respondent with two questions on it. Which question the subject answers depends on a flip of the coin. The subject flips the coin and gives an answer to one of the questions. The researcher does not know which question each subject answers, but with complicated statistics, how subjects in general respond can be worked out.

The general philosophy for protecting the privacy of subjects is to perform the research in such a way that subjects' names cannot be connected with the research information pertaining to them. In those cases where information must be associated with names, this should be done indirectly by using code numbers. Names and code numbers should be kept in a separate place from the other records, preferably in a different geographic location. Names should be destroyed as soon as possible. While there is disagreement about whether or not researchers should destroy data and records, if the privacy of subjects is threatened, we would suggest that this might be appropriate. Finally, the confidentiality of research documents should be protected with every reasonable procedure. Subjects should be made fully aware of the procedures to be used to protect that confidentiality, and subjects should never be told that their responses are anonymous if they are not.

While we have raised various ethical issues as the result of the tension between the value of knowledge and the importance of protecting subjects from harm, there are other issues involved in the question of the ethics of research. In an attempt to acknowledge these additional issues about ethics, the next section will explore a number of ethical "no-no's."

4. ETHICAL NO-NO'S

There are a number of practices about which there is general agreement that they constitute unethical behavior. These practices require little comment, and we mention them in order to alert the student to the possibility that these prohibitions may be violated. While we are aware of their existence, we think (hope) that they are seldom violated by bonafide researchers.

Fabrication of data

There is a strong moral precept against fabricating or falsifying data, but there are sometimes such strong temptations that the human being in the detached scientists may succumb. In the physical sciences the practice of "dry labbing" involves "reporting" what went on in the laboratory while never really getting one's hands or equipment wet. That is, the experiment is reported without actually being conducted. In the social sciences interviewers or assistants on projects may report observations or interviews that they themselves have not conducted in order to please some professor or project director, or to get paid. The classical plot where an overambitious anthropologist files down a bone and claims to have found the missing link may be illustrative of what may sometimes actually go on. Since creativity and discovery are rewarded so much more highly than replication, the temptation to cheat may be great. There is a universal proscription against such practices to protect the sanctity of scientific knowledge. We support it.

Plagiarism

Another kind of ethical violation involves the unacknowledged "borrowing" of ideas or data from others. Unfortunately, the proscription against plagiarism is not always kept. We suspect that there are more violations of this ethic than are discovered or reported. This may take the form of professors under publish-or-perish pressures not properly citing the contribution of their graduate students, or writers purposely ignoring the authors of previous works which have been liberally used. The elaborate system of citations discussed in Chapters 5 and 17 illustrates the great steps that are taken to give researchers and authors the appropriate credit for their work. While plagiarism does not harm people in general or individual subjects, it may hurt researchers, and they count too.

Exploitation of assistants and/or subjects

The final issue to be explored in this chapter deals with the possible exploitation of people. Just as in other human activities, the ethical researcher will not "use" people in a way that will unjustly enrich the researchers' position at the expense of the other individual. For the researcher this means that every precaution will be taken to handle both assistants and subjects with consideration and care. Every precaution must be taken to safeguard their well-being and to insure that the social exchanges involved in the research project are fair and equitable.

5. ETHICAL GUIDELINES

While there is no one set of practices, procedures, or statement of ethics that has been universally adopted by the social/behavioral sciences and education, we feel that any such effort must confront the basic dilemma discussed in this chapter. Somehow subjects must be protected from harm without appreciably affecting the researchers' ability to conduct important studies which might benefit all people for all times. Each of the issues we have introduced should somehow be dealt with.

There are many statements of ethics in the various disciplines which deal with research on human subjects, but many of them are vague and too general to be of much use to the practicing researcher. However, on May 30, 1974, a set of regulations were published in the *Federal Register* (39 FR 18914) relating to the protection of human subjects in research projects which receive funding from the U.S. Department of Health, Education and Welfare. In addition, on July 12, 1974, the National Research Act, Public Law 93–348 was enacted which approved this set of regulations. These regulations along with the public act and the technical amendments that have been added to them comprise a rather thorough statement of what types of procedures must be followed to protect the welfare of human subjects. These documents are too long to be printed here but they can be consulted if the student has a special interest in these issues.

One practice which we believe will go a long way in protecting the welfare of human subjects is the institution of boards of review that will have the ability and authority to approve of or disapprove of particular pieces of research. The purpose of such boards would not be to spread out the blame for poor research procedures or to "whitewash" research projects which did not adequately protect subjects. Rather, their purpose would be to help make wiser and better decisions about protecting human subjects. Hopefully, by sharing the decision making for deciding whether a particular research project adequately protects subjects, the wisest decisions about conflicting interests may be discovered.

6. SUMMARY

Scientists performing research involving human subjects have two potentially conflicting values. They value the types of information that may only be obtainable through research on human subjects. They also value human welfare. The dilemma which research ethics confronts exists when these two values seem opposed. Scientists not only have to be concerned with the welfare of individual subjects in the long and short run, but they have an obligation to be concerned about the welfare of society. In an attempt to provide a framework for ethical decision making we have pinpointed five basic areas where subjects should have "rights."

Subjects should have the right of self-determination. Whenever feasible subjects should be volunteers on the basis of informed consent. Subjects should be provided with equal opportunity when human services are concerned. This opportunity should encompass the right to refuse services and to select services when possible. Subjects have the right to have implied and stated promises fulfilled. They also have the right to maintain their self-respect and to have their privacy respected. Whenever these rights are abridged or delayed, researchers must be certain that in so doing subjects will not be harmed. While there is probably no foolproof method for doing this, it will likely help if decision making in these areas is shared. Boards of review or similar mechanisms should be employed to protect the interests of research subjects while remembering that the knowledge potentially gained from research on human subjects may be crucial in the search for relationships.

EXERCISES

1. Divide into groups to discuss the following:
   a. Under what conditions are "volunteers" not really volunteers for research participation (e.g., the poor, students, prisoners, hospital patients, etc.)?
   b. What kinds of questions are sensitive enough to:

   invade privacy
   create emotional harm

   c. How much is necessary to disclose to get really "informed" consent?
   d. Under what circumstances, and what types of deception are appropriate in social research?
   e. Do you feel that social scientists have the right of free inquiry; that no topic is too dangerous or "sacred?"

   f. What types of ethical _____ should be developed?

   training
   safeguards
   rules and/or standards
   review boards

2. Develop a statement to read the subjects or respondents their "rights" before being involved in a study.

For each of your projects:
1. What ethical issues are anticipated prior to the study?
2. How will they be resolved?
3. Do you feel that these resolutions are adequate for the protection of subjects?
4. Do you feel that you have to make any compromises in your scientific interests for the protection of subjects?

AMERICAN PSYCHOLOGICAL ASSOCIATION. *Ethical Principles in the Conduct of Research with Human Participants.* Washington, D.C.: American Psychological Association, 1973.

AMERICAN SOCIOLOGICAL ASSOCIATION. *Code of Ethics.* Washington, D.C.: American Sociological Association, 1971.

DENZIN, N. *The Research Act.* Chicago: Aldine, 1970.

KELMAN, H. *A Time to Speak: On Human Values and Social Research.* San Francisco: Josey Bass, 1969.

MILGRIM, S. "Behavioral Study of Obedience." *Journal of Abnormal and Social Psychology,* 67, 1963, 371–378.

MILGRIM, S. "Some Conditions of Obedience and Disobedience to Authority." *Human Relations, 18,* 1965, 848–852.

RING, K., WALLSTON, K., AND COREY, M. "Mode of Debriefing as a Factor Affecting Subjective Reaction to a Milgrim-type Obedience Experiment: An Ethical Inquiry." *Representative Research in Social Psychology, 1,* 1970, 67–88.

SJOBERG, G. (ED.). *Ethics Politics and Social Research.* Cambridge, Mass: Schenkman, 1967.

WARWICK, D. "Stimulus Response: Social Scientists Ought to Stop Lying." *Psychology Today,* February, 1975, 38–40, 105–106.

CHAPTER 7
ORGANIZING AND SUMMARIZING
OUR OBSERVATIONS

After studying this chapter, students should be able to:

1. Change simple frequency distributions into cumulative distributions.

2. Identify grouped data distributions and translate simple distributions into grouped distributions.

3. Construct all types of grouped data distributions.

4. Construct frequency polygons, histograms, and ogives for simple and grouped data distributions.

5. Express the general ideas of central tendency and dispersion.

6. Compute values for the mode, mean, median, range, mean deviation, and standard deviation for simple and grouped data.

7. Determine the midpoint of simple and grouped data categories.

8. Compare two different distributions; say what differences might exist between them based on given values for central tendency and dispersion.

9. State the ways in which each measure of central tendency and dispersion may inaccurately describe the whole distribution.

10. Discuss the problems of interpreting central tendency and dispersion.

11. Describe a distribution in terms of skewedness and kurtosis.

Absolute value   A number or computation where the sign is ignored, that is, seen to be positive.

Central tendency   Statistics that identify a category of a variable, either real or hypothetical, around which a distribution clusters, hangs together, or centers.

Cumulative frequency distribution   A frequency distribution where the frequencies of each category are successively added to the sum of the frequencies preceding that category.

Deviation   How far one score is from another.

Dispersion   Statistics that give an estimate of how spread out, scattered, or dispersed the scores of a distribution are.

Frequency polygon   A line graph representing a simple frequency distribution.

Grouped data   Data are recorded in such a way that the categories of the variable include more than one distinct type of observation, or score, or value.

Histogram   A type of graph using bars to represent a simple frequency distribution.

Kurtosis   How pointed the peaks are in a frequency polygon.

Mean   Provides a score that each case would have if the variable were distributed equally among all observations. The arithmetic average.

Mean deviation   A deviation score which tells how far away from the mean each observation would be if all the observations were the same distance away from the mean. (The average distance of each score from the mean.)

Median   A score that separates all of the observations (frequencies) into two equal-sized groups.

Midpoint   The center of a category obtained by subtracting the lower limit of a category from the upper limit, dividing by 2, and adding that figure to the lower limit.

Mode   Score (value or category) of the variable which is observed most frequently.

Ogive   A line graph representing a cumulative distribution.

Range   The difference between extreme scores calculated by subtracting the lower limit of the lowest score from the upper limit of the highest score.

Skewed distribution   A distribution where more scores occur at one end than the other.

Standard deviation   A measure of dispersion, based on deviations from the mean, calculated by taking the square root of the average squared deviations of each score from the mean.

Univariate analysis   The description and/or summarization of the scores (categories, observations) of one variable.

1. INTRODUCTION

In Chapter 4 we presented the first step in organizing and summarizing observation, the construction of simple frequency and percentage distributions. The translation of raw data into simple distributions is mandatory in order to understand what has been observed. It is also a crucial step in preparing data for use in the analysis of bivariate relationships by percentage tables. In addition to the use of summaries such as percentage distributions for analyzing relationships, it is often desirable to more fully examine the distribution of one variable. The term *univariate analysis* is used to denote the application of various procedures and statistics to describe and summarize the distribution of scores (categories, observations) of one variable.

The bulk of this chapter is concerned with univariate analysis and with organizing and summarizing observations. Specifically, cumulative distributions, graphic presentations, and measures of central tendency and dispersion for both simple and grouped data are presented. In addition, a later section deals with using measures of central tendency and dispersion to estimate scatterplots and explore bivariate relationships. The univariate procedures covered are not only important for understanding the distribution of one variable, but they also can be used to compare different distributions.

2. CUMULATIVE FREQUENCY AND PERCENTAGE DISTRIBUTIONS

With simple frequency distributions, the only kind of information presented is the number of observations in each category of the variable in the table. However, sometimes we would like to organize our observations so that other kinds of information are available. For example, a vocational education teacher might want to test the manual dexterity of a group of prospective students. If the test given to measure manual skills has 6 possible scores with 6 being very skillful and 1 being the most unskilled, a simple frequency distribution of the test group might look like Table 7.1.

TABLE 7.1
Simple frequency distribution of manual dexterity test results

Test score	f
6	3
5	5
4	6
3	7
2	4
1	2
N	27

If the teacher wanted to know how many students scored 4 *or more* on the test or 3 *or less* on the test, a simple frequency distribution would not provide answers to these types of questions. However, it is quite easy to translate a simple distribution into cumulative distributions which would provide such answers. In a *cumulative frequency distribution* the frequencies of each category are successively added to the sum of the frequencies preceding that category. Addition can be started at either the top or bottom of the simple frequency distribution in order to construct the two types of cumulative distributions shown in Table 7.2.

TABLE 7.2
Translating simple frequency distributions into cumulative distributions

Simple distribution		Cumulative down		Cumulative up	
Test score	f	Test score	Cumulative f	Test score	Cumulative f
6	3	6	3	6	27 (24 + 3)
5	5	5	8 (3 + 5)	5	24 (19 + 5)
4	6	4	14 (8 + 6)	4	19 (13 + 6)
3	7	3	21 (14 + 7)	3	13 (6 + 7)
2	4	2	25 (21 + 4)	2	6 (2 + 4)
1	2	1	27 (25 + 2)	1	2
N	27				

By cumulating down, we see that 14 people scored 4 *or more* points in the manual dexterity test, and by cumulating up, we see that 13 students scored 3 *or less*. Thus, if we want this kind of information, cumulative frequency distributions will be necessary. When presenting such tables, the figures enclosed in parentheses would not be printed, and the final cumulative frequency in both cases will correspond to N, the total number of observations made.

The same general procedures used to transform simple frequency distributions into simple percentage tables can also be used to change cumulative frequency distributions into cumulative percentage distributions. Using one of the cumulative frequency distributions from Table 7.2, we would have Table 7.3.

The last percentage in such cases will of course always equal 100 percent, since the total of all the cases (observations or frequencies) will always be in the last position in the distribution, either the top or bottom. Cumulative percentage distributions are useful if we want to know what part of all the observations in a distribution are either above or below a certain score or category. Table 7.3 shows

TABLE 7.3
Converting cumulative frequency distributions into percentage distributions

Test score	Cumulative f	Fractions	Proportions	Test score	Cumulative percentages
6	3	3/27	.111	6	11.1
5	8	8/27	.296	5	29.6
4	14	14/27	.518	4	51.8
3	21	21/27	.778	3	77.8
2	25	25/27	.926	2	92.6
1	27	27/27	1.000	1	100.0

that 29.6 percent of all students tested had a score of 5 or more and 92.6 percent of the students had a score of 2 or more, and so on. Cumulating up would provide similar information only in the reverse direction.

3. GROUPED DATA

As was demonstrated in Chapter 2, categories of variables often have "width" and are composed of more than one score. For example, if we wanted to get a distribution of the variable of the weekly income of working college students, we might not wish to record the frequency of people at every income level, but the frequency of people in income groups, for example, between $85 and $90 a week. When data are recorded in such a way that the categories of the variables include more than one distinct type of observation, or score, or value, we call such data *grouped data*.

Grouped data can be presented in simple and cumulative frequency and percentage distributions. The form of grouped distributions is the same as for ungrouped data. Categories within these distributions can be either the same size or different sizes. Using weekly part-time income as an example, we might choose to group our observations as in Table 7.4.

Some of the other types of distributions presented so far can be constructed from the grouped frequency distribution in Table 7.4 (See Table 7.5).

Note here that as we discussed in Chapter 2, each of these categories have upper and lower limits. For example, the upper limit of the 76–80 category would be 80.5 and the lower limit would be 75.5. Therefore, if one of the students in our research earned just over $80 (such as $80.05), that person would be placed in the $76–$80 category.

TABLE 7.4
Grouped frequency distribution

Weekly Part-time income (in dollars)	*f*
Over 85	2
81–85	4
76–80	6
71–75	1
66–70	5
61–65	4
60 and less	3
N	25

TABLE 7.5
Various types of grouped data distributions

Cumulating down		Percentage distribution		Cumulative percentage, up	
Income in dollars	Cumulative *f*	Income in dollars	%	Income in dollars	Cumulative %
Over 85	2	Over 85	8	Over 85	100
81–85	6	81–85	16	81–85	92
76–80	12	76–80	24	76–80	76
71–75	13	71–75	4	71–75	52
66–70	18	66–70	20	66–70	48
61–65	22	61–65	16	61–65	28
60 and less	25	60 and less	12	60 and less	12
		T	100		

4. GRAPHIC PRESENTATIONS

Sometimes it is helpful to present data in graphic form rather than with a set of numbers. When it is thought that such forms of presentation would aid our understanding, interpretation, and/or communication of the data, then we can construct frequency polygons, histograms, and ogives. These three graphic ways of presenting distributions are all quite similar. Each of them is a chart made up of two perpendicular lines or axes, one across the page (horizontal) and one up and down the page (vertical). In all cases the horizontal axis is labeled with the names or values of the categories of *one* variable, along with the name of the variable. The vertical axis of frequency polygons and histograms contain either frequencies or percentages of *simple* distributions. For ogives, the vertical axis is labeled with *cumulative* frequencies or percentages.

Using the simple frequency distribution of manual dexterity scores from Table 7.1, a frequency polygon and histogram would have six categories represented on the bottom axis and at least a frequency of 7 on the side, since the highest f is equal to 7 (Figure 7.1). Notice that the blank graphs look exactly alike. To construct the graphs, we must plot the frequency of each category of manual dexterity directly over each category. In category 1 of dexterity there is a frequency of 2. This frequency is represented on the polygon by placing a dot directly to the right of the 2 frequency and directly above the 1 category of dexterity. In the histogram, a bar is placed over the 1 instead of a dot. Completing this step, we would have Figure 7.2.

There are 4 frequencies in category 2 or dexterity and this would be plotted and added to the previous diagram resulting in Figure 7.3.

Plotting the rest of the frequencies in categories 3, 4, 5, and 6 would result in graphs that would look similar to Figure 7.4.

To complete the charts, straight lines are drawn to connect the dots on the frequency polygon. For the histogram, the area under each bar is enclosed to give Figure 7.5.

There are many variations on these types of charts, but the basic principles presented here are consistent with those variations.

Frequency polygons can be described in several ways. Two of the most common ways are skewedness and kurtosis. *Skewedness* re-

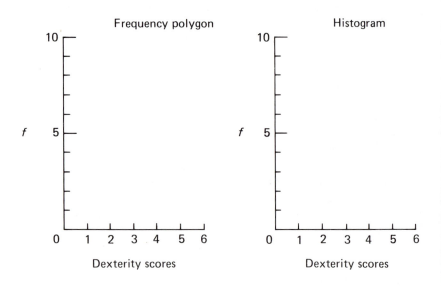

FIGURE 7.1
Construction of frequency polygons and histograms

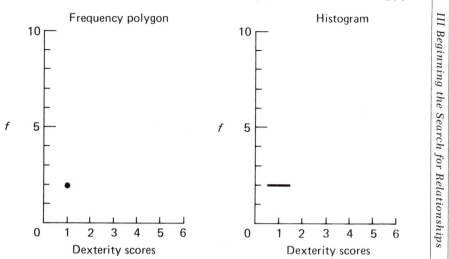

FIGURE 7.2
First step in frequency polygon and histogram construction

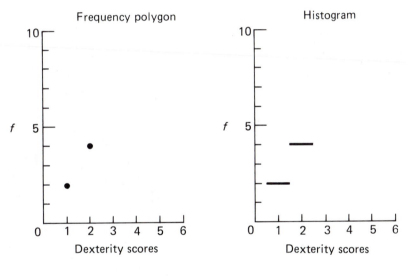

FIGURE 7.3
Continue plotting data

fers to the symmetry of a distribution. In a frequency polygon a distribution is *positively skewed* if more of the scores (cases or observations) are to the left of center (low). Conversely, scores are *negatively skewed* if more of them are to the right of center. If the

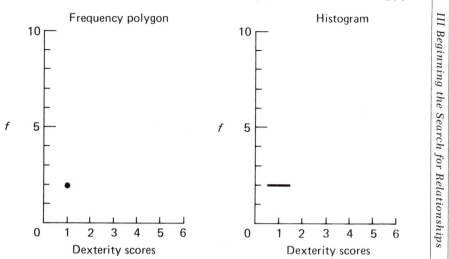

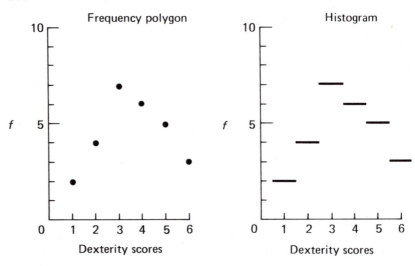

FIGURE 7.4
All data plotted

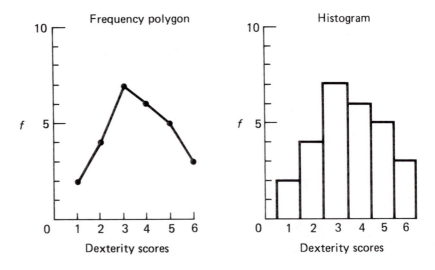

FIGURE 7.5
Completed frequency polygon and histogram

frequency polygon looks approximately the same on both sides, the distribution is *symmetrical*. Figure 7.6 shows some examples of each type of distribution. The lines in the frequency polygons have been smoothed out for ease of presentation.

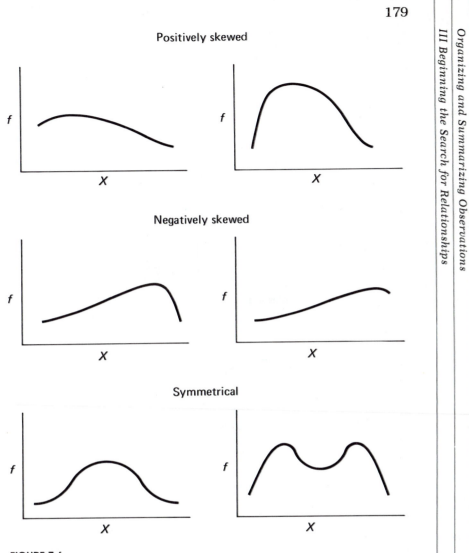

FIGURE 7.6
Skewed and symmetrical distributions

Kurtosis refers to the sharpness of the peaks in a frequency polygon. If the peaks are sharp the distribution is *leptokurtic*. When the peaks are very flat the distribution is *platokurtic*. If peaks are neither sharp nor flat, the distribution is called *mesokurtic*. Figure 7.7 provides an example of each type of kurtosis.

Ogives are merely frequency polygons representing cumulative frequencies or percentages on the vertical axis rather than simple frequencies or percentages. Using the same data, charting the cumulative down part of Table 7.3, the ogive in Figure 7.8 can be con-

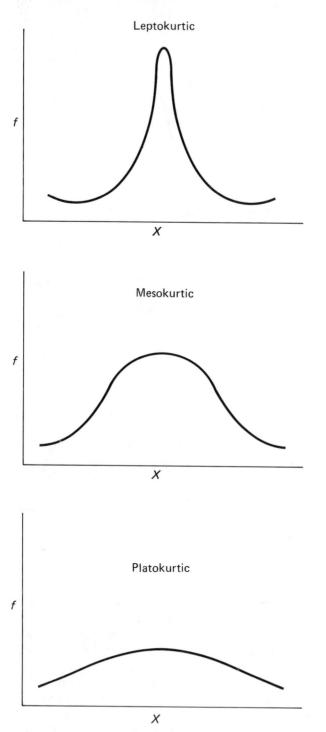

FIGURE 7.7
Examples of different kurtosis

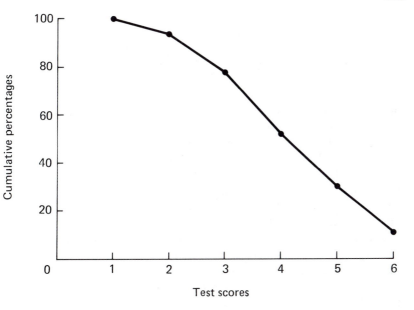

FIGURE 7.8
Ogive

structed. We see that there is a great deal of similarity between ogives and frequency polygons.

5. CENTRAL TENDENCY AND DISPERSION

Despite the fact that the above graphic ways to describe a total distribution of a variable may simplify interpretation of data quite a bit, researchers have other ways of summarizing distributions. Measures of central tendency and dispersion are attempts to *summarize* a total distribution of a variable by calculating one value. The various statistics of *central tendency* attempt to identify a category of a variable, either an actual or hypothetical category, around which a distribution "clusters," or "hangs-together," or is "centered about." They attempt to convey some idea of where the main part of the distribution is. Statistics of *dispersion* attempt to give an estimate of how "spread out," "scattered," or "dispersed" the scores of a distribution are. If most of the frequencies in a distribution are clustered around one point or category, one would expect very low values for measures of dispersion. However, if the frequencies are more spread out among many categories, measures of dispersion would tend to be higher.

All summaries give a somewhat incomplete picture of what is being presented. Consider the following analogy: When a sportscaster presents an after-the-game report of the scoring of a football game, only a limited picture of the pattern of the total game is presented. We know little about each particular play or the performance of any individual athlete. Similarly, when summarizing frequency distributions by using measures of central tendency and measures of dispersion, an overall picture of the distribution is presented, but we know little about particular observations. Therefore we lose detailed information about the pattern of the frequency distributions described by such summary statistics.

Although these summary measures give somewhat incomplete descriptions of frequency distributions, they are of value for answering limited questions. For example, if all we are interested in is which team won the football game, the final scores would be appropriate information. However, if we are avid fans, we would want to know the plays that were carried out, who scored, the condition of the field, number of first downs, field goal distances, punt returns, and so on. Very often when talking about many research variables, simple summaries are meaningful but not adequate for full understanding of the variables. Therefore one should be cautious when exploring a distribution of scores with summary measures. Full understanding of a variable will often not be possible until the total distribution of the variable is more completely explored than summary measures will allow.

General definitions

The mode, mean, and median are the measures of central tendency which attempt to provide a single score or value that is representative of the center of a frequency distribution. Each of the measures is representative in its own way. The *mode* characterizes a distribution by telling the score (value or category) of the variable observed most frequently. There is no calculation involved. One merely examines the distribution to see where the largest frequency is.

The *mean* is an average. It describes the distribution by providing a score that each case would have if the variable were distributed equally among all observations. In other words, the mean is the category of the variable that every observation would be in if all observations were the same score. For example, if we are talking about mean income in the United States and it is $5,000, this could be interpreted that if all the income in the country were split evenly between all families, each family would make $5,000 a year.

The *median* represents a distribution by telling the score (real or hypothetical) that separates all the observations (frequencies) into two equal-sized groups. It is the score for the middle observation and is "positional" in nature. If there is an odd number of cases in a distribution, the median is the score of the middle case, but if there is an even number of cases, the median is the hypothetical score between the two middle cases.

While measures of central tendency are scores or values that any particular observation or person might have, measures of dispersion are not. They attempt to describe *differences between* observations. Although measures of central tendency also rest on comparisons between scores and describe the group of scores, we think of the result in terms of values that a typical observation might have. Measures of dispersion are interpreted solely as group properties which no particular observation could be thought of as having. Measures of dispersion include the *range, mean deviation*, and *standard deviation*. Each provides different kinds of information on the spread of a distribution.

The *range* simply talks about the difference between extreme scores. One finds the total width or size of the distribution by subtracting the lower limit of the lowest category (score) of the distribution from the upper limit of the highest observed score.

The *mean deviation* (average deviation) rests on the mean for its assessment. A *deviation* is how far one score is from another score. The mean deviation focuses on deviation from the mean, that is, it tells the average distance each score is from the mean. The total deviation of all of the scores in the distribution from the mean are divided equally among all observations to give an "average" deviation from the mean. Thus it is sometimes called the average deviation.

The *standard deviation* is also one common statistic of dispersion, but it has no simple interpretation or common sense meaning. However, because of the way in which it is calculated, and because of certain statistical properties and its use in more sophisticated statistics, the standard deviation is used extensively in research reports. It is also based on deviations from the mean. The higher the value of the standard deviation, the greater the dispersion of the variable in question.

The student should remember that by most conventions in statistics none of the measures of dispersion or central tendency presented above are interpretable for levels of measurement below interval level. The exception to this rule is the mode. It can be interpreted for nominal and ordinal as well as interval and ratio categories. Some statisticians do compute a median for ordinal variables, but we do not believe this is particularly meaningful.

Now that we have introduced the ideas of the summary statistics of central tendency and dispersion, we need to understand how actual calculations are made. At this point the student is urged not to get anxious while reading the following computations section. The important thing at this stage is to understand the meaning and *logic* of the statistics and to be able to know how each statistic is attempting to describe a distribution.

Many students are not familiar with the symbols that will be introduced and often it has been a number of years since the student has attempted any "math." Therefore, we suggest that as you read the remainder of the chapter for the first time, you attempt to gain a *general understanding* of each statistic. Do not ponder over the more difficult examples. Once an initial understanding is gained, the more complex calculations will become much easier to comprehend. Also, do not attempt to remember formulas. As you begin to understand the *meaning* of the statistics, you will not need memorized formulas.

Calculations for simple data

The mode

As we have previously stated, the mode can be determined by inspection. You simply ascertain which category(s) of the variable under consideration has the largest frequency. Some distributions and their modes (symbolized by *Mo*) are given in Table 7.6. In order to make it easier to refer to these and the following examples, the symbol of X_i will be used to denote each individual category of the variable.

Note that the mode is the value of the *category* and *not the number of observations*. Often this distinction is forgotten and students will incorrectly say that the mode of the left distribution in Table 7.6 is equal to 16, which is the highest frequency instead of the category "Strongly agree." *Modes are always categories* or values of the variable, *never frequencies*. Usually when there is more than one category with the same highest frequency, each category is reported as the mode. In the distribution at the right there are two modes, 5 and 1. This is said to be a *bimodal* distribution, meaning there are two modes. Sometimes distributions are said to be bimodal if there are two categories with "fairly equal" frequencies.

The mean

The mean is calculated by adding the values of each case in the distribution and dividing by the total number of observations in the

TABLE 7.6
Examples of modes

X_i	f	X_i	f	X_i	f
Strongly agree*	16*	32	4	5*	7*
Agree	5	22	5	4	2
Neutral	2	19*	6*	3	3
Disagree	7	12	1	2	6
Strongly disagree	9	9	2	1*	7*
N	39	N	17	0	2
				N	27

Mo = Strongly Agree *Mo* = 19 *Mo* = 5 and 1

distribution. Remember, to add categories, they must be at least interval level. The distribution of the number of industries closed for pollution control violations during 1984 in selected countries will serve as an illustration (Table 7.7).

In this example, the mean would tell us the number of industries that would have been closed per county if all of the counties studied had closed the same number of industries. We might say that the mean gives us the "typical" number of industries closed in a county. Since we must find out the total number of industries closed in all the counties studied, it will be necessary for us to do some simple arithmetic. We see from the distribution that there are 3 counties where there are 5 industries closed; there are 2 counties where 4 industries are closed; 7 counties where 3 are closed, and so on.

In other words, there are 3 X_i values of 5, 2 X_i values of 4, and so on. To sum all of the X_i's would be a rather long addition problem. Therefore we merely multiple each value of X_i by the number of frequencies that have that value of X_i and then add those products. The total number of industries closed in all the counties studied can be represented by adding up all the frequencies times the category values. If we use the sigma sign Σ to stand for *the sum of*, the first part of our calculation can be represented by $\Sigma (fX_i)$.

In our illustration, the first step in calculating the mean is represented in Table 7.8.

In doing this calculation we find that 56 industries were closed in all of the counties we are examining. Since the mean tells us how many industries would have closed in each county if the same number had closed in each of the 25 counties studied, we must divide the 56 closings equally among the 25 counties. The mean resulting

TABLE 7.7
Number of industries closed per county[a]

	X_i	f	
	5	3	
Number of	4	2	How many counties
industries closed	3	7	had X_i number
in a county	2	5	of industries closed
	1	2	
	0	6	
		25	

[a]The table is interpreted as follows:
    There are 3 counties that have 5 industries closed in each of them (top row). Two countries (second row) have 4 industries closed in them, and soon.

TABLE 7.8
First step in calculating the mean

X_i	f	f times $X_i (fX_i)$
5	3	$3 \times 5 = 15$
4	2	$2 \times 4 = 8$
3	7	$7 \times 3 = 21$
2	5	$5 \times 2 = 10$
1	2	$2 \times 1 = 2$
0	6	$6 \times 0 = 0$
		$\Sigma (fX_i) = 56$

from dividing 56 by 25 is 2.2. The interpretation for this example would be that if all of the 25 counties studied had closed the same number of industries, each would have closed 2.2 of them.

Thus the general formula for the mean (represented by $\bar{X}$) for ungrouped data is:

$$X = \frac{\Sigma (fX_i)}{N}$$

$56 \underline{/ 25}$
2.2

The median

Recall that the median (represented by *Md*) splits a frequency distribution into two equal parts. In our example the median number of industries closed would be that number where half of the counties closed more than that number and half of the counties closed less than that number.

The first step in calculating the median is always to arrange the categories in the frequency distribution from low to high. In order to find out which number of closed industries is the middle case, we simply add 1 to the sum of frequencies and divide by 2. Since there are 25 counties, adding 1 to 25 gives 26 and dividing by 2 gives 13. Therefore, if we find the number of industries closed in the 13th highest county, that number would be the median. The 13th highest county would have 12 other counties closing fewer industries and 12 other counties closing more industries.

The first task is to locate the category in which we find the 13th highest county. To do this we must make a cumulative frequency distribution as in Table 7.9.

The 13th highest county is in category 2 since the cumulative frequency distribution shows the 9th highest through the 13th highest county in that category. The simplest way to report the median would be to report it as equal to "2." Although there are more complicated procedures that are mathematically more difficult and precise, in most cases this procedure will suffice.

The above procedure is only slightly different when there is an even number of cases involved. We still compute $N + 1$ and divide by 2. This procedure will result in a mixed number. For example, if there are 50 cases in a distribution, $50 + 1 = 51$ and $51/2 = 25\frac{1}{2}$. This indicates that the median lies halfway between the 25th case and the 26th case. If the 25th and 26th case are in the same category, simply report the category. If the 25th case is in one category and the 26th case is in another category, the upper limit of the 25th case should be reported.

The range
The range equals the upper limit of the highest value *(UL)* minus the lower limit of the lowest value *(LL),* or

$$Range = UL - LL$$

For the distribution of Table 7.10, the range is found by subtracting 6.5 (the *LL* of 7) from 15.5 (the *UL* of 15). Thus the range = 15.5 − 6.5 or 9.

We can ignore frequency to find the range. Thus, in the distribution in Table 7.11, the range is the same as in Table 7.10, 15.5 − 6.5 or 9.

Mean deviation
If we have calculated the mean of a distribution, it is straight-

TABLE 7.9
Cumulative frequency for computing the median

Number of industries closed	Cumulative number of counties	
5	25	
4	22	
3	20	
$Md \to$ 2	13	9th–13th county
1	8	
0	6	

TABLE 7.10
Distribution for calculating the range

X_i	f
15	1
12	1
10	1
9	1
7	1
N	5

TABLE 7.11
Additional example for range

X_i	f
15	33
12	15
10	67
9	9
7	18
N	142

forward to find out how far away a particular score in our distribution is from the mean. We simply subtract them. Expressing this symbolically, we denote the difference between the mean and any particular score in the distribution by $\overline{X} - X_i$ (the mean minus the score).

Since we are not interested in focusing on any one particular score but on the whole distribution, it makes sense to calculate the "average" distance that scores are from the mean. In order to compute this "average deviation from the mean," or *mean deviation,* we need to add up how far away all scores are from the mean and divide by the total number of scores (N). This is directly analogous to our previous calculation of the mean.

Using the previously calculated mean of 2.2 in our industrial example, we note that because the mean is a measure of central tendency, some of the values for the number of industries closed are higher than the mean and some are lower. For the mean deviation, we are interested in the average *distance* from the mean and not which direction the category is from the mean; we want to disregard the sign of the deviations from the mean. To obtain the deviation of any particular category from the mean, each is simply subtracted from the mean. Symbolically this would be $(X - X_i)$. Ignoring the sign is called taking the *absolute value* of the deviation and this is represented by a set of vertical lines on either side of the deviation value, $|\overline{X} - X_i|$.

To calculate the mean deviation we first find the absolute value of the deviation of each category from the mean. At this point we multiply this value by the frequency in each respective category. Since we are interested in the whole distribution, the deviation points for all categories are added together. Once the total deviation points for the distribution are determined, then they must be divided equally among all the observations. These calculations are shown in Table 7.12. In this case, the deviation from the mean for category 5 is = 2.8; the deviation of category 4 is 1.8; and so on. Finding the deviation points for each category gives us 8.4 (2.8 × 2) deviation points

TABLE 7.12
Calculation of the mean deviation

Score X_i	Frequency f	Deviations $(\overline{X} - X_i)$	Absolute value $\|\overline{X} - X_i\|$	Deviation points $f\|\overline{X} - X_i\|$
5	3	$2.2 - 5 = -2.8$	2.8	$3 \times 2.8 = 8.4$
4	2	$2.2 - 4 = -1.8$	1.8	$2 \times 1.8 = 3.6$
3	7	$2.2 - 3 = -\ .8$	.8	$7 \times\ .8 = 5.2$
2	5	$2.2 - 2 = +\ .2$	.2	$5 \times\ .2 = 1.0$
1	2	$2.2 - 1 = +1.2$	1.2	$2 \times 1.2 = 2.4$
0	6	$2.2 - 0 = +2.2$	2.2	$6 \times 2.2 = 13.2$
N	25			Total deviation points $= 34.2$

$$\frac{56}{25} = 2.2 \qquad \text{Mean deviation} = \frac{\text{Total deviation points}}{N} = \frac{34.2}{25} = 1.4$$

for category 5;3.6 (1.8 × 2) deviation points for category 4; and so on. Since the mean deviation is an average amount of deviation, we must add all the category deviation points together and then divide by the total number of observations. The total deviation points are 34.2 and dividing them equally among all 25 counties results in a mean deviation of 1.4 companies. By interpreting this statistic we would find that if every county were different from the mean county by the same degree, each would differ by 1.4 closings.

By determining the mean deviation, we have a statistic that tells us the "typical" distance that a score is from the mean of our distribution. The interpretation of the mean deviation is then a relative one. If we have different distributions of the same variable, comparisons as to their degree of dispersion are possible utilizing the mean deviation. *The greater the mean deviation, the more dispersed or spread out the scores in the distribution.*

For example, scores in a distribution with a mean deviation of 3.2 would be "bunched-up" much more than the scores of a distribution with a mean deviation of 23.5. Hence, we have a valuable measure of dispersion which gives us some picture of the nature of a frequency distribution.

Standard deviation
The final measure of dispersion is also based on deviations from the mean, and is called the *standard deviation* (represented by *s*). Once the deviations from the mean are computed, each deviation is squared (multipled by itself). The next step is to find the total number of squared deviation units. This is done by multiplying each squared deviation by the number (*f*) of times it occurs. The total number of squared deviation units are then added together. The next step is to find the average number of squared deviation units

by dividing the sum of the squared deviation units by N (sometimes $N - 1$ is used). The final step in the computation of the standard deviation is to take the square root of the average squared deviation units. Table 7.13 shows each of the steps in the computation for the same data as above. Notice that in this example the value of the standard deviation is not too different from the mean deviation. This is not always the case, but just as with the mean deviation, the larger the value of the standard deviation, the more spread out (dispersed) the observations in a distribution.

TABLE 7.13
Calculation of the standard deviation

X_i	f	Deviations $(\bar{X} - X_i)$	Squared deviations $(\bar{X} - X_i)^2$	Sum squared deviations $f(\bar{X} - X_i)^2$
5	3	−2.8	$-2.8 \times -2.8 = 7.84$	$3 \times 7.84 = 23.52$
4	2	−1.8	$-1.8 \times -1.8 = 3.24$	$2 \times 3.24 = 6.48$
3	7	− .8	$- .8 \times - .8 = .64$	$7 \times .64 = 4.48$
2	5	.2	$.2 \times .2 = .04$	$5 \times .04 = .20$
1	2	1.2	$1.2 \times 1.2 = 1.44$	$2 \times 1.44 = 2.88$
0	6	2.2	$2.2 \times 2.2 = 4.84$	$6 \times 4.84 = 29.04$
N	25			Total squared deviations $= 66.60$

$$s = \text{Standard deviation} = \sqrt{\frac{\text{Total squared deviations}}{N}} = \sqrt{\frac{66.60}{25}} = 1.63$$

Calculations for grouped data

The mode
As in the case of ungrouped data, no calculations are necessary to find the mode. The mode is found by locating the category(s) with the largest frequency. There are two common practices for describing the mode for grouped data. Either describe the name of the category, or describe it by the category midpoint. Since a single number is commonly interpreted as representing a category with an interval of 1, and since this would be the implied size if the midpoint were reported alone, we prefer that the whole category be reported. For example, with the data in Table 7.14, the mode could either be reported as 8 (the midpoint of the 6–10 interval) or preferably, 6–10.

The mean
Calculation for measures of central tendency and dispersion for grouped data are simple extensions from calculations for ungrouped data. The main difference is based on the fact that the category of the interval in grouped data is wider than a value of 1. In calculating the mean, we view all cases within the interval as lying at the

TABLE 7.14
The mode for grouped data

	Intervals	f
	21–25	3
	16–20	2
	11–15	6
Mo ⟶	6–10	10
	1–5	4

midpoint of each category. The midpoint is calculated by finding the width of the interval and dividing by 2. This quantity is then added to the lower limit. The formula would be

$$mp = [(UL - LL)/2] + LL$$

The mean is calculated by taking the sum of the midpoint of each category times the frequency and dividing by the sum of the frequencies, thus giving

$$\bar{X} = \frac{\Sigma f(mp)}{N}$$

This can be compared to the formula for the mean for ungrouped data:

$$\bar{X} = \frac{\Sigma (fX_i)}{N}$$

For example in Table 7.15 the mean equals 11.

TABLE 7.15
The mean for grouped data

Intervals	f	mp	f(mp)
21–25	3	23	69
16–20	2	18	36
11–15	6	13	78
6–10	10	8	80
1– 5	4	3	12
N	25	Σ f(mp) = 275	

$$\bar{X} = \frac{\Sigma f(mp)}{N} = \frac{275}{25} = 11$$

The median
The computation of the median for grouped data is very similar to

192

calculating it for ungrouped data. The first step is to determine the interval in which the center of the distribution lies. Given the distribution in Table 7.16, the median lies somewhere in the 16–20 interval since $(63 + 1) \div 2 = 32$, and the 32nd case would be in that interval. Using the simple method presented for ungrouped data, the median would be reported at 16–20. For grouped data the lower and upper scores for the category containing the median can be given for the median. Another method sometimes used for group data is to report the midpoint of the interval containing the median unit. In this example the midpoint would be: $20.5 - 15.5 = 5.0$, $5.0/2 = 2.5$, $15.5 + 2.5 = 18$.

TABLE 7.16
The median for grouped data

	Interval	f	Cumulative f
	21–25	12	63
Md ⟶	→16–20	22	51
	11–15	19	29
	6–10	6	10
	1– 5	4	4
	N	63	

The range

Consistent with the logic for the mean, median, and mode, the extension for calculating the range for group data is straightforward. As is the case for ungrouped data, the range is calculated by subtracting the lower limit of the lowest case (or interval) from the upper limit of the highest case (or interval). Thus, the range of the example in Table 7.17 $= 25.5 - .5 = 25$.

Mean deviation

When computing the mean deviation for grouped data we assume that all the cases within the particular interval are at the midpoint of their interval. The logic of the mean deviation remains the same,

TABLE 7.17
The range for grouped data

Interval	f
21–25	23
16–20	18
11–15	13
6–10	8
1– 5	3

and the practice of assuming that the scores in an interval lie at the midpoint is consistent with previous practices.

In computational formulas, then, we substitute the midpoint of grouped categories (mp) for the score of ungrouped categories (X_i); symbolically, $f(mp)$ substitutes for fX_i and $f \mid mp - X \mid$ substitutes for $f \mid X_i - X \mid$. Making these substitutions would result in computations such as those in Table 7.18.

TABLE 7.18
The mean deviation for grouped data

Intervals	f	$\mid mp - \bar{X} \mid$	$f \mid mp - \bar{X} \mid$
21–25	3	$23 - 11 = 12$	$3(12) = 36$
16–20	2	$18 - 11 = 7$	$2(7) = 14$
11–15	6	$13 - 11 = 2$	$6(2) = 12$
6–10	10	$8 - 11 = 3$	$10(3) = 30$
1– 5	4	$3 - 11 = 8$	$4(8) = 32$
N	25		Total deviation points $= 124$

$$\text{Mean deviation} = \frac{\Sigma f \mid mp - \bar{X} \mid}{N} = \frac{124}{25} = 4.96$$

Standard deviation
Calculating the standard deviation for grouped data is very similar to calculating it for simple distributions. Again the exception is that the midpoint of the interval is used instead of the particular score. Calculations for grouped data are presented in Table 7.19. The interpretation for grouped data is exactly the same as for ungrouped data; the larger the standard deviation, the more the dispersion of the distribution.

Problems of interpretation

Although summaries often provide convenient and brief tools for understanding the distribution of a variable, they do have limitations. Perhaps the biggest problem with interpreting measures of central tendency and dispersion is that they sometimes distort the true distribution. If one really wants to get the most accurate picture of how a variable is distributed, the total distribution as well as summary statistics should be examined. Only after the total distribution is compared to the summary statistics can it be determined if these statistics are "honestly" reflecting central tendency and dispersion. Measures of central tendency are more "trustworthy" for presenting a typical score in a distribution if dispersion is low.

One major source of problems for interpreting central tendency

TABLE 7.19
The standard deviation for grouped data

Intervals	f	$(mp - \bar{X})$	$(mp - \bar{X})^2$	$f(mp - \bar{X})^2$
21–25	3	$23 - 11 = 12$	144	$3 \times 144 = 432$
16–20	2	$18 - 11 = 7$	49	$2 \times 49 = 98$
11–15	6	$13 - 11 = 2$	4	$6 \times 4 = 24$
6–10	10	$8 - 11 = -3$	9	$10 \times 9 = 90$
1– 5	4	$3 - 11 = -8$	64	$4 \times 64 = 256$
N	25			Total squared deviations $= 900$

$$s = \sqrt{\frac{\Sigma f (mp - \bar{X})^2}{N}} = \sqrt{\frac{900}{25}} = 6$$

and dispersion arises from the presence of extreme scores or categories. This distortion can easily be shown for the interpretation of the mean and range.

As you can see, the two distributions in Table 7.20 look quite different. Most of the observations in the left distribution are focused around the values of 5 and 6, but in the right they are at the extremes of the distribution. However, the mean in both distributions is 5.5. Although each distribution tends to center about the same value as indicated by the mean, the total distributions are quite different from one another.

Thus, although the mean describes the average *accurately* in both cases, it does not allow one to realize that the two distributions are

TABLE 7.20
Distortions of the mean

Distribution A			Distribution B		
X_i	f	$f X_i$	X_i	f	$f X_i$
10	2	20	10	40	400
9	4	36	9	1	9
8	6	48	8	1	8
7	12	84	7	1	7
6	20	120	6	1	6
5	20	100	5	1	5
4	12	48	4	1	4
3	6	18	3	1	3
2	4	8	2	1	2
1	2	2	1	40	40
	88	484		88	484

$$\bar{X} = \frac{484}{88} = 5.5 \qquad\qquad \bar{X} = \frac{484}{88} = 5.5$$

very different from one another. A few extreme scores will also tend to make the mean less representative of the data. This occurs when a distribution contains extreme scores that are to one side (above or below) of the mean. Such distributions, as you will recall, are called skewed distributions.

Consider the two distributions in Table 7.21. The mean for the distribution on the left is 13.8. The mean for the distribution on the right is 44.4. A mean of 13.8 more closely represents cases in the left-hand distribution than 44.4 does for most of the cases in the right-hand distribution. A similar problem occurs for the range. The range of the distribution on the right is equal to 522, whereas the range of the distribution on the left is equal to 5.

TABLE 7.21
Extreme scores and the mean

Distribution A			Distribution B		
X_i	f	$f X_i$	X_i	f	$f X_i$
16	2	32	533	1	533
15	3	45	16	2	32
14	5	70	15	3	45
13	2	26	14	5	70
12	4	48	13	2	26
	16	221	12	4	48
				16	754

$$\bar{X} = \frac{221}{16} = 13.8 \qquad \bar{X} = \frac{754}{16} = 44.4$$

$$Range = 16.5 - 11.5 = 5.0 \qquad Range = 533.5 - 11.5 = 522$$

These examples serve to illustrate the hazards associated with attempting to describe a whole distribution of a variable using only the statistics of central tendency and dispersion. In order to avoid such problems of interpretation, we suggest that summary statistics be calculated and presented along with the original distribution. Independent judgments can then be made concerning the appropriateness of each summary statistic in describing the distribution.

Now that we have explored some of the more fundamental ways that researchers use in organizing their findings, we can take a more informed view when examining the many aspects of the research process which precede summarizing data. We shall begin this examination of the research process in the next chapter.

6. USING STATISTICS TO ESTIMATE SCATTERPLOTS

Recall that in Chapter 4 we approximated scatterplots by using percentage tables. This helped us to determine the form, extent, and precision of a relationship. In a somewhat similar manner, measures of central tendency and dispersion can be used to estimate scatterplot-like figures. For example, suppose that we had some comparative information about children who went to summer camp and those who did not. In order to determine any relationship comparisons must be made. Therefore it is manditory that comparative data be available. Let us suppose that the average school absenteeism for students who go to camp is 5 days, and the standard deviation of absenteeism for these students is 3. Furthermore we know that the average rate of absenteeism for children who do not go to summer camp is 8 days with a standard deviation of 6. One way to examine such data would be to simply describe the measures of central tendency and dispersion. Another way would be to con-

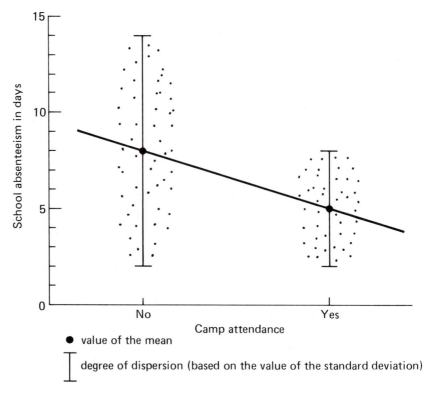

● value of the mean

 degree of dispersion (based on the value of the standard deviation)

FIGURE 7.9
Estimating a scatterplot between camp attendance and school absenteeism using means and standard deviations

ceive of the possibility of a relationship between camp attendance and absenteeism. We could posit that the camp attendance would be an important variable for understanding school absenteeism. In this framework camp attendance would be the independent variable and absenteeism would be the dependent variable. A scatterplot with those variables could be constructed. Since we do not have paired raw data a complete scatterplot could not be completed. However the means of each group could be plotted and a best fitting line drawn through the mean values. In addition, dots could be placed around the mean to correspond to the measures of dispersion. Figure 7.9 shows such a scatterplot. Note that the estimated scatterplot shows an inverse relationship between summer camp attendance and school absenteeism. Notice also that the precision of such a relationship is not high. Precision is somewhat better on the right side of the plot than on the left. Such a procedure is a very useful tool in the search for relationships.

7. SUMMARY

This chapter introduces many of the ways in which researchers organize and report their observations. The techniques described in this chapter are introduced at this point because other methodological practices are structured to produce data consistent with these techniques. By understanding them our ability to comprehend other methodological practices is enhanced. The basic way of organizing both ungrouped and grouped data is to construct simple and cumulative frequency distributions. Frequency distributions can be changed to percentage distributions to allow the scientist to make comparisons between different distributions and/or report a relative proportion of observations. Distributions can be presented pictorially with many different graphic techniques. Simple frequency distributions can be seen pictorially by the use of frequency polygons and histograms. The ogive pictorially describes cumulative distributions. Distributions may also be interpreted in terms of skewedness and kurtosis. Frequency polygons can be easily inspected to arrive at descriptions of these two properties.

In order to briefly summarize the nature of distributions of scores, two sets of statistics are introduced. The first set is composed of measures of central tendency. Each of these summary statistics provides some idea of the category around which observations tend to cluster. The second set is composed of measures of dispersion. Each of these summary statistics reports a value which indicates how spread out observations within a distribution tend to be. The mode, median, and mean are the measures of central tendency, and the range, mean deviation, and standard deviation are the measures of dispersion. First we provided an initial discussion of their general character. Then we presented detailed calculations for each of the statistics. The calculations are provided for all the measures on ungrouped data followed by calculations for grouped data. The chapter concludes with a warning about the interpretation of summary measures of central tendency and dispersion. Their interpretation may be troublesome because of the presence of extreme cases. We suggested that whenever such statistics are used, they be accompanied by a description of the overall distribution of scores. This would allow one to judge whether the summary statistics accurately reflect the total distribution. Finally, measures of central tendency and dispersion can be used to estimate scatterplots. When comparative information is available the approximation of scatterplots serve as a useful tool in describing bivariate relationships.

EXERCISE

1. The following two sets of data supposedly were collected from an introductory sociology class.
   Number of hours a day spent watching TV:
   0, 5, 1, 0, 0, 4, 5, 3, 1, 5, 4, 2, 0, 2, 7, 1, 4, 0, 3, 2, 5,
   3, 2, 4, 5, 0, 0, 1, 6, 5, 1, 0, 2, 5, 4, 1, 3, 4, 2, 6, 5, 0
   Quiz Grades:
   B, C, A, C, C, B, C, D, F, B, F, B, B, C, C, A, C, A, C
   For each:
   a. Construct a frequency distribution.
   b. Construct a percentage distribution.
   c. Construct a cumulative frequency distribution.
   d. Construct a frequency polygon.
   e. Construct an ogive (with frequencies) cumulating both from low to high and high to low.
   f. Construct an ogive in percentages. (*Note:* In order to construct an ogive for percentages it is necessary to construct a cumulative percentage distribution.)
   g. Construct a histogram.

2. From the raw data given below construct two frequency distributions and two frequency polygons.

I.D. number	Motivation	Performance
1	high	low
2	high	high
3	high	low
4	high	low
5	low	low
6	high	high
7	low	high
8	low	low

9	low	high
10	high	low
11	high	low
12	low	high
13	low	low
14	low	high
15	high	high
16	low	low
17	low	high
18	low	high
19	high	low

3. What is the median of the following numbers?

    75   76   77   78   79   80   81   82   83

4. What is the mode for each set of data?

a.	X_i	f		b.	X_i	f		c.	X_i	f
	8	2			25	6			106	21
	7	4			24	7			105	4
	6	3			23	8			104	3
	5	5			22	9			103	2
	4	1			21	8			102	1
	3	1			20	9			101	6
	2	1							100	8
	1	2								

In which group(s) is the mode an adequately representative measure? Why?

5. Find the mean, median, and mode for each of the following:

a.	X_i	f		b.	5		c.	40
	10	5			6			28
	9	5			10			24
	8	1			12			20
	7	1			8			12
	6	1			7			2
	5	1			6			
	4	1						
	3	0						
	2	0						
	1	10						

d. X_i	f		e. X_i	f		f. X_i	f
11	1		10	7		25	10
10	2		9	0		24	0
9	1		8	11		23	8
8	3		7	1		22	1
7	1		6	3		21	1
6	2		5	10		20	0
5	4		4	0		19	5
			3	5		18	1
						16	7
						15	3
						14	4
						13	0
						12	5
						11	3
						10	2

g. 89
15
10
12
9
7
6

For each distribution state which measures of central tendency you feel represent (or does not represent) the data. Why or why not?

6. Compute the range, mean deviation, and standard deviation for Exercise 5.

7. Compute the medians, modes, and means for the following grouped data:

a. X_i	f		b. X_i	f		c. X_i	f
115–119	1		17–20	3		35–44	3
110–114	2		13–16	2		25–34	4
105–109	1		9–12	3		15–24	8
100–104	3		5– 8	1		5–14	10
95–99	4		1–4	4			

d. X_i	f		e. X_i	f		f. X_i	f
115–119	4		17–20	4		35–44	10
110–114	3		13–16	1		25–34	8
105–109	1		9–12	3		15–24	4
100–104	2		55–8	2		5–14	3
95–99	1		1–4	3			

g. X_i	f	h. X_i	f	i. X_i	f
40–49	13	110–119	10	55–59	4
30–39	7	100–109	11	50–54	5
20–29	2	90–99	8	45–49	5
10–19	1	80–89	2	40–44	7
		70–79	10	35–39	5

8. Compute the range, mean deviation, and standard deviation for the grouped data in Exercise 7.

9. Describe the forms of distribution from the data in Exercise 5.

10. What would the following income distributions for different neighborhoods tell you about the nature of the neighborhood?

Average income distributions (in thousands of dollars)

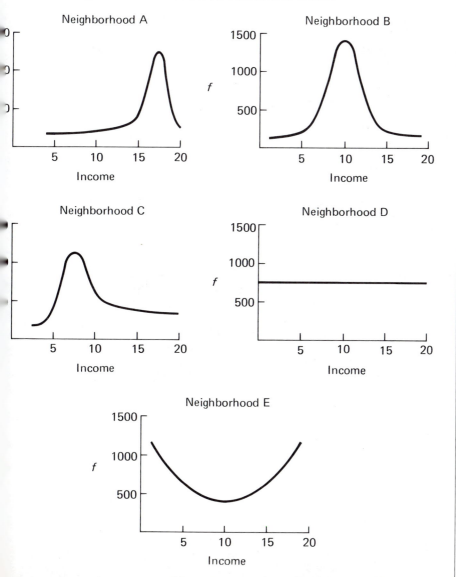

11. A frequently used alternative to scatterplots involves the comparison of data on central tendency and dispersion for the dependent variable between groups which may be ordered (ordinal variables) for the independent variable. Central tendency could be used to approximate slope and dispersion could be used to approximate precision. For example, we might have data on college athletes versus nonathletes concerning the cost of medical care. Let us say that the data are as follows:

	Nonathletes	Athletes
Mean medical care cost per year	$150	$200
Standard deviation	70	45

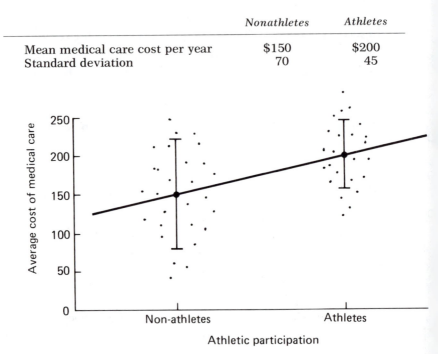

Assuming that we might order people on their degree of athletic participation, we could present the data as follows:

The slope can be represented by comparing means. We note a $50 difference.

The precision can be represented in terms of dispersion. Discuss the adequacy of such an approximation.

a. Which would you prefer: means, medians, or modes? Why?

b. Can you say anything about a relationship if the groups are nominal? If so, what?

List three variables you are considering for your project. Although you will not actually collect the data at this time, discuss how you would numerically describe each variable. Which graphs, measures of central tendency, and dispersion would you use and why?

ANDERSON, T., AND ZELDITCH, M. JR. *A Basic Course in Statistics.* New York: Holt, Rinehart and Winston, 1968.

BLALOCK, H. JR. *Social statistics,* 2d ed. New York: McGraw-Hill, 1972.

MUELLER, J., SCHUESSLER, K., AND COSTNER, H. *Statistical Reasoning in Sociology,* 2d ed. Boston: Houghton Mifflin, 1970.

CHAPTER 8
COMPUTER USE

After studying this chapter, students should be able to:

1. Communicate the uses and functions of the various machines and devices available to computer users.

2. State the three major tasks the user must be able to do to utilize canned programs on a set of data.

3. Use and explain the key (card) punch machine.

4. Use and explain the teletype machine.

5. Describe the layout of an IBM (computer, Holerith) card.

6. Write F-type variable format statements.

7. Discuss the advantages and possible limitations of the use of computers in the research process.

Batch job The method of communicating with the computer by using punched IBM (computer, Holerith) cards.

Canned program Prepared sets of instructions to the computer that allow the user to do manipulations, statistics, and so on.

Card (key) punch A device used to punch holes in IBM cards.

Data deck A number of IBM punched cards that contain punches representing data.

Data files Sets of data that have been stored in the computer for later use.

Disk (core) storage area A space in the computer that is used to store data files.

Line printer A device that prints any output information from the computer at a very high rate of speed.

Marked sense sheets Sheets that have spaces which can be blackened with a number 2 pencil.

Optical scanner A device that converts marked sense sheets into data files and/or sets of punched cards.

Output Materials produced, usually printed, by the computer and given to the computer user.

Program description Sets of instructions to user on how to use canned programs.

Programmer People who write special sets of instructions to the computer.

Project Number and/or password A number that allows the user to gain access to the computer.

Teletype Machine similar to a typewriter that one uses to communicate with the computer over regular telephone lines.

Time sharing The method of many users sharing the computer to do jobs at the same time, usually via teletype.

Variable format statement A set of instructions to the computer about where to find punches on cards in a data file that represent particular variables.

1. THE MYSTERY MACHINE

It is a fact of modern life that nearly everything is computerized to some extent. This is certainly true of the research world. Even the smallest scale research project is likely to employ a computer or computer-like device in the preparation of research findings. Although this usage is often in the data analysis phase of research, computers can and are used in other parts of the research process. For example, we briefly discussed the use of computerized retrieval services in Chapter 5. In this chapter we shall attempt to increase your understanding of how computers work and how researchers use the computer to aid them. For those of you who will be engaged in research, some necessary skills can be acquired with the materials presented here. For those who will consume research results, insights into the process and machines that scientists use will provide a more sophisticated basis on which to evaluate research reports.

Few researchers who use computers really know how computers work. Computer science is a very technical specialty in and of itself which requires a great deal of training to master. Researchers can use computers without knowing a great deal about the electronic components from which they are constructed. There are two general types of computers—analog and digital. Most computers that are used for the social sciences and education are digital computers. They are made by IBM, Westinghouse, RCA, Control Data, PDP, and many other companies. Most of them have some number associated with them to denote the model and the size. The size of a computer is determined by how many bits of information can be stored and processed through and in the computer. For most research procedures, only modest size computers are needed and computers of this size are quite common even in small colleges or research companies.

Although the electronics of computers is a mystery to most of us, what the digital computer does is very simple: It adds and subtracts. The power of the computer is that it does it very, very quickly. It accomplishes the task of adding and subtracting at the speed of light. Because of this speed, it can perform many operations within 1 second. Computer speed has become a useful tool to science because developers have determined how to translate these very fast simple arithmetic operations into various more complicated tasks and procedures.

Once computer systems have been developed, people can be trained to use them. In order to be able to use these systems, it is necessary to be able to activate them, to have them do what you want, to communicate with them. People who are able to tell the computer systems what to do are called *programmers*. We shall discuss computer programs and programmers more fully in a later section.

For computer users the "mystery" is taken out of the machine by the systems specialists who design and build computers, and by the programmers who can use the computer systems to do tasks. The computer user must rely on the expertise of the systems specialist and the programmer in order to use the power of the computer. When the user understands what is required and what is available, the mystery turns into mastery.

2. THE ROLE OF THE COMPUTER USER

Because there are so many different brands and models of computers, no general text can give specific instructions on one particular system. However there are some general principles, procedures, and terminology that are nearly universal. An important part of using a computer is learning these procedures and terms.

Most computers are housed in a special building behind brick and glass walls called the *computer center*. The normal contact for a user is with a person who is called an *operator*. The computer operator is usually at a counter in the center. Exchanges with the operator usually consist of the user giving the operator a set of punched IBM cards and the operator giving the user a set of printed "output" (along with the punched cards which the operator previously received from the user). When punched cards are used the term *batch job* is often employed. Increasingly, however, users never even go near the computer center nor deal directly with an operator. Communication with the computer is accomplished through the use of regular telephone lines via a computer teletype. This is known as *time sharing*. The use of the teletype and other devices will be covered in a forthcoming section. We will attempt to introduce both batch and teletype terminology, but the emphasis will be on teletype.

Machines and devices at your disposal

Table 8.1 shows a list of different machines that are available to most computer users. The usual location and function of each device is also included. Most users would come into contact with or use most all of the devices listed.

These machines and devices are used to do the tasks the user wishes to accomplish with the aid of the computer. To use the computer, the devices are employed at various stages in the process.

What the user must be able to do

In general, there are three tasks that must be mastered by the user in the data analysis phase of the research. This is the phase in which most users employ the computer. The first thing that users must be able to do is to create and store data in the form of data files within the computer. In some systems data are punched on cards and a collection of cards comprise the data file. This set of cards is called a *data deck,* similar to a deck of playing cards. In other systems data files can be created directly from mark sense sheets and/or by using a teletype. Each procedure requires that a unique name and/or number be used to label each file so that it is not confused with other files.

The user must also be able to know which program, either canned or original, must be used to accomplish whatever is desired. That is, the user must obtain a list of available canned programs stored

TABLE 8.1

Various machines and devices available to computer users

Device	Usual location	Function
Project number and/or passward	In user's possession	Allows the user to use the computer and related services.
Card (key) punch	Various	Punches holes in IBM cards and has a keyboard similar to a typewriter.
Teletype	Various	Used to communicate with the computer via telephone lines. Some are portable.
Disk storage area or core area	Inside computer	A space in the computer that is used to store any data files user may wish stored.
Line printer	Computer center	Prints any output or other information from the computer at a very high rate of speed.
"Canned" programs	Inside computer	Prepared sets of instructions to the computer that allow the user to do manipulations, statistics, and so on.
Programmers	Various	People who can write special programs (sets of instructions) for the computer.
Program descriptions	In user's possession, obtained from computer center	Sets of instructions to user on how to use canned programs.
Optical scanner	Various	Converts mark sense sheets into data files and/or sets of punched cards.
Data files	Inside computer	Sets of data that have been stored in the computer for later use.

within the computer and be somewhat familiar with that list. This collection of canned programs is usually referred to as the *program library*. There are several commercially available series of programs that are used by a wide range of computer centers. Since this is the case, many users who avail themselves of more than one computer are already somewhat familiar with program libraries. Once the correct program is identified, the user must obtain a program description and learn how to use the program. If a canned program is not available in the library to do the desired task, it might be necessary to find a programmer to write an original program. This can be quite costly. However, computer centers frequently have such people available at low or no cost. In either case the novice user will have to rely heavily on assistance from personnel in the computer center. Most centers have advanced graduate students who serve as aides to people wishing to use the computer. Our advice to new researchers is to get to know these aides.

Finally, the user must be able to get the data together with the appropriate program so that the computer can do its work according to the program. The results of getting a program to act on data are called *output*. This printed output is produced either by a high speed line printer or a teletype.

It may sound oversimplified at this point, but there are only three things required of the user—to have the data, to obtain a program, and to have the program produce output. Figure 8.1 shows this scheme of things in a pictorial diagram. The diagram assumes that a data file has been created and stored and that a canned program is available.

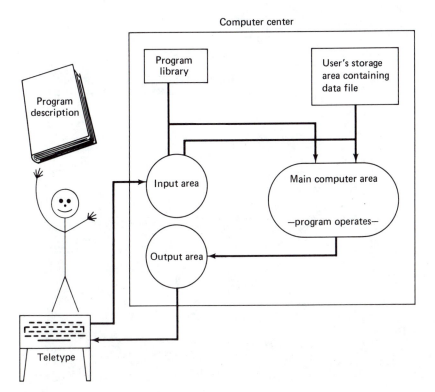

FIGURE 8.1
The user and the computer—a big picture

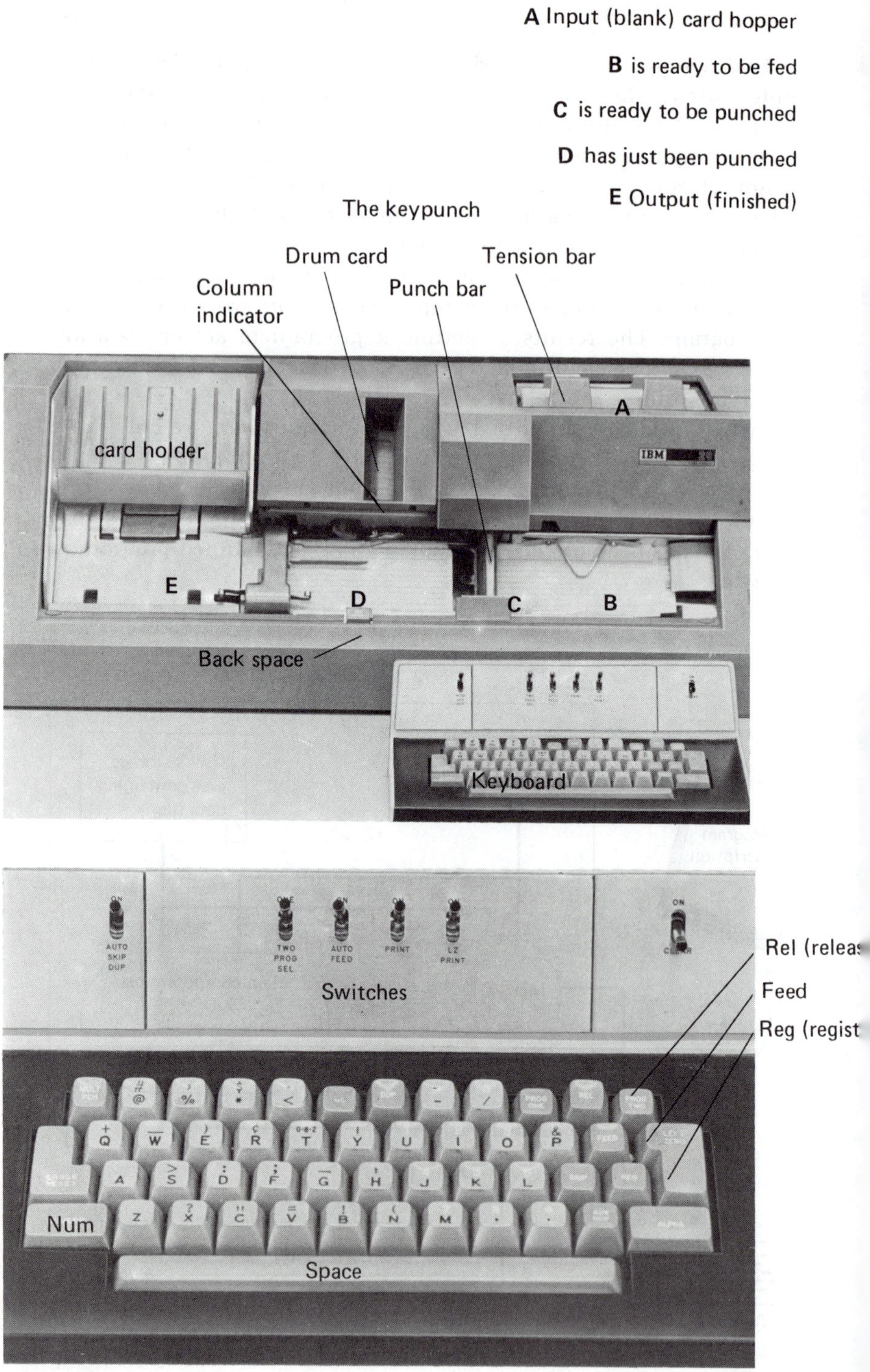

A Input (blank) card hopper

B is ready to be fed

C is ready to be punched

D has just been punched

E Output (finished)

The keypunch

Column indicator

Drum card

Punch bar

Tension bar

card holder

A

IBM

E

D

C

B

Back space

Keyboard

Switches

AUTO SKIP DUP

TWO PROG SEL

AUTO FEED

PRINT

LZ PRINT

Rel (release)

Feed

Reg (register)

Num

Space

FIGURE 8.2
Keypunch machine

Two machines are crucial in accomplishing these three basic tasks. For batch users the keypunch machine is necessary and for the teletype users a teletype is necessary. These two machines are used to enter data into the computer. They are also used to get a particular program to act on your data. The middle step of understanding which program you want to use for what purposes can only be accomplished by the user (with the aid of personnel at the computer center).

The keypunch (card punch) machine

The purpose of the keypunch machine is to make holes in blank IBM cards. These cards are sometimes called Holerith cards after their inventor. A complete description of these cards will be discussed in Section 4. For the moment it is necessary to know that each card has 80 columns into which holes can be punched. These holes can either stand for numbers or alphabetic letters. In most research procedures only numbers are punched on these cards. Figure 8.2 shows a photograph of one of the most common models of a keypunch machine.

Keypunch machines are quite versatile and can be adjusted to do certain operations with great speed, depending on the skill of the user. Such adjustments are accomplished by setting the six switches at the top of the keyboard in different positions and by using a drum card on the drum inside the compartment at the top center of the machine. In most cases set the six switches in the down-up-up-up-up-down position. This will automatically feed blank cards into the machine. The user can determine which column the machine is operating on by looking at the column indicator at the base of the drum holder. To use a drum card one should consult a complete instruction book. For most purposes occasional users can ignore the drum and the drum card (make sure the sensors on the drum card are in an up position).

The keyboard of the keypunch is similar to a typewriter with the exception that there are only capital letters. There are also some unusual characters and some extra keys. To punch letters into the cards simply depress the keys. To punch upper characters (all the numbers) depress the "NUM" key and while holding it down depress the appropriate key. The space bar is located at the bottom of the keyboard similar to a typewriter and when depressed it will move the card one column without punching any holes. There is also a back space key located below the drum. It has "back space" printed on it. There is also a REL key which stands for "release." This key will push the card through either the punch bar or read bar without doing any operation on the card. The FEED key will take one card from the blank card hopper and put in into position B. The

REG key (register) will move a card into the punch bar and/or read bar when depressed (assuming a card is available).

Starting with an empty keypunch machine, observe the following steps to punch cards:

1. Obtain a supply of blank cards and place them in the card hopper with the print facing forward and the 9s at the bottom. The tension bar behind them will hold the cards firmly.
2. Turn the on/off switch located under the keyboard to the "on" position.
3. Set the six switches in the appropriate positions.
4. Press the FEED button to move the first card from position A to position B.
5. Press the FEED button to move the first card from position B to position C (into the punch bar) and the second card from position A to position B.
6. Punch the desired information on the card in position C at the punch bar. This information would either be data that has been properly coded or information necessary for the operation of some program.
7. Assuming that you are not going to use all 80 columns on a card, when you have punched the appropriate information on the card in position C press REL. This will release the card in position C and move a new blank card into the punch bar. (This will also move the card just punched into the read bar.)
8. Continue punching cards by repeating steps 6 and 7 until completed. As you punch more cards the above operation will move punched cards into the output card holder.
9. When all necessary cards have been punched, lift the sixth switch at the top of the keyboard (marked "clear") until all cards have been removed from positions B, C, D, and E.
10. Turn the on/off switch to the "off" position.

If these procedures have been properly followed, the user will end up with a set of punched cards that contain either research data or program instruction cards.

One of the most useful special procedures for the keypunch is the "duplicate" procedure. This process can be used to copy a card that has already been punched or it can be used to correct a punched card. This second feature is helpful because most keypunch operators make mistakes when punching cards and holes cannot be erased. With this procedure all columns on a card can be duplicated, or selected columns can be duplicated, or some columns can be duplicated and others changed (corrected). To duplicate a card it must be in position D registered into the read bar and a blank card must be in position C registered into the punch bar. This will automatically occur when following the previous set of instructions or it can be done by hand-feeding a punched card (make sure all card positions are empty) into the read bar at position D via the slots provided and simultaneously feeding a blank card into position C via the slots provided. After these cards have been hand-fed it is necessary to register them by pressing the REG key.

When the two cards are in the registered position the DUP key can be depressed either once or a series of times or can be held in the depressed position for the appropriate number of columns by noting the column indicator. If you want to duplicate an entire card as it has been punched, simply hold down the DUP button until the job is complete. However, if you want to correct a card you have just punched, the user may follow a procedure similar to the example below.

Suppose the user desires to punch a card with a 1234567 in columns one through seven, respectively. However, when punching the card an error was made and 1234967 was punched instead. To correct this card register it into the read bar and register a blank card into the punch bar. Then press the following series of keys: DUP DUP DUP DUP 5 DUP DUP. In this way the "5" will replace the "9" previously punched, but the other columns will be duplicated. Make sure you discard the original card with the error in it as soon as it is in a cleared position.

With the two procedures described above, users should be able to do most of the necessary tasks associated with the keypunch machine. However, if problems should result, do not hesitate to ask for help from another user or a computer center aide.

The teletype

The three necessary tasks described above can also be accomplished via the teletype. The first operation that might be necessary in a research project would be to create data files. The particular way that this is done will depend on the computer system being used. The user should consult the computer center for this step. Once a data file has been created it is possible to get a canned program to act on a data file by using the teletype as per the description of programs available at the user's computer center.

There are four basic steps in using the teletype to analyze a data file. The first step is to "log in" on the teletype. To accomplish this the user must turn the switch at the lower right hand of the teletype to the "line" position. This switch can be seen in Figure 8.3. This will allow communication over a regular telephone line. A telephone must be near the teletype and a special number is dialed to get in contact with the computer. When this special number is dialed a high tone will be heard. When this tone is heard the telephone receiver is placed on the acoustical coupler. In a moment a period will appear on the teletype paper. This means that the user can send a message to the computer. (Some systems may use another symbol, but the majority use a period.) The user must send the first message which tells the computer that there is a legitimate user on the other end of the telephone line. At some point the user

Paper

Line switch

Acoustical coupler

FIGURE 8.3
Teletype machine

will have to type in a number and/or code word to get through the input part of the computer center into the computer itself.

After the user has successfully logged in, a canned program can be called from the program library by using the appropriate name for the program. With the use of a program description, the user can proceed with the third step by having the program act on a data set. Finally, after the program has completed its work it will be necessary for the user to log off the computer. Upon receiving a period, some message will have to be typed which will terminate the connection with the computer. An example of this message is "KILL JOB." It is also customary for the computer to ask for confirmation that a user wishes to log off. When communicating with the computer via a teletype it is necessary to tell the computer when the user has completed a message to the computer. This is usually accomplished by using a key marked "RETURN." This return key is to the computer what a period is to the user. These symbols indicate when it is the user's turn to type and when it is the computer's turn to type.

Because each system is a little different, the particular commands and messages will have to be learned for each different system.

However the basic procedures and steps discussed above are similar for all systems. Many users prefer teletypes for relatively small jobs because the mode of communication with the computer is often "conversational." That is, the user types in sentences and/or phrases and the computer types back similar sentences and phrases. In this way the user and the computer interact with each other in a manner similar to a conversation. It is therefore called the *conversational mode*. No matter which approach is utilized, it takes a very short time to become familiar with using canned programs on data files. One of the more difficult aspects of computer usage emerges if appropriate canned programs are not available in the computer's library. If they are not available, original programming must be obtained.

3. THE PROGRAMMER AND PROGRAMS

When a user enters data into a computer and uses a canned program to act on that data, the user is not actually communicating with the main part of the computer, only the input and output areas. The program is the means used to get the computer to do desired tasks. Programs are sets of instructions to the computer in a language the computer can understand. This process is similar to using a foreign language, with the exception that all the various computer (machine) languages must be used very precisely. There are many machine languages including FORTRAN, BASIC, and COBOL that can be used by the programmer depending on the system in which the program is being used. With the increasing use of the computer, more and more programmers are being trained and employed in various fields. Some programs are fairly easy to write and take a matter of minutes. Other programs are extremely difficult to write and take months and years to perfect. The difficulty of writing the program depends on the difficulty of interpreting the desired task into a language that the machine (computer) can understand.

When original programs are needed in research there are two alternatives available to the researcher. The scientist can take courses and learn programming, or the researcher can hire a professional programmer to write a program specifically for a particular research purpose. Researchers vary in their opinion about how involved with programming they themselves should become. Although some researchers may find simple programming skills useful early in their career, the vast majority rely upon other people to produce programs for them. Most universities and virtually all private research firms have such professional programmers available to them.

Because researchers often do not have the skills necessary to write programs, there is virtually no way for the researcher to directly "check" the accuracy of the program being used. If unanticipated findings are discovered, the researcher may try another program or mode of analysis to verify the results. However, even when this is done, other programs are being relied on to verify other programs. The results are still being produced via a mechanism beyond the scope of most investigators' ability.

The process of confirming that a program is doing what it is supposed to do is called *documenting the program*. Most canned programs have been used so widely and in so many circumstances that there is no problem in terms of their accuracy. However, when original programs are used the problem becomes more difficult. We know of one researcher who is so skeptical of the accuracy of programs that he always does some of the calculations by hand in order to check the accuracy of the computer. Of course this defeats the purpose of using the computer in the first place. Hand calculation cannot really be done when there is a large set of data or if complicated calculations are necessary. So researchers are left with the reality that most research results rely very heavily on the accuracy of computer programs. Since this procedure cannot be directly controlled by the researcher, it is one area where the potential for error is very real and indeed sometimes occurs.

Although it may appear that there is a great potential for error in such a situation, this is not the case. Most professional programmers are competent in their jobs and will produce reliable and accurate programs. There are many strategies that programmers have developed to check and verify their work. We discuss this issue not so much to raise the potential for error, but to note that it is one part of the research process which is probably least in the direct control of researchers. Since we have stressed the idea that scientists go out of their way to have control over research procedures, this is one area that is an exception. This exception is taken for granted by most researchers and is seldom challenged.

4. BITS AND PIECES

Card layout

As was previously mentioned, a computer (IBM or Holerith) card has 80 columns in which numbers or letters can be punched. Figure 8.4 shows an IBM card with numbers appearing in some columns and letters and symbols in other columns. Notice that the letters and symbols utilize more than one punch in a column. The number or letter can be printed on the top of the card by the keypunch machines as it is being punched. There are twelve different positions where punches may appear in each column. Any of the printed numbers 0 through 9 may be punched as well as two punches at the top of the card where there is nothing printed.

The usual procedure for data cards is to allow a few columns at the beginning of the card for an identification number. The remaining columns can be used for data that have been coded into number equivalents. If more than 80 columns are necessary to hold all of the variables being examined, more than one card per case will have to be punched. If this is done, the usual procedure is to place the case identification number at the beginning of each card with data placed after the I.D. number and the card number punched into the eightieth column. The first data card would have a 1 in column 80, the second, a 2 in column 80, and so on. Even when the teletype is used, many programs call for data in the form of "card images." That is, data are entered via a teletype as though one were punching out a card. Card images are also commonly used on computer tapes when they are used. (See "Use of Tapes" in this section.)

Each card used must have a code sheet that tells what the various punches mean. The construction of a code sheet is explained in Chapter 10. The code sheet lists the columns of each card along with the interpretation of each possible punched code. It is these cards, or images of these cards, that usually compose data files. That is, data files are usually collections of data cards, one or more for each data case. Many variables would have to be involved in order to require that more than one data card be prepared for each case. When multiple cards are used they are placed one behind another.

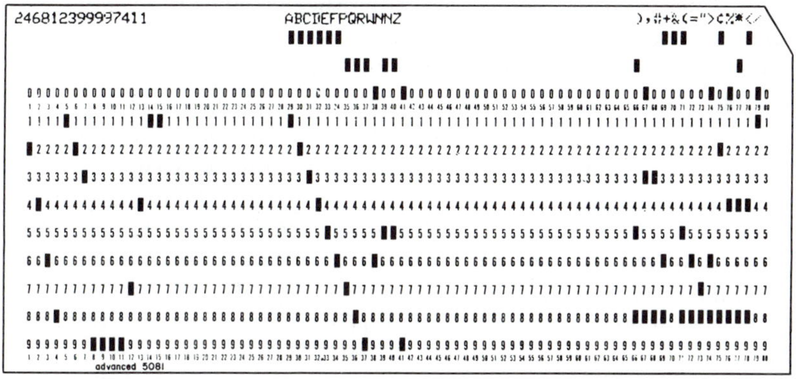

FIGURE 8.4
An IBM card with various numbers and symbols punched

Writing variable format statements

One of the most common aspects of using programs to analyze a data file is the construction of a variable format statement. A *variable format statement* is a set of instructions to the computer about where on the IBM card to find punches that represent particular variables. A variable code might take one, two, or more columns of the card, and this can also be communicated to the computer with the variable format statement.

There are several parts to the variable format statement that mean different things. The following are the symbols used in such statements:

(= the beginning of a variable format statement
) = the end of a variable format statement
/ = go to the next card for this data case (only used when more than one card image exists for each data case)
, = separates SKIP commands and READ commands
X = SKIP command (i.e., do not read these columns)
F = READ command (i.e., this (these) column(s) is (are) a variable(s))

In addition to these symbols, there are numbers preceding X (SKIP) commands and numbers preceding and following the F (READ) commands. The numbers preceding X tell the computer how many columns to skip (not read). Columns are skipped if they do not contain variable codes or if they do not contain variables that are being examined by a particular analysis. The number following F tells the computer how many columns are taken up by one variable code as well as where to put the decimal point if one is desired. The number preceding the F tells the computer how many variables of the same size (number of columns) are to be read at this time. Remember, the number of columns occupied by each variable specified *follows* the F. Although there are other types of variable format statements, a similar format is used in most cases.

Some simple examples of "F-type" variable format statements should make the procedure fairly clear. If the statement is (3X,2F1.0), then there is one data card image for each case. The computer is to skip the first three columns and read two variables each one column wide. There are to be no (0) decimal places in these two variables. In other words, this statement tells the computer that there is a one-digit variable code in column 4 of the data card and a one-digit variable code in column 5 of each data card.

If the statement reads (15F1.0,3X,1F2.1), this would tell the computer that the first 15 columns of each data card are to be read as 15 different one-column variables with no decimal places. The computer should not read columns 16, 17, or 18. Then in columns 19 and 20 there is one two-digit variable and you want the computer to read that two-digit number with one decimal place in it. The usual practice for creating data files is to leave decimal points out. They are put back into the data through the variable format statement.

The variable format statement is usually necessary with a canned program as one of the instructions. It never has any spaces in it.

Use of tapes

Most of you are familiar with computer tapes because of television and the movies. It is quite common to see large computers with rapidly spinning spools of tape as a background for science fiction, the bionic people, and so on. Computer tapes are growing in popularity because of their ease of access and storage as well as their large capacity. The two most common types of computer tapes are the large reels familiar to most of you and a small tape in a cartridge similar to tape cassettes. In most cases, card images are recorded on these tapes in a manner similar to vocal tape recording. The effect of such a procedure is that a series of card images appears on the tape and each image can be "read" by a tape machine in the computer center. These card images are often copied onto the tapes by using a deck of punched cards or input from a teletype. Computer output may also be stored on tapes in addition to being printed on line printers and teletypes. All in all, the use of computer tapes is well accepted and they are used whenever very large computer jobs are necessary. For very large jobs this has become the most practical way to store and handle data.

5. CAN WE TRUST THE COMPUTER?

Modern computer systems are built in such a way that an internal malfunction of a computer component will be quickly detected and corrective action can be taken. Therefore there is little likelihood that errors will be made because of a "broken" computer. There is a much greater chance for an error to be made in the execution of a program and/or the preparation of data files. However, even in these cases, with experience the occasional user will be able to detect when major errors have been made. With the proper training the use of computers in the research act poses no major problem for researchers.

We feel that the more crucial problem for those using research results produced by computers is that a mystique often surrounds such results. When the computer is used it is quite common that consumers of research feel they do not have the knowledge or ability to question it. This is a totally inaccurate perspective to have. In most research procedures the computer only speeds up the calculation of statistics. If the consumer of research becomes at least somewhat familiar with the statistics that are common in research, the mystique can be taken out of computer analysis. When the most common ways of analyzing data are mastered the consumer of research results can become very critical. It will not be necessary to merely "accept" research results produced by the computer. Rather, the consumer can understand what the computer has done and evaluate the adequacy of the analysis and the appropriateness of the conclusions reached.

6. SUMMARY

The computer is a useful tool for the producers of research. If one knows how to create data files and use canned programs, all of the univariate, bivariate, and multivariate analyses presented in this text can be done at the speed of light. It is important for consumers of research not to be intimidated by the computer. Although the electronic components may remain a mystery to most of us, the products of computer use are quite comprehendable.

Teletypes and card punch machines are devices that enable us to create data files. Most data files are in the form of card images. IBM cards have 80 columns. The usual practice is to start each card with a subject I.D. The data follow this I.D. When multiple cards are necessary to store data for one unit, a card number is placed in column 80. The use of the variable format statement tells the computer which columns to read as variables. The specification of these variables allows the program to complete the specified analysis. Output from the high speed line printer or teletype is the product of getting the program to act on the data file.

EXERCISES

Your school's computer facilities should have canned programs, such as SPSS, that can be used to analyze data. After your instructor has provided you with specific instructions about (1) the programs available to you, (2) how you may log in, and (3) how you may enter the data:

1. Create a data file for the following exercises. You may use the data from Chapter 11, exercise 3, or you may use data provided by your instructor. If you use data from Chapter 11, note that your canned program will probably require you to code the sex and driver training variables with numbers (e.g., male = 1; female = 2).

2. For your data use the canned programs to compute the following:
   a. frequency distribution
   b. percentage distribution

c. frequency and percentage ogives
d. measures of central tendency

mean
median
mode

e. measures of dispersion

range
mean deviation
standard deviation

f. scatterplot
(*Note:* Some computer programs use numbers instead of dots since more than one case could have the same value on X and Y.)
g. percentage cross-tab table

3. Compare what you have discovered with the computer with your "hand" calculations in previous chapters.

Determine which computer programs can be used to analyze the data that you will be collecting in your project. Be sure that you know how to use each of them and determine what form your data will have to be in for you to use the computer.

DIXON, W. *Biomedical Computer Programs.* Berkeley, Calif.: University of California Press, 1973.

NIE, N., BENT, D., AND HULL, C. *Statistical Package for the Social Sciences.* New York: McGraw-Hill, 1970.

PROJECT

REFERENCES

CHAPTER 9
THE GRAND MASTER: THE EXPERIMENT

After studying this chapter, students should be able to:

1. Detect, describe, diagram, and give examples of classical experimental design; common sense experiments; one group pretest-posttest design; simple surveys; case studies; Solomon four-group design; and multiple-X experimental design.

2. Differentiate between cross-sectional and longitudinal studies and say why this distinction is important.

3. Describe what manipulation means.

4. Define stimulus, treatment, pretest, and posttest and describe why each is important in experimental design.

5. Describe control groups and experimental groups and discuss how they are used in each of the experimental and quasi-experimental designs.

6. Discuss the similarities and differences between random assignment, frequency matching, and precision matching and describe their role in experimentation.

7. List and describe the sources of confounding in experiments, including subject characteristics, environmental changes, maturation, testing, instrument decay, subject mortality, unreliable measurement, reactivity, and experimenter bias, and discuss how different experimental designs and procedures deal with each of these problems.

8. Discuss the issues and problems associated with the generalization of experimental results.

9. Define and discuss representatives of subjects, setting, manipulation, measures, timing, and other unique characteristics in experiments.

10. Discuss the interplay between random selection and random assignment of subjects.

Before-after design   A design where one quasi-experimental group receives a pretest, a relatively high level of the independent variable, and a posttest.

Case study   A design with one quasi-experimental group having a relatively high value of the independent variable and a posttest only.

Classical (simple) experiment   A design where individuals are randomly assigned to the experimental and control groups with a pretest and posttest in both groups.

Common sense experiment   A design where a quasi-experimental group receives a pre- and posttest and a number of independent variables are present, and another quasi-experimental group which also has a pre- and posttest but where none of the independent variables are present.

Confounded   A situation when unseen and unmeasured variables may be operating and distorting the picture of the relationship between the independent and dependent variables.

Confounding variables   Unseen variables that may confound the original relationship.

Control group   The group in the experiment where the independent variable typically is manipulated so that it has a low or zero value.

Controlling   Removing the possible confounding influences in an experiment by design, matching, and/or statistics.

Cross-sectional studies   Research done at one point in time.

Dependent variable   Variable that happens after the independent (presumed effect).

Differences in subject characteristic   Confounding caused by the lack of random assignment to experimental groups.

Environmental changes   Confounding caused if there are other things happening in the subjects' environment (that are not controlled) other than those which are in the experiment.

Experimental group   The group in the experiment where the independent variable typically is manipulated so that it has a high value.

Experimenter bias   The existence of bias when the experimenter inappropriately influences the subjects' behavior or when an error has been made in observation.

Experimenter effect   The effect when a social characteristic of the experimenter limits the generalization of research results.

External validity   A synonym for generalization of experimental findings.

Frequency matching   Assigning subjects to groups so that the distribution of relevant characteristics are similar.

Generalization   Extending a particular set of research findings to a class of similar phenomena and/or subjects.

Independent variable   Variable that happens first in time (presumed cause).

Instrument decay   Confounding caused by any changes in the measurement process between the pre- and posttests.

Internal validity   A situation where none of the sources of confounding has had an effect on the experiment.

Longitudinal studies   Research where variables are measured over some period of time.

Manipulate   The researcher structures the research so that different values of the independent variable exist.

Maturation   Confounding caused by any unmeasured changes internal to the subject(s).

Multiple-X design   An experiment with several experimental groups that have different levels or values of the independent variable.

Posttest   The measurement of the dependent variable after the independent variable has been manipulated.

Precision matching   Assigning subjects to groups so that there is one subject with similar characteristics in each group.

Pretest   The first measurement of the dependent variable.

Random assignment   The process of placing subjects in experimental groups on the basis of probability so that groups will likely be similar.

Random selection   The determination of subjects for an experiment by using probability.

Reactivity   Confounding caused by subjects realizing they are involved in an experiment and consequently acting differently than they otherwise would.

Replication   Conducting studies over and over again.

Representativeness   The degree to which subjects, setting, manipulations, measures, timing, and other unique circumstances of an experiment are similar to a class of phenomena to which findings might be generalized.

Research design   Ways of structuring the research process.

Simple survey   Design where there are two quasiexperimental groups one of which receives a high value of the independent variable and the other a zero value and both have only a posttest.

Solomon four-group design   Experiment that combines the strategy of a classical experimental design and a posttest only design.

Sources of confounding   Differences in subject characteristics, environmental changes, maturation, testing, instrument decay, subject mortality, unreliable measurement, reactivity, and experimenter bias.

Stimulus   Synonym for independent variable.

Subject mortality   Subjects leaving the experiment prior to its completion which might cause confounding.

Testing   Confounding caused by giving the pretest.

Treatment   Synonym for independent variable.

Unreliable measures of extreme scores Potential confounding caused by inability to reliably measure extreme cases when extreme groups are used in experiments.

1. INTRODUCTION

Ways of collecting data are often referred to as *research designs.* The *classical experimental design* is considered the grand master of research designs because in a relatively simple way the researcher can deal with many of the problems of demonstrating causation. In the classical experiment, time order is directly observed or manipulated; mutual patterned change in variables is observed over a period of time; and unseen or unmeasured variables are considered as fully as possible. This can be undertaken with little or no sacrifice in generality. In other words, the experiment "controls" many areas that create problems with interpreting research observations. Three general design problems confront researchers.

The first problem that often arises with respect to design is being certain about the time order or sequence of the two variables under study. This problem is more difficult if change is not directly viewed over a period of time. For example, in a typical questionnaire survey data are gathered at one point in time. This is referred to as a *cross-sectional* study. On the other hand, when observations are made on variables over some longer time period, called a *longitudinal* study, it is possible to view change directly. Almost all experiments are longitudinal.

A second problem can arise in coping with other variables that may distort what is observed in a scatterplot. If people have different scores on a variable, researchers try to infer why they are different on the basis of past events. For example, if two people have different political attitudes, researchers would try to attribute these differences to variables which differed before these attitudes occurred. Such things as child-rearing practices or educational levels might be considered. The difficulty in doing this is that there were probably many different things that happened prior to the study. The people may have been from different parts of the country, different socio-economic backgrounds, rural or urban residences, and so on. The impact of any of these unseen or unmeasured variables may distort what is observed in a scatterplot. The simple experiment helps eliminate many of these problems.

Finally, even if these difficulties are resolved, the problem of generality remains. Although a scatterplot may have been constructed very carefully, we can never fully determine the degree to which our conclusions can be generalized.

This chapter explores how experiments deal with these three problems of design.

2. THE CLASSICAL EXPERIMENT

Observing the relationship between two variables is the main objective of the classical experimental design. The experiment always occurs over some period of time. This time frame allows the scientist to directly observe changes in variables. Time sequence of change is certain because the experimenter has control over the order of events. The event or variable that changes first is called the *independent* variable, and the variable that changes after the first is called the *dependent* variable. Note that these names reflect causal thinking, that is, changes in the second variable are thought to be "dependent" on changes in the first variable. For shorthand purposes, the first variable is often labeled the X variable, and the second is labeled the Y variable.

To examine change in the first variable, two groups are used. The experimenter *manipulates* the research so that one group has one value of the first variable and another group has a different value of the first variable. Sometimes the variable that is manipulated is called the *stimulus* or *treatment*.

In one group the experimenter controls the value of the first variable in such a way that the value of the first variable is relatively low or zero. This group is called the *control group*. The second group, referred to as the *experimental group*, is manipulated by the experimenter in such a way that the first variable is at a relatively *high* degree or value. In this fashion the first variable will have two values, one relatively low, and the other relatively high. All the people in the control group will be in the lower category of the first variable and all the people in the experimental group will be in the higher category. In this way the first variable is said to have been *manipulated*. Although it is possible to test whether manipulation has actually changed the independent variable, it is usually assumed that the manipulation has been effective.

To examine change in the second variable, both the experimental group and the control group are measured on Y, the dependent variable, or the variable on which the experimental variable is expected to have an impact. The first measurement of Y is called the *pretest*. After the pretest, X is manipulated; that is, set at a low level in the control group and set at a high level in the experimental group. After X has been manipulated and some time passes, Y is again measured. This is called the *posttest*. Comparisons between the pretests and posttests will give an indication of change in the second variable. The timing of the posttest can be quite crucial in this design. Depending on the nature of the variables being studied, the dependent variable may change immediately or may change only after some period of time has elapsed. The simple experimental design is depicted in Figure 9.1.

	Time 1 $\longrightarrow$	Time 2 $\longrightarrow$	Time 3
Experimental group:	Pretest Y	High X	Posttest Y
Control group:	Pretest Y	No X	Posttest Y

FIGURE 9.1
Simple experimental design

Change in X is observed by comparing the value of X in two groups. This procedure will give us a value of X for each person according to group membership. Change in Y is observed by subtracting the pretest value of Y for each person from the posttest value of Y for each person. Each subject will have a "change" score in Y resulting from the difference between the pretest and the posttest. Raw data from an experiment might look something like the data presented in Table 9.1.

TABLE 9.1
Hypothetical data from a simple experiment

Subject I.D. numer	Pretest Y (time 1)	Manipulation of X (time 2)		Posttest Y (time 3)	Change in Y (posttest − pretest)
2234	2	0	*People*	6	+4
1126	3	0	*in the*	5	+2
4434	6	0	*experi-*	6	0
1734	2	0	*mental*	2	0
193	5	0	*group*	5	0
2673	6	0		5	−1
994	2	0		1	−1
805	3	0		1	−2
963	6	0		3	−3
443	0	1	*People*	6	+6
33	2	1	*in the*	8	+6
673	1	1	*control*	6	+5
9548	1	1	*group*	6	+5
3434	2	1		7	+5
8256	4	1		8	+4
371	3	1		7	+4
96	1	1		5	+4
5	2	1		5	+3
1913	3	1		6	+3
326	5	1		5	0
222	5	1		4	−1

These data would indicate that person 2234, referred to as *subject 2234*, is in the control group ($X = 0$) and the difference between 2234's pretest and posttest is +4 (2234 was four points higher in Y at the end of the experiment than at the beginning). Subject 33 is in the experimental group ($X = 1$) and 33's change in Y is +6 (six points higher at the posttest than at the pretest).

Figure 9.2 shows a scatterplot constructed from the raw data given above which is similar to those in Chapter 3. It should be read and interpreted in the same manner as those in Chapter 3: "As X increases what kinds of changes occur in Y?"

The hypothetical example shows data for X changing (from 0 in the control group to 1 in the experimental group) and for Y changing (differences between posttests and pretests). However, rather than simple Y scores, the Y variable is represented by *difference scores* in Y, or changes in Y from pretest to posttest.

In this type of scatterplot an envelope of dots could be determined, the best fitting line could be drawn, and the nature of the relationship between X and Y could be described. The form of this particular example would, of course, be a direct relationship. That is, as X increases Y also increases; or, more precisely, as X increases the changes in Y increase. Estimating the envelope of dots and the best fitting line would give us a scatterplot like the one in Figure 9.3.

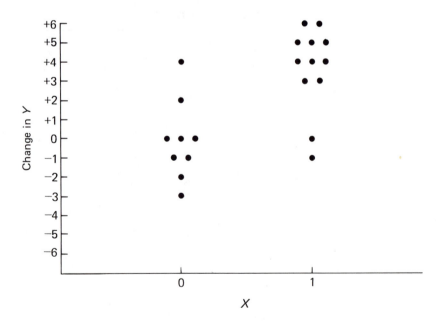

FIGURE 9.2
Hypothetical scatterplot for experiments

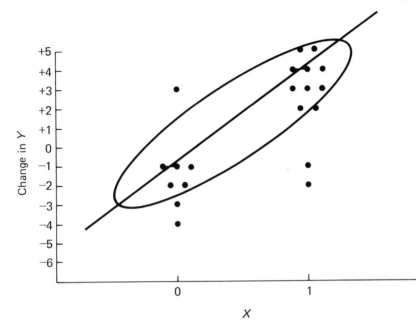

FIGURE 9.3
Completing scatterplot for experimental data

The scatterplot reveals that some of the people in the control group changed with respect to Y even when they were relatively low on X. This happens sometimes just because of the passage of time. The important thing to determine in an experiment is whether or not the people in the experimental group changed differently (on the average) than people in the control group.

When this happens, researchers conclude that a relationship exists between X and Y.

Researchers sometimes draw scatterplots using only mean values of changes in Y. The mean value of the change in Y in the control group of the above example is −.14 and the mean value of the change for the experimental group is +3.67. Constructing a scatterplot using means would yield a scatterplot like the one in Figure 9.4. Of course the conclusions as to the form and extent of the relationship would be consistent with the scatterplot in Figure 9.3.

In any system of variables that researchers want to examine, time order is sometimes difficult to determine. In those cases where experimenters are uncertain about the time order of events in the environment, it would be possible to do two experiments. In one experiment any specific variable may be chosen as the first variable. In another, the order could be reversed. From these experiments,

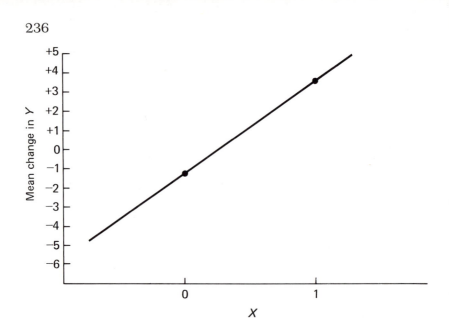

FIGURE 9.4
Scatterplot using the mean change in Y

both time sequences could be explored and reported. Of course in those cases where there is no question of the time order of variables in a system, the time order would be specified by the theory of the system.

By now you may have noticed that there are different people in the experimental group and in the control group. You may have wondered whether the differences in changes in Y between the experimental and control groups may not be due to this fact.

If changes in the dependent variable are partly a result of the fact that the people in the control group are different from the people in the experimental group (aside from the fact that their X values have been manipulated), the relationship described by the scatterplot may be misleading. To make the experimental and control groups as equal or similar as possible on all other variables besides X, experimental design utilizes random assignment or matching.

3. EQUIVALENCY OF EXPERIMENTAL GROUPS

The technique of *randomly assigning* subjects to experimental and control groups is analogous to placing the names of all subjects on slips of paper and putting them into a large bag, vigorously shaking the bag to mix up the slips, and then having a blindfolded assistant reach in and toss the names of people into an experimental pile and a control pile.

Whether a particular person winds up in the control group or experimental group depends solely on the luck of the draw. By using luck, often referred to as probability, random assignment can mix up all characteristics of subjects so that their distributions are usually close to equal in each group. This could create comparable groups.

Another procedure sometimes used to assure that experimental groups are equivalent at the beginning of an experiment is to *match* experimental groups. There are two types of matching—frequency and precision matching. Both types of matching require the experimenter to list the characteristics of subjects that might have an impact on experimental results. The theory behind the experiment should prove helpful in deciding what traits are important. *Frequency matching* is achieved when the distributions of all of the specified characteristics are nearly the same for all experimental groups. Precision matching requires that subjects with similar sets of characteristics are placed in each experimental group. For example, if the characteristics specified were sex, race, and intelligence, frequency matching would require the same percentage of males, the same percentage of blacks (assuming blacks and whites were involved), and the same proportion of people with high intelligence to be in each group. However, in precision matching if there was a male, white, low intelligence subject in the control group, a similar subject would be needed in the experimental group. Random assignment is more often used in experiments than is matching.

The difference between experimental and control groups may always be due to either different values of X between the groups, or the possibility that subjects in both groups are not similar. Sometimes, even with randomization, groups are not made exactly equal. Chapter 16 explores a procedure that experimenters use to determine the odds that randomization has produced similar groups. At this point it is sufficient to understand that random assignment or matching does not *guarantee* that the subjects in the control and experimental group will be similar. The randomization process only gives us better odds that there is no interference from characteristics of the subjects. It is always possible that the difference in the amount of change in Y scores is due to chances of the draw in random assignment. However, by means of statistics, it is possible to make the odds very small that differences will be due to chance. However, since we can never completely eliminate this problem, we can never know for certain that changes in X have *produced* changes in Y. One way researchers can have more confidence in their tentative decisions is to conduct research over and over, or *replicate* their studies. If the results come out the same each time, they have more confidence that the results observed are not due to the accident of assignment of different kinds of people to each group.

We can now completely diagram the classical experimental design as follows:

	Experimental group:	Pretest Y	High X	Posttest Y
Random assignment				
	Control group:	Pretest Y	No X	Posttest Y

An actual example of a classical experiment can be seen in a research study conducted by Edsel Erickson *et al* (1969). The experiment involved "disadvantaged" young children from the inner city. Part of the research consisted of an experiment in adding special verbal-skill training to a regular kindergarten situation. The experiment focused on any changes in measured intelligence that might occur during the kindergarten experience. Some children were assigned to regular kindergarten and some were assigned to kindergartens in which special verbal skills were taught. In other words, the teaching of verbal skills was the experimental or independent variable. Measured intelligence, determined at the pretest and posttest by use of the Stanford-Binet intelligence test, was the dependent variable. The experimental group consisted of all the children who were given special verbal skills training, and the control group were those children who received no special training.

This particular experiment revealed that the average IQ of the children enrolled in regular kindergartens dropped 3.3 points. The average score of the children in the experimental group where verbal skills were taught increased by 10.1 points. Figure 9.5 represents this difference in the change of mean IQ between the experimental group and the control group.

One can easily see from the experimental results that there is a direct relationship between special training in verbal skills and increases in measured intelligence. This is but one example of the types of experimental findings which prove to be most useful to research scientists.

In order to appreciate why experiments are considered the ideal way of collecting data for finding relationships, it would be valuable to have the perspective of some typical nonexperimental or quasi-

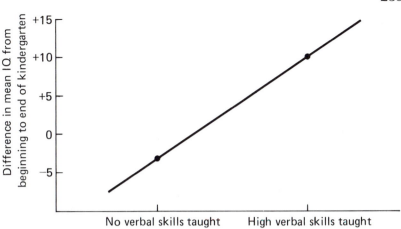

FIGURE 9.5
Actual experimental results

experimental designs. These designs include: the common-sense experiment; the before-after, or one-group pretest-posttest design; the simple survey, or static-group comparison; and the one-shot case study.

4. THE COMMON SENSE "EXPERIMENT"

The following diagram of the common sense experiment looks very similar to that of the classical experiment:

Pretest	X, Z, W, A, B, C	Posttest
Pretest	No: X, Z, W, A, B, C	Posttest

There is a quasiexperimental group which receives a pretest, an experimental treatment, and a posttest. There is also a quasicontrol group which is given a pretest and posttest. Often the pretest and posttest are not as formal as in typical scientific research, but this is not the major problem. Even if this study were conducted like an experiment, the researcher could draw no conclusion about the nature of the relationship between two variables.

Rather than manipulating one variable (X), the researcher has manipulated a large number of variables. An example of this "common sense" experiment would be a student who decides to improve her dating situation by creating a whole new image. She diets (X), buys a new wardrobe (W), changes her hairstyle (Z) and color of hair (A), hangs out with a different group (B), and improves her posture (C). If her dating patterns, as measured by pretest and posttest, change, she cannot clearly relate the change to any specific variable or combination of variables. She may erroneously conclude that the whole batch of changes were necessary when this may not have been the case. She may have been able to get more dates just by dieting.

The dotted line in the diagram separating the quasiexperimental group from the quasicontrol group represents the fact that the two groups may not be equal. No random assignment was used to establish them, and measurement may not occur at the same time. A true experiment involves studying the groups during the same time period.

5. THE ONE-GROUP PRETEST-POSTTEST DESIGN

This design looks like its name:

Pretest   High X   Posttest
on Y   on Y

The problem with this design is that any change in Y must be attributed to the presence of X. However, since there is no equivalent group in which X does not occur, the researcher cannot determine if Y would have changed even if X had not been there. Since this is the case, there is no way to tell whether or not there really is a relationship between X and Y.

An example of this type of study could be as follows: Suppose the director of a teenage recreation center wanted attendance at events to increase. To accomplish this increase a decision was made to install a juke box in the center. If attendance improved (change in the dependent variable), it might be attributed to installing a juke box (the manipulation). The problem is that attendance may have increased anyway, even if the music system were not installed. Perhaps one of the teenagers' favorite hangouts was closed about the same time as installation of the juke box.

6. THE SIMPLE SURVEY OR STATIC-GROUP COMPARISON

This design is labeled "static" because there is no assessment of change; only a posttest is employed.

High X	Posttest on Y
------	-------------
No X	Posttest on Y

Here all subjects are chosen from a larger population. After they have been selected, they are separated into the two groups, depending on their value of X. Natural occurring events, not randomization, determine the subject's score on X. Thus the characteristics of the group who received X may be different from the group who have not received X. Although surveys usually collect data on more than two variables, basically the static-group comparison is nevertheless a fair representation for any two variables in a survey.

There are two major problems with the statistic comparison. The first is that change is not viewed directly. There is no pretest measure so we cannot tell if there has been a change in Y. Furthermore, rather than seeing whether there is a *change* in Y over time, only differences between the two posttests in the quasiexperimental and quasicontrol groups can be used. The second problem arises because there is no random assignment. There is no way to get an estimate of the odds that the groups are similar. Therefore any observed differences may be a product of nonsimilar groups rather than a product of differences in X.

7. THE ONE-SHOT CASE STUDY:

The case study is the simplest design of all:

High X	Posttest on Y

There is only one group. It is measured only after X has occurred. Since there is no pretest and no control group, any comparison between groups must be made on the basis of guesses about what a group without having received X would be like. Researchers do not agree about the value of collecting data in a case study to try to assess the impact of an event. We feel that such efforts are not entirely wasted if the investigator can be fairly certain about the nature of conditions on Y prior to the occurrence of X.

This knowledge of conditions prior to the event may come from knowledgeable and reliable observers who knew about the group being studied prior to the event X. Case study investigators often refer to self-reports from the subjects about their condition on Y prior to X; diaries or other documents such as school files; or reports of other observers such as parents, spouses, friends, neighbors, or teachers. To the extent that this information is valid and reliable, the case study resembles the one-group pretest-posttest design and may thus more closely resemble a "true" experiment.

We have shown that both the common sense "experiment" and the case study provide inadequate information for making a comparison. The other two designs, the one-group pretest-posttest and the simple survey, provide adequate information for making a comparison of Y scores for no X and high X, but they do not take care of some of the unseen variables for which the experiment is designed to control.

The strength of the experiment lies in its ability to produce results which ensure that several unseen variables are not distorting the picture of the relationship observed in the experimental study. When these unseen variables may be operating and distorting the picture of the relationship, the relationship is said to be *confounded*. Correspondingly, the unseen variables are called *confounding variables*. The process of removing confounding influences when examining a relationship is known as *controlling*. There are three methods of controlling commonly employed in research: design, matching, and statistical. We shall treat design and matching in this chapter. Control by statistics will be treated in Chapter 11.

8. SOURCES OF CONFOUNDING INFLUENCES

If data are not collected or analyzed properly, it is possible to have an inaccurate picture of the relationship. We shall classify the major types of conditions which may create distortion and discuss how the experiment is designed to eliminate the influence of such confounding variables. These sources of confounding influence include: *differences in subject characteristics* between comparison groups; history or *environmental changes* simultaneous with changes in X; *maturation* or personal changes; *testing* or giving a pretest; *instrument decay; subject mortality* or differential subject loss between comparison groups; *unreliable measurement* of extreme subjects; *reactivity;* and *experimenter bias.* Controlling sources of confounding is also referred to as internal validity. *Internal validity exists* (ideally) *when none of the sources of confounding have had an effect on the experiment.* Note that this is quite a different use of the term validity than is applied to the validity of indicators and operational definitions. The following material on confounding borrows heavily from the modern "bible" on experimental design: Donald T. Campbell and Julian C. Stanley, *Experimental and Quasi-Experimental Designs for Research,* Chicago, Rand-McNally, 1963. Campbell and Stanley also mention confounding produced by combinations of these sources of confounding.

Differences in subject characteristics

The experimental design controls for differences in subject characteristics between the experimental and control groups by use of random assignment. By randomizing, subjects are mixed up so that the groups are as equal as possible on Y and on all characteristics which could conceivably change Y scores. If this is not done, the comparison between experimental and control group results could not only be influenced by X versus no X, but also by differences in other variables. We have discussed this process above.

You might ask why randomization is used to make groups equal when it is not guaranteed that after random assignment the groups will in fact be equal on all characteristics. Why not make the groups equal on other characteristics by measuring these characteristics and matching subjects so that the groups are for certain equal on these characteristics? Matching is insufficient because there is always the possibility that the researcher will fail to anticipate and match for the most important variables. Thus, random assignment is always necessary to control for possible confounding variables among subject characteristics.

In some quasiexperimental studies differences in subject characteristics are also controlled. For example, in the one-group pretest-posttest design subject characteristics are controlled, or made equal, because there is only one group. Characteristics of subjects are *not* controlled in the survey. Therefore it is always possible that different Y scores in the comparison groups are due to subject characteristics.

Environmental changes

Environmental changes refer to events in the subject's experience which occur between the pretest and the posttest other than the experimental variable (X). In a nonexperimental situation, in addition to changes in X, several other variables may be changing. In the one-group pretest-posttest design, for example, lots of other events may occur between the pretest and the posttest. If other things happen, the variable which really produced changes in Y scores may be one of these other events rather than X. For example, suppose a study were attempting to relate the effects of a television discussion about the President and attitudes toward his handling of some war. If a peace negotiations announcement occurred between the television program and the posttest of attitudes, this announcement, rather than the television program, may have altered people's feelings toward the President. The one-group pretest-posttest design cannot show which variable is related to Y (attitudes). Thus the *external* event (the news about the peace negotiations) was confounded with the *experimental* event (the television program about the President). It is not always possible to put people in an isolated setting where events other than the experimental event will not happen to them.

In the classical experimental design, changes in Y scores for *both* the experimental group and the control group are studied. For both groups, external events may be changing Y scores. However, in the experimental group X *occurs in addition to external events.* In the control group it does not. Both groups are equally exposed to external events. Thus any differences in the two groups must be due to the fact that the experimental group received X and the control group did not.

Maturation

Maturation involves personal changes which take place within the subject between the pretest and the posttest that are not related to X or environmental changes. These changes include all things that would occur over time such as growing hungrier, more tired, more bored, older, and so on. In the case study, the one-group pretest-posttest design, and the survey, we have no way of assessing the degree to which these variables may be influencing Y scores. In the case study and one-group pretest-posttest, all individuals receive X and may also "mature" in various ways. In the survey we have no way of knowing whether those selected with X may have chosen X because of some maturation factor. Maybe having received X had nothing to do with their different Y scores.

In the classical experiment there are two groups (experimental and control) which are equalized as well as possible by chance (random assignment). These two equalized groups should grow tired, hungry, bored, and so on, at equal rates. Both groups may change in Y scores because they have matured. However, the change in Y scores due to maturation should be the same for each group. Thus, any difference in change scores can be attributed to the fact that only one group received X.

Testing

The process of pretesting may alter Y scores in the posttest. That is, Y scores may be higher or lower following a pretest than if no pretest were given. Thus, in the case of the one-group pretest-posttest design, the reason for changes in Y scores between the pretest and posttest might be partially due to giving a pretest as well as due to the presence of X. The pretest is especially likely to be related to Y in instances where the measure of Y involves performance for which practice will improve scores. Giving the pretest provides the opportunity for practice. It is also possible that the pretest will influence Y scores if the pretest may make the person more tired, bored, anxious, or decrease the posttest score in some fashion. Hence the pretest influence is confounded with X in designs where a pretest is given and no comparison groups are used.

In the classical experimental design, since both groups receive the pretest, the influence of the pretest on the Y scores (in the posttest) is equal for both the experimental and control groups. Thus, as we have reasoned for environmental changes and maturation, the only difference in change scores for Y should be due to the presence of X in the experimental group.

Instrument decay

Posttest measures may appear to change or be different from those of the pretest because the measuring instrument may change, over time, in the way it measures Y. Consider, for example, using a tape measure to check your waist size as you diet. If the tape is made of stretchable material, what happens? Your 40-inch waist may measure 36 inches not because your waist is smaller, but because your tape has stretched. A new tape would still show your waist at 40 inches.

A similar phenomenon occurs sometimes to human observers when the observer is used as a measuring instrument. For example, teachers giving essay examinations may change their criteria as they read several examinations; judges in a school art contest may change their assessment of good work after they see several works. In a similar manner, interviewers may ask questions differently after they have interviewed for some time.

A properly conducted classical experiment should control for instrument decay. Changes in instrumentation should occur equally for both the experimental and control groups and, hence, not be related to changes in Y scores. However, a note of caution is in order. If all of the experimental group is measured in the posttest before all of the control group, it is possible that the instrument (such as observation) may "decay" for the control group. Hence the experimenter should alternate the timing of measuring Y in the experimental and control groups.

Subject mortality

Mortality involves subjects "dying out" of the study. Subjects may be lost to the study due to death, moving, quitting during the experiment, failing to return at some later date for a posttest, or becoming ill. In a one-group pretest-posttest design the apparent change in Y scores from pretest to posttest may be due to loss of subjects. For example, if subjects with higher than average scores in some skills drop out of an "experimental" training program, the average for the group skill measure would be reduced. Thus, it is likely that the Y (skill) scores will appear to have been reduced. Mortality can also be a problem in a survey. People who have received X may be more interested in it and more likely to return a questionnaire talking about it than people with no experience with it. This might make the characteristics of those returning the questionnaire in the quasi-experimental and quasicontrol groups different.

If the same number of people are lost to the experimental and the control groups, experimenters assume that they may be safe in concluding that mortality is not a confounding variable. Actually, they should (and often do) check to see if the characteristics of the people lost to both the experimental and control groups are the same. Then it is safer to assume that the effect of mortality is not confounded with X. Experimental design is not a perfect control for mortality. Even if subjects lost to experimental and control groups look equal on the measured characteristics, there is no way to be sure that they are not different on some unmeasured ones.

Unreliable measures of extreme groups

One potential problem in the pretest-posttest design stems from the occasional practice of choosing to study only subjects who have extreme values of the Y variable (those in the highest or lowest category on the particular scale of measurement used). Because of possible mistakes in measurement, subjects from a nearby category may be chosen as part of the extreme group in the pretest. When measured the second time in the posttest, these subjects may be measured correctly. This would make their scores seem less extreme or closer to the mean on Y. Thus the whole group's average score in the posttest would be closer to the mean. Since the posttest score in the pretest-posttest design is compared to the pretest score, it would appear that the value of Y for the group has changed. This apparent change is really due to mistakenly placing some people in extreme groups on the pretest measure and then measuring them correctly on the posttest.

The classical experimental design can control for the confounding influence of extreme groups, yet still study extreme groups. Since both treatment groups could be extreme, any apparent changes in Y due to some degree of measurement error ought to be the same in both groups. Thus differences in changes in Y scores could not be due to unreliable measurement.

Reactivity

Reactivity refers to the problem arising when subjects become aware that they are involved in an experiment and because of this awareness "react" differently than they would have if they were not participating in a research study. This reaction is sometimes called the *Hawthorne effect,* named after the group of experiments where the discovery of this syndrome was first formalized. The only real defense against reactivity in experiments is to conduct "debriefing" interviews of subjects after an experiment. Through these interviews the researchers may be able to determine if the subjects reacted to the experiment. If it appears that reactivity raises questions about the experiment, it may be wise to disregard such findings.

Experimenter bias

Experimenter bias occurs when the experimenter inappropriately influences the subjects' behavior. It also occurs if the experimenter makes a "mistake" while observing or recording an experiment. Bias may result from the experimenter's knowledge of the hypothesis and knowledge of which group (experimental or control) each subject is in. If the experimenter "expects" subjects to behave differently in each group, this may lead to transmitting subtle cues to subjects. Such cues may be differences in voice tone, eye contact, or posture that may be intentionally or unintentionally transmitted. When experimenters make errors in observing, recording, or interpreting data, the errors usually support the experimenter's hypothesis (Rosenthal, 1966). Thus, such errors are considered to be bias.

There are several techniques commonly used to minimize experimenter bias. (1) People who give instructions or actually make observations in the study are not informed about the hypothesis being tested. (2) These same people also are not told which group a subject is in. A common expression for these two techniques is that those conducting the experiment should be "blind" to the hypothesis and/or manipulations. (3) Automated devices should be used whenever possible, for example, videotapes, data recorders, and so on.

Apart from these considerations of sources of confounding, it is important to ask the extent to which experimental results apply to other settings and subjects. This is the question of generalization.

9. GENERALIZATION

Through random assignment and the presence of a control group, experiments deal with many sources of confounding. By doing so we can be confident that in a particular experiment, X is really related to Y. *But a single experiment may not produce much valuable general knowledge* to aid in scientific progress. This is because the classical experiment is designed to assure the investigator that what is observed about the X-Y relationship is as free of confounding influence as possible. The experiment is not designed to demonstrate that the concepts which X and Y reflect will have that same relationship for all subjects in all circumstances. Being able to say that experimental results will hold true for other subjects, measures, circumstances, and the like is a problem of generalization. *Generalization* involves extending a particular set of results to a class of similar phenomena. Generalization involves being able to suggest that what occurs in the experiment reflects the way the concepts X and Y are related in all circumstances. The term *external validity* is sometimes used synonymously with generalization when discussing experimental results. Again, this is quite different from our previous use of the term "validity."

Prior to discussing generalization, the experimenter must have confidence that the observations made in the experiment are accurate. This is essentially the problem of attempting to control for confounding. If one has no confidence in the results of a particular experiment because of possible confounding influences, one could not have any confidence that the results might extend or generalize to similar situations. Thus, in order to be able to generalize, it is first necessary to control for confounding influences. If this is done, the issue of generalization can be confronted.

The issue of generalization is largely an issue of representativeness. Do the arrangements of a particular experiment represent the class of events to which the investigator would like to extend the study? Problems of representativeness can be classified into five different types:

1. Do the *subjects* or *cases* in the study represent all the subjects in which the experimenter is interested?
2. Is the *setting* under which the experiment takes place representative of all settings in which the experimenter is interested?
3. Are the *manipulations* and *measures* of X and Y representative of all measures for the concepts X and Y?
4. Does the *timing* of the measurement of Y represent all the observations of Y in which the experimenter is interested?
5. Do all the other *unique circumstances* under which the study is conducted represent all the circumstances under which the experimenter would like the results to apply?

A discussion of each of these problems is presented in this section. Procedures that experimenters have developed for dealing with each problem will also be presented. Often these procedures will involve a departure from the classical experimental design to a more sophisticated one.

Subjects

Experiments are designed to ensure that characteristics of the subjects in the experiment are mixed up as equally as possible into the experimental and control groups. The experimental group is as much like the control group as possible. However, there is no necessary arrangement to see that subjects in the experimental and control groups are like subjects in general. Social psychologists who have critiqued their own experimental work during the 1960s have become increasingly aware of this limitation in their studies. They were conducted mainly on middle class, white, college underclass volunteers. The 1970s and 1980s should see increasingly more creative experiments conducted outside of university populations.

To be able to generalize to all kinds of subjects from an experiment, all kinds of subjects must be included in the experiment. As Chapter 15 will show, the simplest way to do this would be either to experiment on an entire population (which is typically too costly) or to include in the experiment those who are selected from a population solely by chance. In the *random assignment* procedure, the subjects are selected from anywhere. There is no guarantee that they are in any way representative of any particular group. Yet this process is important. It allows the experimenter to know that the results are not confounded by subject characteristics. The experimenter can trust the experimental results but cannot be certain about the groups of subjects to which the results might generalize.

To be able to specify the groups (populations) to which experimental results might generalize, the experimenter must *randomly select* subjects from all people in those populations. Experiments are rarely conducted in this fashion. This is probably not because of the difficulties involved but because it is a matter of convention. The problems of sampling will be fully discussed in Chapter 15.

Setting

The choice of a setting also presents dilemmas for the experimenter. Should the experiment be conducted in the "real" world, a world other than a laboratory setting, or should the experiment be conducted in the "artificial" world of the experimental laboratory? If the experiment is conducted in the "real" world (often called field experiments), several other variables may be changing at the same time X changes. If the experiment is conducted in the "laboratory," it may be possible to artificially create a setting whereby other variables are controlled by not being allowed to change. Experimenting in a laboratory allows the X-Y relationship to be "purified." X may have a special relationship to Y when combined with changes in other variables which it does not have all by itself. If this is the case, it might be advisable to study the relationship between X and Y as X changes by itself. The laboratory makes it possible to reduce changes in several other variables. However, it is also possible that the laboratory itself may make a difference in the X-Y relationship. X may be related to Y in a special way just because the study is conducted in an "artificial" setting.

The resolution of this dilemma is indeed a difficult one. Researchers have not resolved the question as to whether or not experiments are best done in controlled laboratory settings or in natural field conditions. Therefore, at this point, it would be advisable to conduct experiments in both settings to determine if different conclusions are reached merely on the basis of setting.

Problems of generalization from one setting to another are not limited to differences between field or laboratory. Several other aspects of the setting may limit generalization. The style and social characteristics of the experimenter are also part of the "setting." When this aspect of the setting partially determines the outcome of an experiment, the consequences are called *experimenter effects*. For example, a business-like experimenter may restrict possible emotional reactions in an experiment more than a casual experimenter (Adair, 1973). Other social characteristics may also influence results. These include age, sex, race, dress, and so on.

Experimenter effects are different than experimenter bias because experimenter effects have equal influence on both the experimental and control groups, whereas experimenter bias has an unequal impact. Experimenter effects will "cancel out" and allow one to reach accurate conclusions in one experiment. However the results may not generalize when other experimenters follow the same research design and procedures. Experimenter bias does not cancel out. Indeed, if experimenter bias is present the results of the particular experiment are not accurate.

One solution to this possible limitation in generalization is to employ several experimenters. Studies should be replicated with different experimenters, or the same study should use more than a single experimenter in each group.

Manipulations and measures

One of the most important aspects of generalizing the classical experimental results to the "real" world involves the giving of a pretest of Y. In the real world this kind of an intrusion would be noticed and it might have an impact on the subject's behavior. For example, if we were concerned with an experimental weight reduction program, weighing each subject prior to the experiment may have an impact merely because the subjects then would have knowledge which they might not have otherwise held. In another experiment, if the effects of a movie on prejudice was being studied, a questionnaire on attitudes might change the impact of the movie if it were given prior to viewing the movie.

In order to alleviate this problem experimenters developed an alternative experimental design, called the *posttest-only design*. As its name might suggest, it differs from the classical design in that the measure of Y is conducted only after the manipulation of X. In other words, for both the experimental and control groups, *there is no pretest*. Experimental and control groups are considered to be similar because the subjects in each group were chosen by random assignment. Differences in Y scores between the experimental and control groups can be considered to be related to whether or not the group received X, as in the case of the classical experimental design. However, in the posttest-only design, rather than different scores representing posttest minus pretest, the scores on Y come only from the posttest. Since the experimental and control groups are randomly assigned, any differences in such confounding influences as environmental changes, maturation, or mortality will be randomly mixed among both groups. Thus, differences in posttest Y scores should only be due to the fact that one group received X and the other did not.

The posttest-only design may be diagrammed as follows:

Randomization

Experimental group: No pretest X   Posttest Y

Control group: No pretest   Posttest Y

The posttest-only design might answer questions concerning the nature of the X-Y relationship for cases where Y is not pretested, but it does not allow the experimenter to directly view changes in Y as the classical experimental design does. Some experimenters like to get more complex and ask the question, "will the X-Y relationship look the same for experimental groups where there is a pretest as for groups where no pretest is present?" To answer this question, it would be necessary to conduct an experiment where one experimental and control group received a pretest and a second set of experimental and control groups did not. This results in four groups. The man who first received credit for suggesting such an experimental design was Richard L. Solomon. Hence, the name of the design is the *Solomon four-group design*. It can be diagrammed as in Figure 9.6.

The Solomon four-group design is a combination of the classical experimental design and the posttest-only design. It is used to determine whether the X-Y relationship is the same when there *is* a pre-

Experimental group A:	Pretest	X	Posttest
Control group A:	Pretest		Posttest
Random → Experimental group B:	No pretest	X	Posttest
assignment			
Control group B:	No pretest		Posttest

FIGURE 9.6
Solomon four-group design

test as when there *is not* a pretest. To determine whether the relationship is the same, two scatterplots can be compared, one for groups with a pretest, and one for groups without a pretest. Usually if the slopes (extent) are the same in each table, the relationships would be considered the same. That is, the relationship would not be complicated by the pretest.

Another way in which generalization from an experiment may be limited involves the choice of indicators for X and Y. There are two basic problems for generalization that might occur if the classical experimental design is employed. The first involves the number of experimental groups with different amounts of X. The classical experimental design involves an experimental group in which X is relatively high and a control group in which X is relatively low. Thus only two points on the scatterplot are represented. In constructing a scatterplot with only two categories of X difficulties often arise. Having only two categories of X may lead to mistakes in assessing the relationship between X and Y.

Suppose that the real relationship between X and Y is nonlinear whose scatterplot looks something like Figure 9.7.

An error might be made if, in constructing a classical experimental design, the control group was equivalent to an anxiety score of 1 and the experimental group was equivalent to an anxiety score of 5. The scatterplot in Figure 9.8 would result.

One can easily see that the conclusion as to the *form* of the relationship between anxiety and performance would be different, depending on which scatterplot was examined. Since the classical design offers only two levels of X to be examined, an alternative design for constructing a more complete scatterplot has been devised.

To eliminate this possible misinterpretation of the actual X-Y relationship, experimenters have extended the logic of the classical experimental design to include several experimental groups. These groups are each given different degrees or levels of X. This allows the experimenter to provide data which more closely approximates the full scatterplot where every value of X is represented. An experi-

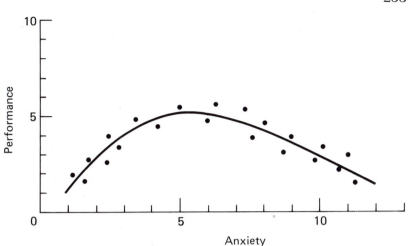

FIGURE 9.7
Actual plot of anxiety and performance

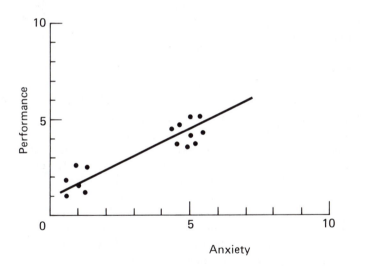

FIGURE 9.8
Experimental plot of anxiety and performance

ment with several levels of X is sometimes called a *multiple-X de-sign.*

Usually multiple-X designs involve three or more levels of X. This may involve two groups with some degree of X and one control group with no X, or this may involve three groups each with differ-ent amounts of X, but none with no X. Multiple-X designs extend the generality of the study by demonstrating that the relationship between X and Y holds for more than one degree or value of X.

An additional consideration in generalizing experimental results has to do with varying the indicators of Y and the manipulations of X. The relationship the experimenter is really interested in involves the *concepts* X and Y.

In order to have confidence that experiments have provided correct information about the concepts, it is necessary to use alternative manipulations and measures. Experiments could be devised so that X would be manipulated differently in different experimental groups. For example, an experimenter examining the effects of a behavior model on the child's performance may use several types of models: a film model, a real life model, an overheard story about someone else, and so on. Each of these can be compared with the control group where no model is used. If modeling behavior is the same in each experiment, we would have more faith in our findings. Unfortunately, this procedure is seldom used.

It is also possible to run a series of experiments where different measurement devices are used to observe Y. It is perhaps more typical to observe Y in several different ways within the same experiment. If results are consistent when different procedures are used, we could increase our confidence even more.

Timing of events

Experiments in the social sciences are usually conducted over very short periods of time. Thus shortly after subjects receive X they are observed or tested or measured on Y. For situations where the change in X is associated with an immediate change in Y, it is possible to generalize from such experimental procedure. But sometimes the relationship between X and Y is not so immediate. After X changes it may take time for Y to change. For example, after an oral reading program is instituted, it takes time to observe a change in reading skills in general. After a diet is started, it takes time to observe a change in belly size. Students of attitude change have often noted a "sleeper" effect, whereby there is no relationship between the message and an attitude change immediately after a message is communicated, but weeks later a change has occurred.

To be able to generalize experiments in which timing may be an important factor, it is necessary to design experiments in such a way that the posttest be given at various intervals after the manipulation of X. If an experiment does not deal with the long-range effects of the experimental variable, then the critic of the experiment could always suggest that the real relationship between X and Y can only be determined after a longer period of time has elapsed.

Unique circumstances

Another sense in which the classical experimental design may not be representative of "reality" is that in an experiment the subject is usually exposed to the experimental treatment, X, only once. In many real life situations people are often changed only after repeated exposure to a variable. Thus several experimental designs have modified the classical experimental design and added repeated exposure to the experimental treatment.

10. EXPERIMENTS: A BRIEF ASSESSMENT

Experimental designs are good data collection strategies which help assure that confounding or unseen variables have not crept in, resulting in distorted research. They are also compelling to researchers because they allow the researcher to present X to a randomly assigned group and actually observe change. Experimentation may also be economical when conducted with relatively few subjects over a relatively short time. Students should not be misled by "false economy," however. They often get the idea that experiments are relatively easy to conduct because they look so simple. Actually, researchers who conduct experiments would spend approximately the same amount of time supervising an experiment as they might supervising the average survey.

A major shortcoming of experimental design is a consequence of the nature of randomization. In some fashion subjects must be randomly assigned to treatment groups. There is no way to guarantee that the randomizing process has created groups equivalent on all relevant unseen variables. Thus there is no way to guarantee that differences are due exclusively to differences in X. This weakness is a limitation of probability, not experimentation.

The major weakness of experiments derives from the inability of experimental design *per se* to guarantee that one can generalize from the experiment. Subjects need not be randomly selected from a larger population. Thus what goes on in an experiment may be free from the disturbance of unseen variables but results may *only* be accurate for the particular subjects selected to participate in the experiment. Situations are in no way randomly selected. All subjects in an experiment enter into the same situation. Therefore, all the experimenter can say for certain is that the results may hold for that situation. In addition, experiments usually are conducted in a brief time period which may not be analogous to that of the "real" world.

All of these difficulties are surmountable with the use of random selection of subjects, combined with replication of experiments in different settings and with different manipulations and measures, employed over different time periods. Thus, as scientists continue to do research on the same topic the experimental design may become the *grand master*.

11. SUMMARY

The classical experimental design is considered the grand master of research designs because it allows researchers to make observations which are useful for causal analysis in a relatively simple way. The classical design uses two randomly assigned groups which receive different degrees of the independent variable. By comparing the magnitude of the changes in the dependent variable between these two groups, a decision about the X-Y relationship can be made. Scatterplots can be used to plot the data from experiments in a manner similar to that discussed in the last chapter. Random assignment, or matching, is used to insure that any differences between the control group and experimental group are solely a result of the manipulation of X and not a product of the characteristics of the subjects. In addition to the classical design, there are many experimental and quasiexperimental designs that can be utilized in research. The common sense experiment uses a pretest and posttest but many variables are different from one group of observations to another. The before-after design is useful when one group can be examined before an event occurs and after an event occurs. The simple survey is similar to the classical design but random assignment is not used and only a posttest is given to subjects. The one-shot case study is convenient for situations where no control group is possible and no pretest can be given.

No matter which design is utilized, sources of confounding must be taken into account when reaching conclusions with experiments. Differences in subject characteristics, environmental changes, maturation, testing, instrument decay, subject mortality, unreliable measurement of extreme subjects, reactivity, and experimenter bias can all potentially impair the internal validity of experiments. Each design can be assessed according to how adequately each source of confounding is handled. Even if confounding does not influence the results of an experiment, one must also be concerned about generalizing results.

It is highly desirable to be able to extend research findings beyond particular subjects and particular times. The issue of external validity centers around whether results will pertain to other subjects, settings, manipulations and measures, time sequences, and circumstances. Random selection of subjects with the replication of experiments in alternative settings and circumstances will do much for the generalizability of findings. In addition, different manipulations and measures should not affect results, nor should different time sequences of measurement.

Some of the inherent problems of the classical experimental design can be overcome by using more sophisticated designs. The multiple-X design allows the investigator to view changes in X over a large range of values. The Solomon four-group design can be used to determine if a pretest is having an effect on subjects. All in all, experimental methods are very compelling if confounding can be controlled and generalization of results is possible. However, even when designs adequately deal with the issues of internal and external validity, they still yield probabilistic statements. It is only through replication that increased confidence can be placed in general conclusions.

1. Using your class for pilot studies (a) design and, if the students and instructor agree, (b) conduct simple experiments to examine the following:

the effect of leader versus no leader on group problem solving for various tasks

the effect of working individually versus working as a group for constructing anagrams (other words) out of the word "superstitions"

the effect of audience versus no audience on the time and accuracy of solving math problems

2. List five sources of confounding influence and explain the function of a control group in controlling for each.

3. Several experimental settings and techniques have been established in psychology and sociology to study conformity. Using the *Psychological Abstracts*, locate articles describing three different manipulations or measures of conformity. Find the descriptions in the original articles. Then assess which technique would have the greatest generalization (external validity) and state why you think so.

4. Design an experiment to study the effectiveness of a review session before your next quiz in your methods course. How has your design controlled for each of the sources of confounding influence? Why might your study be limited in external validity?

EXERCISES

1. Select an hypothesis from your list in Chapter 5 which is suitable for experimental study.

2. Describe a design suitable for examining this hypothesis and state why the design is suitable.

3. Describe how you would manipulate the independent variable and measure the dependent variable. Then assess how well each procedure should generalize. Indicate how generalization of manipulation and measurement is related to validity, as indicated in Chapter 2.

4. Describe a realistic plan to recruit subjects (your classmates, friends, volunteers, and so on). Assess the effects of this recruitment procedure on internal and external validity.

5. Experimenters call the detailed plan and description of taking a subject through the experiment from the time the subject arrives to the time the experiment is completed the *procedure*. It includes a detailed set of instructions for subjects in experimental and control conditions. Create the *procedure* for your experiment.

6. The subject is entitled to some explanation of your experiment and its purpose. This is called *debriefing* (see Chapter 6). What to include in debriefing may become a dilemma in instances (1) where full knowledge of the experiment could alter a subject's perceptions and performance, and (2) when subjects who complete the study may share such information with future subjects. Thus you should consider carefully what to include in your debriefing. Write a potential description of what to say in your debriefing.

7. Consult with your instructor about whether your study is:
   a. adequately designed
   b. feasible
   c. ethical

8. If your instructor approves and requires, conduct a "trial run" of your experiment. Keep a diary of unanticipated problems and changes which you would need to make to successfully complete your experiment after the trial run. Consider such questions as:

   Were your instructions clear and understandable?
   Did your subjects interpret your manipulation as you intended?
   Did the subjects read cues from you, as experimenter, which were unintended?
   Did subjects misinterpret the purpose of the study and act accordingly?

ADAIR, J. *The Human Subject: The Social Psychology of the Psychological Experiment.* Boston: Little, Brown, 1973.

ANDERSON, B. *The Psychology Experiment.* Belmont, Calif.: Brooks/Cole, 1971.

CAMPBELL, D., and STANLEY J. *Experimental and Quasi-experimental Designs for Research.* Chicago: Rand McNally, 1966.

ERICKSON, E. *et al. Final Report: Experiments in Head Start and Early Education: Curriculum Structures and Teacher Attitudes.* (Contract No. OEO-4150). Washington, D.C.: United States Office of Economic Opportunity, November 1969.

JUNG, J. (ED.). *The Experimenter's Dilemma.* New York: Harper & Row, 1971.

ROSENTHAL, R. *Experimenter Effects in Behavioral Research.* New York: Appleton-Century-Crofts, 1966.

WUEBBEN, P., STRAITS, B., and SCHULMAN, G. *The Experiment as a Social Occasion.* Berkeley, Calif.: Glendessary Press, 1974.

CHAPTER 10
THE OMNIPRESENT SURVEY

After studying this chapter, students should be able to:

1. Define what is meant by a survey.

2. List and discuss each of the steps of the survey design.

3. Describe what a descriptive study is.

4. Discuss and differentiate between research populations and samples.

5. Describe and do simple coding operations.

6. Develop questions for surveys which are free of the errors enumerated in this chapter.

7. Evaluate questions in terms of how bias free they are.

8. Describe and construct response categories that are mutually inclusive and mutually exclusive.

9. Discuss the importance of residual categories.

10. Describe and discuss the uses of open-ended and fixed alternative questions.

11. Discuss the issues surrounding nonresponse rates.

12. Discuss the issues and procedures of face-to-face interviews, including interview do's and don'ts.

13. Describe, differentiate, and discuss the differences between structured, semistructured, and unstructured interviews.

14. Compare mailed questionnaires and face-to-face interviews.

Coding   The process of changing answers into usable data.

Data reduction   Translating answers into numbers or other forms for analysis.

Descriptive studies   Research which does not set out with the idea of testing hypotheses about relationships, but wants to find distributions of variables.

Double-barreled question   Questions that really ask two questions or presume some fact or opinion upon which to base the question.

Fixed alternative question   Type of question where the subject has a set of answers from which to choose.

Follow-up   Additional requests of respondents to fill out and return questionnaires and/or participate in interviews.

Interviewer bias   The possible problem of respondents answering questions because of something about the interviewer instead of responding accurately to the questions.

Mutually exclusive   Having only one possible response for each subject when asking a fixed alternative question.

Mutually inclusive   Exhaustive responses such that each subject is provided with a response in fixed alternative questions.

Nonresponse rate   The proportion of the original sample from which data were not collected.

Open-ended question   Type of question that does not have particular answers that the subject can select.

Pilot study   A trial run of the survey using similar questions and similar subjects.

Research population   The group of people to which the survey is supposed to pertain.

Research sample   A smaller number of people from the research population which has been selected to participate in the survey.

Residual categories   A response that allows a subject who does not feel comfortable with any specific alternative provided to select an answer including either "other," "none," "uncertain," or "don't know."

Semistructured interview   An interview in which some of the questions are specified.

Structured interview   An interview in which all of the questions are specified.

Survey   Any way of making observations where the indicators of variables are answers to questions presented either verbally or in writing in situations where the investigator has not controlled or manipulated the situation.

Unstructured interview   An interview that only specifies the area or subjects to be explored.

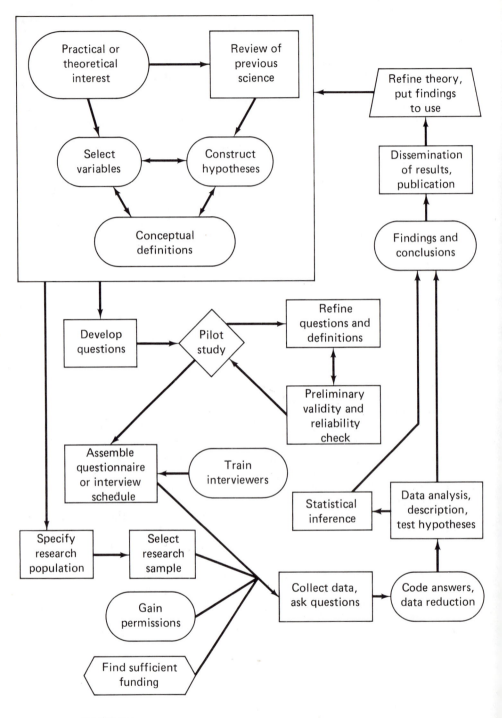

FIGURE 10.1
Flow chart of survey diagram

The last chapter presented a research design which is most likely the ideal way to make observations leading to scientific conclusions about the nature of relationships. This is primarily because of the high degree of control the researcher has over the data collection process. Despite the fact that the classical experiment and the modifications that were proposed in the last chapter are the "ideal" way to make observations, they are not the most widely used techniques in the social sciences, education, or perhaps even in the behavioral sciences. The predominant mode of making observations is the survey.

1. SURVEY DESIGN

As with many words in research the word "survey" carries a very specific connotation. One dictionary defines survey as "the act of measuring and estimating." However in the research process the term *survey* refers to any way of making observations where the indicators of variables are answers to questions presented either verbally or in writing. In surveys investigators have not controlled or manipulated the situation. Surveys are usually conducted at one point in time. The questions pertain to things in the subjects' own experience. In experiments changes in independent variables are a result of manipulation by the experimenter. In surveys, however, changes in variables are a result of naturally occurring events. In the experiment the scientists control changes in the independent variables, while in the survey the scientist must discover circumstances where the variables are of different value.

Figure 10.1 shows a flow chart for survey design which provides a complete overview of the survey process. Notice that the flow chart forms a circle. This is done deliberately to remind you that the research process has no particular beginning or end but is a continuous *process*. In addition, there is no set order of events that occur in survey designs, other than some common sense order of events. For example, it is not possible to tell people about findings until after the research has been completed. Beyond these obvious types of things, many parts of the flow of work represented in the flow chart go on at the same time, or in mixed order.

Beginning the survey

A convenient place to start examining the flow chart is at the upper left-hand corner with the area of theoretical or practical interest. All researchers have motivations for what they do. The idea that investigators have a purpose in mind is not unique to those who do surveys. By "theoretical interest" we mean that there is some abstract or "disciplinary" reason for wanting to do research. In other words, there is usually some theory that is present in a particular academic discipline about which the researcher wants to know more. The scientist may want to test, refine, modify, or elaborate the ideas presented in some scheme or theory, or the scientist may be trying to establish a theory. For example, the educational psychologist may want to confirm the idea that people from different size communities perceive the attainment of a college degree quite differently; or a sociologist might want to refine the theory that unstable family structures lead to delinquent behavior of children.

"Practical Interests" refer to all of the motivations for doing research that have immediate application to some ongoing activity. A marriage counselor may want to know what "causes" divorce. The criminologist may want to be able to spot children who are likely to get into trouble so that something can be done to prevent it. The social worker may want to know how to break the chain of poverty that ties many people to economically disadvantaged ways of life. A demographer might want to find out why people desire particular sized families.

Whether or not a motivation is labeled as theoretical or practical is of no great importance to us. All motivations essentially lead to the same result, that is, research that helps us describe and understand systems of variables. Of course that is what the search for relationships is all about — trying to understand systems of variables.

Review of published material

To begin the search for relationships with surveys, researchers will often do reviews of published materials. This procedure was fully elaborated in Chapter 5 but should be noted as a central part of most surveys. Although it was suggested in Chapter 5 that some feel reviewing the literature limits the kinds of innovative and exploratory work that researchers might do, this is probably not true in the case of surveys. Most scientists feel that surveys are more fruitful when some knowledge of variables is already available. In other words, if scientists knew almost nothing about a system of variables the survey technique would most likely not be employed. The following chapters will explore research designs used to make observations that would be most appropriate in the case where little was known about the variables under consideration.

Selecting variables and stating hypotheses

Out of a combination of the "need to know," either theoretical or practical, and a review of past research, the particular variables to be studied will be selected. These include the major independent and dependent variables and all appropriate "control" variables. The exact choice of variables is often the result of the researcher's motivation combined with awareness of previous work in the area. Hypotheses will also be very often constructed at this point. As you will recall, hypotheses are statements about the expected relationship between variables. Usually research hypotheses only predict the direction or form of the relationship between variables which the researcher expects to find as a result of performing a survey. It is undoubtedly more typical to see surveys which test particular hypotheses than to see ones which do not have expectations about the form of contemplated relationships. Studies that do not set out with the idea of testing hypotheses but want to find distributions of variables selected are often called *descriptive* studies.

Closely integrated into the above procedures is the matter of carefully stating conceptual definitions of the variables selected for study. At some point prior to the development of questions that serve as indicators, the investigator must explicitly or implicitly define research variables. If the researcher cannot clearly articulate what is being measured and observed, there will be neither a way to judge the validity of the indicators nor a way to evaluate the meaning of what is discovered. This matter of stating clear and explicit definitions for variables is often an area of weakness in research, not only in surveys, but for all research. One must be able to communicate an imagery with conceptual definitions of variables in order to have research findings that are useful.

Developing indicators

Hopefully, after variables have been selected and defined, it will be possible to develop indicators to accurately represent the concepts under study. In the case of surveys these indicators will be subjects' answers to questions posed by the researcher. In the survey one task is constructing clear, understandable questions whose answers can be interpreted. In order for questions to be good indicators it is necessary that the researcher be able to place subjects in categories of variables based on the subjects' answers. The problem of question construction will be considered at length later in this chapter.

Pilot studies

In order to find out if people can understand the wording of questions, if directions are clear to subjects, if interviewers are adequately trained, if the questions and answers mean the same thing to subjects as they do to the researchers, and if there is a variation in the dependent variable, a pilot study of indicators (questionnaires or interviews) is often done. In a pilot study, people who are similar to those in the research population are asked to respond to the assembled questions.

From this "trial run" of the survey it can often be determined if people understand the directions provided; if they will follow them; if they understand the questions; if the answers provided are clear and easy to use; and if there are any other "technical" changes that need to be made in the survey. In addition, the pilot study makes it possible to do a preliminary check on the validity and reliability of the questions.

A necessary part of the pilot study consists of assembling the questions which form the basis of the survey. This would be the total questionnaire if it were a written survey or the interview schedule if it were an interview survey. In either case the exact arrangement and presentation of questions should be determined prior to conducting the pilot study. The arrangement would be altered if the pilot study revealed it was necessary to do so. In addition, if the study were to be an interview, it would be necessary to develop the ability to train staff to do the actual interviewing. Interviewer skills could also be checked in the process of the pilot study, and further training could be devised if necessary.

Specification of the research population

Several additional things must be accomplished before starting the actual asking of questions in the survey. First, the researcher must determine the research population. That is, a decision must be made specifying *the group of people to which the survey supposedly pertains*. This group of people is called the *research population*. This choice will often be associated with the researcher's theory or practical interest in the study. The criminologist might want to survey all criminals in the United States; the social worker might want to survey all poverty families in a particular city; and so on. Until the decision is made we will not know to whom we will address the questions in our survey.

Sampling

Once we know the general group of people we are interested in learning about (the research population), it will very often be necessary to select a smaller number of people from that population to actually answer the survey. The procedure of deciding who is actually going to be asked the questions in the survey is called selecting the research sample. *The research sample* is that smaller number of people from the research population which has been selected to participate in the survey. Different ways of selecting research samples will be described in Chapter 15. In addition, Chapter 16 presents techniques that allow the researcher to generalize findings from the research sample to the members of the research population.

Gaining access to subjects

Very often, in order to ask the people in a research sample the questions you desire, it will be necessary to get someone's permission. This is the general problem of gaining access to subjects for the purpose of conducting surveys. For example, if we desired to sample a group of school children, it would be necessary to gain the permission of the schools involved, the parents of the children, and perhaps the children themselves. If the survey were to be conducted in a factory, the managers of the factory would have to give their permission. Perhaps the unions involved and the actual subjects would also be directly contacted for their permission prior to doing the survey. In any case there is often the need to obtain "official" permission to do research. The ultimate decision makers, of course, are the subjects themselves. If the subjects selected for the research sample do not participate in surveys, they are called *nonrespondents*. The problem of alleviating nonresponse by gaining legitimacy in the eye of the subjects will be discussed below.

Legitimate and important sponsorship is one technique used to gain cooperation in surveys. Such sponsorship can be effectively communicated in a cover letter. *Cover letters* precede questionnaires and provide subjects with an introduction to the research.

It is more likely that subjects will cooperate and other permissions will be gained if the research is being conducted by a well-known scientist, a university or college, some nationally known group, or other prestigious person or association. Such sponsorship will prove advantageous in the initial stages of negotiation and in the final act of data collection. Appropriate letterheads and other such devices can be used to communicate the sponsorship of research.

Another useful procedure is for the cover letter to appeal to the self-interest of those involved. For example, if the research is somehow going to benefit the industry in which the survey is done, there is a greater likelihood that the controllers of that industry will cooperate. If a particular survey in schools will potentially result in a better kind of school, teachers will be more receptive to the study. Often research not only serves scientific interests but particular self-interests as well, and an appeal to healthy self-interest is a technique frequently used in survey research. In a similar vein, if the sponsors of research can appeal to some "higher purpose," the probabilities of gaining cooperation are increased. For example, if a particular survey in a community could possibly result in improvements that would make the community "a better place to live," this could be pointed out. Hopefully, increased cooperation with the researcher would result. The purpose of research can often be phrased in such a way that the findings will help improve life, create a better society, aid individuals, or in some other fashion be beneficial to people or organizations.

There are several other techniques that are often employed to help researchers gain access to places and subjects. One such practice is to promise to report conclusions of the research to subjects who cooperate. It is often the case that summaries of findings could be distributed to cooperating organizations, groups, and individuals as a sort of "trade-off" for their cooperation. This is particularly true when there is appreciable self-interest potential in the research. Other types of promises which are often made include the promise that only the scientists involved in the study will have access to the data and that records will be kept so that subjects cannot be identified, or that responses cannot be matched with subjects. Finally, unless there is some particular need to know which subjects responded in particular ways, many objections to surveys can be lessened if the researcher will guarantee anonymity of subjects. Sometimes there is a need to match subjects with their responses. However, if this is not the case, most people will be more at ease with surveys if they do not have to write their names on the questionnaire or if there is no code number which could be used for identification. People are often sensitive to preserving their privacy and, if the research can respect this, then cooperation is easier to obtain. Of course any promises made should be honored. In short, the problem of gaining access to subjects will be significantly decreased if the researcher can gain legitimacy in the eyes of those who control access to subjects and in the eyes of the subjects, if the research can be made to appeal to self-interests or higher purposes, and if the survey can be structured to protect and inform those who participate.

Financing surveys

Surveys are often expensive to conduct. This is particularly true if large samples are used or if the subjects are geographically distant. Money is needed for salaries of assistants, secretaries and other staff, printing, postage, data processing, computer use, telephone, travel, and supplies. If the survey is to be conducted by interview, field staff must also be trained and paid. These costs are in addition to normal overhead expenses such as heat, electricity, rent, and other sorts of costs which most scientific enterprises incur. The failure to get money is very often cited as the reason for not conducting particular pieces of research.

Data collection

Once all of the above considerations have been successfully dealt with, it is possible to actually start asking subjects questions and getting their answers. The process of asking the survey questions and recording subjects' answers is called *data collection*. This is the point at which observations are actually made. Although the remaining steps take place after data have been collected, good researchers have considered each of them prior to the time of actual data collection. Each has been anticipated in the total research act. To some extent the nature of initial steps depends on planning for the later stages of the survey design.

Data reduction

Before any use can be made of the answers to questions, it is necessary to put those answers in a form that can be easily understood and communicated. The process of changing answers into usable data is called *coding* and/or *data reduction*. This process includes translating answers into numbers, interpreting responses to open-ended questions into categories of variables, and any other process which might be necessary to prepare frequency distributions or other statistics. The process of coding is often a time consuming, costly, and difficult task. This is especially true if the researcher has not thoroughly considered coding at the time of question construction or has not participated in complete coding at the time of the pilot study. As we have previously discussed, even when variables are at the nominal or ordinal level, researchers often translate categories of variables into numbers. This makes them easier to handle and most importantly, if coded into numbers the computer may be used to aid in analysis.

Even if answers are not changed to numbers and placed into a computer, data reduction may still be necessary to arrive at desired categories. For example, when dealing with a subject's occupation, a researcher might change the response of "carpenter" into the category of "skilled labor."

The most difficult type of question to code is the *open-ended question*. This is the type of question which does not have particular answers that the subject can select. An example of an open-ended question would be, "What is your opinion of how the government is handling the national budget?" On a questionnaire there would be a space left for the respondent to fill in an answer. In an interview, the interviewer would either record the answer word-for-word or put a few words down to summarize what the subject said. In any case the researcher must determine which sets of verbal answers go together to form a particular category of a variable. Unless the question is worded very carefully and has been thoroughly pre-tested, chaos can occur at the time of coding and data reduction.

The other type of question asked in surveys is the *fixed alternative question*. A fixed alternative question is one for which there is a set number of answers provided. Subjects must select the one answer which best fits their desires or opinions. When this type of question is used in surveys the number translations of answers should be fixed before collecting data. Sometimes these codes are printed on the questionnaire or interview schedule so that it is easier to feed the information into the computer. Another technique that is sometimes used with fixed alternative questions (when the subjects have previous experience) is to use "marked sense sheets" with the answers printed on the sheet. This is the type of "IBM" sheet that is used for exams, for applying for some licenses, and for similar purposes which require you to fill in a space with a number 2 pencil. These sheets can be "read" by an optical scanner and the information can then be transferred into a computer. If this method can be used, human coding errors can be kept to a minimum as long as the subjects cooperate. In the cases where coders must translate answers into numbers, the possibility for many errors exists. In order to keep these errors at a minimum a *code book* must be constructed, along with a set of instructions that can be followed by those doing the coding. Table 10.1 shows a page from a code book. This book should contain the variable index number, that is, the order in which the variable appears, a one-word label for the variable, a description of the variable (possibly the question itself), the different categories of the variable, the card and column numbers where the data appear in the computer (this was explained in Chapter 8), and possibly the frequency of each response in the data.

In addition it is often necessary to provide coders with special instructions which describe how to handle problems in coding. Sometimes coders prepare large sheets that contain the number translations for answers. These sheets are then used by a key punch operator to to prepare cards that the computer can "read." It is understandable that because of so many operations the possibility of errors is quite large. The prudent researcher will devise methods to check on the accuracy of coding prior to doing any analysis on the data. This often involves checking a percentage of questionnaires with the coders' and keypunchers' work to detect any systematic errors. If there is a large proportion of errors, then corrective measures must be taken.

Data analysis

The analysis part of the survey design requires testing hypotheses, computing statistics, summarizing observations, and handling any

TABLE 10.1
Example code sheet

Card no.	Column no.	Variable name	Variable index	Item and code	f
3	38	ALIEN1	125	In spite of what some people say, the lot of the average man is getting worse, not better. 1. Strongly agree 2. Agree 3. Undecided 4. Disagree 5. Strongly disagree	
3	39	ALIEN2	126	It's not fair to bring children into the world the way things look for the future. 1. Strongly agree 2. Agree 3. Undecided 4. Disagree 5. Strongly disagree	
3	40	RELIG1	127	I believe that men working and thinking together cannot build a just society without supernatural help. 1. Strongly agree 2. Agree 3. Undecided 4. Disagree 5. Strongly disagree	

other procedures that are employed to reach conclusions about what is being studied. It is also at this point that you would conduct tests of statistical inference to determine how safe it would be to generalize your sample findings to the research population from which the sample was selected. Chapter 16 deals with specific types of statistics which are used for generalizing sample results to research populations.

Dissemination of findings

Most researchers are not content to keep their findings to themselves, so reporting their research findings becomes an important part of the total enterprise. Findings are reported by presenting papers at professional meetings, by writing journal articles, or by incorporating the findings into a book or monograph. By sharing with others the findings can be used for solving practical problems and/or contributing to the understanding of a phenomena from a theoretical perspective. In this way findings can add to our knowledge about the world in which we live and become a part of the literature which helped spawn the research at hand. This final step completes the circle we have called the survey design. The remainder of this chapter deals with question construction and a comparison of the different types of surveys.

2. QUESTION CONSTRUCTION

One task common to all types of surveys is the difficult job of constructing good questions. There are several specific errors that are often made in constructing questions for surveys which will be explored in this section. The general goal behind each of these issues is to end up with a question that will effectively communicate to the subjects and that will allow the subjects to answer in a way that the intent of the answer will be clear to the researcher. It is the problem of good communication which is at issue in question construction. In addition, the scientific researcher wants to ask questions so that the subject is not led to any particular answer. The wording of the question should not bias the subject to answer in any particular way. Finally, when fixed alternative questions are used, a set of mutually exclusive and inclusive categories must be constructed. If the following issues are considered when constructing questions, it is more likely that good question construction will result.

Word meaning

There are several aspects of word meaning that are crucial to good question construction. The first concerns the difficulty of the words used. Although for some special subjects difficult words might be appropriate, in general one should be careful to only use those words that are common and easily understood. For example, instead of using the term "prestidigitator" it would be preferable to use the word "juggler" or "one who practices sleight of hand." A rule of thumb is to use vocabulary at the level usually found in most newspapers or magazines.

Another problem area deals with the possible double meaning of words. For example, the term "high" might refer to height or a condition of the mind. When constructing questions for surveys questions should be screened with an eye toward double meanings. What the question asks, should be clear to the reader. Although double meanings are often employed in sarcastic humor, they have no place in the research act.

Double-barreled questions

There are three types of double-barreled questions that are often seen in research. The problem with double-barreled questions is that it is not possible to determine the intent of the subject from the answer. The first type of double-barreled question asks two questions in one. For example:

"Are politicians dishonest or do you think they are just like other people?" ___YES ___NO

In this question the subject may or may not feel that politicians are dishonest, and the subject may or may not feel that other people are dishonest. A "yes" answer may mean that the subject thinks politicians are dishonest and so is everyone else, *or* it may mean that the subject feels that politicians are dishonest and that everyone else is honest, *or* it may mean that the subject views politicians as not being dishonest but as being like other people. There is no way to determine the intent of the answer. Similarly a "no" response is also confusing.

The second type of double-barreled question makes a statement of fact that a person may or may not agree with and then goes on to ask a question using that supposed fact as a premise. For example:

"College administrators have more facts than students; students should therefore not question the decisions they make." ___Agree ___Disagree

In this case an "agree" answer may mean that the subject feels that administrators do have more knowledge but that students should question decisions, or a subject may feel that administrators do not know more but students should not question their decisions anyway. Perhaps even more confusing is the idea that a "disagree" may be a reflection that administrators don't know more, *or* that students should not question their decisions. The researcher has no way to accurately determine the meaning of responses to these types of questions. Therefore the potential for error in interpreting responses is great.

A third type of question is one with a hidden premise, confirmed by any answer to the question. For example:

"Have you stopped drinking alcohol?" ___YES ___ NO

This question assumes that you drank alcohol no matter what you answer.

Double negative questions

One of the most difficult aspects of linguistics is the double negative. Strictly speaking a double negative results in a positive statement. (That is, it is not that a double negative is not positive.) However, we have enough experience to know that people often get confused when asked questions in the double negative mode. For example, subjects may be asked to say whether they would agree or disagree with certain kinds of statements such as:

> "I don't think it is not a wise policy to continue foreign aid to dictatorships." ____YES ____NO

Does a "yes" response mean that the subject feels that foreign aid should or should not be continued to dictatorships? Sufficient confusion is generated by this type of question so that we can never be sure. The best advice is to avoid using double negatives. Either phrase questions clearly in the positive or clearly in the negative. In fact, it is often suggested that questionnaires and interviews should be constructed using a mixture of positively and negatively worded questions. This practice will avoid getting the subjects into a pattern of agreement or disagreement. Such a pattern is called a *response set*.

A better way to ask the above question would be:

> "Do you think foreign aid should be provided to dictatorships?" ____YES ____NO

Prestige bias (socially acceptable response)

In some cases it is difficult to find the true feelings of respondents. The nature of the question may be such that a particular response seems most appropriate, or information in the question may give the reader the idea that one answer is more likely "right" or "wrong" (Of course, in surveys there are no "right" or "wrong" answers, merely accurate or inaccurate description of subjects and/or subjects' perceptions.) For example:

> "Would you agree with scientific studies that show that people who are married are happier than people who are divorced?" ____YES ____NO

In this question there are two types of prestige bias. The first is the reference to "scientific studies." In the western world science enjoys a fairly high status in most people's minds. To disagree with scientific findings would not be openly admitted in many circumstances. Therefore it would be difficult to determine whether the subject really agrees with "scientific findings" or is merely going along because of the prestige value of such findings. In addition, there is still a certain amount of stigma associated with being divorced. If subjects feel this type of stigma, then they might answer this type of question in the affirmative even if they themselves do not really believe it. In this case perhaps a more socially acceptable answer would be to agree that married people are happier. A bias-free approach to the question would give the respondent the impression that any answer is acceptable and that one is not preferred over another. A question such as,

> "We know that many things go into being happy, but do you feel that married people are generally happier than divorced people?" ___YES ___NO

attempts to eliminate the prestige bias and the existence of a possible stigma that might be attached to being divorced. Questions must be carefully constructed so that respondents do not just answer in a manner they think is "good" or "desired."

Leading questions

A similar type of error in question wording is the notion of leading questions. This type of question, by the way it is asked, lets the reader know that a particular response is the desired response. The leading question is undesirable because it may influence the subject's answers. Subjects may want to "go along" with the question just to be nice, or they may choose not to "go along" with the question just because they are angry that the researcher is trying to get a certain kind of answer. A question such as

> "Have you read or heard about the massive famines that are predicted for the near future?"

indicates to the reader that they would be quite uninformed if they had not read such predictions. In most people's minds this type of question is seeking a "yes" response. The problem, of course, is that if the question points to a particular answer, the possibilities of misinterpretation are increased. A better question which would elicit similar information from respondents would be:

> "Some writers have argued that famines are very likely in the future, while others have said that this is not very likely. How familiar are you with the writings which surround this controversy?"

Emotionally loaded questions

Many of the errors of question construction occur simultaneously. One such example would be the use of emotionally loaded questions. Questions that use words or phrases in ways which get subjects upset or disturbed are undesirable. It is not known whether subjects' responses are due to true feelings and perceptions or to an excited emotional state. Such questions are also often leading questions. The following question is taken from an actual survey conducted by a state representative within his congressional district.

"Should the state ignore the principles of the Bible, which is the law of God and morality and legalize murder by abortion?"

Regardless of how one feels about abortion, this kind of question could sway a subject purely on the basis of its wording and phrasing. If the survey is attempting to determine if subjects are for or against legalized abortion, then a more bias-free question would be:

"Do you believe that the state should legalize abortions?"

Of course the questionnaire might have been attempting to find out people's position on the relationship between the state and the Bible, or people's definition of when life begins, or people's opinions about whether abortion constitutes murder. It is not really possible to determine what was the exact nature of the information sought in this question. In any case the answers to this type of question would be difficult to interpret, assuming subjects would be willing to answer such a question.

Embarrassing questions

It may be important for scientists to study phenomena that most people consider very personal or confidential. If this is the case, a decision might be made that such matters could best be researched by methods other than surveys. However, if one wishes to pursue personal issues in a survey, appropriate care must be taken to assure subjects that their identification will be protected. In addition attempts should be made to word questions in a manner that respondents will not be so embarrassed, angry, or shy that they will either not participate in the survey or answer the survey inaccurately. For example, instead of asking the question:

"Are you sexually impotent?"

it would be preferable to phrase the question:

"It is a well established fact that many men experience impotency at various times. This often occurs if males are overly tired or have been drinking or have important matters on their minds. Would you say that impotency has been a problem for you in your sexual relationships?"

In this fashion the respondent can be assured that if he has impotency problems, he is not alone. Also, such a question would help to relieve the stigma that the respondent may associate with impotency.

Assuming prior knowledge

Survey researchers must be careful when asking questions which require some prior knowledge on the part of respondents. In the situation where some knowledge is necessary in order to meaningfully answer a question, it should be established ahead of time that the respondent possesses such knowledge. Asking a respondent

"Do you think that an "eta-mason" nuclear accelerator should be built in this community?"

assumes that the respondent knows what an eta-mason nuclear accelerator is. In many cases this would be a faulty assumption. If the respondent is not aware of what such a device is, the response might be due to some general feeling about nuclear matters or about civic improvements or about science. The response may be given just to appear knowledgeable. The response to such a question might mean different things to different people.

Use of jargon or slang

Generally speaking questions should not use words that are slang or jargon. An attempt should be made to use everyday language that is clear and that most everyone will understand. It might be appropriate to ask a sample of research specialists:

"Do you feel that after the demographic transition occurs fertility rates will automatically decrease?"

However, only someone familiar with demography will have the jargon to understand the issues involved in such a question.

The use of slang should also be avoided. A question like:

"How often do you get stoned?"

would be less desirable than a question like:

"How many marijuana cigarettes would you estimate you smoke in a typical week?"

Some subjects may not know what "stoned" means. Some subjects may think "stoned" means getting drunk or using drugs other than marijuana. Such confusion is eliminated when slang or jargon are omitted from questions.

3. RESPONSES FOR FIXED ALTERNATIVE QUESTIONS

The task of providing respondents with good sets of answers, when dealing with fixed alternative questions, is as important as constructing good questions. Even if the questions asked in a survey are worded well and without bias, the range and wording of answers must be considered with as much care. The problem is again one of trying to make sure that communication occurs without error. That is, the researcher must provide alternative answers that the respondents feel provide the answer which "fits" with their position or feelings. If the scientist does not provide an appropriate set of answers, then several possibilities exist for miscommunication. First, the respondent may simply choose not to participate in the survey. This may mean total nonresponse or perhaps just not answering particular questions. Another possibility is that the respondent will choose one of the available alternatives that would not accurately reflect the respondents' perceptions. A final possibility is that the subject may write an answer or respond verbally in such a way that the researcher has no way to interpret the response within the framework of the survey. We shall examine several aspects of specifying alternative answers below.

Mutually inclusive (exhaustive) categories

The first consideration is that you provide an answer for every respondent. For example, if you were asking subjects what their religious affiliation was and you did not have as one of the available answers, "Catholic," those respondents who considered themselves to be Catholics would not be able to indicate their affiliation. In other words, for responses to be exhaustive each respondent must be provided with an appropriate alternative.

Mutually exclusive categories

In addition to having one category or answer for every respondent, it is equally important to have *only one* response possible for any subject. For example, if we were seeking religious affiliation and gave the following possible answers:

Lutheran
Methodist
Catholic
Protestant
Jewish

a Methodist or a Lutheran could answer in the exact category but could also answer in the "Protestant" category. The problem comes when some Methodist respondents answer in the "methodist" category while others answer in the "Protestant" category. The researcher would have no way of separating out the Methodists from the other Protestant denominations such as Presbyterian or Baptist. Presumably there would be some reason for wanting to do this, or there would be no purpose served by providing the category of Methodist or Lutheran. A simple Protestant category would have been sufficient. Responses should be structured in a way that a respondent cannot possibly choose more than one of those provided. Combining the ideas of mutually inclusive and exclusive categories results in the following rule for constructing answers for fixed alternative questions: *Always structure the set of alternatives in such a way that all respondents will be able to choose one and only one alternative.*

Residual categories

Researchers generally use fixed alternative questions when they are fairly confident that they know just about all of the possible ways respondents will answer. As a precaution against the possibility that some subjects may choose to answer a question in an unanticipated way, it is customary to provide a "residual" response. A *residual response* allows a subject who does not feel comfortable with any specific alternative provided to select an answer. Typically, residual responses will be something like, "don't know" or "uncertain" or "none." Perhaps the most common type of residual category is "other." The provision of an "other" response is often helpful in refining sets of responses so they are more useful. In general it would be beneficial to refine the list of alternatives provided so that only a very small proportion of respondents choose the residual response. One technique often used to aid researchers in refining response sets is to include a space after the "other" response for respondents to write in (in the case of questionnaires) or verbally add (in the case of interviews) what they consider to be a better response. The format of the response would be something like:

_____ other (please specify: _____)

With this format all respondents will be able to select one category, thus satisfying the mutually inclusive condition, but they may also provide the researcher with the information necessary to refine the list of specific alternatives provided.

Balanced responses

Just as questions may bias the response from subjects it is also possible that the set of alternatives provided may bias an answer. To avoid that possibility, fixed alternative questions should allow for an approximately equal number of responses on either side of an issue if the question calls for the respondents to take a value position. This is probably not a particular problem when a question asks for a report of "facts" or "experiences" of subjects. For example, if a survey were seeking peoples' attitudes toward the younger generation in the 1960s, it might have been appropriate to ask people what they thought of "hippies." A question such as:

> Hippies are: Crazy ＿＿
>
> Dangerous ＿＿
>
> Dirty ＿＿
>
> Lazy ＿＿
>
> O.K. ＿＿
>
> A Nuisance ＿＿

is not particularly biased but the available responses are. There is only one positive answer, "O.K.," and this is a very mildly positive term. The other terms are all negative and some are quite strong terms. In addition, they are not mutually inclusive or exclusive. The general point is that responses should be equally balanced in terms of number and emotional loading so that they will not bias the respondents.

Special exceptions

On occasion researchers will want to ask questions that are designed to have multiple answers, or they may desire respondents to rank certain kinds of preferences. On these special occasions categories may not be mutually exclusive. The major problem with this type of question is to construct them so they are clear and can be meaningfully coded after the survey has been conducted. This type of question is extremely difficult to construct. Even if the researcher is able to do this, the task of coding responses in such a way as to produce meaningful measures of a variable is problematic. Using this type of question appropriately requires experience. Beginning surveyors are discouraged from using such questions, particularly in questionnaires. The task, however, becomes somewhat simplified in the interview.

All of the steps, issues, and concerns discussed thus far in this chapter have general utility for all types of surveys. There are many settings and procedures for asking people questions. Telephone surveys and passing out questionnaires to a group are common techniques. The two main types of surveys employed by scientists are the face-to-face interview and the mailed questionnaire.

4. THE MAILED QUESTIONNAIRE

Many of the practices and procedures presented in this chapter have not been developed through scientific research but rather through the experience of many generations of scientists who have utilized mailed surveys. The major goal of many of the points made in this section is to increase the response rate of subjects. Since the problem of nonresponse is the single-most troublesome aspect of mailed surveys, scientists have developed strategies to avoid this problem. It is thought that a low percentage return will lead to inaccurate conclusions in research using mailed questionnaires. There is some research (Goudy, 1976) which suggests that distributions of variables, as well as relationships between variables, may not be as adversely affected as some have contended. Nevertheless, most researchers prefer a high response rate. A review of the literature in this area by Linsky (1975) showed that there were several factors that have been shown to increase response rate. They are:

1. follow-ups
2. precontact of respondents
3. "high powered" postage such as special delivery
4. prepaid cash rewards
5. sponsorship by an important agency/institution/person

No simple conclusions can be reached about the effects of personalized cover letters, the assurance of anonymity, the appeal to the respondent for help, the length of the questionnaire, the notification of the respondents about their importance, printed versus mimeo reproduction, precoded versus open-ended questions, the color of the questionnaire, and the provision of a deadline for respondents (Henley, 1976).

Questionnaire construction

In addition to an attractively arranged format, the usual order of questions is to place first those questions which ask respondents for factual information. Demographic characteristics such as age, occupation, and so on, are the type of question initially asked. After these, other "noncontroversial" questions follow. Finally, any questions which may be especially touchy or highly emotional are usually placed at the end of the questionnaire. The idea behind this ordering of questions is that the respondent can "warm up" on questions that are not offensive or difficult to answer. By the time the respondent gets to the more difficult questions enough time and energy will have already been invested in filling out the questionnaire that the respondent will be more likely to finish the task.

One of the often overlooked aspects of questionnaire construction is the provision of simple, easy to follow instructions for completing the questionnaire. Sometimes researchers overlook the fact that many people are not used to following directions and filling out questionnaires. This may be because so much research is conducted on students who are familiar with such procedures. It is always best to assume that the respondents are totally inexperienced in filling out questionnaires. Therefore it is desirable to supply very explicit, clear, and concise instructions. It is better to give too many directions than not enough. In addition, arrows, heavy print, lines, or special arrangements can aid the respondents a great deal. Pilot studies are especially useful for determining the adequacy of directions.

Follow-ups

In social research it is quite common to have only a part of the sample respond upon first receiving a questionnaire. Percentage responses of 50 to 60 percent are fairly typical for "first time around" respondents. Since this is the case, a practice often employed is to conduct follow-up studies. A *follow-up* constitutes additional requests of the respondent to fill out and return the questionnaire. There are many different techniques employed in follow-up procedures.

One of the most common procedures is to send a second letter to all respondents after about two weeks have elapsed since the original mailing. In this letter the researcher asks those who have not responded to do so, usually reminding them of how important their responses are, and also expressing appreciation to those who have responded. This procedure is especially appropriate if the researcher has no way of determining which respondents have returned the questionnaire and which have not. Of course it is costly to follow-up on all subjects. This procedure is sometimes done more than once and if cost is not a problem, a second or third questionnaire might be enclosed in case subjects had discarded or misplaced the original questionnaire. The follow-up often results in an additional 10 to 20 percent response. On occasion this difference may determine whether or not the study is considered adequate.

If respondents are identified by some code number or similar technique another type of procedure is more efficient. Along with each originally mailed set of materials a stamped return addressed post card is included. The post card is addressed to the researcher and has on the reverse side the code number of the respondent or the name of the respondent. The subjects are instructed to mail the post card at the same time they mail back the questionnaire; not in the same envelope, but at the same time. By comparing the post cards returned with the list of subject names or numbers, the researcher can determine which subjects have returned their questionnaires and which have not. Unfortunately, nothing prevents a subject from returning the card but not the questionnaire! The advantage of the post card technique is that follow-up efforts can be concentrated on those respondents who have not returned their questionnaires. Perhaps more importantly, by knowing which subjects have responded and which have not, it may be possible to determine if there is some bias in response rates. For example, if the researcher knew that 75 percent of the responses in the sample were female, the post cards could be examined to see if approximately 75 percent of those returned were from female respondents. If that were the case more confidence could be placed in the answers. If it were discovered that only 40 percent of those responding were female, questions could be raised. Perhaps there is something about the questionnaire that offended female subjects. If so, the results of the questionnaire would be biased and any conclusions reached would be questionable. One of the most persuasive ways to determine if responses are biased is to compare the characteristics of respondents with some known features of the sample. This can be done with the post card method or by using questions in the survey.

Inducements

The problem of inducing people to participate in surveys is not unique to the survey design. The same issues confront any data collection procedure that involves cooperation of subjects. Hopefully the subjects will be pursuaded to cooperate on the basis of appeals made in cover letters and by the interest generated in the survey. However, it is possible to offer subjects additional rewards for participating in the survey. Usually such procedures are discouraged by scientific researchers because they fear that such procedures might affect the responses of subjects or would determine which people responded and which did not. Tiny pencils or trinkets could be included with the questionnaires but the most common type of inducement utilized to get subjects to respond is money (Armstrong, 1975). The sum of money is usually small and is not intended to "pay" subjects for their answers but rather to acknowledge that respondents have gone out of their way to participate in the study. This practice is viewed with such great suspicion on the part of some scientists that it is seldom used by them, but it is a possibility.

5. FACE-TO-FACE INTERVIEWS

Many of the procedures and techniques discussed for mailed surveys are appropriate for face-to-face interviews. However, since interviewing involves human interaction, the potential for problems is perhaps even greater than with mailed surveys. The main reason is that in addition to the characteristics of the subjects, the scientist must consider the characteristics of the interviewers. Research conducted using face-to-face interviews must be designed in such a way that the results of the study are not a consequence of the behavior, appearance, or interference of the interviewer(s). The possibilities of this occurring are so great that there have been many books written concerned solely with the interviewing process. In this text we have devoted little discussion to this extremely technical matter and the best we can hope for is a sensitization to some of the procedures employed. The following is a list of "do's" and "don'ts" that may be useful in this context.

Do's:

1. If the subject is not receptive or available to the interviewer when initially contacted, set up a future appointment.
2. Establish good rapport with the respondent.
3. Know the questions to be asked and be very familiar with the responses possible.
4. Be sure you are interviewing the right subject.
5. Practice using an interview schedule and interviewing.
6. Follow the interview schedule; do not improvise.
7. Read all questions *exactly* as they are written.
8. Faithfully record the responses of subjects. If coding procedures are not clear or appropriate, record responses verbatim.
9. Ask all questions; do not skip.
10. Be courteous and thank all subjects and leave the door open for possible follow-up interviews.

Don'ts:

1. Don't take positions on a question or issue. Be friendly but neutral.
2. Don't give a quiz.
3. Don't take a friend with you.
4. Don't lie in your responses about the nature of the study.
5. Don't interview more than one subject at a time.
6. Don't interview friends or acquaintances.
7. Don't let untrained people do interviewing.

8. Don't reveal the whole purpose of the study, that is, hypotheses, and so on.
9. Don't argue with the subject or with others present during the interview.

Two major potential problems with the interview technique are interviewer bias and biased interviewers. *Interviewer bias* refers to the possible problem of respondents answering questions because of something about the interviewer instead of responding accurately to the question. The physical appearance, behavior, side comments, facial expressions, sex, age, and dress of the interviewer are all possible reasons for subjects answering questions in certain ways. Researchers attempt to eliminate interviewer bias by thorough training of interviewers and by pretests and pilot studies to determine if interviewer bias seems to be occurring. It is probably safe to say that one can never be certain that interviewer bias has been totally eliminated from any particular piece of research which relies on the interview for data collection.

The problem of biased interviewers is similar to the problem of experimenter bias. *Biased interviewers* inappropriately influence different respondents. For example, interviewers may treat "poor" subjects impolitely and "rich" subjects respectfully. Biased interviewers also may make "mistakes" in data collection. They may miscode responses, incorrectly report answers, report false data, or make up phoney data for some reason.

Interview structure

One of the major ways that interviews vary has to do with the extent to which they are structured. Degree of "structure" refers to the extent to which the interview contains specific questions with fixed alternative answers. An interview schedule which prescribes all of the questions an interviewer is to ask and specifies their order, is said to be *structured.* A schedule which has some questions specified is called *semistructured,* and an interview which only specifies the area to be explored is called *unstructured.* The terms *standardized* and *focused* are sometimes used instead of the term "structure." Table 10.2 summarizes these distinctions.

There are advantages and disadvantages to each of the types of interview schedules. The major advantage of the structured schedule is ease of coding and the reduction of interviewer bias. Since standardized interviews specify exactly what the interviewer is to say, they tend to minimize stray comments by interviewers and reduce the bias produced by such variations from interview to interview. In terms of coding, the problems of questionnaires also apply to interviews. Fixed alternative questions are easier to code while open-

TABLE 10.2

Characteristics of interview schedules

Type of schedule	Description
Structured (standardized or focused)	The content and order of questions is completely specified.
Semistructured (semistandardized or semifocused)	Some questions are specified but some latitude is left to the interviewer to explore areas of concern.
Unstructured (nonstandardized or unfocused)	Only the areas of concern are specified and the interviewer is free to ask various questions to obtain appropriate information.

ended questions present greater difficulties in coding. Problems of coding are also reduced when all subjects are asked the same set of questions.

The major disadvantage of the structured interview is that the interviewers are not free to explore subjects' answers, or to clarify them, or to expand them with information which might be helpful to the research. This is, of course, the major strength of the unstructured interview. For this type of schedule, interviewers are trained in terms of the variables, concepts, or phenomena under study, and in techniques used to explore these areas. Interviewers are often provided with opening questions and with possible probing questions to help get at the areas being investigated. This technique relies very heavily on the expertise of the interviewer. The interviewer must win the confidence of the subject and must have the skill to know when, how, and what to ask the subject to elicit the desired responses. This type of interview creates many problems of coding for researchers. Therefore the tendency in interviews is to use standardized interview schedules. However, if the subject matter of the research is very sensitive, or if the scientists do not know much about the phenomena being studied, unstructured interviews are often seen as desirable. In exploratory studies the attempt is not so much to test hypotheses or to accurately measure variables but to discover hypotheses or to uncover potentially useful research procedures. One technique often used in this type of interview situation is to ask questions which "funnel" the respondents' answers from very general issues to very specific points. The funneling procedure starts at a very general level and, with subsequent probing questions, gets increasingly more specific.

6. COMPARING MAILED QUESTIONNAIRES WITH INTERVIEWS

There are many advantages and disadvantages of the two survey research techniques discussed above. The decision to use one procedure over another is often made on the basis of the topic under study. Practical considerations may also weigh heavily in this decision. In order to compare mailed questionnaires with interviews, Table 10.3 presents considerations relevant to various stages of the flow chart.

Aside from these particular aspects of the survey design, some general comments about these data collection strategies can be made. Interviews offer the scientist the highest degree of control of the data collection process. However, one must carefully guard against the potential for interviewer bias or cheating. Mailed questionnaires, once they have been distributed, are essentially out of the control of the researcher. However, the bias due to nonresponse may be great. One can see that many of the advantages of the questionnaire are the disadvantages of the interview, and many of the advantages of the interview are the disadvantages of the questionnaire. Mailed questionnaires are used much more often than interviews, probably because of their ease of administration and their relatively lower cost.

TABLE 10.3

Comparison of the major survey data collection methods

Stage of the survey	Mailed questionnaire	Interview
Develop questions	Subjects may be less embarrassed and more open in their responses Probing questions cannot be used Questions must always be direct	Can explore areas where specific questions are difficult to construct Can use probing and funneling tech niques
Specify research population and select sample	Wide variety of subjects are potentially available May cover large geographic areas with ease Some subjects would not be approachable by an interviewer If there is nonresponse it may be	Identity of respondents is known Some subjects may take the time to answer if confronted by an interviewer but would not respond by mail

TABLE 10.3 (*continued*)
Characteristics of interview schedules

Stage of the survey	Mailed questionnaire	Interview
	difficult to determine who answered and who did not	
Funding	Cost per questionnaire is low	Probably the most expensive
Data collection	No field staff necessary Subjects have more time to think and may respond when they want to Nonresponse may be great	Very flexible if using semi- or unstructured schedule Nonresponse is usually very low Must train and supervise field staff
Data reduction and analysis	It is difficult to deal with missing data Easier to use computerized analysis Interpretations often more clear-cut	Responses from unstructured schedules must be handled Results often a matter of interpretation
Statistical inference	May be difficult to generalize findings if large nonresponse rate May not be able to generalize to certain types of people	Since more control is possible may be more certain of generalization of findings

7. SUMMARY

While many steps in the survey process can be enumerated, six general areas form the basis of activity. Activities may take place in different order but every survey must: provide a statement of the problem, develop questionnaires or interview schedules, collect data, reduce data, analyze data, and disseminate the findings of the survey. A review of the literature is often helpful for the specification of research variables in a survey. Through the development of indicators and conducting pilot studies, sound questionnaires or interviews should emerge. After the research population is specified and the sample is selected, necessary permissions must be obtained to gain access to subjects. Many of these considerations are partially determined by the source and amount of funding for surveys. Data collection is the task of collecting answers to the questions posed to subjects. The reduction of data may be relatively simple if precoded fixed alternative questions are used. However, if open-ended questions are used, the coding of answers may be a tremendously difficult task. Data analysis is made relatively simple if coding can result in reducing answers to number labels. When this is possible, the computer can be used to calculate distributions, scatterplots, and other types of statistics. The dissemination of findings is accomplished mainly through publication in professional journals.

The task of constructing questions and responses that are bias free is of primary importance to surveys. Word meaning, double-barreled questions, double negatives, prestige bias, leading questions, emotionally loaded terms, inappropriate personalization, assuming prior knowledge, and the use of slang or jargon all may lead to miscommunication in question construction. Responses for fixed alternative questions must be mutually inclusive and exclusive. This is often accomplished by providing a residual category for respondents. Responses should also be balanced in their presentation.

Mailed questionnaires are one major method of conducting surveys. An important problem for mailed surveys is to reduce the percentage of nonresponse. There are many techniques that have been found to reduce nonresponse. For example, follow-ups, precontact of subjects, and high powered postage have been found to be effective. The question of inducements can also be considered to reduce nonresponse. In any event, when nonresponse occurs it is necessary to consider the degree to which it has biased results. Face-to-face interviews are thought to be very useful when in-depth information is necessary or when a topic is initially being explored. Interview procedures are very important. The major potential problem with interviews is the bias that may be introduced by the presence of the interviewer. The advantages and disadvantages of each of the techniques should be examined before a method is decided upon.

1. Determine (estimate) what concept each question is attempting to measure. State what is "wrong" with the question. Construct a "good" question to measure the specified concept.
a. Do you think that Congress should enact gestapo-type laws that would reward citizens for spying on other citizens for such offenses as air or water pollution?
b. I would rather:
(1) have everybody in the class get a "C" at the beginning of the course than

EXERCISES

(2) be graded at the end of the course with the possibility of getting a higher or lower grade.

c. The administration has more facts about a given situation than we do; therefore we should not question the decisions they make.

Strongly agree ____ Agree ____ Disagree ____
Strongly disagree ____

d. How compassionate do you feel (political candidate) is?
(1) Very compassionate
(2) Moderately compassionate
(3) Not compassionate
(4) No opinion

e. About how often did you attend religious services during the past year?
(1) Never
(2) 2 or 3 times
(3) 2 or 3 times a month
(4) About once a week or more

f. Socialists have historically advocated free trade among nations. Do you think we should eliminate some of the tariff barriers that have been erected against free trade?

g. How do you feel about blacks invading your neighborhood?

h. In view of the fact that the United States is the guardian of the free world, do you think that the defense budget should be cut as much as 25 percent?

i. Do you think this book is:
(1) Excellent
(2) Superb
(3) Fantastic
(4) Very good

j. Should the elementary schools return to a punitive model of socialization?

2. Write a cover letter for one of the following:
   a. Work and leisure attitudes of union members who have undergone a recent layoff
   b. Children's attitudes toward a new mathematics program in the schools
   c. The religious practices and attitudes of a local congregation

3. Construct a set of questions to measure the two concepts you examined in the exercises in Chapter 5.

4. Construct a code sheet for your questions in Exercise 3.

Design a pilot study for a survey to study (one of) the dependent variables you and your instructor agreed upon for a project assignment for Chapter 5. In order to facilitate analysis, we recommend that you find a dependent variable which has an interval or ratio level of measurement.

1. List three to five hypotheses you feel worthy of investigating, based on your library search.
2. Because you will be able to use these data in later chapters, add sex, age, socioeconomic status, religion, and others recommended by your instructor to your list of independent variables for this study.
3. Create operational definitions for each variable you will examine. Since this is a survey, it will involve constructing questions for your questionnaire. Be sure your questions follow the suggestions for good questions in this chapter. Unless the concept is very simple, you should make at least three questions for each concept.
4. Assemble your questions into a questionnaire or interview schedule including a cover letter.
5. Describe your plan for gathering data (phone, mail, interview, or possibly in this case, dropping off and picking up personally). You might consult with your instructor about combining questionnaires from several students in this class. This could give each student more returned questionnaires with which to work.
6. a. In order to anticipate the analysis you may do when the data are returned, develop a code sheet. List which questions might be combined into a single index or scale (see Chapter 2).
   b. Describe your plan for analysis. This is important to do *before* you gather data because it might point to something you omitted. If the independent variables are interval or ratio, set up the scatterplots you will wish to examine. If the independent variables are ordinal or nominal, set up blank percentage tables.
7. Before you actually gather data, be sure to consult with your instructor about adequacy, ethics, and feasibility. If your instructor says it is permissible to proceed, collect the data.
8. When the data are returned, code them according to your prearranged plan (Number 6) and any changes you find necessary at this point. Analyze each hypothesis in terms of a scatterplot or percentage tables.
9. What tentative conclusions are you willing to make on the basis of your pilot study?
10. What improvements would you suggest on the basis of your pilot study?

294

ARMSTRONG, J. "Monetary Incentives in Mail Surveys." *Public Opinion Quarterly, 39,* No. 1, Spring 1975, 111–116.

BABBIE, E. *The Practice of Social Research.* Belmont, Calif.: Wadsworth, 1975.

BACKSTROM, C., AND HURSH, G. *Survey Research.* Evanston, Ill.: Northwestern University Press, 1963.

HENLEY, J. "Response Rate to Mail Questionnaires with Return Deadline." *Public Opinion Quarterly, 40,* No. 3, Fall 1976, 374–375.

KAHN, R., AND CANNELL, C. *The Dynamics of Interviewing.* New York: Wiley, 1957.

KERLINGER, F. *Foundations of Behavioral Research,* 2d ed. New York: Holt, Rinehart and Winston, 1973.

LINSKY, A. Stimulating Responses to Mailed Questionnaires: A Review." *Public Opinion Quarterly, 39,* No. 1, Spring 1975, 82–101.

MILLER, D. *Handbook of Research Design and Social Measurement.* New York: David McKay, 1970.

OPPENHEIM, A. *Questionnaire Design and Attitude Measurement.* New York: Basic Books, 1966.

PAYNE, S. *The Art of Asking Questions.* Princeton, N. J.: Princeton University Press, 1951.

SELLTIZ, C., WRIGHTSMAN, L., AND COOK, S. *Research Methods in Social Relations,* 3d ed. New York: Holt, Rinehart and Winston, 1976.

SHAW, M., AND WRIGHT, J. *Scales for the Measurement of Attitudes.* New York: McGraw-Hill, 1967.

WILLIAMSON, J., KARP, D., AND DOLPHIN, J. *The Research Craft: An Introduction to Social Science Methods.* Boston: Little, Brown, 1977.

CHAPTER 11
MEASURING AND ACCOUNTING FOR OTHER VARIABLES

After studying this chapter, students should be able to:

1. Define a control variable.

2. Discuss in general terms why multivariate models are important.

3. Describe how to partition data for exploring three variable models.

4. Describe what the original and control scatterplots and percentage tables would look like for spurious, intervening, complicated, joint-effects, and no-effect models.

5. Give examples of the various types of three variable models presented in the chapter.

6. Analyze data with scatterplots and percentage tables to determine what type of three variable model exists in the data.

7. Discuss how conclusions about the relationships between variables could be altered by controlling for a third variable.

Antecedent variable   The first variable in a three variable causal chain.

Clarification model   A type of complicated model.

Complicated model   The X-Y relationship in the control plots are different from one another and different from the original X-Y relationship.

Contingent model   A type of complicated model.

Control table   An X-Y table which is the result of partitioning (separating) units on the basis of their score(s) on the control variable(s).

Control variables   Other variables included in a model or analysis aside from the independent and dependent variables.

Controlling   Adding a third variable to any bivariate analysis.

Description model   A type of complicated model.

Intervening model   An original X-Y relationship disappears with the introduction of a third (control) variable and the third (control) variable occurs between the first and second.

Joint-effects model   The best fitting lines in the control tables have the same slope but are at different heights.

Multivariate models   The conclusion reached when analyzing three variable models.

No-effect model   The control plots are the same as the original X-Y relationship.

Partitioning data   Controlling for a third variable by separating the units being studied into groups depending on their value on the third control variable.

Specification model   A type of complicated model.

Spurious model   An original X-Y relationship disappears with the introduction of a third variable and the third variable occurs first in time.

Statistical interaction   The relationship between three variables in a complicated model.

Suppressor variable   The third variable in a complicated model where the original X-Y relationship shows no relationship.

1. INTRODUCTION

One major problem of searching for relationships concerns the difficulty of interpreting research findings when two variables are viewed in isolation from other important variables in a system. Very early in this text we introduced the idea that the ultimate goal of any science is to understand important *systems* of variables. That is, research and theory work hand in hand to discover and interpret sets of interrelated variables which help to explain some phenomena. Until now, we have focused on either one (univariate) or two (bivariate) variables. A number of statistics were introduced in Chapter 7 that can be used to describe various aspects of the distribution of one variable. In Chapter 3 the scatterplot was introduced as one technique that can be used to determine the form, extent, and precision of bivariate relationships. Chapter 4 presented percentages as an additional technique. The purpose of this chapter is to use the scatterplot and percentages to show how conclusions about bivariate relationships may be misleading if viewed in isolation.

A system of relationships may contain any number of variables. The number of variables is usually dictated by past research and present theory. In this chapter the first step is taken in exploring more complete systems of variables. Instead of focusing on two variables in isolation, we will focus on three variables in isolation from any other possibly important variables.

Before getting into a detailed discussion of three variable models, let us explore a hypothetical situation. This example will show the importance of such a discussion. The data for the illustration include people from two different countries. The variables are income and educational attainment. We want to search for the relationship between income (the independent variable) and educational attainment (years of schooling, the dependent variable). We hypothesize that there is a direct relationship between income and educational attainment. Figure 11.1 shows data on a bivariate scatterplot. The best fitting line clearly indicates a direct relationship with fair precision. It would seem our hypothesis is supported by these data.

We just viewed income and educational attainment in isolation from other variables and reached a conclusion about the nature of the relationship between these two variables. However, remember that these data are from two different countries. Suppose, for the il-

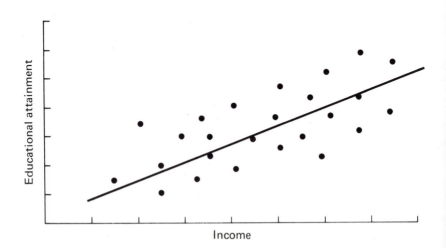

FIGURE 11.1
Bivariate scatterplot of income and educational attainment

lustration, that these two countries have different kinds of educational systems. One country has a system where people pay for their education. The other country has totally free education, all the way through the highest degree level. We can expand our two variable system to a three variable system by taking this fact into account. The variables would be income, educational attainment, and type of educational system. We examine this three variable system with the same type of scatterplot we used for the bivariate system. The only difference is that circles are used to represent those cases from the country where people must pay tuition (similar to some parts of the U.S. system), and triangles are used to represent those people from the country with free education (similar to some countries with more socialized education).

The scatterplot at the top of Figure 11.2 is a scatterplot of three variables, but it is a little difficult to see what is happening. Therefore at the bottom of Figure 11.2 we have taken the data and partitioned it into two parts. If the two bottom tables were superimposed on each other, they would look exactly like the top plot. Notice what has happened by including a third variable. When focusing on the "free system" (left bottom plot), there is no relationship between income and educational attainment. When focusing on the "tuition system" (right bottom plot), the relationship between income and educational attainment is still direct (the slope may be a little different).

The point is inescapable. If we examine the bivariate relationship, we come to one conclusion about the relationship between income and educational attainment. If we examine the three variable system, our conclusion about the relationship between income and educational attainment is more complicated. The norms of science dictate that, if possible, the most complete system of variables should be examined. Discussing the relationship between income and educational attainment in the three variable system is seen as superior because a more complete understanding of the variables can be attained.

Taking a third variable into account when analyzing a system of variables is called *controlling for a third variable*. The techniques used to explore three variables, and the lessons that can be learned by adding a third variable, are somewhat similar no matter how many variables are added. The analysis of systems with at least three variables is called *multivariate analysis*.

2. WHAT IT MEANS TO "CONTROL" FOR A VARIABLE

There are two strategies for explicitly introducing a third variable (often called Z) into one's analysis of an X-Y relationship. The first

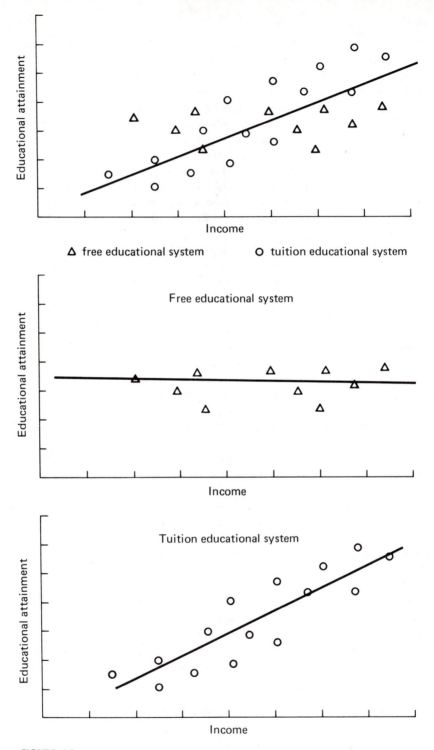

FIGURE 11.2
Three variable scatterplot of income, educational attainment, and type of educational system

is to be concerned mainly with the X-Y relationship and to introduce a third variable to see if the X-Y relationship still has the same characteristics. This third variable can be either a second independent variable or a "control" variable.

The second is to think in terms of a system of variables considering three variables at one time. The analysis procedures for both strategies are similar. Both end up by looking at the three variable model (system) and interpreting the relationships among three variables. The difference is that some authors first look at the two variable case and then introduce the third variable to see what happens, much as we did in our hypothetical illustration. Others, if interested in three variables, simply start with three. Each technique should result in the same interpretation of relationships between the three variables. We suggest that for the moment you start with the two variable relationship, then add the third variable. Note that some research articles do not examine the two variable case, but go directly to looking at the three variable model.

Research designs used to explore three variable models generally have one of two structures. The first type of design structure does not allow Z to have different values. Therefore Z cannot vary. If Z cannot vary, then it is not a "variable," but a "constant." It is thought that if Z is controlled in this manner, it cannot have an effect on the X-Y relationship. Therefore any conclusion about the X-Y relationship has accounted for the presence of the third variable, Z. For example, an experimenter may always conduct an experiment with the room at the same temperature. In this way, temperature as a variable would be "controlled" by not allowing it to change. Temperature would be *held constant*. A survey researcher could make sure that every subject in a mailed survey receives the same cover letter explaining the research. By doing this, any effect of different words or phrasing in the cover letter will be "controlled" because the words are not allowed to be different. They are held constant by design.

The problem with this type of control is that it limits the type of information available to the researcher about the three variable model. For example, suppose an experimenter were studying the relationship between frustration and aggression. It may be that the results of an experiment studying these two variables conducted in a room where the temperature was 22°C would be different than the results of an experiment conducted in a room where the temperature was 37°C. Perhaps the difference in temperature makes a difference as to how much aggression results from the same amount of frustration. Maybe this is why motorists honk their horns at other motorists more often in the summer than in the winter. If all such experiments were conducted at the same temperature, this type of information would not be obtained. Any conclusion about the X-Y relationship will only be correct at the value of Z at which the experiments took place. (In our first example this approach would amount to only looking at one of the plots at the bottom of Figure 11.2.)

In the second type of design structure the research is conducted so that Z is allowed to operate. That is, Z will vary as X and Y are varying. For example, in surveys, since the data are collected after all of the events being studied have occurred, it is not possible to structure the world so that some Z(s) will remain constant. In this situation, Z will be operating unevenly. At times it will have had one value and at other times it will have had another. In some experiments yet another situation exists. When randomization or precision matching is used, Z will not be held constant. Rather, all Z's will be operating evenly. The idea behind randomization is that Z will vary but it will vary in a random fashion. Since Z changes in a random fashion in both experimental and control groups, any effect of Z operating is thought to cancel out when comparing the control and experimental groups. In some instances the effect of Z does cancel out. However, if the system of variables is like our illustration of income, educational attainment and type of educational system, this type of even variation in Z will not allow us to fully understand the system. (See the subsection on "Complicated models.")

In all cases where the design of the research is such that Z is allowed to operate (vary, have different values), it is necessary to "artificially control" for Z. This artificial control for Z is called *partitioning*. In partitioning, the data are treated in a way that Z is statistically held constant. Only the units with the same value of Z are examined to determine the relationship between X and Y. This means that a separate analysis of the X-Y relationship is needed for each value of Z. By comparing and contrasting these different analyses of the X-Y relationship, a conclusion can be drawn about how Z is affecting the X-Y relationship. This partitioning is also necessary when randomization is used, if one wants to detect certain kinds of three variable models. Figure 11.3 shows the discussion presented above in graphic form. Thus, if controlling is done by designing a study in such a way that Z does not vary, you will be limited in what you can say about the three variable model (system). If Z is allowed to vary, the final step in exploring a three variable model will be partitioning of the data. In the case of randomization and precision matching, some three variable models will be revealed, but in order to fully explore and interpret the possibilities of all three variable models, the data must be partitioned. The following section will explore how to partition data using the scatterplot and how to interpret the different sets of scatterplots that may result from partitioning data.

FIGURE 11.3
Two strategies for controlling for a third variable

(a).		(b)
Let Z operate (vary)		Do not let Z operate (vary)
↙ ↘		↓
Even variation in Z	Uneven variation in Z	No variation in Z
↓	↓	↓
By randomization or precision matching	Must partition data	*Problem* = cannot observe if X-Y relationship will stay the same at other values (levels) of Z
↓		↓
Problem = cannot observe certain types of three variable models		Limited in conclusions about the effects of Z
↓		
Must partition data		

3. EXPLORING THREE VARIABLE MODELS WITH SCATTERPLOTS

Partitioning is a statistical operation that has the effect of holding Z constant. We would like to analyze the X-Y relationship at each value (level) of Z and compare these analyses with the original X-Y analysis. Since we cannot literally prevent Z from varying, the statistical procedure used must approximate this for us. The original X-Y relationship is determined using the same techniques presented in Chapter 3. After this is done the units for which we have data on X, on Y, and on Z are separated into different groups depending on their value for Z. For example, if the units being studied are people and we have a value of X, a value of Y, and a value of Z for each person, the subjects will be separated (partitioned) into groups according to their score of Z. If there are two possible values of Z, say high and low, this partitioning results in two groups of subjects. One group has a low Z and one group has a high Z. Each group would probably have people with different values of X and Y. These smaller groups of units are then analyzed separately using the same techniques employed for looking at the original X-Y relationship. The result of this partitioning will be three scatterplots of the X-Y relationship: the original X-Y relationship, the X-Y relationship for only those units with low Z, and the X-Y relationship for only those units with high Z. For the last two analyses Z is being held constant by partitioning the data. Z is being controlled "statistically."

Figure 11.4 provides some hypothetical data to show how to construct scatterplots while controlling for a third variable.

Data:	Unit	X = number of fire trucks	Y = damage in dollars	Z = size of fire
	A	3	$ 400	Small
	B	2	500	Small
	C	4	600	Small
	D	1	500	Small
	E	5	500	Small
	F	9	900	Large
	G	7	800	Large
	H	8	1,000	Large
	I	10	900	Large

Original *X-Y* relationship—all units

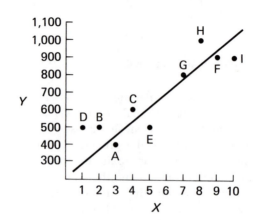

Only units with *Z* = small   Only units with *Z* = large

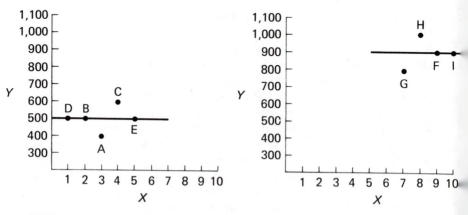

FIGURE 11.4
Hypothetical data for controlling for a third variable using scatterplots

Note that all the units are used in the scatterplot for the original X-Y relationship. However, in the scatterplots where Z is controlled, only those units with the appropriate values for Z are included. The left lower plot is only for units with Z = Small. The right lower plot is only for units with Z = Large. In this manner, Z is statistically held constant in the lower control (conditional) tables. The best fitting line in the original plot clearly shows a direct relationship between the number of fire trucks at a fire and the amount of damage done. Examining all the control tables shows that all of the best fitting lines show no relationship between X and Y. In other words, the original appearance of a strong direct relationship between X and Y disappears when Z is controlled. When this occurs the model can be a spurious one, or an intervening one.

There are virtually an infinite number of possibilities that may occur when data are partitioned to control for a third variable. Through experience, researchers have found that there are certain types of findings that continually occur. Since this is the case, we are able to present a relatively small number of basic types of conclusions that can be drawn from multivariate analysis. We will follow the strategy of examining the main X-Y relationship without controlling for Z. We will then partition the data and reexamine the resulting X-Y relationships. We will categorize each three variable model as being one of the following types:

1. spurious model
2. intervening model
3. complicated model
4. joint-effects model
5. no-effect model

Although authors and researchers sometimes use different labels for these five categories, the principles of analysis as well as the conclusions about the three variables under consideration are the same.

Spurious model

A spurious model may occur if a relationship is found to exist when examining a bivariate X-Y relationship, but when controlling for Z, the original X-Y relationship no longer exists. That is, by considering three variables, we now conclude there really is no relationship between X and Y. This type of third variable is one of the unseen variables discussed in Chapter 1.

There are really two types of spurious relationships, depending on the causal reasoning. One type exists because the third variable could happen prior in time to both X and Y and could "cause" changes in both of them. Our earlier example of the size of the fire causing both the number of fire trucks and the degree of damage is this type of spurious model. Figure 11.5 diagrammatically shows this causal reasoning. The solid lines are "real" relationships and the dotted line is the spurious relationship.

The second type of spurious model has no such time order requirements. The reasoning is *not* that the third variable "causes" X and Y. Somehow the third variable is covering up the real relationship between X and Y. The third variable is seen as "confusing" the X–Y relationship. For example, the statement, males have more auto accidents than females, implies a relationship between sex and driver safety. However, if we introduce a third variable, distance driven, we discover that there is no relationship between sex and driver safety. There originally appears to be a relationship between sex and driver safety only because males drive more miles than females. Causally, we do not think that miles driven "causes" sex. However, the relationship between sex and driver safety is spurious because miles driven confuses that bivariate relationship.

In the above model we conclude that the originally observed bivariate relationship was spurious because it can totally be explained by controlling for Z. If an experiment is properly conducted, randomization will control for the possibility of spurious relationships between X and Y. Therefore, in these cases it is not necessary to partition the data to try to determine if perceived relationships between X and Y are spurious. However, in field experiments, quasiexperiments, surveys, and most other research designs, partitioning would be necessary.

Intervening model

The results of partitioning the data when the third variable is an intervening variable are similar to the results obtained when partitioning a spurious model. The original X–Y relationship will seem to exist before controlling for Z, but upon partitioning, all of the X–Y relationships will disappear. However, these models are very different if viewed from a causal perspective. In an intervening model

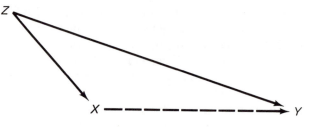

FIGURE 11.5
Spurious model

the variations in X lead to variations in Z, and variations in Z lead to variations in Y. This can be diagrammed as in Figure 11.6.

There are many three variable sociological systems that can be viewed as intervening. For example, the relationship between social class and school achievement may have opportunity as an intervening variable. Likewise, a politician's popularity may produce more campaign funds which may allow the candidate to be elected. On first glance it may appear that the candidate's popularity was the "cause" of winning. However, without the presence of funds, popularity may not lead to being elected. Figure 11.7 gives an example of the best fitting lines for an intervening or spurious model. The important thing is that an original X–Y relationship disappears when controlling for Z.

In some contexts the variable we are referring to as X is called an antecedent variable, Z is called the independent variable, and Y the dependent variable. It really makes no difference what letter or word labels are attached to the different variables. The model remains the same and the scatterplots will turn out the same. In both cases, one variable "causes" another and that variable "causes" the third. There is a special circumstance that needs to be mentioned at this point. If we have a three variable model that we believe to be like an intervening model, that is, three variables in a row, it would not be appropriate to examine the relationship between the second two variables while controlling for the first. You would always control for the middle variable. Although the reasoning is too technical for this book, this point is important. We only want to control for a possible intervening variable, not an antecedent variable.

Notice that a problem is created in the interpretation of spurious and intervening models. Scatterplots look similar for both models. In order to tell whether a three variable model that produces these types of scatterplots is a spurious or an intervening one, you must decide about the causal reasoning.

Complicated model

In the case of a complicated model, it is not possible to draw a simple diagram that represents how the three variables in the model

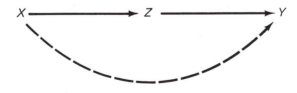

FIGURE 11.6
Intervening model

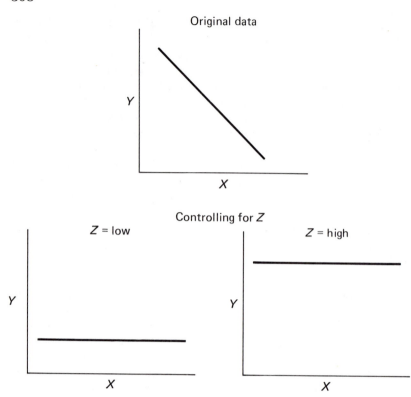

Original data

Controlling for Z

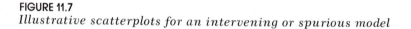

FIGURE 11.7
Illustrative scatterplots for an intervening or spurious model

are interrelated. The link between X and Y cannot be seen as one kind of link or one type of relationship. When the partitioned scatterplots of a complicated model are constructed, the extent (slope) of the conditional (control) X-Y relationships will be different from one another. Some may be direct relationships, some inverse, and some no relationship. Figure 11.8 shows one illustration of the types of best fitting lines that might be obtained for a complicated model.

Complicated models go under many different names in other textbooks and in research reports. They may be called nonadditive models, systems in which there is statistical interaction, specification models, clarification models, description models, or contingent models.

When the original X-Y analysis shows no relationship but where the control tables show a complicated model (different extents), the third variable is called a suppressor variable. An example may help to clarify what is meant by a complicated model.

Zajonc (1965) has noted that for those who have had much expe-

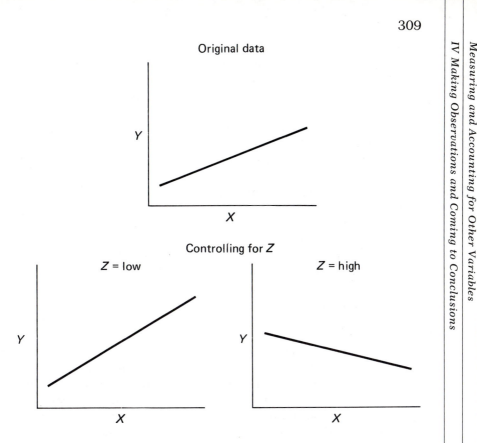

FIGURE 11.8
Illustrative scatterplots for a complicated model

rience at a task (high Z), the presence of an audience will improve task performance. For those who are inexperienced at a task (low Z), the presence of an audience will reduce proficiency in task performance. If the original X-Y (audience-task performance) relationship were investigated without controlling for experience, and an equal number of experienced and inexperienced people were in the experimental and control group, the original X-Y relationship would show no relationship. However, the low Z table would show an inverse relationship and the high Z table would show a direct relationship.

This example enables us to illustrate several things about complicated relationships. First, this is an example of a suppressor relationship. The true X-Y relationship is "suppressed" by the control variable. It does not appear until the third variable is brought into the analysis. Second, this complicated situation may exist whether data are collected in a nonexperimental or experimental design. A simple experiment would not really control for the influence of such variables. Conclusions about the complicated model could only generalize to populations where the control variable would have the same value as in the experiment. Third, in a complicated model, not only is there a relationship between X and Y, but there is also a relationship between Z and Y.

In our example, how experience affects task performance depends on the presence of an audience, or we could say that how an audience affects task performance depends on experience. The situation is truly a complicated one.

There are, of course, many different types of complicated models. A complicated model exists anytime the best fitting lines (slope, extent) in the control scatterplots are nonparallel (in the case of linear relationships), or when one or more control plots have different curvilinear relationship from the other control plots. Figure 11.9 shows a number of control tables for different complicated models.

Joint-effects model

In a joint-effects model the originally observed X-Y relationship is also modified in the control tables. It is also quite difficult to draw a simple diagram representing this type of model. The control scatterplots will have the same extent (slope), but the best fitting lines will be at different levels (if the same categories are marked on the coordinates). In other words, if the control tables were superimposed on one another, the best fitting lines would be parallel. Figure 11.10 shows an example of the type of scatterplots which would be produced from a joint-effects model.

An example of a joint-effects model can be drawn from the supermarket. Marketing specialists have discovered that items placed closer to the end of store aisles sell more than items near the middle of the aisle. There is a direct relationship between how close an item is to the end of the aisle and its sales volume. In addition, items that are sale priced sell more than similar items that are not on sale. Viewing the sale status of an item as a control variable, the relationship between the location of an item and its sales volume will be the same in both cases. However, the sales volume of the sale priced items will always be larger. Thus, there is a joint effect between these three variables. Figure 11.11 illustrates this model.

No-effect model

In all the models presented thus far there has been a different best fitting line in the control scatterplots than in the original X-Y scatterplot. In a no-effect model, as the name implies, Z has no effect on the X-Y relationship. That is, the best fitting line in each control scatterplot will be the same as in the original X-Y plot. For example,

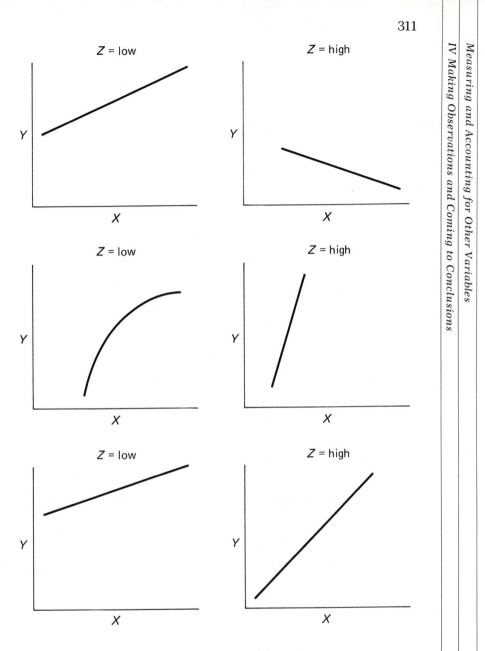

FIGURE 11.9
Additional illustrations of complicated models

an original direct or inverse relationship remains the same in all control plots, or an original X-Y analysis showing no relationship would also be found if Z were controlled. Figure 11.12 provides an illustration of scatterplots for a no-effect model.

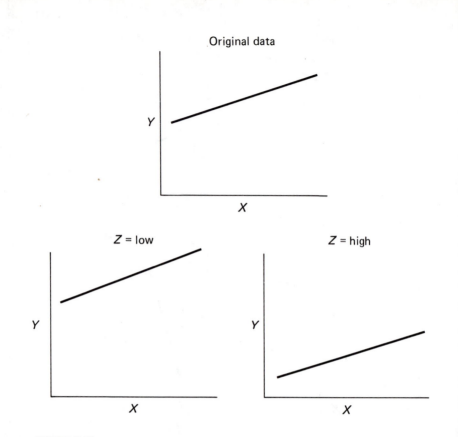

FIGURE 11.10
Illustrative scatterplots for a joint-effects model

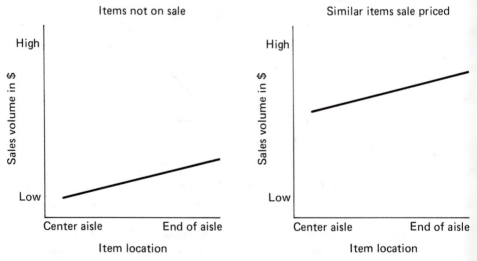

FIGURE 11.11
Example of a joint-effects model

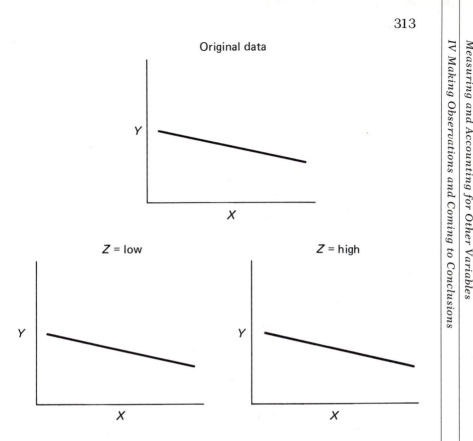

FIGURE 11.12
Illustrative scatterplots for a no-effect model

An example of a no-effect model would be the introduction of religion into the analysis of the relationship between social status and marital adjustment. The bivariate relationship between social status and marital adjustment would not likely change when religion is introduced as a control variable. That is, religion does not influence the link between social status and marital adjustment.

4. ANALYZING THREE VARIABLE MODELS WITH PERCENTAGES

Analyzing systems of more than two variables with percentage tables is directly analogous to exploring them with scatterplots. The two main variables of interest are still called the independent and dependent variable, and any other variables that we include in the model to be analyzed are often called control variables. In order to do a multivariate analysis with percentage tables, one first examines the main X-Y relationship. After this has been done it is necessary to construct "control" or "conditional" tables by separating the units into two or more groups depending on the units' value on the control variable(s). After the data have been partitioned, an X-Y analysis is constructed for each group of units. In a three variable model, if the control variable has three values, there will be three control tables. If the control variable has four values, there will be four control tables. In a three variable analysis there will be a main X-Y table composed of all the units measured plus a number of control tables composed of only units with the same value on the control variable. The total number of units in all of control tables will of course add up to the total number of units in the main table. By doing this it is possible to determine what impact the control variable is having on the relationship between X and Y. If the nature of the relationship in the control X-Y tables is the same as in the main X-Y table, the control variable is having no effect on the main relationship. However, if the control tables show a different relationship between the independent and dependent variable than the main table, the control variable is having an effect on the main relationship. If this is the case, any conclusions reached about the X-Y relationship will be distorted unless the control variable is included in the analysis.

Suppose we wish to explore the relationship between people's religious background and the degree of authoritarianism in their personality. Although common sense may tell us that there would be a relationship between these two variables, sociological theory might suggest that the nature of the relationship between these two variables will depend on what type of socialization experiences people have had. If this were the three variable model we wished to explore, religious background would be the independent variable, authoritarianism the dependent variable, and type of socialization background the control variable.

Table 11.1 illustrates the type of data that might result from a survey of subjects concerning these three variables. The data on all three variables must be available for each subject and they must be matched so that the subjects can be properly placed in the various tables.

Table 11.2 shows a typical multivariate analysis of these types of data. Both frequencies (in parentheses) and percentages are displayed in each table to conserve space. This is a very common practice in research journals. Notice that in all the tables the percentages in each column add to 100 percent. In addition, note that the frequencies of the two control tables add up to the total of the frequencies in the main table. This will always be the case if the data have been partitioned properly.

The main table shows a curvilinear or inverse relationship between religious background and authoritarianism, and if no further analysis was done on these data, that would be the conclusion. How-

TABLE 11.1
Typical data for a three variable analysis

Unit I. D.	Religious background[a]	Authoritarianism[b]	Socialization background[c]
0045	F	H	T
1254	M	H	T
5467	R	L	P
1126	M	H	P
•	•	•	•
•	•	•	•
•	•	•	•

[a] Independent Variable – Religious Background
    Categories: F = Fundamental, M = Moderate, R = Radical
[b] Dependent Variable = Authoritarianism
    Categories: H = High, L = Low
[c] Control Variable = Socialization Background
    Categories: P = Permissive, T = Traditional

ever, on further analysis, controlling for socialization background shows that there is no relationship between religious background and authoritarianism for those subjects who come from a permissive socialization background. For those who come from a traditional background the relationship is either curvilinear or inverse. It is difficult to determine if the relationships in this illustration are curvilinear or inverse because there are so few categories of Y. In general, the more categories of both variables, the easier it is to come to conclusions about the form of a relationship. The relationship between the independent and dependent variables is considerably different depending on the value (category) of the control variable. Recall that this type of three variable model is called a "complicated" model. It may also be said that there is statistical interaction between the control and independent variable.

In addition to the types of tables displayed in the above example, it would be possible to construct a percentage table between the variables of socialization background and authoritarianism (Z-Y), or socialization background and religious background (Z-X). The third variable in each of these analyses could be considered a control variable. This would necessitate constructing seven additional tables. The reason that this is not done is that the theory behind our analysis specified which variable was the independent, dependent, and control variable. It is quite easy to see that without this kind of specification, the task of analyzing data would be considerably increased.

If more than three variables compose the model being analyzed, it would be necessary to construct control tables for every combination of the categories of the control variables. For example, if a

316

TABLE 11.2
A multivariate percentage analysis

MAIN TABLE — ALL UNITS

Religious background

	F	M	R
H	93%	61%	16%
	(28)	(52)	(10)
L	7%	39%	84%
	(2)	(33)	(51)
	100%	100%	100%
	(30)	(85)	(61)

Authoritarianism

(N = 176)

CONTROL TABLES

Only units with P socialization

Religious background

	F	M	R
H	80%	80%	83%
	(8)	(12)	(5)
L	20%	20%	17%
	(2)	(3)	(1)
	100%	100%	100%
	(10)	(15)	(6)

Authoritarianism

(N = 31)

Only units with T socializati

Religious background

	F	M	R
H	100%	57%	9%
	(20)	(40)	(5)
L	0%	43%	91%
	(0)	(30)	(50)
	100%	100%	100%
	(20)	(70)	(55)

Authoritarianism

(N = 145)

(31 + 145 = 176)

model had two control variables, one with low, medium, and high categories and one with categories of 1, 2, and 3, nine control tables would be constructed, as follows: (1) low on the first control variable and 1 on the other, (2) low on the first and 2 on the second, (3) low on the first and 3 on the second, (4) medium on the first and 1 on the second, (5) medium on the first and 2 on the second, (6) medium on the first and 3 on the second, (7) high on the first and 1 on the second, (8) high on the first and 2 on the second, and (9) high on the first and 3 on the second.

The number of control tables increases considerably as the number of control variables increase in the model. Nevertheless, to be complete a multivariate analysis must present all the appropriate control tables along with the main *X-Y* table.

Now that we have described the general procedures for analyzing multivariate relationships with percentage tables, let us review the decision making criteria for interpreting such relationships. Note the special difficulties of interpreting percentage tables. If controlling for a third variable does not change the percentages in the control tables from the original bivariate table, then there is no effect. If the tables are very similar, we still would interpret this as no change. (When reading journals, you might note that one of the criteria used to see if the control tables are different are tests of significance.) If controlling shows that the *X-Y* relationship virtually vanishes in each control table, then the best interpretation would be spurious or intervening. If the percentage tables display different forms of relationships after controlling, then the multivariate relationship is probably complicated. The most difficult case to interpret is when the percentage tables show relationships of the same form but different strength. Since percentage tables combine extent and precision, it is difficult to know if this is a case analogous to different slopes (which would reflect a complicated relationship), or parallel slopes at different heights (which would reflect joint effects). We have adopted the rule that if the percentages are different but the strength is the same, we shall interpret the multivariate relationship as one of joint effects. If the form is the same but the strength is different, we shall interpret the relationship as complicated. Table 11.3 provides some examples.

5. CONCLUSIONS

When additional variables are added to any model the relationships between the variables being considered may change. It is important to include variables that are thought to be important in an analysis before conclusions about relationships are made. Ideally all analyses in research should be multivariate. For various reasons (some good and some not so good), this is not always done. Viewing sets of variables in isolation from other important variables may result in errors of interpretation about relationships in systems of variables. This is perhaps one of the most important connections between theory and research. It is customary to decide on the basis of theoretical issues and concerns whether important control variables have been considered. Although there is never any guarantee that all relevant variables have been included in any model, theory and experience will allow us to have a certain amount of confidence.

In this chapter we have followed the strategy of first examining

TABLE 11.3
Examples of joint and complicated relationships

JOINT EFFECTS

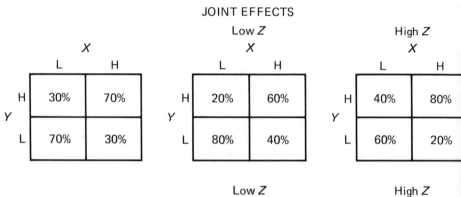

X

	L	H
Y H	30%	70%
Y L	70%	30%

Low Z — X

	L	H
Y H	20%	60%
Y L	80%	40%

High Z — X

	L	H
Y H	40%	80%
Y L	60%	20%

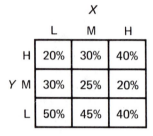

X

	L	M	H
Y H	20%	30%	40%
Y M	30%	25%	20%
Y L	50%	45%	40%

Low Z — X

	L	M	H
Y H	10%	20%	30%
Y M	30%	25%	20%
Y L	60%	55%	50%

High Z — X

	L	M	H
Y H	45%	55%	65%
Y M	20%	15%	10%
Y L	35%	30%	25%

COMPLICATED RELATIONSHIPS

X

	L	H
Y H	30%	70%
Y L	70%	30%

Low Z — X

	L	H
Y H	20%	80%
Y L	80%	20%

High Z — X

	L	H
Y H	40%	60%
Y L	60%	40%

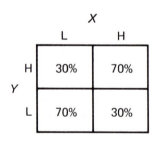

X

	L	M	H
Y H	20%	30%	40%
Y M	30%	25%	20%
Y L	50%	45%	40%

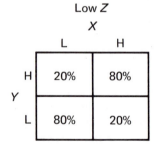

Low Z — X

	L	M	H
Y H	10%	40%	60%
Y M	30%	20%	10%
Y L	60%	40%	30%

High Z — X

	L	M	H
Y H	45%	55%	65%
Y M	20%	15%	10%
Y L	35%	30%	25%

the original X-Y relationship and then preparing control (conditional) scatterplots. It is common to find all three variables considered simultaneously. The way that this is done is to plot both of the control scatterplots on the same set of coordinates. This may be done with different color ink. One color is used for units with low Z and one for those with high Z. Different symbols besides dots can also be used to represent the partitioned data. Or, different types of best fitting lines can be used. This has the same effect as superimposing the control scatterplots on one figure. The technique is particularly popular when reporting experimental results. It may make describing complicated models and joint-effects models a little more clear. Figure 11.13 shows some typical results using this technique for the various types of models we have discussed.

If we are to understand our environment through the scientific study of important variables, it is necessary for us to be able to study models which go beyond simple bivariate systems. This chapter has introduced the concept of multivariate models and has presented the most common types of three variable models. Although we have exclusively used the scatterplot and percentages in this chapter, there are other techniques that are commonly employed to describe and analyze multivariate models. The most common techniques are measures of association. Chapter 13 presents some common measures of association which are used to analyze bivariate and multivariate relationships.

6. SUMMARY

Whenever a variable is added to a system there is a possibility that conclusions already reached about relationships will have to be altered. Specifically, adding a third variable to a bivariate analysis may alter the relationship between the original two variables. Adding a third variable to the analysis is called controlling for the third variable. The goal of controlling for a third variable is to remove the effects of that variable from the X-Y relationship. There are five main types of three variable models: spurious, intervening, complicated, joint-effects, and no-effect models. In the spurious model the third variable is either "causing" both X and Y or is confusing the bivariate relationship. In either case, what appears to be a relationship between X and Y disappears when controlling for Z. In an intervening model the original X-Y relationship also disappears when controlling for Z. The causal reasoning in the intervening model is that Z is an intermediate causal variable between X and Y. Complicated models are not easily described. In these models it is necessary to describe the X-Y relationship within each conditional scatterplot. The bivariate relationship is different depending on the

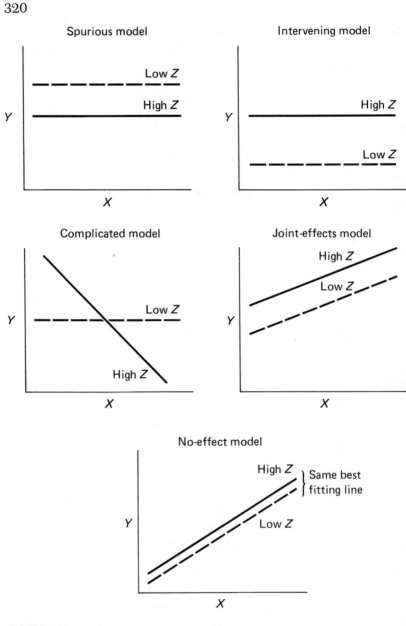

FIGURE 11.13
Illustrative scatterplots for different models resulting from considering three variables simultaneously

value of Z. Each control relationship between X and Y can also be compared to the original X-Y relationship. In the joint-effects model the slope of the X-Y relationship is the same for all conditional scatterplots; however, the level of the best fitting line is different for different control tables. In the no-effect model, as the name implies, Z has no effect on the original X-Y relationship.

In order to detect the various three variable models it is necessary to partition the data. This is true even if experimental designs utilizing randomization are used. By partitioning data it can be determined if the third variable added to the analysis is having an impact on the X-Y relationship. If it is having no effect, the original analysis can be reported with the confidence that knowledge of the third variable will not increase our understanding of the systems of variables under study. However, if controlling for a third variable results in finding either a spurious, intervening, complicated, or joint-effects model, simply reporting the original X-Y relationship would be an unsatisfactory description of the system of variables. In our search for relationships we must always be alert to the idea that a complete understanding of a system of variables will not be obtained until we have satisfactorily controlled for all important variables. Theory, replication, and the exploration of many alternative systems of variables are the guides we can use in searching for relationships in systems of variables.

EXERCISES

1. For each example below, if possible:
   a. Identify the dependent variable.
   b. Identify the independent variable and the control variable; for models with two independent variables state which variable you would partition (use as if it were the control variable).
   c. Identify the multivariate model.
   (1) The direct relationship between status and IQ is unaffected by sex.
   (2) Propinquity (being nearby) is directly related to frequency of interaction. Frequency of interaction is directly related to attraction.
   (3) Possibly greater frequency of interaction only leads to greater attraction if people share similar values. If not, the interaction–attraction relationship may be inverse.
   (4) For women who work fertility is lower than for women who do not work. Industrialization is another variable which directly affects fertility.
   (5) When education is controlled, the direct relationship between being authoritarian and being prejudiced disappears.
   (6) Mixed marriage is likely to create value conflicts which in turn are likely to lead to divorce.
   (7) In Chapter 9 we pointed out that experimental results may differ if the experimenter is businesslike as opposed to being casual.
   (8) In the experimental study of attitudes, persuasive techniques are likely to be more effective on attitude change if a pretest is employed than if there is no pretest.

(9) Recent reports suggest that the relationship between age and theft is equal for males and females.

(10) Controls for status do not change the relationship between urban crime and youth. Middle class youths are as likely to be "delinquent" as working class youths.

(11) Both good looks and status are directly related to attractiveness.

(12) Marriage seems to diminish the appetite for motion pictures: fewer married than single people attend films. However, when age is controlled this relationship (marriage–film going) disappears.

(13) Emotional sermons seem to have greater appeal to the working class than to the middle and upper classes.

(14) Psychological depression is affected by physical health and social success.

(15) The lower the surveillance the greater the temptation. The greater the temptation the greater the probability of cheating.

(16) Economic conditions are inversely related to the crime rate. When unemployment is controlled there is no relationship between economic conditions and crime.

(17) The relationship between race and achievement may be explained by social class.

(18) The two-step-flow-of-communications hypothesis suggests that the media has an influence through opinion leaders.

2. a. Determine whether the data in the following scatterplots support the hypothesis that the father's occupational status influences the son's occupational status by providing the son with educational opportunity (and of course, motivation to take advantage of the opportunity).

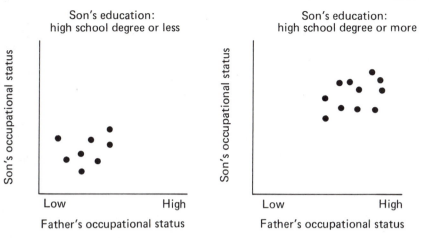

For each of the following, what would you conclude about the three variable model?

b.

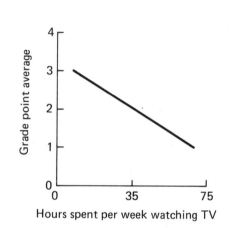

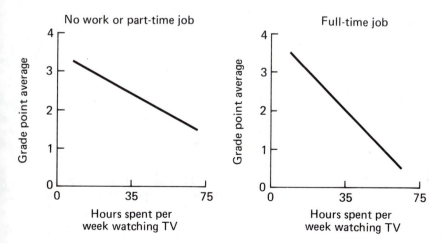

c.

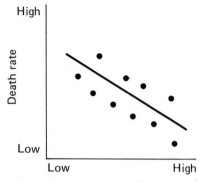

Country's average per capita income

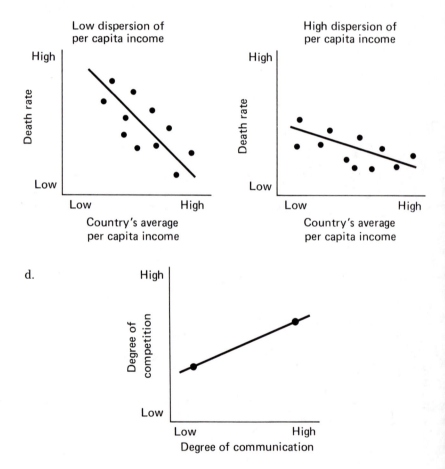

Low dispersion of per capita income

Country's average per capita income

High dispersion of per capita income

Country's average per capita income

d.

Degree of competition

Degree of communication

(*Note:* The slopes for these experimental data are means. The control variable involves the experimenter's stress on cooperation in the instructions.)

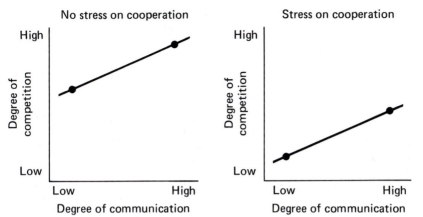

3. Below is a set of data on driving accidents over a three-year period, along with information on several other variables.
a. Construct a scatterplot to examine the relationship between average miles driven per week and accident rate.
b. Control for whether the driver would be considered "drunk." For your operational definition of drunk, use Blood Alcohol Level of .07 or better. Make two scatterplots, one for "drunk" drivers and one for "sober" drivers.
c. Examine the effect of sex and the effect of driver training, separately, on the relationship between miles driven and accidents.

Subject	Number of accidents in a three-year period	Average miles driven per week	Amount of alcohol in system when accident occurred (blood alcohol level)	Sex	Driver training
1	10	40	.17	M	No
2	7	35	.10	M	No
3	5	10	.07	F	Yes
4	12	75	.22	M	No
5	3	60	.04	M	No
6	2	40	.00	F	No
7	10	90	.19	F	No
8	4	105	.02	M	Yes
9	3	110	.01	M	Yes
10	11	60	.20	F	Yes
11	7	50	.11	F	Yes
12	7	120	.03	F	No
13	9	110	.14	F	Yes
14	2	90	.02	F	Yes
15	3	30	.03	F	No

Subject	Number of accidents in a three-year period	Average miles driven per week	Amount of alchohol in system when accident occurred (blood alcohol level)	Sex	Driver training
16	1	50	.00	M	Yes
17	11	105	.21	M	No
18	3	77	.02	F	Yes
19	6	75	.07	M	No
20	8	70	.12	F	No
21	1	60	.01	M	Yes
22	0	20	.00	F	Yes
23	9	25	.16	M	Yes
24	5	80	.07	M	No

4. a. Construct bivariate tables and interpret the relationship between religious background and authoritarianism.

b. Control for socialization and interpret the multivariate relationship.

Religious   F M R R M M F F R F F R M F F M
  background: R R M M F R F R M

Authoritarianism: H H L L L L L H H L L L L L L H H L L L
L L H L L L

Socialization: T T P P P P P T T P P P P P T T P P P P
P T P P P

Complete the following tables:

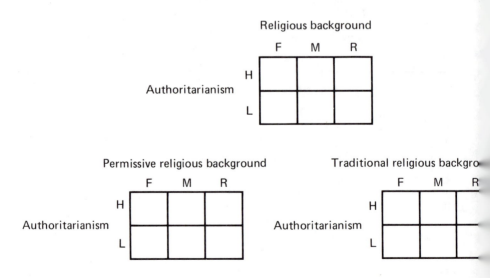

Religious background

Authoritarianism

Permissive religious background   Traditional religious backgro

5. A sociologist was interested in the relationship between a father's occupation, his son's occupation, and his grandson's occupation. The following are the data he obtained:

Father's occupation: B B W W P P W B B W W P P P W B W B W B W P B W B W W B P

Son's occupation: P W W W W W P P B W W B P W P P B W B W B W P W W B P W B P

Grandson's occupation: P W P B P P P P B W B P B B P P W P P W B P P P P W P W B W

P = professional; W = white collar; B = blue collar.

a. What multivariate relationship(s) can be examined with these data?

b. Construct the appropriate percentage tables to examine such relationships.

c. What do you conclude?

6. In the case of experiments where data typically involve comparing means rather than scatterplots, describe how you could control for a third variable.

1. From your survey data:

a. Select a main hypothesis on which to focus (this must involve two interval or ratio variables). Treat the independent variable as X. Re-examine this relationship by controlling for all other "independent" variables in your study.

b. Are there other variables that you should have controlled which you did not include in your study?

2. Re-examine each of your other projects. Are there instances in which a multivariate perspective might have altered your results? Describe how you would have redesigned your study to include such variables.

BLALOCK, H. *Theory Construction*. Englewood Cliffs, N.J.: Prentice-Hall, 1969.

HYMAN, H. *Survey Design and Analysis*. New York: Free Press, 1955.

ROSENBERG, M. *The Logic of Survey Analysis*. New York: Basic Books, 1968.

ZAJONC, R. "Social Facilitation." *Science, 149,* 1965, 269–274.

ZEISEL, H. *Say It with Figures,* 4th ed. New York: Harper & Row, 1957.

CHAPTER 12
OTHER RESEARCH DESIGNS

After studying this chapter, students should be able to:

1. Generally describe participant observation, content analysis, simulation, evaluation research, and unobtrusive research.

2. List and discuss three general reasons for conducting participant observation studies.

3. Discuss the problem of selection in participant observation.

4. Describe the uses of informants in participant observation as well as discuss some of the problems of their use.

5. Discuss some of the possible applications of participant observation.

6. List and discuss four uses of content analysis.

7. Briefly describe how content analysis is done and give examples.

8. Discuss the issue of whether the mass media are a cause or an effect in social analysis.

9. Discuss the role of models in simulation research.

10. Describe game simulation and computer simulation and say how they differ and how they are similar.

11. List some uses of simulation and provide examples of each use.

12. Describe the chain of program events with which evaluation research is largely concerned.

13. Discuss the nature and purposes of formative and summative evaluation and say when and why each type is used.

14. Discuss some of the problems of the role of the researcher in evaluation.

15. Discuss the problem of determining whether a program is a "success" or not on the basis of evaluation research.

16. Describe the problem of reactivity and give examples of the types of research in which reactivity would be a problem.

17. List and describe the major types of unobtrusive measures.

18. Give examples of some unobtrusive measures.

19. Discuss the possible uses of unobtrusive measures in the research process.

20. Discuss how each of the research methods presented in this chapter can aid in the process of searching for relationships.

Accretion measures   Any type of data which results from human behavior that leaves some physical traces.

Back region   Places, situations, behaviors, and phenomena which occur out of the sight of outsiders.

Computer simulation model   A set of mathematical equations which specifies the relationships between variables into which certain values for some of the variables can be inserted.

Content analysis   Any systematic procedure devised to examine the content of recorded information.

Disguised observation   Hiding the fact that you are doing research from those whom you are observing.

Document research   A type of content analysis involving the use of recorded documents as a data base.

Erosion measures   Any type of data resulting from human behavior which results in the "erosion" or "wearing away" of some physical evidence.

Field setting   Place or setting in which people normally interact.

Formative evaluation   The examination of the implementation of some program plan and the initiation of the activities that the plan was supposed to produce.

Game simulation model   A set of rules for subjects to use as they "play" a game according to the rules.

Gatekeepers   People or organizations which control people's activity.

Indirect observation   Observations involving informants or other techniques.

Informants   People who observe for the participant observer.

Jargon   Technical words or special words not part of everyday language.

Macroscopic approaches   Attempts to get an overall perspective of some phenomena, beyond that which could be obtained by examining individual behavior.

Participant observation (P/O)   A set of data collection strategies involving some degree of direct observation by the researcher.

Projective techniques   Measurement procedures used to assess subject characteristics by their responding to some stimulus such as a picture, description, or event.

Reactivity   The phenomena of people (subjects) behaving differently (reacting) because they realize they are involved in the research process.

Simulation   Techniques scientists use to artificially build some situation or set of circumstances to determine how they work or what would happen if certain events or changes would occur.

Summative evaluation   Focusing on the achievement of the goals, outcomes, result, or outputs of some program, both intended and unintended.

Unobtrusive research (nonreactive measurement)   Any technique of doing research where subjects do not know that they are being observed or researched.

332

1. "LEFTOVERS" OR "GOLDEN OPPORTUNITIES?"

Although the vast majority of scientific research studies employ either experimental or survey designs, there are many other approaches that have been developed to produce research data. In most textbooks these other methodologies are covered much less intensively than are surveys or experiments. We shall also spend less space on these alternative data collection strategies but our reasoning is a little different. It seems to us that many of these methods are often discussed merely in terms of their being the "leftovers" of research design. Judging from their predominance in the literature, surveys or experiments will be used if at all possible. If for some reason these designs cannot be used, then perhaps some other designs might be considered. It is our conviction that these other designs represent "golden opportunities" for researchers to explore problems, issues, and phenomena that have not been adequately studied with experiments and surveys, and perhaps cannot adequately be studied with them. The reality in much research today is that only a small part of changes in the dependent variable are usually explained by changes in the independent variables. That is, even when good experiments and surveys have been done in the past, it is common to find that we still do not fully understand the system of variables that has been examined. The alternative designs explored below offer the potential of contributing a great deal to our understanding of the world around us. Indeed some classical research has been produced by these "alternative" methods. We treat these methods briefly not because they are less desirable ways to do research, but because we want to integrate an understanding of statistics with the most frequently used research designs—experiments and surveys. In trying to keep this text to a reasonable size this combined undertaking limits the space available to us to explore other methods. You might ask why the customs of research have developed the way they have if these other methods are potentially so useful. We think the answer to that is twofold. First, the "soft" sciences have attempted to be like the "hard" physical sciences. Experimental methods are the most acceptable way of doing physical science research. Second, surveys and experiments are the easiest research designs to plan and carry out. Experiments are relatively easy because we have borrowed heavily from the physical sciences for our model of experiments. Surveys are relatively easy because the skills necessary to do them are widely held, even though they may often be poorly done. To do a study using other methods requires a bit more creativity and imagination. The steps and procedures are not quite so clear-cut and the obstacles in carrying them out may be greater than when employing traditional research designs. There are many specialized books that deal specifically with each of these alternative research designs and we would encourage the aspiring researcher to read them. We offer this chapter to the consumers of research to enable them to gain a broader perspective of research involving human systems.

2. PARTICIPANT OBSERVATION / FIELD RESEARCH

Perhaps the most widely used alternative research design is *participant observation,* sometimes referred to as field research. There are, however, other types of field research. Anthropologists, cross cultural analysts, and sociologists are the most likely users of this technique.

What is participant observation?

Like experimental or survey designs, participant observation is a set of data collection strategies. Most notably *participant observation* (sometimes denoted by P/O) involves the collection of data in a "natural" or "field" setting by some degree of direct observation by the researcher. Field or natural settings are places and situations that are familiar to the subjects being observed. They are the settings in which people normally interact. They are not contrived solely for the purposes of research as are most laboratory experimental settings, and there is no manipulation of the setting or events by the researcher. In general, the settings are part of the everyday life of the group being observed. The observations are made during the subjects' ongoing activities. Although most participant observation takes place in these everyday settings, we may be interested in conducting P/O before, during, or after events that are *not* everyday events, such as disasters (floods, earthquakes, tornadoes), festivals (Mardi Gras, New Year's Eve), or other special occurrences.

Observation may take several forms. The forms vary on at least three dimensions: (1) degree of researcher's participation, (2) degree of disclosure to subjects, and (3) degree to which events and subjects are viewed directly by the researchers. Degree of participation ranges from complete participation as a person completely involved in the setting, to simply being an outside observer who happens to be there. Complete participation may take such forms as becoming a new member, initiate, or trainee of some group such as a fraternity or sorority, a medical school, or a prison. Partial participation may involve external observation of some foreign tribe, religious group, and so on, either with or without the approval of the people being observed.

The degree of disclosure of one's research project, and possibly its specific aims also varies from none to all. Some researchers opt to totally conceal that they are conducting research during the data collection or observation phase of a study. (We shall discuss the pros and cons of this practice in a later section.) It may be advantageous to participate with partial concealment. This partial concealment could mean informing selected members of the group being observed about your purposes while leaving others uninformed. It is felt that through partial concealment a compromise can be reached between letting a group know it is being studied and preventing the possibility that the researcher will get treated preferentially because a study is being conducted. The researcher does not want the subjects to act differently during P/O than they would at any other time. Participant observation may also take place with total disclosure to everyone involved in the setting in which the research is being conducted.

P/O always involves some degree of direct observation but varies in the degree to which other sources of information and data are also relied upon to reach conclusions. One of the most common supplemental sources of data in field work is reports by informants. *Informants* are members of the group being studied who are either representative of the group or are in a special position to have valuable information about the group being observed. Although the use of informants is not direct observation, it is a special technique of participant observation.

There are also other types of "indirect" observation that can be employed in conjunction with direct observation. These include the inspection of any written records available, the viewing of pictures or films involving the subjects, and so on.

Why participant observation?

It is important to keep in mind that there is no reason to consider any research strategy as competing with others. Whatever scientific reality there is to observe, it should look the same no matter what technique we use to see it. Each data collection technique has various problems in dealing with internal and external validity. The "why" of participant observation is that some researchers feel it has some advantages over other designs in terms of exploration, access, and richness of data.

Exploration
Sometimes we know so little about a specific group, structure, process, or other dependent variable that it would be extremely difficult, perhaps impossible, to design a good experiment or survey to study it. Therefore we need to design a research project to explore the problem before other more structured research can mean-

ingfully take place. For example, we may be interested in the socialization process of various professional groups such as medical students. If we know little about this process, it would be helpful to learn more before we can explore any specific research hypotheses.

If there is little or no previous research on this subject, then one of the best ways we might learn about such a group is by P/O. Similarly we may discover a new tribe in some remote area. A comparison of the social structure of this tribe with our "modern" society might provide valuable insights, but what things do we compare? To answer this question we must first learn something about the tribe and P/O is one way to do this.

Participant observation can also be useful for exploring theory or measurement. Sometimes there is not sufficient theory to design a structured research project and P/O can be useful in developing theory. In addition if we do not have enough experience to develop good indicators and operational definitions, there is a possibility that P/O can be used to explore how to describe and measure some types of variables. Field studies can also be used for validation or possibly invalidation of information gathered by other research techniques.

Access to subjects

Even if we know what we wish to study and how to measure the variables, participant observation can sometimes be used when we feel it is the best way to gain access to the data or subjects. For example, it may be relatively difficult to gain rapport quickly with some groups such as professionals. In this case it might not be possible to do surveys or experiments because the subjects would not cooperate. We would expect noncooperation, for example, when the research question pertains to nonprofessional practices or misconduct. However, if it were possible to live and work with such a group for some time, this information might become available. Professionals might become so accustomed to the researcher that they feel comfortable enough with the "ex-outsider" to divulge such information. Secret societies may also be unwilling to disclose certain information. By joining such an organization one could potentially use P/O to become privy to such data. Goffman (1959) refers to various types of behind-the-scenes values and practices as behavior and norms of the "back region." It is this type of behavior that participant observation may be effective at uncovering.

The possibility of establishing rapport is one reason why P/O may be particularly advantageous. Subjects may also be unable to see some of the events or phenomena which may interest the researcher. First, they may be too involved to see what is really going on. This seems to be true for some of the new quasireligious movements in this country whose major purpose seems to be fund raising as opposed to spirit raising. Of course the participants probably do not see it that way. Second, participants may find reporting on-the-scene information too troublesome or find that it interferes with their regular activity. Because of this they may be unable to give a good account of events after they have occurred. In other words, recall may be difficult. For example, interviewing "stoned" subjects at a rock concert may irritate them, yet they may not be able to recall their feelings or perceptions experienced during the concert. Third, respondents simply may not see what is happening. In *Street Corner Society,* White (1955) pointed out that bowlers' scores matched their group status, rather than their ability, only when they bowled together. None of the bowlers were aware of this or could say why it happened.

Another problem of access involves subjects who are unable to use self-reports to inform researchers. We may wish to study an illiterate population which could not read a questionnaire. A research population could be mute or inarticulate, such as those with severe developmental disabilities or mental illness. Subjects may also be unable to report because of the fear of possible retribution if they give information to a researcher. Even if subjects are willing and able to communicate they may not have sufficient comparison frameworks to be adequate observers of their own situation. Students, prisoners, or soldiers, for example, may not be able to adequately assess what "fair" treatment is if they have only participated in one school, prison, or army program. Mothers may be biased about their children's performance simply because they do not know how good other children are, and so on.

A final consideration may suggest that participant observation is the advisable strategy for gaining access to subjects. There may be much potential benefit in gaining social science data about people's reaction to disasters, but few of us would like to simulate or actually cause some disaster just to study how people respond. Thus we must await events outside the researcher's control. Of course information gained from this type of situation would be lost if not studied while the event was occurring, or shortly thereafter. People would likely be too involved or unwilling to respond to an interview or survey in such a situation, and P/O provides a good option in such cases.

Richness of data

A third general rationale for using participant observation is characterized in terms of the "richness" of the data gathered. In the natural settings where P/O occurs everything going on is a potential research variable. Through participant observation it is possible to see and measure variables that might have been overlooked in a more structured design. Viewing variables in the context in which they naturally occur may shed light on important interpretations which might otherwise be missed. In settings familiar to subjects it is felt that they may act less on guard and more spontaneously. Data may be observed before it is filtered through some coding process. As a result, there is less chance for measurement error. The cliche "you had to be there" is indicative of the idea that by experiencing, to some degree, the phenomena being studied the researcher can potentially capture the richness of the experience.

How to do participant observation

No book the size of this one can give you complete instructions on how to do participant observation. You should realize that many of the considerations for P/O are the same as those for other research designs. You need to be concerned about reliability and validity of measurement, about internal and external validity, about sampling or subject selection procedures, and about ruling out alternative explanations for what is observed. However, there are some special concerns of participant observation that can be identified.

Problem selection
The procedures for selecting a problem or topic of study are the same as those outlined in Chapter 5 where we discussed utilizing previous research. The less well-defined your problem, the less you can count on previous science. Yet in some sense every participant observation utilizes previous research. Every participant observer uses frameworks of comparison with, and questions about, information which is the result of past research. The "reality" observed in P/O is partially a reflection of the discovery view discussed in Chapter 2. For example, if a study were to involve examining a new tribe or social group that has not been previously studied, there is still a great deal of previous work that should be consulted. Before going into the field anthropologists would get a great deal of training in what to observe and how to make contacts and observations. They may have no information on the specific tribe about to be studied but they already "know" what kinds of things to look for. There are standard things we wish to ask about any special group being studied. The list of such things is too detailed to enumerate here but the types of areas to be considered include:

1. How are the major institutions organized? These include the family, economy, politics, education, and religion.
2. What is the nature of the social relationships with other tribes or groups? For example, how much contact is there, what kinds of wars, what is traded, or do they intermarry?

3. What is the nature of their technology and its relation to their social organization? That is, what kind of tools, medicine, housing, transportation, and so on, are employed?
4. What is the nature of their art and leisure?

Sociologists who do field studies are also likely to have general frameworks which come from their involvement in or study of previous research. For example, students of delinquent gangs might be concerned with the nature of the status systems of the gang, or how one gains status, or the relationships with other gangs, or how "turfs" are established, or the specification of various role relationships in the group. All of these concerns have established traditions in other types of research. Specialists probably go into participant observation studies with concerns pertinent to their specialties. Thus even if a researcher goes into a P/O study with a completely exploratory framework, certain issues are likely to be considered more important than others.

Another way in which some participant observers narrow their exploratory focus may be somewhat more free of influence from past research. The research problem is determined by cues from the subjects one is studying. These cues indicate what the subjects regard as problems. One obvious way to determine this, which is often overlooked, is to simply tell the people being observed that you are a researcher and that you want to know what problems or situations in their group are worth studying. People may simply tell you. A second approach focuses on *jargon* — technical words or special words that are not part of everyday language. Such jargon may refer to social situations or to individuals that are particularly important to the subjects. For example, in a study of medical students, Becker (1958) found that the word "crock" was used rather frequently. It referred to a type of complaining patient for whom symptoms could not be demonstrated. The word "crock" also refers to a problem sale in the women's shoe business. A third good source of problem definition may be to focus upon the complaints of the participants. A fourth may be to examine the amount of time spent on various issues at social gatherings. Finally, focusing on unusual norms, customs, or practices may be an excellent way to determine an interesting problem to study with P/O.

Choice of setting

If the purpose of the P/O is to examine a certain location or group, then the choice of setting would be determined. The choice of setting will depend on the nature of the problem to be explored. If a researcher has identified a problem, it is crucial that the situation observed contain that problem. For example, it would be unwise to spend a summer in a boys' camp waiting for conflicts when there is no guarantee that such conflicts would occur. Another consideration involves the degree of access one may have to information. One may be incumbered by various distractions or inconveniences such as transportation difficulties. Or one may be unable to get past leadership or other "gatekeepers." Finally, it may be worth emphasizing that the researcher must be somewhat comfortable in the setting in which the study is to be conducted.

Establishing social relationships

Since all types of participant observation studies involve relatively greater social interaction with subjects than other research designs, a key part of P/O involves establishing social relationships. First it is necessary to pave the way to gain entry into the research settings, to gain access to the data, and to ward off external intrusion or control. Second, it is necessary to establish relationships at all levels of the group's organization to build rapport with members being observed. It is difficult to be precise in providing instructions for establishing good relationships. There are many variables to consider that are different in different settings and for different people. We shall sketch out some general considerations and briefly comment on variations in strategy that can be used.

PRIOR TO THE STUDY. At each phase of the study there are some general things that can be considered about the nature of social relations. Prior to the study one must touch several bases to gain access, permissions, support, and so on. If a researcher is observing part of a formal organization in the United States, it is likely that the permission and confidence of upper management must be obtained. Other "gatekeepers," such as unions, may also have to be consulted. If one is able, a series of lunches or other informal gatherings could be planned to discuss the nature of the project. Students might ask their professors to pave the way for them or to go with them. Many projects are stopped at the last minute by a person in a higher position who was not consulted in the early stages of research. Some bureaucracies such as school systems have units in the administration that are set up to handle outside research. In those cases it may not be necessary to take the superintendent out to lunch. Of course many a project has been approved by supervisors and other top personnel but sabotaged by some other internal or external group. In a factory the researcher should consult the shop steward responsible to the union, as well as the supervisor. Other types of people such as parents might be consulted if the study is being conducted in a school or camp. In such cases getting the endorsement of formal groups like the PTA is potentially quite valuable.

Establishing initial contacts and permissions for field research in other countries is similar to the process of making contacts prior to doing P/O in a formal organization. Problems in the study can be avoided by using official and unofficial contacts. Government agencies, universities, and other such groups are both necessary and helpful assets in cross-cultural research.

INITIAL CONTACT WITH SUBJECTS. Regardless of the nature of the P/O several general rules seem to apply. In no case does the observer want to change the nature of events being observed. Since this is always a possibility, observers try to minimize this by remaining somewhat reserved and in the background of events. One should attempt to disclose little about the specific nature of the research. It is appropriate to be vague and general. One should probably not disclose too many options or specific hypotheses. Another reason for not getting too involved in this phase is that you may impede getting information at a later stage in the study by committing yourself earlier to opinions or to others in the group. For this reason it is not a good idea to form strong personal friendships at this point. In this phase it is not always possible to assess the friendship, cliques, or political networks in the group. Befriending some people or groups may cut off access to others who disagree or do not associate with others.

Finding informants

Once the problems to be studied have begun to be defined and the researcher has gotten used to the nature and structure of the setting or group being studied, it is possible to select those who may be particularly knowledgeable about the situation in which the observer is interested. These people are selected to observe *for* the participant observer to suggest to the observer particular areas of focus, to confirm in more depth what the observer has noticed, and generally inform the observer about the group and/or situation. We call such people *informants*. Informants may be selected for a number of reasons. If the researcher is doing field research in a foreign culture, common norms and practices must be learned. The same could hold for learning special norms in a delinquent gang or other unusual settings. Some informants are selected because they may be in a unique position to observe. For example, one may be the survivor of a disaster, or another may have been a consultant to a president, and so on. An informant may also be chosen because the participant observer notes that the informant appears to be particularly articulate and understanding.

For whatever reason the informant is chosen, it is important to establish the "credibility" of the informant. How is the researcher to know that the informant's reports are accurate or valid? Becker (1958) suggests that appropriate responses to the following questions may give the researcher more confidence in an informant: (1) Is the informant in a position to know? (2) Is the informant reporting to enhance his security, vanity, or self-concept? (3) Does the informant have any feelings on the issues which may bias perceptions or reporting? (4) Did the informant actually witness the reported events? (5) Were there people around who may have influenced the report when the informant reported? (6) Was the informant's statement volunteered? One may also check the reliability and validity of the informant by asking questions about some events the researcher has actually witnessed, or by checking one informant's report against another, or by observing similar events at a time after the informant has reported. Even inaccurate reports by informants may still be valuable data. It may be as important to discover what is misperceived, misunderstood, or missed entirely, as it is to find informants that accurately report data.

Establishing rapport
In P/O there are various degrees of rapport. There are degrees of closeness one establishes with others, degrees of trust, and degrees of confidence others develop in the researcher. In the initial stages of the research the observer must develop some degree of rapport with all participants. As the study proceeds, those in special positions, those working most closely with the observer, and those who become informants must be singled out for development of even closer relationships. We have adapted some suggestions for building rapport from Bogden and Taylor (1975):

1. Be yourself.
2. Dress in a manner comfortable for you. You need not dress like the other participants (unless you are doing disguised observation), but if comfortable and appropriate, dress similarly to the others.
3. Start relationships slowly. Don't be pushy.
4. Don't make a big deal out of your expertise or sophistication. This may scare off or threaten the participants and keep them from opening up to you.
5. Establish common interests with the participants.
6. If appropriate, participate in common events and activities.
7. Don't disrupt the participants' routines.
8. Don't assume that initially hostile, distant, or reticent subjects will remain so.

Rapport in complete and disguised observation
One may be able to learn more about private matters and gain more intuitive and subjective data by observing as a complete participant while hiding the fact that you are a researcher (disguised observation). However, there are some possible serious drawbacks to such an approach. Active and involved participant observers may establish relationships or conduct research in such a way that their obser-

vations become invalid. Because they must keep the research secret they may become too self-conscious and act accordingly. They may be afraid to ask certain questions which would raise suspicions. They would find recording data difficult or impossible because this would appear unnatural and raise suspicions. As a result, their recall may be less accurate. By being fully involved it is more likely that they may influence others. Furthermore there is a danger that by "going native" they become involved and lose perspective.

After the study

Not only is it important to establish good relationships before and during the study, it is also important to maintain relationships after the data are collected. The nature of the material discovered in P/O studies may be sensitive. Thus it is important to discuss the nature of the results with certain subjects prior to the publication of findings. This will insure that no one is adversely affected by the disclosures of the researcher. It is also valuable to return to selected subjects and ask them to read any reports so they can check them for accuracy.

Recording of data

The nature of data may vary so much from study to study, and even from phase to phase of the same study, that specific guides for data collection and recording are difficult to specify. Some studies, being very exploratory, may require only impressions. Others may require the same rigor as observations in laboratory experimental settings. Most field and P/O researchers keep some type of daily log, journal, or diary. This may be in the form of recording tapes, written summaries, or on some occasions, coded records. The purpose of writing in code may be to keep secret the fact that research is taking place. One may also keep notes in some form of code because the material is sensitive. It may also be possible to film or videotape events, but this becomes very expensive, both in terms of equipment and material costs and in terms of editing and coding the material later. Therefore most observations are coded on the basis of the recall of the observer. Since recall is often difficult, there are some general tricks which P/O people have developed. Bogden and Taylor (1975) have created a general list of hints that we have adapted:

1. "Look for 'key words' in your subject's remarks." We mentioned earlier that one way to locate problems worthy of study is to watch for jargon, or special words. These words, plus key phrases, are easier to remember. With practice you can learn to reconstruct whole sentences or episodes from them.
2. "Concentrate on the first and last remarks in each conversation." Since conversations generally follow a certain sequence, by remembering the beginning and end you can learn to recall the whole episode.
3. "Leave the setting as soon as you have observed as much as you

can accurately remember." The length of time involved depends on the nature of the data you are collecting. Bogden and Taylor suggest that novice observers may find an hour a good starting point, unless they know that they have developed good recall abilities or unless they know that special events will never reoccur.

4. "Record your notes as soon after the observation session as possible."
5. "Don't talk to anyone about your observation session until you have recorded the field notes." Although this may be very tempting, it is likely that you may cloud your memory and lose the ability to recall events accurately.
6. "Draw a diagram of the physical layout of the setting and attempt to trace your movements through it." A diagram or seating plans, organizational charts, the physical layout of a place, and so on, will enable you to retrace steps and recall events which you might otherwise have forgotten.

Summary of participant observation

Participant observation remains one of the most powerful designs for exploratory field research. In addition, this strategy can potentially be used to supplement more structured research designs. P/O requires very careful planning and perhaps more commitment than some other types of research. This commitment entails not only more time and effort but more personal involvement. It is quite common for researchers engaged in P/O to become involved with the people being observed. It is difficult to "participate" in any ongoing social group without becoming somewhat involved. This is one of the major problems with the method. If this involvement occurs the possibility of biased results increases. In the past, however, P/O has produced research monographs that have become classics in the social sciences. There is no reason why this data collection technique cannot continue to provide us with valuable insights about our environment.

3. CONTENT ANALYSIS

We mentioned earlier that one way to supplement observation in P/O is to examine documents or records of a group or association. Because examination of written materials has proved to be so useful and important in the past, there is a special technique that has been developed to examine recorded materials for research purposes. This technique is called *content analysis*.

What is content analysis?

Content analysis is any systematic procedure which is devised to examine the content of recorded information. The data can be written documents, films, audio recordings, video presentations, or any other type of interpretable communication media. These could include any of the mass media of radio, television, movies, billboards, books, magazines, records, eight track tapes, newspapers, and so on. Content analysis might also involve focusing on all types of documents, diaries, and private communications such as letters or speeches. For example, one study (Morris, 1973) examined all of the articles in two Los Angeles newspapers over a two-year period. The purpose of the analysis was to attempt to determine how the public defined the women's liberation movement. The analysis was done by counting the articles dealing with women and categorizing whether they were neutral, favorable, or unfavorable toward this social movement. Table 12.1 shows the results of this particular content analysis. It is but one example of how researchers might analyze the content of materials.

Of course the decision as to whether or not these percentages show the public orientation to women's liberation is somewhat arbitrary. Content analysis can have many purposes and can be done in many different ways. The following sections deal with these issues.

What are its various uses?

In general content analysis is used to study variables or phenomena that are "bigger" than individual people. The designs we have discussed thus far tend to be used to study individuals and their interaction. There are many variables or conditions that are reflective of a total society or subpart of society. Although measuring individuals may help us to measure such variables it is felt that a more macroscopic view can often be obtained with alternative methodologies. *Macroscopic approaches* attempt to get "the big picture," an overall perspective which could not be obtained from looking at small parts of society. Specifically, content analysis has been useful for the following purposes.

Cultural comparisons
To the extent that literature, art, and the mass media reflect and create social conditions, the analysis of the content of such materi-

TABLE 12.1
Example of a content analysis: attitude toward women's liberation

	Los Angeles Times	Herald Examiner
Total articles	996	409
Neutral	837 (84%)	360 (88%)
Favorable	121 (12%)	13 (3.2%)
Unfavorable	38 (3.8%)	36 (8.8%)

als may give insight into the values, orientations, and norms of a culture. Government documents and official papers can also be analyzed to determine the general orientation of a society. These analyses can be conducted in different societies and comparisons can then be made. Since such materials are often somewhat available, they can be used in place of more expensive and time-consuming designs. In fact, it might not be possible to carry out other designs simply because subjects would not be accessible.

Meanings and intentions

A "behind the scenes" story often surrounds observable phenomena. For example, most legislation passed in government is *intended* to accomplish particular ends that are not clear and obvious in the legislation itself. If Congress were to institute a national pickle day, we might not be able to tell *why* such a bill was passed unless we were to read press reports or perhaps the *Congressional Record*. Propaganda also can be analyzed to determine the motives and intentions of a culture or political regime. Diaries and private papers could be examined to determine the inner motivation of famous people and linguistic analyses could be done to "read between the lines" of important public pronouncements. Although imputing motives and intentions on the basis of content analysis can be very tricky, conclusions reached through contact analysis can be quite credible.

Indirect measurement of character and personality

Many of us feel that personality (both individual and collective) is often revealed through various kinds of documentary material. Such things as novels, plays, newspapers, and diaries have been used to attempt to determine the "personality" of nations and individuals. For example, content analysis of newspaper editorials could reveal what character traits are (or at least appear to be) valued and honored by a particular people. Patriotic novels could tell us the hopes and aspirations of the political life of a society, or a diary might enable a researcher to determine the innermost thoughts and motivations of the writer. Of course a great deal of care must be taken to insure that such documents are not only genuine but spontaneous and not the product of some type of propaganda campaign or other type of pressure.

In addition to assessing collective types of character or personality, content analysis is used in conjunction with other techniques to assess individual personality. For example, there are a number of different approaches to the study of personality which are called *projective techniques*. Projective procedures sometimes involve the subject telling or writing a narrative (story) about some picture, description, or event. Content analysis must be used to examine the narratives produced in projective measurement to reach a conclusion about an individual subject's personality. In each particular test there are careful instructions on how narratives are to be interpreted. A similar approach to understanding personality is sometimes used in psychoanalysis when dreams are analyzed for their meaning. The idea behind the "content analysis" of dreams is that the subconscious, through dreams, will reveal the true, inner personality of the subject (patient); conscious thoughts and expressions may not. Exploring personality by use of the well-known "inkblot test" is probably the most familiar examples of this type of content analysis.

These types of analyses of personality tend to be quite subjective and many scientists disagree about the utility of such approaches. One of the problems with projective techniques is the determination of their validity and reliability. However, much individual counseling and therapy relies on such techniques and they have been used from time to time to conduct more general research studies. Such uses of content analysis are generally made by those researchers who believe that language and the use of language can be used as one key to unlock the personality of individuals and societies.

Social trends
Historically, one of the most useful products of content analysis has been the analysis of social trends over some relatively long period of time. The same types of documents which were appropriate for other purposes of content analysis can be used for this purpose as well. For example, it would be possible to examine newspapers over the nine years of the Viet Nam war. This could verify that the national sentiment changed dramatically during that period of time, from one of support for the United States' involvement, to one of extreme aversion to any type of entanglement in Viet Nam. Another such historical trend could be documented by examining the image of women portrayed in textbooks over the past several decades. Over this period of time we could likely find that women have been increasingly portrayed in other than subservient, housewife roles. Such a study could effectively determine the extent of such changes. In addition, we could predict future changes based on projections of past occurrences. The broad social trends cited in these two examples are quite difficult to capture with an experiment or survey. Content analysis provides a relatively inexpensive way to approach an objective measurement of social trends. Social values, intentions, motivations, and sentiment as well as phenomena, such as racism, international isolationism, and sexual orientation, can potentially be explored. This could be done at one point in time or at various times to verify if changes and trends are occurring in society.

How is content analysis done?

Many of the steps involved in content analysis research are similar to those used in doing research by use of surveys and experiments. All of the various points and problems discussed in previous chapters also apply to content analysis.

There are some special problems, however, which confront researchers using content analysis. Some are unique to this method.

Selecting a sample

The decision as to which elements are most appropriate to examine in content analysis is often made on the basis of common sense or a hunch. If we wished to explore the role of women in textbooks, which textbooks should we look at? Perhaps a general sampling of texts would be the most appropriate. Perhaps social studies and history texts would be better than mathematics texts. Would it make any difference? It is almost inevitable that sampling will have to be done when using content analysis. In addition to sampling of certain types of content, a sampling in time will also have to be taken. For example, suppose we decide to determine a social trend on the attitudes toward the Viet Nam war by examining editorials in the *New York Times*. We would still have to decide which editorials to examine. Should we take every other Monday's editorials, or the first Sunday of the month?

Coding of material

The recorded information used in content analysis must be categorized in a manner similar to that used for coding the answers to an open-ended question. Once the appropriate categories have been developed or established, it is quite common to record the frequency and intensity of the occurrence of each category of phenomena in the information being studied. The frequency simply refers to counting the number of times that a particular category may appear. Intensity refers to the strength of feelings about a particular matter that written material may convey by using adjectives or similar techniques. The idea of intensity enables a researcher to refine the analysis beyond just "counting."

In addition to counting the frequency and evaluating the intensity of the material, associations in the data can be determined. For example, in a novel, a particular trait may be associated with virtue or honor. In another source the same trait may be associated with moral degradation and dishonor. Without looking for these associative connections, simply recording the frequency and intensity of a comment would not allow for the proper interpretation of events.

The need for comparisons

Content analysis is often used for comparison purposes rather than for the purpose of causal analysis. Note that the example at the beginning of this section compares editorials in two different newspapers. Most content analyses would make some type of comparison. It is difficult to use the products of content analysis for causal analysis. If used causally, it is usually in the form of verifying some causal finding established by another scientific technique. Although content analysis might be used in conjunction with other methods in causal analysis, this is not the major use that the method has enjoyed in the past.

Advantages and disadvantages of content analysis

There are three major advantages of content analysis. The first is that materials for analysis are readily available, usually at very little cost. That is, data are accessible and inexpensive. The second advantage is that many sources of available recorded materials cover a long period of time. Such things as newspapers, books, magazines, movies, diaries, and government publications often are available over a period of years. This makes the analysis of trends and other historical comparisons relatively easy. The third major advantage is that content analysis is usually unobtrusive. Unobtrusive measurement will be discussed in Section 6 of this chapter, but the general idea is that unobtrusive measurement does not interfere with the ongoing activity of subjects. Therefore a more "natural" flow of events might be observed. In other words, there is little chance that content analysis itself may be "causing" what is observed.

One of the major problems of content analysis is that most materials available for analysis have already been screened, selected, or edited by some other person for some other purpose. For example, editors make selections as to what appears in books, magazines, and newspapers; television executives and movie executives exercise great control over what is contained in their media; individuals are somewhat selective and biased in their reports for diaries or private papers; and so on. The researcher really has no way of knowing what kinds of selection processes have occurred and what distortions these processes may produce for the particular research objectives. One can easily imagine that a government censored newspaper may not be the best source of unbiased information about the political orientation of a society. This may also be the case in less obvious instances. In addition, content analysis is very time consuming. It takes a great deal of effort to digest and analyze most available materials. Other types of studies can be conducted with relatively less time and effort. Finally, there is a great deal of judgment required for content analysis. Dealing with language is always difficult, but when the language itself is the focus of attention, the soundness of the researchers' judgment becomes even more critical. There is a high degree of subjectivity involved in making many of the inferences that are made by most content analyses. Finally, most content analysis studies are descriptive in nature and tend not to explore relationships between variables. Although this is not inevitable, it has been the case historically. To the extent that scientists are generally more interested in exploring relationships, this technique has been somewhat limited in the past.

Are the mass media a cause or an effect?

Since many of the materials used for content analysis are part of the "mass media," one question has become crucial. Where does the mass media fit into the causal sequence—as a cause or as an effect? If we wish to use content analysis to try to understand social change, or as an element in a causal analysis, the question takes on special importance. Although this question concerns all media, in recent years the focus has been on the impact of television and movies. The issues of violence and sex have become the center of the public debate. There has been increasing public concern that the expression of violence and sex in the media may be having a detrimental effect on the morals of society. Another area of concern has to do with the role of the media in the political process. Televised debates took on special importance during the Kennedy-Nixon campaign and again during the Carter-Ford election. There has been some research in experimental settings on the effects of media on certain types of behavior but this type of research really does not address the question of the role of mass media in society. The crucial question for content analysis is whether the material analyzed is a *reflection* of social condition or a *cause* of social conditions. Focusing on political activities, the question becomes whether the media reflect public attitudes and orientations toward a candidate, or whether the media shape those attitudes. Does the way the media present a candidate actually determine whether the candidate succeeds or not? It seems we can find instances of both types of occurrences. There is no final answer to this question. We bring it up here so that you, as consumers of such research, can become sensitive to the issue when using content analysis in a causal explanation. It is very likely that other types of information will have to be used in conjunction with content analysis when issues of this type are to be decided.

4. SIMULATION *see Monte Carlo*

As the name implies, all simulations are essentially artificial. By various types of techniques scientists attempt to artificially build (simulate) some situation or set of circumstances. They want to determine how they work or what would happen if certain events or changes occur. In other words, simulation involves the construction of a "model" of some sort. This model might be a situation, a society, a device, or an organization that is artificially created by some means. The two most common types of techniques used to build a model are *gaming* and *computer*. After models are built either by gaming or by computer, they are "operated" to see how they work.

In gaming, the model is developed by constructing a set of "rules" for people (subjects) to use as they "play" a game according to the rules. Several commercial games are currently available to use in simulation. Among them is one called *SIMSOC*, which is a game simulation of society—as well as the title of a book (Gamson, 1969). In this game players are assigned to certain social roles like senator, president, union head, military leader, and so on. The game prescribes certain circumstances and conditions. The players then go ahead and act out the situation to see what happens. In gaming the rules of the game are the model. The model is operated by people "pretending" to act out certain prescribed roles. The rules are flexible enough so that each player is somewhat free to make decisions and alter the situation. In any game the rules or situation can be altered to see if such changes make any differences in terms of what the players do in their respective game roles.

In computer simulation the model is a set of mathematical equations. In order to construct a computer simulation model, it is necessary that researchers specify ahead of time by some mathematical formula the relationship between variables. The computer model is "operated" by filling in certain values for some of the variables in the equations to see what values the other variables will have. Because the computer is so fast at calculations, models of this type can contain many equations with many different unknowns. The model can also be operated using many different initial values. There are many different simulation models that have been devised by researchers to explore different problems. One of the most well-known simulation models was developed by a group called the Club of Rome. In this computer simulation model researchers attempted to build a mathematical model of world population growth. They wanted to predict what would happen to world population if different events would occur in the future. In their attempts they predicted that no matter what types of changes in behavior would occur, the world would become overpopulated. Many people were upset with their conclusions and felt that they were wrong. In order to argue that such predictions were in error, critics had to argue that the model the scientists used was an incorrect one.

The crucial aspect of simulation—the model

The goal of any simulation model, whether a game or computer model, is to construct a model that is realistic and accurate. That is, putting the model into operation should produce correct results. For example, if a game simulation were supposed to represent a family situation and the problem was to discover what effect having a baby would have on the family, playing the game should result in the players behaving in a way that is close to how they would behave in such a real situation. If a computer simulation was supposed to predict how polluted a river would become if certain environmental protections were enacted, the model should accurately predict pollution levels after such protections were put into effect. You might think, at this point, that there really is not much sense to simulation if you can only determine its value after waiting to see how accurate the predictions were. Why not just wait and see what happens without simulation? The idea is to develop a model that works in such a manner that *different* situations can be explored. In the game example above, we could change the income level of the family to see what might happen. If we had a good model we might be able to use it to determine the appropriate level of public assistance for indigent families in such circumstances. In the computer example, it would be very beneficial to try different types of environmental protections to see which one might be most efficient in cleaning up a river. A crucial part of simulation is to develop the model. A big part of that problem is the testing of the model. The question becomes how to demonstrate the accuracy of the model.

The two major ways that models are developed are constructing a model from past experience or data and constructing a model by using some theory, assertion, or intuition. If we are building a model using past occurrences, we would need some historical data with which to build the model. For example, if we were constructing a model to predict the growth of industry in some state, we would need to determine the growth rate of industry in that state over some historical period. In constructing the model we would have to search for other variables in the state or in the economy that could explain the growth rate of the past. Tax structure, population size, and development in transportation might be variables that could explain industrial growth. If such a model could be developed to explain growth in the past, we could use it as a basis to predict growth in the future. Calculations could include changes in tax structure, population, and transportation. This is one way that a model gains

352

credibility and earns the confidence of consumers of simulation research. Of course it is necessary for the scientists to discover the variables that are historically related to industrial growth in order to construct such a model.

Many times researchers may not have adequate historical data to do such a test on a model. In these instances the model would have to be constructed using some theory or supposition. Theory can also be used to develop models that are tested against historical data.

The relative importance of theory in model building varies considerably. In the cases where the major foundation of a model is some theory, credibility and trust in the model will depend on how much faith people have in the theory. Simulation is a methodological area where the wedding of theory and research is explicit and important. Consumers of research based on simulation have the opportunity to see the importance of theory in research.

Simulation models are not merely intellectual curiosities or the product of esoteric irrelevance. They have been successfully used for many purposes in many scientific areas.

Some uses of simulation

Prediction
The hope of all simulation model building is to explain some series of events or behavior. Most scientists are not content to explain historical events but would like to have a model that will predict the future. The most general purpose then is prediction. Prediction by simulation has many advantages. Among the advantages is the fact that simulations are usually cheaper than doing the real thing. Perhaps more importantly, if the real thing would harm or injure people, perhaps this can be detected in the simulation and thus be avoided. Excellent examples of this can be found in the aerospace industry. In nearly every case in this industry devices are designed and then simulated. Every rocket engine or aircraft has been described mathematically before it is built. It is only after such simulations are successful that production goes into full swing. Of course such models could be incorrect. Therefore prototypes are built and tested before people actually begin to use them. In the social sciences such models have not become as useful, but those who believe in simulation have great hopes that someday models of society can be built that will aid decision makers in planning.

Planning
More and more, society is beginning to recognize the importance of planning prior to the initiation of some social policy. In recent years this has become most visible in the area of ecology. In many jurisdictions it is now necessary to do an environmental impact study

prior to the building of certain types of industrial or energy enterprises. Computer simulation offers the potential of providing an excellent tool for social planners. Such things as energy, education, transportation, unemployment, and taxation are areas where decisions are made every day. The bases for these decisions are often political in nature. This may not be solely because politicians are sensitive to special interests, but because they do not have the types of scientifically derived information that would allow them to make decisions based on other types of data. Simulation, particularly computer simulation, has the potential to do research on large social processes which would otherwise be impractical to explore. If successful models of important social processes can be developed to the point where the decision makers and the public can have trust in them, then this type of research could prove to be as useful in the social sciences as it has been in the physical sciences.

Quasiresearch purposes

Simulations are also used for purposes which could be classified as "quasiresearch" in that the activities do not result in the types of data usually associated with "research." Game simulation in particular has been used for such things as sensitization of social groups and individuals, individual and group therapy, and conflict resolution. In these contexts, game simulation is sometimes similar to social role playing. A situation is described or given to participants; rules for the game are outlined; roles are assigned to participants; and the game is carried on either until completion or until some prearranged time. For example, game simulation has been used to lessen social tensions in school settings by allowing white students to play the role of blacks and the black students, to play the role of whites. Sometimes the increased awareness and sensitization gained through these experiences can prove quite useful. Political science students have also gained some insights about international relations by simulating a game of international politics. In more intense settings and under the proper supervision such game situations can and have been used for individual therapy.

It also has been suggested and some experimentation has been conducted on the idea that both personal and group conflicts might be settled by game simulation as opposed to open hostility or warfare. Through simulation it might be possible for settlements and/or compromises to be worked out without the threat of real consequences that might exist if such settlements were worked out in the "real" world. Whether or not such simulation can ever be developed to the point where serious problems could be solved with their aid is an unanswerable question. The possibility does exist and the development of models for these and other purposes will likely benefit from the contributions of social and behavioral scientists.

5. EVALUATION RESEARCH

Evaluation research uses many of the same skills, procedures, and techniques as any of the more traditional research designs previously discussed. However, there are some particular aspects of evaluation research that have a different emphasis from that in other types of research. First, in one sense, evaluation research tends to be more focused than other types of research. Populations of subjects tend to be narrowly defined and the questions being asked by the research tend to be very specific in nature. In fact, some researchers consider evaluation research less "worthwhile" because they view it as being less relevant in the general sense. Although one may argue against this perspective, many pieces of evaluation have not been interpreted beyond a narrow frame of reference.

The second way that evaluation can vary from other types of research is that it tends to be oriented to particular social programs. This second factor is somewhat associated with the first in that, since the usual focus of evaluation is a particular program, the scope of the research tends to be limited to that program. For this reason such research is bound by a particular setting and a particular time. There is seldom any attempt to structure evaluation research so that results can generalize to other settings in other times. Indeed the question of generalization is not even of concern in most cases. Basically, evaluation research has as its goal the determination of the effectiveness of a program. This may sound simple but it is not always easy to determine what a program is for and how one would determine whether a program is effective or not. In addition, evaluation research often tries to find out how efficient a program is relative to other similar programs and this complicates things even further. One of the reasons this determination may be difficult is that programs often have many purposes and some of them are not made explicit. Indeed sometimes the purposes of programs are hidden and people do not want to admit to or talk about all of them. For example, most educational programs have as their purpose the education of students, but another thing schools do is keep young people out of the labor force. Even though this might have been a purpose of education at one time and might still be today, few educators would say to the public, "look what a good job we're doing keeping children out of the labor force."

Just as many programs have multiple purposes, the initiation of evaluation research also may have many purposes. Evaluation may be done because funding agents require it. It may be done in an attempt to placate critics. It may be done for public relations purposes or it may be done to justify decisions that have already been reached. Because evaluation research is almost always done for money, questions can be raised as to who paid for the evaluation and why were they willing to pay money to have such research done? Although it is our belief that the vast majority of evaluation research is conducted by ethical researchers who could not be "bought" for such sums, the fact that there are direct payments for services raises this question from time to time. Of course most significant research is funded by someone. The norms of most disciplines, however, pay less attention to the possibilities of bias in traditional research than they do in evaluation research. We suspect that as many researchers have produced biased research as a result of pressure from research funding agencies as from pressure from programs being evaluated.

The general purpose of most evaluation research is to examine a chain of events. The chain starts with some sort of program, the program is supposed to lead to some activity, and the activity is supposed to produce some desired outcome. In order to be evaluated as a "success," a program must lead to the activities to which it was designed to lead and the activities should produce the outcome that the activities were supposed to produce. There are several places where this chain can break apart. The first place is where the actual implementation of the program may be different than the design of the program. The second place is where, even if a program is implemented properly, it may not lead to the activities to which it was supposed to lead. Third, even if the activities were carried out according to plan, it is always possible that such activities lead to other than the desired outcomes. These factors have led to differentiating at least two types of evaluation research.

Formative versus summative evaluation

In many cases evaluation research is an integral part of the initiation of a program. In fact, the continuation of many social action programs depends on achieving a successful evaluation. In addition to this fact, many programs are continually undergoing changes in their structure. With each of these changes evaluation is frequently necessary. Because many evaluations are conducted on emerging or newly changed programs, it is very likely that the last part of the chain of events described above has not had time to occur. The last step of course is desired outcomes. In addition to this factor, many desired outcomes of social programs are quite global and often long ranged. For example, programs to eliminate poverty, to eliminate illiteracy, to improve the mental health of a community, to improve the penal system, or to decrease the crime rate would be expected to take a number of years to accomplish — even if they were very effective. Therefore evaluation is sometimes limited to the first two parts of the programmatic chain described: the implementation of the plan of the program and the initiation of the activities that the plan was supposed to produce. This type of evaluation is sometimes referred to as *formative* evaluation. The evaluation focuses on the "formation" of the program. In formative evaluation, actual programmatic features might be compared to the "plan" of the program design. For example, a plan to implement a voluntary probation officer program for juvenile offenders might include the idea that 50 volunteer probation officers would be recruited. One way to evaluate the formation of such a program would be to see if indeed 50 volunteers had been recruited. If only five had been recruited after a period of some months, the success of implementing the plan could be questioned. Another aspect of formative evaluation is often the examination of "process." *Process* refers to the activities of the program and not necessarily the effect of the program. Using the volunteer probation example again, the program might have proposed that volunteers would visit the homes of juvenile offenders in an attempt to improve the home environment. Formative evaluation might examine the records of the volunteers to see how often they have made home visitations. If volunteers had visited homes in 90 percent of the cases, this might be considered "success." If volunteers had visited homes in 40 percent of the cases, this might be considered a lack of success.

We must note here that it is seldom the job of evaluation research to come to a conclusion as to the "success" of a program. Ordinarily a researcher would try to avoid such labels. In the above illustration, the decision as to what percentage of home visitation is indicative of success would be left to those persons who were responsible for the program. This might be the Director of the program, a funding agency, or a governmental body, but it would usually not be the evaluator. The major goal of the evaluation researcher is to provide the kind of *information* necessary to reach conclusions about the success of the program and possibly the kind of information which would allow the program to be improved. Decisions as to overall success often depends on a relative perspective and knowledge which only "experts" in such programs possess. For example, if there were information that in most cases volunteer probation programs only involved home visitations in about 30 percent of the cases, one which had a 40 percent rate might be considered highly successful.

In summary, *formative evaluation* would examine any aspect of the program which would involve the "set-up" or initiation of the program. This is sometimes referred to as "effort" or "input." It would involve examination of the number and qualifications of staff, the acquisition of equipment and facilities, the expenditures called for by budgets, the behavior of staff, and any other activity or actions which could be construed as being appropriate for the program being evaluated.

Of course all programs have goals or objectives, that is, expected outcomes. Ideally the full evaluation of a program would focus not only on the formative aspects of the program but also on the summative aspects. *Summative aspects* are goals, outcomes, results, or outputs of the program, both anticipated and unanticipated. For example, the volunteer probation program probably would have as one objective the reduction of repeat offenses by the juveniles in the program. Whether or not the program achieved this objective would be part of summative evaluation. In addition to these obvious types of objectives there may be other, less obvious ones. One example could be that such a program could be part of an effort to have more community support of the police and courts. Summative evaluation should also consider these types of "indirect" goals and objectives. Finally, there may be unanticipated or undesired outcomes of programs. Focusing on the probation program, it could be that the volunteers in the program learn to participate in illegal behavior and as a result tend to become involved in such activity. Certainly if the probation officers of such a program would start helping the probationers commit crimes, this should be noted in the evaluation as one of the consequences of the program. One can quickly see that summative evaluation should look beyond the obvious to discover the outcomes of any program being examined. This examination should not only look to the obvious and not so obvious, but also to the short-term and long-term outcomes. For example, if the program we have been illustrating would result in the volunteers having a nervous breakdown about two years after they left the program, this should be considered. One of the things that makes evaluation research so interesting and at times frustrating is that the identification of formative and summative aspects may not be very easy. Programs are often vague in their objectives and not too specific as to how those vague objectives are to be achieved. No matter how vague the program or illusive the outcomes and processes, the ideal evaluation would attempt to compare the effectiveness of the program under study to some model program or to the situation where there was no program. This type of comparative frame of reference implies consideration of experimental and quasiexperimental designs.

Experimental design and evaluation

From one point of view, the evaluation of any program should take place within the context of an experimental design. Prospective clients or consumers of programs would be randomly selected and randomly assigned or not assigned to the program. Those in the program would constitute the "experimental" group and those not in the program would constitute the "control" group. Of course there could be more than one experimental group if there were more than one program being considered. In this way a comparison could be made between the consequences of being in the program versus not being in the program, or the consequences of being in one program versus being in another. However, it is quite *uncommon* for an evaluation to take place in the framework of an experiment. There are several reasons for this. First, it is probable that conducting an experiment would take more time and money. Usually money for such purposes is scarce and the priority is to spend what there is on direct services. Second, the expertise necessary to set up such evaluation may not be present among those in programs. Perhaps the most important consideration is the question of ethics.

Usually people believe that the program they are setting up will accomplish what they want it to. They tend to be committed to the purposes of the program and *to the program itself*. Because of this they usually feel that people will benefit from being in the program. Most social action programs will try to serve as many clients as possible; and, because there is a belief in the program, the desire is to serve all people who could benefit from the program. Using an experimental design would require clients who might benefit from the program to be deliberately kept out of the program in order to be in the control group. It is sometimes felt that it is unethical to purposefully withhold a service "merely for purposes of evaluation" from someone who might benefit from it. We believe this is false logic for the following reasons. First, programs are seldom so large that they can serve the entire population of potential clients. Few programs ever "run out" of clients. Second, any possible loss of benefits to prospective clients is probably outweighed by the potential benefits of evaluation conducted using experimental designs. Conclusions as to program effectiveness are much more sound when viewed in an experimental situation. There could be tremendous savings by eliminating ineffective programs, supporting effective programs, and changing programs to more efficiently achieve their goals. Without such comparatively derived information the chances of ineffective programs or inefficient programs continuing is greatly increased. The losses to potential clients associated with poor programs probably far outweigh any loss of not serving some clients during the evaluation of a program.

Even if these two arguments were not strong enough, there is still a third important argument. Over the past several years researchers have come up with several close approximations to classical experimental designs which will allow services to be delivered. These designs are called "quasiexperimental" designs. Some examples of possible experimental or quasiexperimental designs involve: (1) letting a randomly selected group of subjects start services at a later date than the first group and using the second group as a control group in the meantime; (2) in multiple approach programs, introducing different phases in succession; (3) in multiple approach programs, giving different phases to different groups at different times; or (4) letting subjects serve as their own quasicontrol group. (Observation of subjects before a program could simulate a control group and observations after the program would be analogous to those in an experimental group.)

If evaluations are not carried on using experimental or quasiexperimental designs, a comparative framework will still likely be used. The difference is that the comparative data will come from other people's experience. A relativistic perspective will come from either the evaluator's experience and background and/or from those who are participating or sponsoring the program. The important thing to note is that this comparative framework is essential for sound evaluation. The basis of comparison can be either experimentation or the experience of others. From a purely scientific perspective we would probably prefer that the comparative information be derived from experimentation but, as the saying goes, "there's no substitute for experience."

The uses of evaluation

As we mentioned in a previous section, there are many reasons for doing evaluation research. Some motivations are noble and some not so noble. From an ethical standpoint, it is important that the researcher behave in such a way that the data are collected, analyzed, reported, and used in a manner consistent with sound scientific procedures. Evaluations should be as free from bias as possible. Variables should be carefully selected and measured and only the most appropriate analyses should be conducted. In evaluation research, however, there is an additional question: "What becomes of the report of evaluation research?" That is, how are the results to be utilized? Views on this subject differ considerably. Some feel that once the research has been done as well as possible, it is no longer the province of the researcher to decide what is done with the research. Others feel that since the consumers of evaluation research may have somewhat limited abilities to critique such research, the researcher has additional responsibilities. The feeling is that there is a responsibility to see that the research is used properly and not distorted.

Perhaps more central to the purpose of this book is how evaluation research can be used in the search for relationships. All of the methods described in this book for determining relationships between variables can be and are used in evaluation research. However, since the major interest of evaluation is to describe the process and outcomes of *programs*, there is seldom a focus on relationships per se. Of course if there is a link between some activity in a program and some outcome, we are in essence talking about a relationship. If home visitation by voluntary juvenile probation officers reduces the degree of delinquency, we have demonstrated a relationship between the variable of "home visitation" and the variable of "delinquency." Unfortunately, most evaluation research is not disseminated very widely. Most are kept quite confidential and seldom go beyond the people or group that commissioned them. However, sometimes researchers have some use of evaluation data beyond the report to the sponsors of the research. When such data are used either for reports at professional meetings or for journal articles, it is very possible to present data that are of general importance to some discipline. Our feeling is that as more and more programs are required to be evaluated, particularly government sponsored programs, there will be increased use of evaluation research to contribute to general theory. As with some of the other alternative methods discussed in this chapter, we view evaluation research as a golden opportunity to add another dimension to the quest for knowledge.

6. UNOBTRUSIVE MEASURES

The problem of reactivity

One of the intrinsic problems of doing research on people is that when they know they are being researched, there is a possibility that they will behave differently. *Reactivity* refers to the phenomena of people (subjects) "reacting" to being studied. When reactivity occurs there is a possibility of biased research conclusions. Any type of research procedure which is conducted in a way that the subjects of the research do not know they are being observed (researched, measured) is called unobtrusive. *Unobtrusive research* or measurement refers to that set of possible procedures in which reactivity could not or would not occur. Sometimes unobtrusive research is called nonreactive research to indicate the absence of subject reactivity. At first this may sound somewhat sinister and may raise the question of unethical behavior. However, the same basic set of research ethics applies to unobtrusive research that apply to all research involving human subjects. We are not talking here about putting tape recorders under beds, tapping telephones, or bugging private residences. Ethical researchers have developed many ways of doing research on the "natural" products of human society and interaction which do not require any type of deception.

Major types of unobtrusive measures

The first major type of unobtrusive measurement is research by documents. *Document research* is any investigation that uses recorded information of any type as its basis for data. This includes use of records, publications, media, newspapers, government publications, and archives. Using this definition, one type of unobtrusive research is content analysis. Indeed content analysis using documents is one of the most widely used unobtrusive measures. There are additional ways that documents can be used for research purposes. For example, Herriott and Hodgekins (1973) used the proportion of families with telephones as a measure of how modern a region was. This could easily be done without "intruding" into the lives of the people in that region. It is probably safe to say that the most widely used documents used for this type of research are the various publications produced by the U.S. Department of the Census. The Census Bureau produces literally hundreds of publications every year. A following section will deal further with using census data.

The second major type of unobtrusive research is *disguised observation*. This of course is one type of participant observation discussed in the beginning of this chapter. People being observed without their realizing there is a study in progress would constitute unobtrusive measurement by observation.

The third major type of unobtrusive research is research using physical evidence as data. There are two types of physical traces that are used for this type of research: erosion measures and accretion measures. *Erosion measures* include any type of data occurring from human behavior which results in the "erosion" or "wearing away" of some physical evidence. For example, museums could tell which exhibits are the most popular by how fast the floor in front of them needs replacing. Street departments could determine the busiest streets by noting which streets need repaving first. Libraries could tell which comic books are the most popular by determining which ones wear out the quickest. These variables may seem rather simplistic and not too worthy of serious theoretical research. However, the inventive researcher can use such measures as proxy variables for other, more important, variables. The use of erosion measures is limited only by the imagination of the researcher.

Accretion measures include any type of data which result from human behavior that leaves some physical traces. People use lots of things and devices and many of them result in some sort of discharge or traces. For example, garbage could be examined to learn a great deal about various types of phenomena. Anyone who has driven about a city on "clean up" days or right before trash pickups can testify that the type of garbage left in front of homes differs a great deal by social class. You could also tell the drinking habits of people by examining their refuse. You could tell which radio stations they listen to by determining where their radio push-buttons were located on the car radios. Again, these may seem to be trite variables but the imagination and creativity of researchers can transform such evidence into worthwhile research data. Many of the examples cited above and a thorough discussion of unobtrusive measures can be obtained from Webb (1966).

The future of unobtrusive research

There are three conditions which lead us to predict that researchers will increasingly use unobtrusive measures in the research process. First, there is an increasing flood of documents which contain almost an infinite amount of information. This massive volume of information, particularly in government publication, is attractive to researchers because, to begin with, it is almost free. That is, it was collected for other purposes by other people and/or agencies and most of it is in the public domain. This means the researcher may have access to it. Also, the information collected may be the type that no single researcher or research agency could collect. For example, it would be virtually impossible for any researcher to conduct a complete census of the population similar to the U.S. Bureau of the Census. There are increased examples of research using such data. These examples may aid the creative process and lead to more studies utilizing unobtrusive measures.

The second condition which may spawn more unobtrusive research is that subjects are becoming more and more sophisticated about research. Some subjects have been "overresearched." There are a very large number of surveys conducted every year and a large number of evaluations and experiments. Subjects are becoming increasingly knowledgeable about what is going on. In addition, there is increased sentiment that researchers have relied too heavily on college students as research subjects. As subjects become more aware and as easily available subjects become less attractive to researchers, it is likely that more unobtrusive research designs will be developed.

The third condition is that nonreactive research has a type of credibility which reactive research designs lack. Research conducted in natural settings (nonreactive research designs) is attractive because the subjects can be "trusted." They do not know they are being researched. Since it is always possible for research to be sabotaged by subjects, nonreactive designs eliminate this possibility. However, scientists are extremely concerned with *control,* and because nonreactive designs allow the researchers very little control, they remain less desirable in the minds of many researchers.

A note about census data and secondary analysis

This chapter and those dealing with experiments and surveys have stressed data collection. Constructing and carrying out research designs that effectively provide information about a system of variables is very difficult. It is expensive, time consuming, and often impractical. Many researchers feel that data collection is a task which should be avoided if at all possible. This does not mean that researchers lack the interest to conduct research, but if data are already available they should be used. Literally thousands of research projects are conducted every year, often for particular purposes. However, it is common to collect data beyond the specific purposes of a study. Such data often become available to other researchers. The analysis of data after the original purposes is called *secondary analysis.* The idea of secondary analysis is that data are useful for many purposes and should be explored and exploited as much as possible. Secondary analysis is sometimes referred to as "mining" the data.

There are three major sources of data that can be used for secondary analysis. The first source is individual researchers. It is almost a universal practice for individual researchers, like college professors, to store their data using the computer. Stored data may take the form of a set of data cards, a computer tape, or other storage devices. It is quite common for such researchers to use data for more than one study. It is also quite common for them to share data that have already been used for original research. For example, many master's theses and doctoral dissertations have used secondary analysis.

The second source of data for secondary analysis is data banks. There are many organizations in this country and abroad which collect and store data as part of their ongoing activities. For example, many universities, such as the University of Chicago and the University of Michigan, have research centers which construct data banks on various subjects. In addition to universities many associations collect data for various purposes. These data are often accessible to bonafide researchers. For example, many professional associations, unions, churches, and so on, have much information at their disposal. One such example is the data contained in the *Yearbook of American Churches.*

The third source of data for secondary analysis is government or quasigovernment agencies. We have already mentioned the possibility of using government documents for research, but it should be stressed that such sources of data are rich with the potential for secondary analysis. For example, the United Nations collects massive amounts of data from its member nations. Such data are often available through the various agencies in the United Nations. Many municipalities, counties, and states have data that are usable for research purposes. The U.S. Bureau of the Census is perhaps the producer of the most accessible data for secondary analysis. Virtually all college, university, and many municipal libraries purchase copies of all census data. With the aid of the documents librarian such data are free for the asking. In addition, special sets of data can be ordered and purchased from the Census Bureau. The possibilities of using such data should be considered before collecting new data. The detail is often amazing. For example, the data available in many libraries will allow one to examine as small a unit as a city block in many larger urban areas. One can easily imagine that the availability of such data for secondary analysis creates the situation where original data collection is often unnecessary.

7. CONCLUSIONS

The major theme we would like to stress after we have discussed the "other" research designs in this chapter is that they should not be viewed as competing designs. It is not uncommon to hear or to read that one design is "better" than another. We would dispute this claim and suggest that all designs, if carried out properly, can and do add to our understanding of a system of variables. The search for relationships is often a difficult task as witnessed by the lack of understanding of so many variables, situations, and phenomena. If we are to make progress in understanding, we must use all of the tools at our disposal. The more tools one has to solve a problem, the more likely a solution can be found. Consumers of research must be "eclectic;" that is, they must look at all types of available evidence and data, judge each piece of research according to the standards discussed in this text, and then synthesize all the data with as much clarity and understanding as is possible.

In our search for relationships, either as producers of research or as consumers of research findings, we tend to have more faith in conclusions reached when we have studies which use different operational definitions and different operationalizations, different measurement devices and techniques, and different modes of analyses. Because each research technique has its strength, some can be used in situations where others cannot. The rich variety of designs that are available to us provides a golden opportunity to search for relationships.

8. SUMMARY

Six strategies for producing research other than the experiment and survey are presented in this chapter. Participant observation offers the potential for producing data rich in the "personal" qualities of social situations. It is often used in the exploratory phase of research. Establishing and maintaining social relationships with those being observed is one of the major difficulties with this method of data collection. Content analysis can be useful for studying phenomena which transcends individuals. Such things as social trends and national character can be meaningfully explored by examining the content of various types of media. The role of the mass media has become an increasingly important topic for researchers. Simulation offers the potential to be a powerful research tool, particularly for social planning. The focus of simulation research is the model being used. Verification that a particular model is accurate is sometimes difficult to produce. The focus for evaluation research is the functioning of particular programs or activities. Formative and summative evaluations are useful types of research to be conducted at various phases of a program's existence. While experimental designs may provide the most desirable way to conduct evaluations, there are some useful alternatives which approximate the experiment. Unobtrusive measures offer the greatest chance to produce research free from the problem of reactivity. Without violating research ethics it is often possible to examine the effects and remains of human activity in order to come to conclusions about variables. The inventiveness of researchers using unobtrusive measures may be the greatest limitation to this technique. Finally, much data are already available for use in research. Secondary analysis of data is to be encouraged. The mining of data already collected can prove to be most profitable in the search for relationships.

1. Describe what concepts and hypotheses you would consider if you were to become a participant observer in your next class; meeting; meal; party; shopping trip; sports event; or trip home (or to relatives if you live at "home" now).

2. Pick one of the examples from Exercise 1 for an actual participant observation. Describe what plans (if any) you have for observation beyond the concepts and hypotheses mentioned above.

3. Complete the observation. Compare what you observed and concluded with what you planned.

4. Pick an available group, event, or setting on campus or in your

community with which you are unfamiliar. The following are
only suggestions.

a revival meeting   a neighborhood bar
a special interest club (ski club)   an open conference
the music lounge   political group or rally

Become a participant observer for a short time. Note such things
as power structure, coalitions of participants, deviant values or
behaviors, and so on. Describe your participant observation.
Assess the conclusiveness, insightfulness, richness, and so on, of
your data and conclusions compared to your experimental and
survey experience and/or knowledge.

5. Design and conduct a brief content analysis to study one of the
   following.
   a. Differences between two of the following in the treatment of a
   major governmental official or controversial political issue in
   your community:
       the local press versus the local television
       a community paper versus a large city paper
   b. The treatment of one of the following in children's shows
   versus adult television:
       violence   politics
       sex roles   ethnic groups
   c. Trends in American values in:
       country or folk music   ecology
       rock   energy
       comedy

6. Locate the recent publications on the *Census of Population
   and Housing* in your library. Select two standard metropolitan
   statistical areas for comparison (for example, a large town and a
   small town or your college community and your home town).
   a. Compare the dispersion (standard deviation) of individual
   income in the two areas.
   b. Find the mean income for each census tract in each area and
   compute the standard deviation for the census tract means in the
   two areas. How adequate is this measure of dispersion in showing
   differences in the two areas relative to your data in part a?
   c. Using the maps at the back of each publication, construct your
   own maps to make comparisons of the two areas. Compare the
   income data for census tracts in downtown areas with selected
   suburbs. Is there a similar pattern in both communities?
   d. Make a second map of one community for which you are able
   to locate important social services for the poor and elderly. Locate
   on one map where there are relatively higher proportions of
   elderly. On the other locate where there are higher proportions of
   people below the poverty level. On each map locate crucial social
   services for the elderly and the poor. Are these agencies well
   located (near clientele, centrally located, dispersed into the
   appropriate regions, and so on)?
   e. Now that you are becoming familiar with census tract

information, describe how it might be useful for preliminary data for content analysis, evaluation research, other research projects.

7. Describe an evaluation research design for one of the following. Compare that design with what you might focus on if you were examining relationships. Discuss whether the distinction is necessary or valuable.
   a. your methods class
   b. the campus infirmary
   c. the campus advising system
   d. the campus parking system
   e. campus food services

8. Describe at least two possible unobtrusive measures for each of the following:
   a. socioeconomic status of college students
   b. the popularity of a professor
   c. a person's interest in another person

Examine as a dependent variable one of the dependent variables you studied in your project in Chapters 9 and/or 10.
1. Assess how each additional collection technique could examine the concept.
   a. Is the technique feasible? Is the technique adequate? Why or why not?
   b. Could the variables in previously examined hypotheses be reliably measured?
   c. What might be replicated?
   d. What might be newly learned or examined?
   If it is possible to continue with the same dependent variable, do so. If not, negotiate additional choices with your instructor.
2. Describe in detail a plan for a participant observation or content analysis. After appropriate approval from your instructor, complete your study.
3. Compare the results of your study with your experiment and survey.
4. Describe which measures in your previous projects have been unobtrusive and which have not. For the "obtrusive" measures, suggest possible unobtrusive ones.

PROJECT

REFERENCES

BECKER, H. "Problems of Inference and Proof in Participant Observation." *American Sociological Review*, 23, 1958, 625–650.

BELCH, J. *Contemporary Games: A Directory and Bibliography Covering Games and Play Situations Used for Instruction and Training by Schools, Colleges, Universities, Government, Business and Management.* Detroit: Gale Research Company, 1973–1974.

BOGDAN, R., AND TAYLOR, S. *Introduction to Qualitative Research Methods.* New York, Wiley, 1975.

BRUYN, S. *The Human Perspective in Sociology: The Methodology of Participant Observation.* Englewood Cliffs, N.J.: Prentice-Hall, 1966.

CARNEY, T. *Content Analysis: A Technique for Systematic Inference from Communications.* Winnipeg, Canada: University of Manitoba Press, 1972.

FILSTEAD, W. *Qualitative Methodology: First Hand Involvement in the Social World.* Chicago: Markham, 1970.

GAMSON, W. *Simsoc.* New York: The Free Press, 1969.

GOFFMAN, E. *The Presentation of Self in Everyday Life.* Garden City, N.Y.: Doubleday, 1959.

GOUDY, W. "Nonresponse Effects on Relationships between Variables." *Public Opinion Quarterly, 40,* No. 3, Fall 1976, 360–369.

HERRIOTT, R., AND HODGKINS, B. *The Environment of Schooling: Formal Education as an Open School System.* Englewood Cliffs, N.J.: Prentice-Hall, 1975.

HOLSTI, O. "Content analysis." In Lindsay, G., and Aronson, E. (eds.). *The Handbook of Social Psychology.* Reading, Mass.: Addison Wesley, 1968.

MCCALL, G., AND SIMMONS, J. *Issues in Participant Observation.* Reading, Mass.: Addison Wesley, 1969.

MEADOWS, D. *et al. The Limits of Growth: A Report for the Club of Rome's Project on the Predicament of Mankind.* New York: Universe Books, 1972.

MORRIS, M. "Public Definitions of a Social Movement: Women's Liberation." *Sociology and Social Research*, 1973, 57, 520–542.

MUEHL, D. (ED.). *Content Analysis at the Survey Research Center: A Manual for Coders.* Ann Arbor: Institute for Social Research, 1961.

POOL, I. (ed.). *Trends in Content Analysis.* Urbana, Ill.: University of Illinois Press, 1959.

ROSSI, P., AND WILLIAMS, W. *Evaluating Social Programs.* New York: Seminar Press, 1972.

SUCHMAN, E. *Evaluation Research.* New York: Russell Sage, 1967.

WEBB, E., CAMPBELL, D., SCHWARTZ, R., AND SECHREST, L. *Unobtrusive Measures: Nonreactive Research in the Social Sciences.* Chicago: Rand McNally, 1966.

WEISS, C. *Evaluation Research.* Englewood Cliffs, N.J.: Prentice Hall, 1972.

WHYTE, W. F. *Street Corner Society,* 2d ed. Chicago: University of Chicago Press, 1955.

ZUCKERMAN, D., AND HORNE, R. *Guide to Simulation and Games for Education and Training.* Lexington, Mass.: Information Resources, 1973.

REFERENCES

CHAPTER 13
MEASURES OF ASSOCIATION

After studying this chapter, students should be able to:

1. Discuss the basic notions of association in terms of describing a relationship with measures of association.

2. Provide the logic of proportional reduction of error measures of association.

3. Discuss how to determine original error and new error for lambda and how to calculate and interpret lambda for various bivariate tables.

4. Describe what is meant by asymmetrical and symmetrical measures of association.

5. Discuss how to determine original error and new error for r^2 and how to calculate and interpret r^2 for simple sets of data.

6. Discuss the interpretations and meaning of correlation coefficients.

7. Describe the relationship between explained variation and PRE measures of association.

8. Explore various three variable models with measures of association.

9. Interpret partial correlation coefficients.

10. Provide simple interpretations of multiple regression analysis and path analysis.

Asymmetrical measure of association A statistic that will take on different values for the same data depending on which variable is specified as the independent variable.

Coefficient of determination A PRE measure of association that can be calculated from interval level data (a scatterplot), represented by r^2.

Correlation coefficient A measure of association, not a PRE type, represented by r.

Explained variance (variations) Phrase referring to the strength of association similar to a PRE interpretation which emphasizes the prediction of scores on Y.

Lambda A simple PRE measure of association that can be used on bivariate tables.

Measures of association Statistical calculations which result in obtaining one number that is an index of the strength of the relationship between two variables.

Multiple correlation coefficient Analogous to r but for more than one independent variable.

Multiple regression analysis Statistical procedure used to analyze a multivariate model when all variables but the dependent are considered to be unrelated independent variables.

New error Mistakes in predicting when the X-Y relationship is known.

Original error Mistakes in predicting Y without knowing about the X-Y relationship.

Partial correlation coefficient Measure of association similar to r but with other variables controlled.

Path analysis A method of multivariable analysis which can be used to specify a model of how a number of variables are related to each other.

Path coefficients Measures of association similar to slope.

Path model Diagram representing how variables are interrelated.

Proportional reduction of error measures of association (PRE measures) Measures of association which are concerned with how much better one can predict values of the dependent variable (Y) with knowledge of the relationship between X and Y than with knowledge of the Y distribution only; a measure of the relative (proportional) improvement in prediction knowing the relationship as opposed to knowing only the distribution of the dependent variable.

Regression coefficient (b or beta weights) The slope when other variables are controlled.

Standardized variable A variable where the categories have been standardized by dividing each category value by the value of the standard deviation for the distribution of the variable. The resulting values are called standard scores or Z scores.

Symmetrical measure of association A statistic that will have the same value regardless of time order considerations.

1. THE BASIC IDEA OF ASSOCIATION

In the search for relationships, scatterplots can be used to clearly differentiate the various characteristics of a relationship. Form, extent (slope), and precision are relatively easy to describe. Percentage tables can also be effectively used to describe relationships. However, it is somewhat more difficult to clearly separate extent and precision and in some tables conclusions about form is a problem. In order to deal with this difficulty of interpreting percentage tables, the idea of the strength of a relationship was introduced. Strength of a relationship refers to a combination of extent and precision and is a measure of how strong the link is between variables. *Measures of association* are statistical calculations which result in obtaining one number that is an index of the strength of the relationship between two variables. One of the reasons that measures of association are popular techniques for reporting the strength of relationships is that only one number has to be reported.

The purpose of this chapter is to introduce some measures of association. Although there are many different measures of association, their interpretations are all somewhat similar.

2. THE LOGIC OF PROPORTIONAL REDUCTION OF ERROR

Proportional reduction of error (PRE) measures of association are a group of statistics that calculate the strength of a relationship by emphasizing the idea of prediction. PRE measures are concerned with predicting the value (score, category) of the dependent variable for each unit being observed. PRE measures tell us *how much better* we can make the prediction of Y knowing about the relationship than not knowing about the relationship. A simple example should make this idea clear. Suppose we wanted to predict the weight (Y) of a number of research subjects. If we knew the subjects' height (X) we could better predict their weight than if we did not know their height. This is because we know height is related to weight (X is related to Y). Our knowledge of this relationship helps us to predict weight.

In order to determine how much better we can predict Y, we must first make some predictions of Y without knowing about the relationship between X and Y. Second, we would make some predictions of Y knowing about the relationship between X and Y. Each of these sets of predictions of Y could then be checked against the correct values of each unit on Y. Assume that the units are people. We will first try to predict their Y value without knowing their score on X (i.e., about the relationship between X and Y). We would need to have some strategy for making these predictions. Suppose in this example we know that there are two categories of Y, low and high. When the predictions are made about each unit the prediction would have to be either low or high. We could always guess high or always guess low. We could alternate guessing low and high, or we could try to intuit each person's score on Y. There are any number of strategies which we might develop. No matter what strategy we use for guessing each person's value of Y, we will likely make a number of mistakes. By comparing our guesses of Y to each person's actual score on Y we could count the number of errors we made not knowing about the relationship between X and Y.

Now suppose we know the relationship between X and Y is a direct one. Before we make our prediction about each person's score on Y, if we would know their score on X, we could better predict their score on Y. If we know a person's score on X is low and the relationship between X and Y is direct (i.e., as X increases, Y increases), it would make sense to predict that person's score on Y as also being low. Furthermore, for all units that have low X we would predict low Y, and for all units that have high X we would predict high Y. This is the idea of a direct relationship, when X is low, Y is low, and as X increases, Y increases. After we predict in this manner we could compare our predictions with the actual value of Y for the people and count the number of errors we made. The stronger the relationship between X and Y, the fewer errors we will make in this second set of predictions. In other words (by knowing about a relationship), we will have a proportional reduction in errors in predicting Y when there is a relationship between X and Y.

Let us return to the example where X is height and Y is weight. We know from experience that there is a direct relationship between these two variables. Generally speaking, the taller a person is, the heavier a person will be. Without knowing about a person's height it would be difficult to predict whether the person is light or heavy. However, if we know a person's height, we probably would make fewer mistakes by guessing a person is heavy if their height is tall and light if their height is short. By comparing our two sets of predictions we could calculate how much our error is reduced by knowing about the relationship between height and weight. PRE measures of association calculates the proportion by which our error is reduced.

At this point it may seem like we are playing some kind of game that does not make much sense. If we already know each person's actual score on Y (which is needed to calculate the number of errors we have made), why are we "predicting" each score? This is because we really are trying to make a statement about the relationship between X and Y in general, not just for the particular units involved in our analysis. Through these procedures what we know about the relatively few units in our data can be used to make a more general statement about the nature of the relationship between the *variables* under study, not the people, or other units.

Before presenting specific PRE measures of association, the logic and procedures of this type of statistical method for assessing the strength of a relationship between variables can be summarized.

1. Make a prediction of each unit's score on Y based only on knowledge about the overall distribution of Y.
2. Compare these original predictions with the actual value of each unit on Y and determine the amount of error in these predictions. This error will be called *original error*.
3. Make a prediction of each unit's score on Y based on knowledge from a bivariate table or scatterplot about the relationship between X and Y.
4. Compare these new predictions with the actual value of each unit on Y and determine the amount of error in these predictions. This error will be called *new error*.
5. Compare the original error to the new error by calculating a ratio of how much the original error has been reduced. This ratio is called the proportional reduction in error and equals the value of the particular measure of association. The computation can be represented by the general equation below.

$$\begin{matrix} \text{Strength} \\ \text{of} \\ \text{association} \end{matrix} = \begin{matrix} \text{Proportional} \\ \text{reduction of} \\ \text{error (PRE)} \end{matrix} = \frac{\text{Original error} - \text{New error}}{\text{Original error}}$$

3. COMPUTATION OF LAMBDA

Many PRE measures of association use Greek letters as names. Lambda (λ) is one of the simplest measures of association using the logic presented in the preceding section. It can be calculated from any bivariate frequency table. Variables can have any level of measurement including nominal and/or ordinal. A hypothetical example of the relationship between workers' perception of job security (X) and their willingness to strike (Y) can be used as an example. The data for this illustration are presented in Table 13.1.

Determining original error

In determining original error we know the overall distribution of Y. This overall distribution is the right-hand *marginal* of Table 13.1; that is, the row totals. The Y marginals appears in Table 13.2. The data show that there are 28 observations in the high category of Y and 20 units with a score of low Y. There are 48 workers in this investigation.

We now make predictions of Y just knowing this information. The strategy used for making original predictions when calculating lambda is to predict the mode of Y. This is the way lambda is defined. If we always predict that each worker is "high" on the will-

TABLE 13.1
Table of frequencies

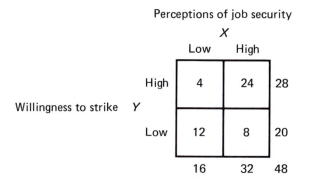

Perceptions of job security
X

		Low	High	
Willingness to strike Y	High	4	24	28
	Low	12	8	20
		16	32	48

ingness to strike (the value of the mode), we would be predicting correctly for 28 of them (the number with high Y). However, we would be wrong for 20 of them (the number that are not high). Therefore we have made an original error of 20.

Determining new error

The process of making new predictions of Y for each worker when the relationship between X and Y is known is similar to predicting when only Y is known. If we know the relationship between X and Y, we know the information in Table 13.1. Thus we know that for those workers who have the perception that their job security is low (first column), 4 of them have a high score on Y (willingness to strike) and 12 have a low score on Y. Calculations for new error separately consider each column of any table being analyzed. In this way knowledge of the X–Y relationship is being used to make predictions. Focusing on the 16 subjects who are low on X, we would again predict the mode of Y in order to calculate the new error. The mode of Y in the first column is low Y. If we predict that each of the 16 units in the low X column also have low Y, we would be correct for 12 of the units (those that are in the modal category) and incorrect for 4 of them (those not in the mode).

TABLE 13.2
Y marginals for computing lambda

Y	f
High	28
Low	20
Total	48

Continuing this logic, the second column of X would be inspected. There are 32 units in the high category of X. Predicting the modal category of Y in this column (high Y) for each of them we would be correct for 24 of them and wrong for the remaining 8 units. To find the total new error, the number of errors in each category of X are added together. Since there were errors for 4 observations in the first column and for 8 in the second column, the total number of new errors is 4 + 8 or 12. Table 13.3 shows how the new error has been calculated in each of the columns of X, that is knowing about the relationship between X and Y.

Comparing original error to new error

In order to compute lambda, the original error must be compared to the new error. A ratio of that value to the original error must be computed. This would result in

$$\text{Lambda} = \frac{\text{Original error} - \text{New error}}{\text{Original error}} = \frac{20 - 12}{20} = \frac{8}{20} = .40$$

The computation shows that for the table of the relationship between perceived job security and willingness to strike, the association between these two variables according to lambda is equal to .40. This is a relatively easy and straightforward calculation. The question remains as to how to interpret this number. All PRE measures of association can be interpreted in terms of increased ability to correctly predict the value of the dependent variable for the units

TABLE 13.3
Calculating new error for lambda

First column of X   Second column of X

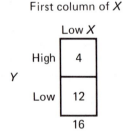

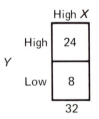

Mode of Y for this column = low Y.   Mode of Y for this column = high Y.
Frequency in modal category = 12.   Frequency in modal category = 24.
Frequency not in modal category   Frequency not in modal category
(i.e., the number of cases where   (i.e., the number of cases where
predicting the mode would be in   predicting the mode would be in
error) = 4.   error) = 8.

Total new error = 4 + 8 = 12

being studied. The top of the PRE general equation is the improvement in prediction based on knowledge of the X-Y relationship versus not knowing about the relationship. In general, the higher the measure of association, the more improvement in prediction. In order to provide a more thorough understanding of how to interpret lambda, we must consider some characteristics of the statistic.

Characteristics of lambda

It seems that lambda could have a minimum value of zero. This would mean that we gain nothing in predicting Y by knowing X. The maximum value could be 1.0. This would mean that we would make no errors when predicting if we knew about the relationship between two variables, lambda would be equal to zero. If there was a perfect relationship (i.e., all dots in the scatterplot analogy would be exactly on the best fitting line) it would be equal to 1.0. This is generally true for PRE measures of association.

This regularity is one reason why they are popular. In fact, some PRE statistics vary between −1.00 (for a perfect inverse relationship) and +1.00 (for a perfect direct relationship). The sign of such measures signifies the form of the relationship. The magnitude of the number indicates the strength of the relationship. Lambda is defined in such a way that it cannot have negative values, thus the sign of lambda will always be +. The form of the relationship between X and Y will have to be determined by looking at the percentage table.

There is a problem with lambda, however. Sometimes the nature of the table being analyzed and the definition of lambda work in such a way that it would be impossible for lambda to ever reach a value of 1.00. To illustrate this phenomenon we will construct two different tables with the same marginals as in Table 13.1. We will arrange the cases inside the cells of the tables so that the strongest possible relationships between X and Y are shown. Table 13.4 shows these tables with a direct relationship on the left and an inverse relationship on the right. Given the marginal distributions of both X and Y, the creation of a cell with zero frequencies results in the strongest relationship that could exist.

Notice that in the left-hand case (direct relationship), the lambda works out to .80. In the right-hand case (inverse relationship), lambda works out to be a value of .40. In other words the maximum lambda would be .80 in one case and .40 in another because of the way the marginals are arranged. Because of this situation, it is sometimes difficult to understand exactly what a particular value of lambda really means. In those tables where the maximum lambda could reach 1.00, the closer the value to 1.00, the more perfect the relationship between the variables. However, in those cases where

TABLE 13.4
Calculating the maximum values for lambda

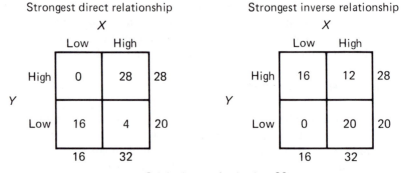

	Strongest direct relationship					Strongest inverse relationship		
	X					*X*		
	Low	High				Low	High	
High	0	28	28		High	16	12	28
Y				*Y*				
Low	16	4	20		Low	0	20	20
	16	32				16	32	

Original error for both = 20

New error:
For low X, zero errors.
For high X, 4 errors.
Total new error = 0 + 4 = 4
Lambda:

$$\frac{20-4}{20} = \frac{16}{20} = .80$$

New error:
For low X, zero errors.
For high X, 12 errors.
Total new error = 0 + 12 = 12
Lambda:

$$\frac{20-12}{20} = \frac{8}{20} = .40$$

the maximum is less than 1.00, interpreting how strong the relationship is becomes somewhat difficult.

Causal assertions are important for lambda. The previous illustration stated that perceptions of job security was the independent variable. It could be argued that it should be the other way around. It makes some sense to claim that willingness to strike could "cause" perceptions of job security. We can arrange the data in Table 13.1 to reflect this causal reasoning. Table 13.5 shows the rearranged table along with the computations for lambda.

It can be seen from the calculations that with these assumptions of time order or causation the lambda is equal to .25 instead of .40. When a measure of association is defined in such a way that a different value will be calculated depending on which variable is considered independent and which is considered dependent, the measure of association is called *asymmetrical*. Lambda is asymmetrical but not all measures of association are. Those that result in calculating the same value no matter which variable is considered the independent one are called *symmetrical measures of association*. To signify this difference, it is somewhat common to see a subscript together with the lambda. This subscript refers to which variable is considered the dependent variable. A λ_y would mean that the lambda is being calculated with Y as the dependent variable, that is, the predicted variable.

TABLE 13.5
Calculating lambda with different time order assumptions

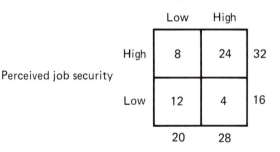

Willingness to strike

		Low	High	
Perceived job security	High	8	24	32
	Low	12	4	16
		20	28	

Original error = 16.
New error;
For left column, new error = 8.
For right column, new error = 4.
Total new error = 8 + 4 = 12.
Lambda:

$$\frac{16-12}{16} = \frac{4}{16} = .25$$

Since only the cell frequency of a bivariate table is needed to calculate lambda, relationships between nominal level variables can be analyzed using this measure of association. Although there are other measures of association that are also appropriate for nominal level variables, lambda is one of the more commonly used statistics. Not all measures of association can be used with variables of all different levels of measurement. Indeed this is one consideration which must be made before a particular statistic of association is chosen to analyze particular data.

A lambda of zero may be calculated even when percentage analysis would lead to a conclusion that there was a relationship between variables. This will occur whenever 50 percent or more of the cases for each category of X fall in the same Y category. Table 13.6 provides a number of examples of the types of tables where this phenomenon occurs. In all cases there is at least a 20 percent difference between the columns and yet because of this peculiarity of lambda, there is no improvement in prediction. This means that even in those cases where lambda equals zero, the percentage table should be consulted to make certain that there really is no relationship in the table.

Finally, lambda can be used to calculate a measure of association for any sized bivariate frequency table. Although all of our examples have been for a four-cell table (in order to make calculation easier), the same basic principles presented above can be applied to larger tables. Table 13.7 shows how lambda would be calculated for a nine-

382

cell table. The first step is to determine original error by inspecting the Y marginals. The mode of the Y marginals would be predicted if we did not know about the X-Y relationship.

Similarly the mode of each column is used to predict the Y value for all cases in each column. Errors in such cases are the sum of the frequencies *not* in the respective medal categories. Lambda is then

TABLE 13.6
Examples where lambda equals zero but where a relationship exists

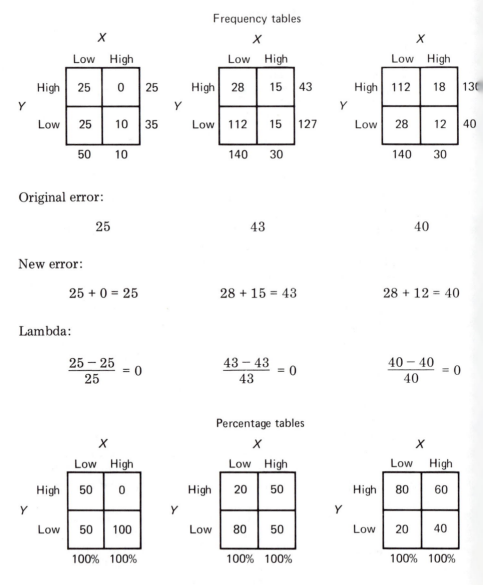

Frequency tables

	X Low	X High	
High	25	0	25
Low	25	10	35
	50	10	

	X Low	X High	
High	28	15	43
Low	112	15	127
	140	30	

	X Low	X High	
High	112	18	130
Low	28	12	40
	140	30	

Original error:

25   43   40

New error:

25 + 0 = 25   28 + 15 = 43   28 + 12 = 40

Lambda:

$$\frac{25 - 25}{25} = 0 \qquad \frac{43 - 43}{43} = 0 \qquad \frac{40 - 40}{40} = 0$$

Percentage tables

	X Low	X High
High	50	0
Low	50	100
	100%	100%

	X Low	X High
High	20	50
Low	80	50
	100%	100%

	X Low	X High
High	80	60
Low	20	40
	100%	100%

TABLE 13.7
Calculating lambda for a larger table

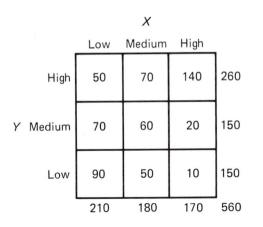

		X		
		Low	Medium	High
	High	50	70	140	260
Y	**Medium**	70	60	20	150
	Low	90	50	10	150
		210	180	170	560

Original error:
    Since the mode of the Y marginal is "high," there will be 150 + 150 = 300 errors made if high Y is guessed for all cases in the table.
New error:
    For the low X column the new error would = 50 + 70 = 120.
    For the medium X column the new error would = 60 + 50 = 110.
    For the high X column the new error would = 20 + 10 = 30.
    Total new error would = 120 + 110 + 30 = 260.
Lambda:

$$\frac{300 - 260}{300} = \frac{40}{300} = .13$$

computed using the general equation for all PRE measures of association.

It is not too difficult to see that interpreting lambda is difficult for some tables. Although it can be a very useful statistic for nominal level variables, there is another PRE statistic that is often used for interval and ratio level variables (and sometimes original variables).

4. COMPUTATION OF CORRELATION AND COEFFICIENT OF DETERMINATION

This section will explore another PRE measure or association called the *coefficient of determination*. It is quite common to hear people ask, "What is the *correlation* between two variables?" They really are asking, "What is the *association* between the variables?" Technically, the use of the term "correlation" in this way is incorrect.

Correlation is a specific statistic of association. It is formally known as the *Pearson product moment correlation coefficient* and it is represented by a small letter r. Unfortunately, r does not have a PRE interpretation, but if r is squared, the resulting r^2 is a PRE measure of association. This statistic (r^2) is called the *coefficient of determination*. Because it is a PRE statistic, the basic procedures for computing r^2 are similar to lambda.

The coefficient of determination is defined in such a way that a mean value of Y must be calculated. Since the calculation of a mean requires interval level data, a scatterplot can be used to illustrate the statistic instead of relying on a bivariate table. This statistic cannot be used with nominal or ordinal level variables. (Some people relabel ordinal categories with numbers and "pretend" the variable is interval level.)

Determining original error

The prediction rule for determining original error with r^2 is to use the mean value of the overall Y distribution to predict the Y for every unit in the analysis. Original error would be determined by examining the difference between each unit's actual score on Y (Y_i) and the mean value of Y ($\overline{Y}$). Figure 13.1 shows a hypothetical scatterplot. Below the plot is the total distribution of all units on Y based on data in the scatterplot. In addition, a dashed line represents the mean value of Y which has been computed from the overall Y distribution.

The value of the mean (5.3) is what we would predict for each unit if we did not know about the relationship between X and Y. We do not need to know about X to compute the mean. Focusing on one case, say unit J, we could determine how far off from the actual value of Y (for unit J) we would be if we predicted that J had a Y value of 5.3 (the mean). Since J has an actual value of 8.0, this is 2.7 ($8.0 - 5.3$) away from the mean of Y. By definition, the original error for r^2 is defined as being this difference squared. This could be represented algebraically by the expression $(Y_i - \overline{Y})^2$. The original error for unit J would be $(2.7)^2 = (2.7 \times 2.7) = 7.29$.

Because we want total original error, this same operation is conducted for each unit. The sum of these calculations equals total original error. Figure 13.1 also indicates how the distance between each dot on the scatterplot and the mean line can be used to compute original error. Table 13.8 carries out this calculation for all the cases in the scatterplot.

Notice that the difference between Y_i and $\overline{Y}$ for every dot below the mean line is negative. When these negative values are squared the result is a positive number.

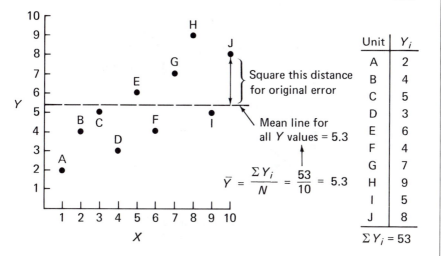

FIGURE 13.1

Constructing the mean line for determining original error for r^2

Determining new error

The next step in computing any PRE measure of association is to define what predicting rule we are going to use to find new error. For r^2 we use the *regression line* of the scatterplot. As you will recall, the estimate of the regression line that we can draw on a scatterplot is called the best fitting line. For this illustration we use the best fitting line. If a computer did the calculations, the true regression line would be used. Both lines are a result of knowing the X–Y relationship. Figure 13.2 shows the previous scatterplot with the best fitting line drawn in.

TABLE 13.8

Computation of original error for r^2

Unit	Y_i	$Y_i - \overline{Y}$	$(Y_i - \overline{Y})^2$
A	2	$2 - 5.3 = -3.3$	$-3.3 \times -3.3 = 10.98$
B	4	$4 - 5.3 = -1.3$	$-1.3 \times -1.3 = 1.69$
C	5	$5 - 5.3 = -\ .3$	$-\ .3 \times -\ .3 = .09$
D	3	$3 - 5.3 = -2.3$	$-2.3 \times -2.3 = 5.29$
E	6	$6 - 5.3 = \ .7$	$.7 \times \ .7 = .49$
F	4	$4 - 5.3 = -1.3$	$-1.3 \times -1.3 = 1.69$
G	7	$7 - 5.3 = \ 1.7$	$1.7 \times \ 1.7 = 2.89$
H	9	$9 - 5.3 = \ 3.7$	$3.7 \times \ 3.7 = 13.69$
I	5	$5 - 5.3 = -\ .3$	$-\ .3 \times -\ .3 = .09$
J	8	$8 - 5.3 = \ 2.7$	$2.7 \times \ 2.7 = 7.29$

$$\text{Total original error} = \Sigma\ (Y_i - \overline{Y})^2 = 44.10$$

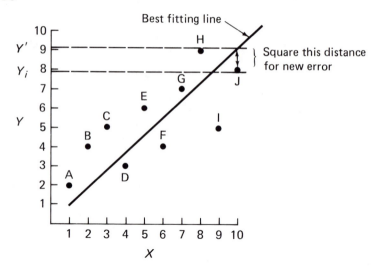

FIGURE 13.2
A scatterplot for computing new error for r²

Calculating r^2 is legitimate only if there is a linear X–Y relationship. (There is a statistic called *eta*, analogous to r^2, which can be used if the relationship is not linear.) One way to determine if the X–Y relationship is linear is to examine the scatterplot. We can again focus on unit J for determining new error. For this calculation the distance we are interested in is the vertical distance between each dot (the true value of Y_i) and the value of the Y on the best fitting (regression) line. To find this distance a line is drawn parallel to the Y-axis and perpendicular to the X-axis which connects the best fitting line and the dot representing each case. The value of Y at the best fitting line is sometimes referred to by the symbol Y'. For case J, $Y_i = 8$ and Y' equals approximately 9.1. Therefore the distance between these two values $(Y_i - Y')$ equals $8 - 9.1 = -1.1$. To calculate new error, this distance is squared, which gives $-1.1 \times -1.1 = 1.21$. This is the value of the new error for unit J. The same procedures are followed for each case. The sum of all the calculations is equal to the total new error. These computations are provided in Table 13.9. The total new error equals 28.93.

Comparing original error to new error

Applying the general formula for PRE measures of association will reveal the value of r^2 as a measure of the strength of the X–Y relationship.

$$r^2 = \frac{\text{Original error} - \text{New error}}{\text{Original error}} = \frac{44.10 - 28.93}{44.10} = \frac{15.17}{44.10} = .35$$

In other words, by using the best fitting line to predict Y_i we can improve our ability to predict over using the mean value of Y by a ratio of .35. We have a proportional reduction of error (of predicting Y) of .35 (35 percent). This would be considered a moderate strength X–Y relationship by most researchers. As with all measures of association, r^2 confounds extent and precision. Another way of saying this is that both extent (slope) and precision (goodness of fit) contribute to the magnitude of r^2. Although there are no formal guidelines that say what a strong or weak association is, Table 13.10 presents a rough approximation of how extent and precision would work together to give various strengths of association. In addition, the table provides an approximation of what we believe most researchers would say the r^2 equivalents would be for various strengths of association.

For example, if a scatterplot had a high extent (slope) but only low precision, the resulting measure of association would be only moderate to strong strength. The best way to determine whether the size of a coefficient of determination is largely due to extent or precision or both is to examine the scatterplot.

Characteristic of r and r²
Although r^2 is the PRE measure of association that is connected with correlation, it is very common to find just r reported in research publications. In these cases, r is often treated as a measure of association. This is appropriate as long as a PRE interpretation is not used. The question of how to interpret r then becomes relevant. It could be squared to obtain r^2 and then that could be interpreted.

TABLE 13.9
Computations for new error for r^2

Unit	Y_i	Y' (approx.)	$Y_i - Y'$	$(Y_i - Y')^2$
A	2	1.2	$2 - 1.2 = .8$	.64
B	4	2.2	$4 - 2.2 = 1.8$	3.24
C	5	3.0	$5 - 3.0 = 2.0$	4.00
D	3	4.0	$3 - 4.0 = -1.0$	1.00
E	6	4.5	$6 - 4.5 = 1.5$	2.25
F	4	5.6	$4 - 5.6 = -1.6$	2.56
G	7	6.5	$7 - 6.5 = .5$	.25
H	9	7.3	$9 - 7.3 = 1.7$	2.89
I	5	8.3	$5 - 8.3 = -3.3$	10.89
J	8	9.1	$8 - 9.1 = -1.1$	1.21

Total new error $= \Sigma\ (Y_i - Y')^2 = 28.93$

TABLE 13.10
The relationship between extent, precision, and association

Degree of extent	Degree of precision	Strength of association
Low	Low	Weak
Low	Medium	Moderately weak
Low	High	Moderate to strong
Medium	Low	Moderately weak
Medium	Medium	Moderate
Medium	High	Moderately strong to strong
High	Low	Moderate to strong
High	Medium	Moderately strong to strong
High	High	Strong

Strength of association[a]	Approximate values of r^2
Weak	.15 or less
Moderately weak	.16–.30
Moderate	.31–.41
Moderately strong	.42–.63
Strong	.64 or greater

[a] These values depend on the type of design utilized and the kind of variables studied.

This is the solution that we favor. We suspect that there are four reasons why this may not be done.

First, there is a tradition of reporting r, so people are used to comparing strength of relationship in terms of r. We do not know whether people realize that r is the square root of strength, but we suspect that often a PRE interpretation is given to r and some do not realize their misinterpretation.

The second reason for reporting r may have to do with the fact that there may be a psychological advantage to reporting r as opposed to r^2. Most researchers want to find strong associations in their research. Since this is the case, they would like to present large numbers to represent strong association. Unfortunately, for this purpose, when a decimal is squared one obtains a smaller number. Thus r^2 is always smaller than its corresponding r (except when $r = 1.0$). For example, an r of .60 equals .36 when squared, only a moderate association according to Table 13.10.

The third reason that r may be reported is that there are several interpretations of r as a statistic in its own right and people may have one of these in mind. Although the mathematics involved are not particularly appropriate for this text, r can be interpreted as kind of a slope (extent)—a slope between standardized variables. A *standardized variable* is one where the value of the category has been divided by the value of the standard deviation for the distribution of that variable. Values are thus standard deviation units (often called Z scores) instead of regular category values. Slope in this context would mean that as one variable changes one standard deviation unit, the other variable changes by some number of standard deviation units. The problem with this situation is that it is difficult to say what a standardized slope means in terms of a relationship between variables.

A fourth consideration for reporting r is that, unlike many measures of association, it has the potential to reflect the form of the relationship being investigated. If r is positive, the assumption is made that the relationship is direct, and if r is negative, there is an assumption that the relationship is inverse. The reason we say that these are assumptions is that r assumes a linear relationship. When that is not the case, to claim this would be an error.

Figure 13.3 illustrates how r would be misleading in the case of curvilinear relationships. In the left plot a very definite U-shaped curvilinear relationship exists. The resulting r from such data would be equal to zero. For the right plot a very small positive r would result. This is the case since precision is low and the "tilt" of the S curve is slightly up at the right. In both cases the r obtained would not satisfactorily describe the relationship between the two variables being studied. This situation again highlights the importance of inspecting the actual scatterplot.

In addition to the considerations listed above, there are several features of r and r^2 which are important. First, they both require interval level variables for their calculation. Thus more detail of the data is examined than in the case with measures based on tables. Second, unlike lambda, r^2 can always vary between zero and 1.0. Finally, r^2 is a symmetrical measure of association. Therefore no assertions need to be made about time order or causal sequence.

5. ASSOCIATION AS EXPLAINED VARIANCE

Sometimes when assessing the strength of a relationship, researchers refer to the proportion (percentage) of variance (variation) explained. This is a technical term which has its roots in formal statistics. For the statisticians to explain variance simply means to be able to predict Y scores. Variance refers to dispersion or variability in the Y distribution. If we can predict when Y will be high and when it will be low some say we have explained why Y takes each value. Thus, predicting the dispersion of Y by knowing about the X–Y relationship is equivalent to explaining variation. To talk of explained variance is to talk of how well we can predict Y knowing the X–Y relationship. To talk of the proportion of variance explained is

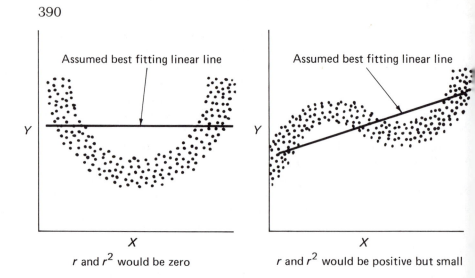

FIGURE 13.3
r and r₂ as they relate to curvilinear relationships

to talk of how much better we can predict Y knowing X than without knowing X. This is no more than the definition of association with which we have been dealing.

When the term "explained variance" is used by researchers, it is easy to get the impression that they are referring to explanation in a different sense. They may refer to how much of the change of Y is caused by X. This would be an erroneous interpretation. Although the mathematics involved is beyond the scope of this text, some statisticians think that since the variance in X and the degree of joint effects from other variables may affect measures of association, it would be better to use a simple measure of slope (extent) as an index of how important variables are in the determination of causing Y.

6. MULTIVARIATE ANALYSIS WITH MEASURES OF ASSOCIATION

There are several ways that we may account (control) for other variables with measures of association or techniques which are similar to association. The first of these is by partitioning data. The second is by using a special type of measure of association called a partial association. Finally, some additional methods are introduced.

Controlling by partitioning

When we account for other variables with partitioning, the data are separated into groups according to the various units' score on the third variable (Z) (just as was done for percentages and scatter-plots). However, rather than comparing scatterplots or bivariate tables, we simply look at the measures of association calculated for each group of data. This technique will work satisfactorily for three variable models where the X–Y relationship disappears when Z is introduced (spurious and intervening models), but it will not clearly allow you to determine if the three variable model under study is a no-effect, joint-effects, or complicated model. Since measures of association confound extent and precision, we cannot examine the slopes of the main X–Y relationship and compare it to the slopes of the control data. Thus two parallel slopes (joint-effects model) may or may not have the same association as two nonparallel slopes (complicated model).

Since these three models are not clearly separable, what appears to be a no-effect model may really be either a joint-effects or complicated model. The problem again points to the necessity of examining scatterplots when possible. Table 13.11 gives some illustrations of how some three variables models might appear when using measures of association. Remember, however, that some models may not be easy to interpret if only measures of association are used.

Controlling by partial measures of association

Perhaps a more common way to assess the interrelationship of three variables is by using a statistical procedure called a partial association. One common partial association statistic is a partial correlation coefficient denoted as a "partial r." For this statistic a multidimensional scatterplot is envisioned. For the case of three variables, another axis would be added to a regular scatterplot and that axis would be perpendicular to the page and would start at the origin of the coordinate system. Each case would then be placed in space (this space could be seen as the corner of a cardboard box) and a surface, analogous to a best fitting line, is computed. From that

TABLE 13.11
Examples of three variable models explored with associations

Model	Association of all data	Association of cases with high Z	Association of cases with low Z
Spurious	$r^2 = .35$	$r^2 = 0$	$r^2 = 0$
Intervening	$r^2 = .35$	$r^2 = 0$	$r^2 = 0$
No-effect[a]	$r^2 = .35$	$r^2 = .35$	$r^2 = .35$
Joint-effects[a]	$r^2 = .35$	$r^2 = .40$	$r^2 = .40$
Complicated[a]	$r^2 = .35$	$r^2 = .65$	$r^2 = .12$

[a] May be difficult to determine and clearly distinguish.

three-dimensional best fitting plane a partial r is calculated. It can be interpreted very similarly to a regular r except that it is a measure of association for the X–Y relationship controlling for Z. It is represented by $r_{YX \cdot Z}$. Rather than having three or more measures of the X–Y relationship to compare, a partial association is statistically removing the effects of a third variable. When this effect is statistically removed, any spurious or intervening model will reduce the partial to zero. Unfortunately it is impossible to determine what other model might be operating aside from these two cases.

The simultaneous examination of multivariate models

There are several other multivariate techniques based on aspects of association which comprise the better part of most courses in advanced multivariate statistics courses. Two of the most common are multiple regression analysis and path analysis.

Multiple regression analysis
Multiple regression is a special technique used to analyze certain kinds of multivariate models. The assumption of multiple regression is that there are no complicated relationships in the system of variables under examination. We can diagram one such system as in Figure 13.4.

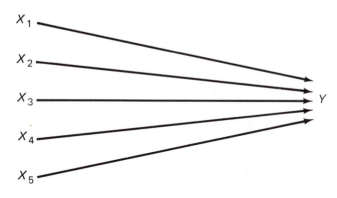

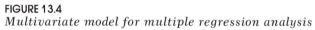

FIGURE 13.4
Multivariate model for multiple regression analysis

As you can see from the diagram, each variable aside from the dependent variable is viewed as an independent variable. One important statistic obtained from multiple regression analysis is called the multiple correlation coefficient, represented by R. When R is squared it has a PRE interpretation. R^2 would be interpreted as the total amount of variation of Y that is explained by all of the independent variables taken together. In our model it would be a measure of how much better we could predict Y knowing about the X_1–Y, X_2–Y, X_3–Y, X_4–Y, and X_5–Y relationships. If we could perfectly predict Y from knowing all of these relationships R^2 would equal 1.0. It is interpreted very similarly to r^2 but it is for more than one independent variable.

Another important set of statistics obtained from multiple regression analysis is a number of regression coefficients. The coefficients (sometimes called b or beta weights) are very much like extent and slope. Their value is the degree that Y changes for a unit change in X, eliminating the change produced by the other independent variables. They are slopes that have controlled for the other variables in the analysis. If unstandardized variables are used, the coefficients are interpreted just like slopes. If standardized variables are used, they are interpreted as slopes with standard deviation units.

Path analysis

Path analysis has gained increasing popularity in the past decade and we feel you should be able to follow its general idea. You might approach it as sort of a combination of examination of association and slopes for several variables at a time. Since we are talking about several variables, we must slightly reorient our views of multivariate relationships. For path analysis we assume that there are no complicated relationships. Rather than thinking of spurious, intervening, or joint effects, we view a set of variables as these types combined. Note in Figure 13.5 that X_1 and X_2 are jointly related to X_3, which in turn is the intervening variable for X_1 and X_2 to X_4, which is intervening for X_1, X_2, and X_3 to X_5. Note also that X_2 is related to X_5 in two ways by means of X_3 and X_4 as intervening variables and directly to some degree. Path analysis treats the nature of relationships between these variables in terms of standardized slopes, similar to an r. The numbers in the path diagram in Figure 13.5 are called path coefficients and are a type of measure of association. Thus, for example, the coefficient between X_1 and X_3 is .47, which

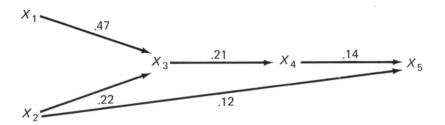

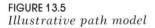

FIGURE 13.5
Illustrative path model

means that as X_1 changes by 1 standard deviation, X_3 changes by .47ths of a standard deviation. Although there are several problems with path analysis, it is a useful illustration of how we can combine previous concerns to look at several variables operating at a time and thus approximate a fuller picture of the systems of variables in which we are interested.

7. SUMMARY

Measures of association are commonly used to indicate the strength of relationship between variables. One common type of measure of association provides a proportional reduction of error interpretation. The idea of PRE measures is that the magnitude of the association will depend on how well we can predict a unit's value of the dependent variable. A comparison is made between predicting Y not knowing the relationship between X and Y, and predicting Y knowing the relationship. These sets of predictions are then compared to research data. On the basis of these two sets of errors the PRE equation is completed. While the measures of association use actual data to compare the predictions of Y, the idea of the measure is to talk about the relationship between the variables, in general.

Lambda is a very useful measure of association for percentage tables. Predictions for this statistic utilize the mode. The coefficient of determination (r^2) is another common PRE statistic. For r^2 guessing the mean value of Y is compared to guessing the regression value of Y. Each of these statistics have certain characteristics and problems which must be considered when analyzing a bivariate relationship. For multivariate systems, measures of association can be used similarly to percentage table analysis by partitioning the data. When data are partitioned, the measures of association computed on the conditional data can be compared to the measure for the original data. These comparisons will allow us to categorize the three variable model.

In addition to partitioning data, three variable models can be explored with partial measures of association, multiple regression analysis, or path analysis.

Partial measures, like partial r, will give us a measure of association between X and Y, controlling for the effects of Z. While such measures will summarize the information obtained by partitioning, they will not allow us to determine some three variable models. Only spurious and intervening models can be detected with partial measures of association. Multiple regression analysis treats a number of variables as independent and provides us with an R^2 and regression coefficients. R^2 will tell us the PRE of predicting Y knowing all of the relationships between the independent variables and Y versus not knowing any of them. Regression coefficients are either slopes or standardized slopes which tell us the degree of change in Y produced by a change in X. Path analysis is somewhat similar to multiple regression analysis. A theoretical model must be specified ahead of time for path analysis. The results of this analysis are path coefficients. Path coefficients can be interpreted as the slope between standardized variables.

All the techniques presented in this chapter help us in our search for relationships. They are useful for summarizing a great deal about the nature of the relationship between variables. As summaries they do not allow us to fully explore the nature of the relationship between variables. Many of the measures do not allow us to separate the extent and precision of relationships. Some of them do not allow us to fully explore all of the possible three variable models we have discussed in previous chapters. As with any analysis tool, measures of association serve their purpose. They are one way to enable us to search for relationships.

1. Give an example when you would use lambda rather than r^2 and explain why you would do so.

2. Compute lambda for the following tables:

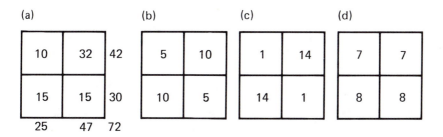

(a)

10	32	42
15	15	30
25	47	72

(b)

5	10
10	5

(c)

1	14
14	1

(d)

7	7
8	8

3. Compute lambda for the tables in Exercise 2, Chapter 4.

4. For each of the following, state what you are able to interpret about the nature of the multivariate relationship.
a. The r^2 between childhood personality and adult personality is .6. When the degree of similarity of social environment is controlled: for those adults in an environment similar to childhood, $r^2 = .71$; for those adults in an environment different from childhood, $r^2 = .34$.
b. The standardized regression coefficient for the contribution of the father's occupational status on the liberalism of the son's voting behavior is .34. The beta weight for the mother's occupational status influence is .21.

EXERCISES

c. The correlation between status and achievement is .4. When motivation is controlled, the partial correlation is .5.

d. The coefficient of determination between the degree of persuasiveness of communication received and a subject's attitude change is .4. When the subject's personal stated commitment is opposed to the position expressed within the communication and this position is controlled, the partial correlation between persuasiveness and change is 0.

5. a. If the original $r = .4$ and the relationship when controlling for a third variable is complicated, will the partial r's differ? Why or why not?

b. In the case of controlling for an intervening variable, if the $r = .4$:

(1) What should the partial r's equal?

(2) What should the r's look like if the data were partitioned into two control scatterplots?

(3) What would r^2 equal?

Compute lambda for all tables you developed for your various projects. Do your conclusions reached using a measure of association match those reached with scatterplots and/or percentage tables?

ASHER, H. *Causal Modeling.* Beverly Hills: Sage, 1977.

BLALOCK, H., JR. *Social statistics,* 2d ed. New York: McGraw-Hill, 1972.

BLALCOK, H., JR. *Theory Construction.* Englewood Cliffs, N.J.: Prentice Hall, 1969.

DAVIS, J. *Elementary Survey Analysis.* Englewood Cliffs, N.J.: Prentice Hall, 1971.

CHAPTER 14
RELIABILITY AND VALIDITY

After studying this chapter, students should be able to:

1. Define and discuss the meaning and importance of reliability and validity.
2. Discuss the relationship between reliability and validity.
3. Describe and differentiate between stability and equivalence reliability.
4. Describe how test-retest methods and split-half techniques are used to test reliability.
5. Define and discuss the importance of interobserver reliability.
6. Define and describe the determination of face, content, criterion, concurrent, and predictive validity.
7. Define and give examples of concepts which are constructs.
8. Define and describe the determination of construct validity.
9. Discuss the role of judgment in the determination of validity of all types.
10. Discuss the importance of reliability and validity in the research process.

Concurrent validity Type of criterion validity which uses an established measure of the same variable to compare with a new one.

Consistency reliability See "Equivalence reliability."

Construct A concept created by some combination of other concepts and/or is composed of several dimensions or characteristics and/or is relatively difficult to observe directly, or possibly unobservable.

Construct validity To demonstrate the relationship of various indicators to one another; to demonstrate the construct's relationship to hypothesized other variables; and to demonstrate the lack of relationships to other variables that are hypothesized to be unrelated.

Content validity Validity based on the representativeness of the measurement (a type of face validity).

Correlation coefficient (r) A statistic sometimes used to reflect reliability which equals 1 when there is a perfect comparison in reliability tests, and 0 when there is no similarity when testing reliability.

Criterion validity Either concurrent or predictive validity.

Equivalence reliability To obtain the same relative value with different types of measures at the same time.

Face validity To determine validity by examining the measurement device and/or procedure and using common sense and experience to judge their adequacy.

Factor analysis A set of highly technical mathematical procedures which allow researchers to examine a large number of items to determine if they are related.

Interobserver reliability The degree to which observers or coders are consistent in their categorization of subjects.

Predictive validity Type of criterion validity which uses the ability of a measure to predict events or behaviors as a basis of validity.

Reliability The consistency of measurement.

Split-half technique To demonstrate reliability by dividing a set of indicators into two parts and comparing the relative score of subjects on each part.

Stability reliability To obtain the same or a similar value for each person or unit measured every time you measure.

Test-retest method To demonstrate reliability by using the same measure (test) at one point in time and readministering the measure at a later point in time.

Validity The degree of fit between a given conceptual definition and an operational definition which has been developed.

1. INTRODUCTION

In Chapter 2 we touched on the idea that for research to be accurate, it is necessary to have reliable and valid indicators of the variables being studied. No matter what the research design, be it experimental, survey, or some other, the problem of accurate observation (measurement) must be adequately handled. Although each design must deal with this problem a little bit differently, there are some general considerations that can be explored. The purpose of this chapter is to examine the processes used to assess reliability and validity of research indicators. While the emphasis here is on the validity and reliability of indicators and measures, it must be remembered that all aspects of the research process must be carried out carefully and accurately in order to obtain research results we can trust.

Sometimes the terms reliability and validity are used in reference to a total study or research project. If for some reason a person does not trust research conclusions or feels a study was done poorly, it might be said that the study was not "reliable" or "valid." We would encourage students not to use these terms in this way. Chapter 17 fully discusses the evaluation of published research, but for now it is preferred that the terms validity and reliability be used solely as they pertain to indicators and operational definitions. Notice also that internal and external validity refer only to the *design* of experiments. We must also consider the validity and reliability of indicators in all experiments.

Remembering the archery analogy from Chapter 2, assessing reliability is a necessary part of demonstrating validity. Since reliability refers to consistency of measurement, it is a necessary condition for demonstrating the validity of a measure of a variable. That is, reliability must be present in order to have validity but it does not guarantee validity. It is possible to have a consistent measure which measures the wrong thing. For example, you could use height to measure IQ. You might have a consistent measure in centimeters of height, but this would not reflect intelligence. The basic idea behind testing the validity of an indicator or measure is to assess the degree of fit between a given conceptual definition and an operational definition which has been developed.

In the following sections we shall first review procedures for assessing reliability and then review those for validity. However, before we proceed we wish to note one sad reality of the research in education, behavioral sciences, and the social sciences. If you were to go to the major journals in your field of interest, you would note that very few articles actually report assessments of reliability or validity. In fact, many do not even report conceptual or operational definitions. We suspect that there are several reasons for this. First, many terms have well accepted definitions for which there is high consensus in the field; status, reinforcement, and gross national product are examples. Second, some measures employed may have been validated frequently in the past. Third, and we suspect this is the major factor, researchers have not been sufficiently strict on themselves in formally testing reliability and validity. Even in those cases where reliability is demonstrated, validity is often assumed rather than actually tested. We hope that as consumers of research become more knowledgeable through coursework and texts such as this, researchers will be forced to confront these difficult problems head on.

2. RELIABILITY

If a measure is reliable, we should get the same score for each unit measured every time we make an observation if the characteristic of the unit being observed does not change in value during the time we are measuring it. There are two general ways of assessing reliability or two major types of reliability: stability reliability and equivalence reliability. *Stability reliability* involves getting the same or a similar value for each person or unit measured every time you measure. It involves using the same indicator, operational definition, and data collection procedure each time and measuring at different times. To have stability reliability, scores should be the same or nearly the same each time a unit is measured. *Equivalence reliability* involves getting the same relative value with different types of measures at the same time. It involves using the same conceptual definition but one or more different indicators, operational definitions, collection procedures, and/or observers.

Since the procedures used to observe the variable may be different, it is not likely that the same unit (usually a person) would get exactly the same score by each procedure. What is important for assessing equivalence reliability is not obtaining the *same* score, but the same *relative* score on each measure. Stability reliability involves the same measure at different times, and equivalence reliability involves different measures at the same time. The following sections discuss, in detail, each type of reliability.

Stability reliability

The most common assessment of reliability of this type is the test-retest method. The *test-retest* method involves using the same measure, or "test," of a variable at one point in time and readministering the measure at a later point in time. In Chapter 2 we mentioned that intelligence has been traditionally thought of as a characteristic that is not supposed to change over time. Therefore we would expect that if an IQ test measures intelligence, one should get the same relative IQ score taking the same IQ test at two different times. Another way to demonstrate stability reliability, if using a survey, is to include the same question in two different parts of a questionnaire or interview. For example, the Minnesota Multiphasic Personality Inventory (MMPI) has a test-retest reliability check within a single questionnaire by repeating certain questions at various places in a long questionnaire.

Test-retest reliability is only an appropriate technique when you are willing to assume that the variable you are measuring has not changed between the first and second measurement. Making this assumption is somewhat difficult at times because between the first and second measurement several factors may alter the characteristic being measured. A variable might change because of events in the environment, maturation, or the first test. Attitudes are very susceptible to such changes. For example, people might change their attitudes because they have received new information from the environment. Thus a person may favor a political candidate during the first interview and not favor the same candidate during the second interview because that person learned that the candidate does not take the "right" stand on several issues. People might also change attitudes because they grow bored with or tired of something (maturation). For example attitudes toward fads and fashions undergo frequent changes as do attitudes toward various forms of entertainment. Attitudes may also genuinely change as a function of having received the first test. The way a questionnaire is worded may make a person reconsider their response and change their mind at some later time.

The major difficulty of demonstrating stability reliability is making the assumption that the trait being measured has indeed remained stable over time. Since it is very likely that there is no other reliable and valid measure available (otherwise why would we need a new one?), there may be nothing the researcher can use to support the assumption that the phenomenon has not changed. The only thing that may be helpful in making this assumption is experience, theory, and/or trained judgment. In any event, this assumption can always be challenged and it is difficult to defend the assumption on objective grounds.

Equivalence reliability

Because a person's score may actually change between measurements, a second type of reliability assessment is often used: equivalence reliability. Checking reliability by means of using an equivalent measure at the same time takes several forms. The most common form is called the *split-half* technique. It is often used in surveys. When a series of questions measuring one variable are included in a questionnaire, the questions are divided (split) into two parts (halves) by some process. (Randomization or alternation is often used for the split-halves technique.) The results of each half of the questions are summarized into a score and then the scores produced by each half are compared. If both scores are relatively the same, split-half reliability has been shown.

Equivalence reliability can also be assessed by using *different measurement techniques*. Anxiety, for example, has been measured by self-report, blood pressure, general fidgeting, perspiration, and pulse rate. Relative scores from one such indicator should be consistent with scores from another. Thus, if a subject appears anxious on a "fidget measure," that person should reflect the same relative anxiety if blood pressure is measured.

Reliability may also be assessed using the same measurement process but using *different observers*. For example, sometimes more than one member of a household could be interviewed about household morale or behaviors. Each respondent would then be an observer of the respondent's own household. We can treat each observation in the same household as different indicators of what is being measured. A reliable measure should obtain consistent responses from each observer. Psychologists often collect data by having observers monitor various behaviors. For example, they may send two or three observers onto a school playground to measure the degree of aggression expressed, or they may have more than one observer watching a child behave during an experiment that manipulates the degree of aggression. In each case, high observer reliability is required as a prerequisite of an assessment of validity. Obviously, if the observers can not agree on how much aggression is expressed, they must not be measuring the same thing. This is an example of *interobserver reliability*.

Another example of interobserver reliability which is crucial would be when responses to open-ended questions are used to measure variables. These types of questions do not give the respondent fixed responses. Instead, the respondents may answer in any way they choose and the responses are classified by the judgment of coders. *Coders* are people who assign subjects to categories of a variable after their responses have been examined. For example, rather than a series of specific questions on child rearing practices, an interviewer might ask, "How do you discipline your child?" If we wanted to determine the punitiveness of the parents, a great deal of judgment would be required. Alternatively, if fixed choices had been used, the coder would simply have to add up the number of punitive responses according to some very specific directions provided by the investigator. The more judgment required, the more room there is for inconsistency. Thus, there is more chance for low interobserver reliability. The method used most frequently to assure this type of reliability is through training of observers and the use of trial runs and pilot studies.

The major problem of demonstrating equivalence reliability is that there must be alternative ways of measuring the same variable. A comparison between "halves" or tests or observers may appear unreliable simply because one of the measures is unreliable. If a reliable measure is compared to an unreliable measure, it appears as though the measure is unreliable. In addition, measures would not be "equivalent" if one measure was not assessing the same thing as the comparison measure – not necessarily because it alone is unreliable, but because the comparison measure is not a valid measure of the variable in question.

Notice that in all types of reliability there is a comparison being made. In stability reliability the comparison is between the same indicator at different times and in equivalence reliability the comparison is between different indicators at the same time. There is one statistic which is often used to reflect these comparisons. The statistic is called a correlation coefficient and is represented by the small letter r. (This statistic was thoroughly explored in Chapter 13.) The coefficient is calculated in such a way that if there is a perfect match when two measures are compared, $r = 1.0$, and when there is no match, $r = 0$. Perfect reliability would result in an $r = 1.0$, but an r equal to or greater than .80 is usually considered indicative of reliability. One simple way of interpreting this rule of thumb is that when about 70 percent of the time the same relative score is obtained when doing reliability comparisons, the measure being questioned can be called reliable.

What produces unreliability?

There are several sources of unreliability, some of which we have already mentioned. One major source of unreliability is invalidity. A checklist of other possible sources follows:

1. From the first measurement to the second the person or unit may have actually changed. (This, of course, should be interpreted as change in scores, not unreliability.)
2. During an interview the unit being measured changes because:
   a. an interviewer gains experience.
   b. an interviewer fatigues.
   c. subjects experience things which may make their interpretation of questions change (as opposed to actual changes in what is being measured).
   d. mistakes are made.
3. Aspects of the situation in which measurement takes place may change from the first measurement to the second measurement.

Such things as time of day, place where measurement takes place, people in the immediate environment who might influence responses, and so on, may differ.
4. Questions may be ambiguous and therefore interpreted differently at different administrations of a questionnaire.
5. Coders and/or observers may not make the same interpretations.
6. What appears to be an equivalence technique is not really because of a poor choice of the comparison.
7. Errors in recording observations or coding may occur.
8. Some combination of the above is possible.

Although we have made a distinction here between assessing reliability and validity, in reality these are often evaluated simultaneously. Logically, once reliability has been demonstrated, then the questioning of validity can proceed.

3. VALIDITY

Determining validity requires an assessment of the link or match between a conceptual definition and an operational definition; this includes how that operational definition is carried out. The assessment of this link is a problem of a very different nature from that of examining data to determine reliability. In the latter case we can get data from an original measure and some comparison. We can place the data in a scatterplot or table, or compute statistics like a correlation coefficient (r). The question is, "how can we test the validity of the measurement of a single concept when there is only one set of data to examine – that implied by the operational definition?"

We must rely on judgment to assess the link or match between the conceptual definition and the operational definition. In fact, whatever procedure we use to assess validity, ultimately we have to rely on *judgment*. As you examine the methods we use to assess validity, note that each rests at its base on judgment. Table 14.1 shows how each type of validity relies on judgment.

We want to emphasize that there is no "direct" way to assess the validity of a measure. There may be techniques to aid or bolster one's judgment, but when all the fancy maneuvers to assess validity have been completed, you should note that holding together every procedure to assess the validity of indicators is judgment. This does not mean that assessing validity is an arbitrary manner. Quite the contrary. When a member of the scientific community moves into a new area of research, typically a great deal of time will be spent examining previous measurement and consulting experts in the field to become familiar with how important concepts might be measured. For example, when a student takes a course in social stratification or personality, much of the course characteristically is spent on measurement procedures. If a researcher is to use a measure of

408

TABLE 14.1
Brief description of validation procedures

Type of validity	Basis of procedure
Face validity	*Judgment* of match between operational and conceptual definitions.
Content validity	*Judgment* of content of items or indicators in operational definition and their match to those in the conceptual definition.
Criterion validity	
Concurrent	Matching of one measure to another which was *judged* valid by face or content validity.
Predictive	Matching of one measure to events which can be presumed or *judged* to be a valid indicator of the variable.
Construct validity	Checking the relation of a set of indicators and if they are related: 1. Checking their relationship to other variables which are *judged* to be related and *judged* to be measured validly. 2. Demonstrating that they are *not* related to other variables which are *judged* to be *un*related and *judged* to be measured validly.

socioeconomic status, personality, or some other concept in a research study, time is spent becoming familiar with previous measurement techniques.

In fact, one research professor (Babbie, 1975) refers to this process of sharing skills and judgment when it comes to measurement as the "intersubjectivity" of science. The process of validation is one of shared judgment and openly communicating procedures of measurement.

Experts may not completely agree on what is a good measure, but in each case they are using similar kinds of criteria for making their decision. These criteria are based on examining the measure itself to see if the items appear to be reflecting the concept and seeing if the measure relates to measures of other variables as expected. The first two procedures discussed emphasize the examination of the indicators used. The second two types also include the exploration of the role of the variable in theory and previous measurement attempts.

Face validity

The most basic kind of assessment of validity is face validity. *Face validity* is ascertained by examining the measurement device and/or procedure and using common sense and experience to judge its adequacy. Using good judgment, the question becomes, "do the indicators appear to be measuring what one has defined the concept to mean, and does the operational definition reflect what is intended by the conceptual definition?" To assess validity in this manner, the first step is to refer back to the conceptual definition of the concept. If the definition is clear, the next step is to determine if there are observable indicators implied by the definition. If so, we can examine the operational definition to see if it is tapping an appropriate range of indicators. If so, on the face of it, the measure is valid.

Let us review a hypothetical example using social class as the concept. A typical conceptual definition of social class would be a person's position in the economic status hierarchy. This definition is fairly clear and we can think of lots of possible indicators. We might consider income to be one indicator of this definition of social class. Different incomes would place people at different levels on the economic status ladder. The first step in the face validation process would be to look at the indicator(s) chosen by the researcher to see if it (they) reflects the conceptual definition provided.

Once the indicator(s) is (are) selected and judged appropriate, the next step is to examine the operational definition. Most indicators can be operationally defined in several ways. Income could be operationally defined in terms of gross or net income, in terms of total family or individual income, in terms of money, or in terms of real income (money plus other goods and services received or grown). Next, cutting points need to be specified. Using income to measure social class, the measure is not of income but of a position in a hierarchy. Researchers must be able to assess how differences in dollars reflect differences in class. The cutting points should reflect these class distinctions. For example, incomes between $0 and $8,000 may have the same value in terms of social class. Suppose gross family income is used to operationalize income. Furthermore, suppose that three categories are specified by our operational definition. They are: $0–$4,000, $4,001–$15,000, and $15,001 and up. The second step in assessing face validity would be to make a judgment about how accurately these categories reflect differences in social class—as we have conceptualized it. The final step would be to examine the procedures used to observe gross family income to determine if the procedures seem legitimate. If a judgment is made that income is not an appropriate indicator of an individual's level in an economic status hierarchy, *or* if operationalizing that indicator into three categories of gross family income does not reflect different levels of a hierarchy, *or* if the procedures used to report gross family income are faulty, face validity would not be demonstrated.

Some feel that all possible indicators, or some subset of all possible indicators, should be identified and used to measure each concept. Others, we among them, feel that if a good single indicator is discovered, this can lead to a valid measure. Of course, if the single indicator is not representative of a concept, it would not be judged a valid selection. Income, for example, would be considered a superior single indicator of social class when compared to dress style because it is more likely to reflect one's economic position. All indicators are not created equal.

Because the determination of face validity involves only judgment, many people are probably able to make an assessment of face validity. The researcher uses it when initiating a study; readers and reviewers use it when examining the work; and science uses it (in a way) by whether or not particular measurement techniques survive the test of time. Despite the fact that science tends to formalize all its techniques and processes, there are no explicit rules for arriving at consensus in the determination of face validity. This does not mean that face validity is completely arbitrary and can be claimed any time someone wants to. Knowledge and training in the particular subject being studied is often necessary to adequately judge whether an indicator reflects a given concept.

Thus face validity, if properly used, is not entirely arbitrary and it can be a powerful tool. The power of face validity is determined largely by the power of the logic and arguments used by the researcher to claim face validity. The burden of the proof is placed on the scientist, not on the consumer of the science.

How to argue for or against the face validity of an operational definition and its application can be learned just as the process of conceptualization can be learned. It is helpful to practice this skill when reading about research studies. Once you are provided with a conceptual definition – either by the researcher or by theory – you can intellectually go through the process of moving from concept to indicator to operational definition. In moving through the explication process, you can make judgments about how well the researcher has done. If you can raise concerns about the process and back them up with sound logic, it is legitimate to question the face validity of the measure.

Content validity

Content validity is a technique so similar to face validity that we view it as one type of face validity. It is similar to face validity in that it involves all the same judgmental procedures as face validity. The difference between face and content validation procedures is one of focus. The major focus of content validity is on the content of the items of a paper and pencil or verbal measure used to reflect a conceptual definition.

Content validity is defined as validity based on the representativeness of the measurement. It is employed for those concepts for which one question or observation is insufficient to reflect the concept. In such cases, more than one indicator or observation must be employed. Such concepts are either multidimensional and require an indicator per dimension for adequate measurement, or have different qualities which a single indicator or question would not be able to capture. For these concepts, it is important to adequately measure all dimensions or qualities. The first step in determining content validity is to list all the dimensions of qualities thought to be appropriate for the conceptual definition. Then an assessment is made as to how well the operational definition represents the dimensions.

Figure 14.1 illustrates the process of content validation of a measure of the "authoritarian personality." Here the various dimensions or qualities of authoritarianism are listed and described, along with the questions in the test which are supposed to reflect each dimension. If on the face of it the questions reflect the appropriate dimension and if all the necessary dimensions are present, then the measure would be considered valid in terms of content validity.

Although this process is similar to face validity, it is more systematic. In this procedure it is necessary to enumerate all possible indicators and then to assess the adequacy of each part of the operational definition. For this reason, some researchers prefer to use content validity over face validity.

Criterion validity

Criterion validity assesses the accuracy of a new measurement procedure by comparing it with some criterion *assumed* to be valid. The "test" of criterion validity is a good match between the criterion (standard, comparison) and the old one.

The most crucial aspect of demonstrating criterion validity is often the assertion of the validity of the comparison. Validity of the criterion is seldom tested with data, numbers, and the like. Rather, it is simply *judged* to be valid. This assumption is supported by either face validity, past practices, or just an assertion. In any event, the case for criterion validity rests on the validity of the standard.

There are several ways to select a comparison or standard. The two major strategies used lead to two distinct types of criterion validity. They are called concurrent validity and predictive validity.

Concurrent validity
Concurrent validity uses an established measure of a variable to compare with a new one. There are three major reasons why a new measure might be needed when one valid one already exists. First, the new measure may be necessary for ease of administration, for ease of coding, or for other similar purposes. For example, "short

FIGURE 14.1
Illustration of content validity

COMPONENTS OF AUTHORITARIANISM

1. *Conventionalism. Rigid* adherence to and *overemphasis* upon middle-class values, and overresponsiveness to contemporary *external* social pressure.
    Sample item: "A person who has bad manners, habits, and breeding can hardly expect to get along with decent people."
    Sample item: "No sane, normal, decent person could ever think of hurting a close friend or relative."
2. *Authoritarian submission.* An exaggerated, emotional need to submit to others; an uncritical acceptance of a strong leader who will make the decisions.
    Sample item: "Every person should have a deep faith in some supernatural force higher than himself to which he gives total allegiance and whose decisions he obeys without question."
    Sample item: "Obedience and respect for authority are the most important virtues children should learn."
3. *Authoritarian aggression.* Favoring condemnation, total rejection, stern discipline, or severe punishment as ways of dealing with people and forms of behavior that deviate from conventional values.
    Sample item: "Sex crimes, such as rape and attacks on children, deserve more than mere imprisonment: such criminals ought to be publicly whipped, or worse."
    Sample item: "No insult to our honor should ever go unpunished."
4. *Anti-intraception.* Disapproval of a free emotional life, of the intellectual or theoretical, and of the impractical. The anti-intraceptive person maintains a narrow range of consciousness: realization of his genuine feelings or self-awareness might threaten his adjustment. Hence he rejects feelings, fantasies, and other subjective or tender-minded phenomena.
    Sample item: "When a person has a problem or worry, it is best for him not to think about it, but to keep busy with more cheerful things."
    Sample item: "There are some things too intimate and personal to talk about even with one's closest friends."
5. *Superstition and stereotypy.* Superstition implies a tendency to shift responsibility from within the individual onto outside forces beyond one's control, particularly to mystical determinants. Stereotypy is the tendency to think in rigid, oversimplified categories, in unambiguous terms of black and white, particularly in the realm of psychological or social matters.
    Sample item: "It is entirely possible that this series of wars and conflicts will be ended once and for all by a world-destroying earthquake, flood, or other catastrophe."
    Sample item: "Although many people may scoff, it may yet be shown that astrology can explain a lot of things."
6. *Power and toughness.* The aligning of oneself with power figures, thus gratifying both one's needs to have power and the need to submit to power. There is a denial of personal weakness.
    Sample item: "What this country needs is fewer laws and agencies, and more courageous, tireless, devoted leaders whom the people can put their faith in."
    Sample item: "Too many people today are living in an unnatural, soft way; we should return to the fundamentals, to a more red-blooded, active way of life."
7. *Destructiveness and cynicism.* A rationalized aggression. For example, cynicism permits the authoritarian person to be aggressive himself because "everybody is doing it." The generalized hostility and vilification of the human by the highly authoritarian person permits him to justify his aggressiveness.
    Sample item: "Human nature being what it is, there will always be war and conflict."
    Sample item: "Familiarity breeds contempt."

8. *Projectivity.* The disposition to believe that wild and dangerous things go on in the world. In the authoritarian personality the undesirable impulses that cannot be admitted to the conscious ego tend to be projected onto minority groups and other vulnerable objects.

> *Sample item:* "The sexual orgies of the old Greeks and Romans are nursery school stuff compared to some of the goings-on in this country today, even in circles where people might least expect it."
> *Sample item:* "Nowadays when so many different kinds of people move around so much and mix together so freely, a person has to be especially careful to protect himself against infection and disease."

9. *Sex.* Exaggerated concern with sexual goings-on, and punitiveness toward violators of sex mores.

> *Sample item:* "Homosexuality is a particularly rotten form of delinquency and ought to be severely punished."
> *Sample item:* "No matter how they act on the surface, men are interested in women for only one reason."

Source: Social Psychology (2d ed.), by Lawrence S. Wrightsmen, copyright © 1972, 1977 by Wadsworth Publishing Company, Inc., as adapted from "The Approach of the Authoritarian Personality," by N. Sanford. In J. L. McCary (ed.), *Psychology of Personality.* Copyright 1956 by Grove Press, Inc. Reprinted by permission of the publisher, Brooks/Cole Publishing Company, Monterey, California.

forms" of several personality tests have been developed and found to satisfactorily compare with longer ones. A second reason for developing a new measure is that an indirect or unobtrusive measure is needed. For example, asking respondents about their social status may put them on guard or offend them and thus ruin any rapport which an interviewer may have developed. For this reason Chapin's (1935) living room scale which can unobtrusively measure status was devised. To validate it, the scale was compared with some traditional measures of status. The relationships were sufficiently strong for researchers to sometimes assume that the living room scale is validly measuring social status. A third rationale for developing new measures is to attempt to reach subjects who might not otherwise be measurable with an established technique. Nonverbal subjects or subjects from other countries might not be able to be tested by standard English questionnaires or other schedules of observation which use language. Ingenious tests are often created for this purpose. For example, Aronson (1958) developed a scheme to code people's doodles in terms of their need for achievement. He found that the scheme is relatively valid when related to more traditional verbal measures of the need for achievement.

Predictive validity

Predictive validity assesses validity by seeing whether we can predict events or behaviors on the basis of the measure (operational definition) we have developed. If we predict well, we assume the measure is valid. For example, we could validate the use of Scholastic Aptitude Tests (SAT) or the test of the American College Testing Program (ACT) by seeing how well scores on these tests predict future college performance of students. If the tests are valid, students who do well on these tests should do well in college. Similarly, we would expect that a diagnostic test like the Minnesota Multiphasic Personality Inventory (MMPI) should predict various personality problems which would "show up" in the future if it were valid. Note that in each of these examples we neglected to state a conceptual definition for the variable being predicted. Thus, we could not demonstrate that the criterion we were using is a good or valid one by comparing it with the conceptual definition. Even if we can predict well, we have no way of knowing if we are measuring a particular concept. This method is not sufficient for showing that we are validly representing a particular concept.

The *known group method* is a second way of determining predictive validity. Group membership is used as the criterion against which a measure is compared. For example, we might use members of the Socialist Workers Party to validate a questionnaire on economic liberalism. Members of such a group should score quite high on this questionnaire — by definition. The crucial aspect of this procedure is the judgment that some group has a certain characteristic.

A third and less frequent approach to predictive validity is to use a known relationship of one variable to another. For example, one might attempt to validate an IQ scale by showing that a new measure of IQ is related to school performance. This would be a test of criterion validity *only* if we "knew" that there was a relationship between IQ and school performance. This form of predictive validity is more frequently used as a part of construct validity, but it does necessitate that the relationship is certain and that the measure of the second variable is valid. These two conditions are sometimes difficult to obtain.

The major problem with all of the types of criterion validity is the selection of the criterion and the demonstration that the criterion is legitimate, effective, valid, and appropriate. The defense of this choice is largely judgmental.

Construct validity

Construct validity has been developed as a technique to attempt to validate the measurement of constructs. *Constructs* are concepts with one or more of the following characteristics:

1. *The concept is created by some combination of other concepts.*

For example, in physics, force = mass × acceleration. That is, force is a property "constructed" out of mass and acceleration.

2. *The concept is composed of several dimensions or characteristics.* For example, in sociology the concept of religiosity includes piety, ritualism, knowledge, ideology, and so on.

3. *The concept is relatively difficult to observe directly, or possibly unobservable.* Examples of concepts which are relatively difficult to observe include intelligence, creativity, group cohesion, the superego, many forms of personality, mental illness, and so on. Examples of possibly unobservable constructs include the id, psychological drives, charisma, the self, and so on.

Constructs typically are more difficult to conceptualize and to measure than other concepts. Usually the measurement of a construct must be relatively indirect. For example, group cohesiveness may be defined as a total group force producing closeness of the members. Unfortunately, such a force is not directly observable. Instead we may use people's admitted feelings of closeness or their preferences of people in the group relative to those outside of the group. Since constructs are more difficult to conceptualize and measure, procedures of construct validation are more involved and complicated than face, content, or criterion validation procedures. Although there are many technical variations on the theme, construct validation basically involves:

1. Demonstrating the relationship of various indicators to one another.
2. Demonstrating the construct's relationship to other variables which are assumed to be related.
3. Demonstrating the lack of relationships to other variables which are assumed to be unrelated.

The fact that constructs are complicated concepts means that it is usually necessary to use more than one indicator to measure the construct. The unobservable nature of constructs means that researchers are often more interested in an underlying trait or property than on the observable indicators. In fact construct validity is often attempted when judgments about content validity would be difficult or when no appropriate criterion can be found. The three aspects of construct validity focus on these complexities.

Showing the interrelationship of indicators
Since constructs are typically multidimensional concepts, it may be necessary to use many indicators to attempt to capture the underlying idea of the concept. When dimensions of constructs are assumed to be interrelated, each indicator used is supposedly a measure of some aspect of the construct. As such, they are all measuring the same concept. Therefore the indicators should be related to each other. They should be associated. For example, if the

construct in question is "liberalism" and one part of liberalism is political and another is ethical, we would expect indicators used to measure political liberalism to be related to indicators used to reflect ethical liberalism. If they are not related, the possibility exists that one or more of the indicators is not valid, that is, they do not tap the underlying idea of the same construct.

All of the indicators used to "get at" a construct must be related in order to claim construct validity. The statistical and graphical procedures that have already been discussed to search for relationships can be used in the attempt to show the interrelatedness of indicators.

In developing measures for constructs, researchers sometimes start out with a large number of indicators (often questions in a survey or interview). This pool of indicators is thought to be representative of the construct on the basis of tradition, theory, common sense, or face validity. There is a set of highly technical mathematical procedures called *factor analysis* which allows researchers to examine a large number of items to determine if they are interrelated. This procedure is highly flexible and requires the researcher to make many assumptions, but it is often used to try to discover the underlying dimensions of a large number of items.

The use of such procedures does not directly constitute a "test" of construct validity. It offers a way of constructing an interrelated set of indicators — hence meeting one of the conditions necessary for construct validity.

It should be noted that the interrelatedness of indicators is not a crucial test of the validity of the measure of a construct. It is possible to have constructs which by definition have dimensions which are not related.

It is also possible to have a set of interrelated indicators all of which are assessing the wrong thing. Therefore this is just one part of the process that must be interpreted with the following two demonstrations.

Showing relationships to hypothesized variables

Since the interrelatedness of indicators does not conclusively demonstrate that such indicators are valid, a second condition must be present. Usually constructs have been invented (discovered) in the process of developing a relatively complete theory to explain some phenomena. Because this is the case, a part of the development of the construct is the development of a set of interrelated propositions which make up the theory. Each of these propositions could be translated into a hypothesized relationship between two variables. When one of the variables in such an hypothesis is the construct in question, it is possible to proceed with the second part of demonstrating construct validity (assuming there is a valid measure available for the other variable in the hypothesis).

The second part of demonstrating construct validity is to collect data using the known valid indicator of one concept and the questionable indicator of the construct. The data are then analyzed to see if the hypothesized relationship exists. If it does, another aspect of construct validity has been demonstrated. If it does not, then several possibilities exist. The theory that suggested the hypothesized relationship could be wrong. The supposedly valid indicator of the other variable might not really be valid. Finally the indicators of the construct may not be valid. There is really no way to tell which of these possibilities has actually occurred. The relationship being tested does not necessarily have to come from a complete theory but there must be some reason for believing the relationship exists prior to the time that it is tested. You should note the similarity of this part of construct validity to predictive validity. The difference is the extent to which there is a theoretical emphasis. Predictive validity could be tested without any underlying theory but this is seldom the case in construct validity.

Showing the lack of inappropriate relationships

To complete the picture of construct validity we need to remember our initial discussions of conceptualization. Concepts not only help organize phenomena but they also help separate them. If we are attempting to demonstrate the validity of a measure of a construct, we should be able to demonstrate that the measure "separates" phenomena as well as organizes them. To do this we can examine relationships that we "know" do not exist between the proposed measure of the construct and measures of the other variable. Of course we must have valid measures of these other concepts to use in testing for the lack of such relationships. The knowledge that concepts are unrelated may come from many sources. Often such knowledge is implied by the theory from which the construct has been drawn. For example, the theory of intelligence (a construct) clearly implies that intelligence should not be related to sex. Therefore if a set of indicators of intelligence is to be validated we should be able to demonstrate that it is not related to sex. Such a measure should not have a "sex bias." This final demonstration "rounds out" the process of construct validation.

4. CONCLUSIONS

The problem of reliability and validity of indicators in education and the social and behavioral sciences is a particularly troublesome one for researchers. It is such a basic condition necessary for scientific research that without it we cannot legitimately function. However, because many of the concepts used in these fields are abstract and not directly observable, validity is sometimes very difficult to demonstrate. The more skeptical consumers often argue that such research is seldom worthwhile because it is so difficult to demonstrate validity. Of course it is much more possible to obtain reliability and consumers of research should insist that scientists use reliable measurement procedures. At least if reliability is shown, the possibility of validity exists. There is no such possibility if reliability cannot be shown.

Assuming researchers have reliable tests, measures, operational definitions, indicators, and procedures, there is no escaping the fact that trained judgment must be employed in determining the validity of indicators. As we have previously stated, if the validity of indicators is demonstrated using more than one approach or strategy, we tend to have more faith in such indicators. We particularly favor going beyond face validity because that procedure is so open to possible bias. Although we encourage researchers to spend more time and attention in demonstrating the validity of their measures, the consumer of research results must somehow deal with the fact that in many studies the validity of indicators has not been demonstrated. We caution consumers that this does not automatically mean that the indicators used are not valid. It is our belief that many operational definitions which are currently being used in research are valid. There must be some faith in the supposed experts, but the consumer is warned to make independent judgments about the validity of measures used in research. If these judgments are favorable then we can have more trust in the accuracy of particular studies. Even if we trust particular studies, the question of generalizing results remains a major problem. One important consideration in the problem of generalization has to do with the adequacy of sampling – the topic of the next chapter.

5. SUMMARY

This chapter focuses only on the reliability and validity of indicators and operational definitions. It is recommended that other uses of these terms be avoided. The basic idea of reliability refers to the consistency of measurement. The basic idea of validity refers to the accuracy of measurement. Since consistency is necessary in order to achieve accuracy, reliability of measurement (observation) is a necessary condition for validity of measurement. The elaboration of the archery analogy presented in Chapter 2 results in specifying two types of reliability and four types of validity.

Stability reliability is often assessed by the test-retest method. Equivalence reliability is often assessed by the split-halves technique. In either approach there are several possible sources of unreliability. Subjects' characteristics may change over the time reliability is being determined. The situation in which observations are made may be altered. There may be errors in coding or recording. Finally, the measure in question may not be valid.

While there is no direct way to assess validity, several strategies have developed to determine the accuracy of measures. Judgment of one sort or another always plays a crucial role when examining the validity of indicators and operational definitions. Face validity is asserted on the basis of the examination of the measurement device or procedures. Content validity is more systematic in specifying the dimensions of a concept and making a judgment about the adequacy of indicators. However, it is very similar to face validity. There are two types of criterion validity, concurrent and predictive. Concurrent validity tests a questioned measure against an established measure. Predictive validity is determined by how well a measure forecasts a future event. Construct validity is the most difficult and complicated procedure used to assess validity. First, a set of interrelated indicators must be developed. Second, these indicators must be related to other variables as predicted. Third, these indicators should not be related to variables when such relationships are thought not to exist.

The demonstration of reliability and validity of measures is a very difficult task in the social sciences. In the past, these questions have often been avoided. However, as the search for relationships continues and as producers and consumers of research become more sophisticated, the demand for measurements with established reliability and validity will increase.

1. Examine your discussion of the external validity of the three manipulations or measures of conformity in Chapter 9, Exercise 3. How is this related to the validity of an operational definition as discussed in this chapter? What do the experimenters say about the validity of their concept? How might you design research to assess the validity of the measurement of conformity employed in the studies you examined earlier?

2. Re-examine two of the operational definitions you constructed in Chapter 2, Exercise 8, on the basis of this chapter's discussion of validity.

3. Reassess the validity of your operational definition of aggression, achievement motivation, or conformity in Exercise 1, Chapter 2.

4. Select two scales from Robinson and Shaver's *Measurement of Social Psychological Attitudes.* (See references for Chapter 2.)
   a. Make your own assessment of the face validity of the concept being measured.
   b. Report on how reliable the authors suggest the scale to be.
   c. Do you feel that the measures of reliability have been adequate? Why or why not?
   d. Describe how validity has been assessed.
   e. Do you feel that the validity assessment has been adequate? Why or why not?

PROJECT

   Review each manipulation and measure you have employed in your previous projects.
1. Do you have sufficient information to assess the reliability of any? List the variables for which a reliability check is possible.
2. Describe what procedures would be necessary to assess the reliability of the remaining operational definitions.
3. Assess the face validity of each concept in your projects.
4. a. Describe what other means you have available to assess the validity of any of your concepts.
   b. On the basis of your present information, how might you redesign your measures (change your operational definitions) to increase the validity of your measures?
5. How might you wish to redesign any of your projects to more adequately study the validity of your operational definitions?
6. Pick a major concept in one of your studies. Go to the library and assess how previous researchers have determined the reliability and validity of the measures of that concept.
7. Has the examination of validity and the explication process revised your feeling about any of your conceptual definitions? If so, how?

AMERICAN PSYCHOLOGICAL ASSOCIATION COMMITTEE ON PSYCHOLOGICAL TESTS. 'Technical Recommendations for Psychological Tests and Diagnostic Techniques.' *Psychological Bulletin*, supplement *51*, part 2, 1954, 1–38.

ARONSON, E. The Need for Achievement as Measured by Graphic Expression, in Atkinson J. (ed.) *Motives in Fantasy, Action, and Society*. Princeton, N.J.: Van Nostrand, 1958.

BABBIE, EARL R. *The Practice of Social Research*. Belmont, Calif.: Wadsworth, 1975.

BONJEAN, C., HILL, R., and MCLEMORE, S. *Sociological Measurement*. San Francisco: Chandler, 1967.

CAMPBELL, D., and FISKE, D. "Convergent and Discriminant Validation by the Multitrait–Multimethod Matrix." *Psychological Bulletin, 56,* 1959, 81–105.

CHAPIN, F. *Contemporary American Institutions*. New York: Harper, 1935.

CRONBACH, L., and MECHL, P. "Construct Validity in Psychological Tests." *Psychological Bulletin, 52,* 1955, 281–302.

CHAPTER 15
SAMPLING

After studying this chapter, students should be able to:

1. Define and differentiate between research populations and samples.

2. Define sample bias.

3. Define and differentiate between parameters and statistics.

4. Discuss the issues of sampling.

5. Describe a sampling distribution and discuss how it is used to generalize.

6. Describe the generalization process.

7. Discuss what is a representative sample.

8. Define and differentiate between nonprobability and probability sampling and say why this difference is important.

9. Describe the process of statistical inference in general terms.

10. Use simple sampling distributions to make decisions about statistical inference.

11. Define what is a Type I error and discuss the importance of knowing this error.

12. Define level of statistical inference.

13. Describe, discuss, and identify simple random, systematic, stratified, cluster, and purposive samples.

14. Discuss the role of sampling in surveys and experiments.

15. Discuss the advantages and disadvantages of the various types of samples.

Availability sample   A purposive sample where elements are sampled on the basis that they are easily accessible to the researcher.

Cluster sample   A sample requiring that subjects be located in various geographic locations and be selected from these locations.

Generalization   The process of concluding that the results reached as a result of examining units in a sample are the same results that would have been reached if the population was examined.

Level of statistical significance   The chances of making a Type I error.

Nonprobability samples   Samples that result from techniques which do not utilize the laws of probability.

Parameter   A characteristic or property of the population.

Probability samples   Samples that result from techniques which utilize the laws of probability.

Purposive sample   A sample whose procedure cannot easily result in a probability sample.

Quota sample   A purposive sample in which the researcher desires a certain proportion of elements to have certain characteristics.

Representative sample   A subpart of the population which has characteristics similar to the population.

Research population   A population consisting of all the units about which we would like to make scientific statements.

Research sample   A sample composed of all the units actually observed (measured) in the research process.

Sample size   The total number of units drawn from the population which are to be examined (measured).

Sampling   To select a sample from the population.

Sampling bias   Error produced by a sampling procedure that, in the long run, will systematically result in faulty conclusions about the population.

Sampling distribution   A list of all possible values of a statistic along with the proportion of times (probability of) each result would be obtained from a particular type of population just as a matter of chance.

Simple random sample   A sample in which every element of the population has an equal and independent chance of being selected.

Statistic   A characteristic or property of the sample.

Statistical inference   The procedures of using a sampling distribution of a statistic to help make the decision about generalization.

Stratified sample   A sampling procedure in which the population was separated into categories or strata prior to the selection of elements.

Systematic sample   A sample in which every nth element from a listing of the population is selected.

Type I error   The error made if one generalizes sample results to a certain type of population when the sample really is not like that population.

1. THE GENERAL PROBLEM OF SAMPLING

The goal of scientific investigation is to learn something about a general class of events, subjects, phenomena, or variables. For example, if we are investigating the causes of delinquency, we would like to know about all delinquents, not just a few. If we would like to know about the relationship between social class and educational attainment, we want to know about these variables for all people and for all time, not just a few people at one point in time.

A *research population* consists of all of the units about which we would like to make scientific statements. Statements could be descriptive or they could involve relationships between variables. Because of financial, time, and personnel limitations, it is usually impossible to observe all of the units in any particular research population. It would be almost impossible to study all delinquents in the United States or to observe the social class and education of all people at all times. If it is not impossible, it would at least be impractical. Because of this problem, researchers rarely observe all of the units they would like to know about. That is, observations of all units in the research population are seldom made. The dilemma for the researcher is how to make statements about the total research population without observing or measuring all of the units. The most often used technique to confront this problem is to observe a part of the population. The part of the research population actually observed is called the research sample. A *research sample* is composed of all of the units that are actually observed (measured) in the research process.

Another way to conceptualize the distinction between a research sample and population is to use "set" terminology and Venn diagrams. Using set terminology we would say that the research population consists of all of the elements of a set that are to be investigated by the research. An element could be a person, a city, a corporation, or any other unit that could be measured. In this vein a research sample would be a subset of the set. A subset is a specified smaller number of elements from the set. Using Venn diagrams (Figure 15.1) to represent a set and subset, the area of the larger circle would be proportional to the total number of units in the research population. The area of the smaller circle would be proportional to the number of units in the research sample. Note that even if the size of the set remains constant, the size of the subset can vary. A research sample can be a small part of the population or a large part of the population and still be a sample. The bottom of Figure 15.1 depicts the process of selecting a sample from the population, *the process of sampling*.

If sampling is involved in the research process, and it almost always is, the big question becomes "how do we know that what we

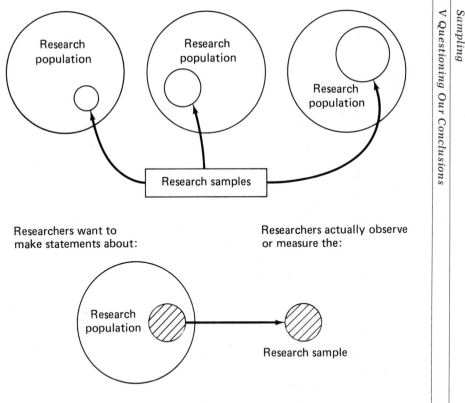

FIGURE 15.1
Venn diagrams depicting research populations and samples

observe in the sample is the same as what we would have observed in the population?" In other words, the possibility exists that we would come to one conclusion based on measuring units in the sample, but a different conclusion if we observed *all* of the units in the population. If sampling is necessary, we never observe all of the units in the population. Therefore we can never say for certain that the conclusions based on the sample are the same as our conclusions would have been if we had observed the population. If we could observe all of the units in the population, sampling would not be necessary. It would be a purposeless exercise. Therefore direct comparisons between sample results and population values are rarely made.

Before proceeding to a concrete illustration of the sampling problem, it is helpful to introduce some terms. The characteristic of the research population that we would discover if we were to observe all of the units in the population is referred to as a *parameter*. The characteristic of the units in the sample that are actually observed is called a *statistic*. Parameters and statistics can be simple descriptions or complex statements about relationships. Parameters are usually unknown. Whenever sampling is done in such a way that "in the long run" sample results will correspond to the parameter of the population, the procedure is called *bias free.* Although *sampling bias* technically refers to the *process* of sampling and not the result, sometimes people do not use the term carefully. You may hear people say that a sample is biased if the statistic does not correspond to what they "think" is the value of the parameter. The lack of bias simply refers to the idea that there is nothing in the process of sampling which will *systematically* result in faulty conclusions about the population. Let us look at an example now to get a clearer picture of the process and problems of sampling.

In this example the "units" of our population are marbles. Some of the marbles are green and some are yellow. There are 40 marbles in the population, 20 are green and 20 are yellow. All the marbles are placed in a cardboard box. One way to describe this population would be to determine the percentage of green marbles. The percentage of green marbles would then be one parameter of the population. The parameter of this population of marbles is *50 percent green.*

In keeping with the usual research process, suppose that a scientist would like to determine the proportion of green marbles in the box (population). However, for some reason all the marbles in the box cannot be observed. Therefore a sample of marbles must be drawn from the box. (In practice, for most studies only one research sample is drawn from a population.) A decision must first be made about how many marbles will be drawn from the population. In other words we must decide on sample size. *Sample size* refers to the total number of units drawn from a population that are to be examined (measured). Sample size is usually referred to by the letter N. For our illustration we use the sample size of 4. Four marbles will be drawn from the box and then examined. The size of a sample is somewhat arbitrary. (Some statistical procedures for making a decision about sample size are discussed later.) Before going any further we can determine all of the possible results that could be obtained by drawing four marbles from the box. Assuming the marbles are all the same size, are all mixed up in the box, and the person who draws the 4 marbles is blindfolded, we would have a bias free sampling procedure. We could conceivably get any of the results in Table 15.1. The possible statistics range from 0 percent (no green) to 100 percent (all green). The only statistic that would correspond to the parameter would be 50 percent. If we get any of the other possible results, the statistic will differ from the parameter. Only in the one type of sample would our conclusions about the

TABLE 15.1
Possible results from sampling

Number of green marbles	Number of yellow marbles	Statistics (% green)
0	4	0
1	3	25
2	2	50[a]
3	1	75
4	0	100

[a] This is the value of the parameter.

units in the sample be the same as our conclusions about the population (were we to look at the population).

If we were to describe the population using data about a sample, our descriptions would be wrong in 4 out of the 5 types of possible samples. It might appear that if we sampled in this fashion we would make an error 4 out of 5 times, just because of sampling. Fortunately this is not the case. Even at the common sense level we know that it is probably not too likely that a blindfolded person would draw all yellow marbles. Nor would it be very likely to draw all green marbles. The reality of the situation is that we would much more likely draw a sample close to the characteristic of the population. Mathematicians have developed formulas for computing the chances of getting each type of possible sample from a population where the parameter is equal to 50 percent. The formula is called the *binomial*. Using the formula gives the results in Table 15.2.

These results show that if we were to draw one 4-marble sample

TABLE 15.2
The theoretical chance of obtaining each type of sample[a]

Sample statistic (percent)	Percentage of time obtained just by chance, in the long run
100 (all green)	6.25
75	25.00
50[b]	37.50
25	25.00
0 (all yellow)	6.25

[a] There are two types of sampling techniques. The first is called sampling *without* replacement. In this procedure when one unit is selected from the population, it is never placed back into the population. The second procedure is called sampling *with* replacement. In this procedure after a unit has been selected for a sample and measured, it is placed back into the population. In so doing, it would be possible to draw a particular unit more than once. The numbers in this table are for sampling with replacement.
[b] Value of the parameter.

out of our box, we would obtain an accurate picture of the population 37.5 percent of the time just by chance. Notice that this type of sample has a higher chance of being selected than any other particular type of sample in the distribution.

In Table 15.2 we calculated a sampling distribution. A *sampling distribution* is a list of all possible values of a statistic along with the proportion of times each result would be obtained from a particular type of population just as a matter of chance. Before showing you how this sampling distribution can be used in this illustration, we need to discuss the issue of generalization.

2. HOW TO GENERALIZE

Generalization refers to the process of concluding that the results reached as a result of examining units in a sample are the same results that would have been reached if the population was examined. If the conclusion is that sample results are applicable to the population, the sample results are said to be generalizable to the population. Another way of asking this question is to ask whether the sample is "representative" of the population. A *representative sample* is a subpart of the population that has characteristics similar to the population. The *hope* of the researcher utilizing sampling is to draw a representative sample from the population. We can use the mathematical laws of probability to help us arrive at representative samples.

There are two general classes of sampling techniques. Those samples resulting from techniques which do not utilize the laws of probability are called *nonprobability samples*. Those resulting from the use of probability mathematics are called *probability samples*. The mathematics of probability can become quite complex. The basic idea of probability samples is that the researcher knows the chances of an element in the population being selected for the sample. If, because of the sampling technique, the researcher does not know anything about the chances of some element from the population being selected, the sample is a nonprobability sample.

The importance of this distinction is that sampling distributions can be used only when probability sampling occurs. In the marble example above, we have a probability sample. That is, the chance of drawing any particular marble from that box is about equal. If the chance of drawing any particular marble is about the same, then we can make a statement about the probability of an element appearing in the population. The probability of any one marble being drawn is approximately equal to the probability of any other marble being drawn. Because of this we can use the binomial equation to compute the sampling distribution in Table 15.2. If the person drawing the marbles was not blindfolded and that person liked green marbles better than yellow ones, we would have no way of knowing the information in the sampling distribution. Indeed we would expect that such a person would draw a sample with more green marbles because that color was preferred.

The procedures of using a sampling distribution of a statistic to help make the decision about generalization is called *statistical inference* (see Chapter 16). Focusing on the marble example, suppose we obtained 4 green marbles in our *one research sample*. In addition, let us assume we would like to know whether that sample came from a population where the percentage of green marbles is 50 percent. Common sense may tell us that the chances of getting a sample of 100 percent green marbles is remote. It would not make too much sense to say that the box has 50 percent green marbles. The problem with this common sense procedure is that we would have difficulty defending it to someone who does not share our same common sense. Besides, we know from the sampling distribution that sometimes we do get 100 percent green marbles from such a box, just by chance. How do we know this is not one of those times? The logic of statistical inference provides a systematic decision making procedure similar to the following:

1. Table 15.2 contains a sampling distribution from a population where the parameter is 50 percent green marbles. We can use this sampling distribution to compare our sample result.
2. Using probability sampling we obtain a research sample statistic of 100 percent green marbles.
3. Comparing this statistic with the sampling distribution in Table 15.2 shows that a statistic of 100 percent green would be obtained from a population (where the parameter is 50 percent green) 6.25 percent of the time just by chance.
4. This means that if the population is really 50 percent green we still get 100 percent green 6.25 times out of every 100 times we draw samples — in the long run.
5. Since we never directly compare the sample with the population, we can come to one of two conclusions:
   a. Our sample is from a population where the parameter is 50 percent and our particular sample is one of the 6.25 percent of this type sample we would expect just by chance, *or*
   b. Our sample is *not* from a population where the parameter is 50 percent. That is, it is *not* one of the 6.25 percent samples of this type we would expect just by chance from a population where the parameter is 50 percent.
6. If we go with conclusion a, the odds are against us. There is only a 6.25 percent chance that such a sample would be obtained in the long run just by chance.
7. If we go with conclusion b, the odds are with us. If we say that our population is not one where the parameter is 50 percent, we will be wrong only 6.25 percent of the time just by chance, in the long run.
8. We would likely decide that our sample is not from a population

where the parameter is 50 percent green. But in doing so we would know that 6.25 percent of the time we would be wrong in making this decision over the long run. This chance of making an error is called the *level of statistical significance* and this type of an error is called a *Type I error*.

By using the logic of statistical inference we have come to the same conclusion as by using common sense. The big advantage is that we know the probability of making an error in the long run if we do come to this conclusion. By comparing the sample statistic to the sampling distribution we have learned that the probability of making a Type I error in the long run is .0625 (the decimal equivalent of 6.25 percent). As we stated previously the logic and statistics of inference will be fully explored in Chapter 16, but the marble illustration serves to show the advantage of probability sampling. *Probability sampling is the only sampling procedure that allows us to create sampling distributions that can be used to obtain the chances of making an error in generalizing sample results to populations.*

You may be left with an uneasy feeling at this point. What does all this mean? Let us review it. The general idea is that we never really know if one research sample accurately represents a research population. If we use a bias free sampling procedure, that is, a probability sample, a sampling distribution can be calculated. This tells us the probability of getting each type of statistic from a population with a specified parameter. We can compare the statistic from our sample with the values in the sampling distribution. The comparison allows us to know the likelihood of getting our sample statistical value from a population with a given parameter. A decision must then be made. We can decide our sample probably came from a population with the given parameter or we can decide that our sample probably did not come from a population with the given parameter. To make this decision we go with the odds. No matter what decision we reach, we might be wrong. If we make the second decision, we know the probability of our making an error in the long run. Since we never know whether we have made a mistake, we have no choice but to go with the best odds. Confidence in sample results can be achieved through replication. Every time the same conclusion is reached, the odds get better and better that we are accurately inferring the characteristic of the research population from our sample results.

Although all types of research designs may use sampling procedures, in surveys sampling is almost always present. The next section will be devoted to the different types of sampling procedures commonly employed in survey research. The last section of this chapter will discuss the issue of sampling in the other major research designs.

3. SAMPLING FOR SURVEYS

All of the sampling procedures discussed in this section can be used for any research design. However they are very commonly used for surveys.

Simple random samples

A simple random sample is the most straightforward way of maximizing the chances of selecting a representative sample from some specified research population. A *simple random sample* is defined as a sample in which every element of the population has an equal and independent chance of being selected. This would of course be a probability sample since the probability of each element being selected is defined as equal. In order to select a random sample all of the elements in the research population must be enumerated. That is, we must be able to assign some number to each person, school, and so on, which comprises the population we want to know about. After the population has been defined and each element numbered, it is necessary to decide about sample size. Although there are statistical procedures for deciding sample size, the decision is often made on the basis of practical considerations like money and staff available to do the study. Table 15.3 shows one reference table that can be used to decide about sample size. The assumption of this table is that the parameter of the research population equals 50 percent (just like our marble example). The table is read as follows:

TABLE 15.3
Sample size for various levels of risk and accuracy

Desired accuracy	Risk of sample estimate being outside accuracy limits				
	1%	2%	5%	10%	20%
±1%	16,587	13,533	9,604	6,765	4,108
±2%	4,147	3,384	2,401	1,691	1,027
±3%	1,843	1,504	1,067	752	457
±4%	1,037	846	600	423	257
±5%	663	541	384	271	164
±6%	461	376	267	188	114
±7%	339	276	196	138	84
±8%	259	212	150	106	64
±9%	205	167	119	84	51
±10%	166	135	96	68	41
±15%	74	60	43	30	18
±20%	41	34	24	17	10

Source: E. Terrence Jones, *Conducting Political Research.* New York: Harper & Row, 1971, p. 64.

TABLE 15.4
Random numbers

25 80 72 42 60	71 52 97 89 20	72 68 20 73 85	90 72 65 71 66	98 88 40 85 83
06 17 09 79 65	88 30 29 80 41	21 44 34 18 08	68 98 48 36 20	89 74 79 88 82
60 80 85 44 44	74 41 28 11 05	01 17 62 88 38	36 42 11 64 89	18 05 95 10 61
80 94 04 48 93	10 40 83 62 22	80 58 27 19 44	92 63 84 03 33	67 05 41 60 67
19 51 69 01 20	46 75 97 16 43	13 17 75 52 92	21 03 68 28 08	77 50 19 74 27
49 38 65 44 80	23 60 42 35 54	21 78 54 11 01	91 17 81 01 74	29 42 09 04 38
06 31 28 89 40	15 99 56 93 21	47 45 86 48 09	98 18 98 18 51	29 65 18 42 15
60 94 20 03 07	11 89 79 26 74	40 40 56 80 32	96 71 75 42 44	10 70 14 13 93
92 32 99 89 32	78 28 44 63 47	71 20 99 20 61	39 44 89 31 36	25 72 20 85 64
77 93 66 35 74	31 38 45 19 24	85 56 12 96 71	58 13 71 78 20	22 75 13 65 18
91 30 70 69 91	19 07 22 42 10	36 69 95 37 28	28 82 53 57 93	28 97 66 62 52
68 43 49 46 88	84 47 31 36 22	62 12 69 84 08	12 84 38 25 90	09 81 59 31 46
48 90 81 58 77	54 74 52 45 91	35 70 00 47 54	83 82 45 26 92	54 13 05 51 60
06 91 34 51 97	42 67 27 86 01	11 88 30 95 28	63 01 19 89 01	14 97 44 03 44
10 45 51 60 19	14 21 03 37 12	91 34 23 78 21	88 32 58 08 51	43 66 77 08 83
12 88 39 73 43	65 02 76 11 84	04 28 50 13 92	17 97 41 50 77	90 71 22 67 69
21 77 83 09 76	38 80 73 69 61	31 64 94 20 96	63 28 10 20 23	08 81 64 74 49
19 52 35 95 15	65 12 25 96 59	86 28 36 82 58	69 57 21 37 98	16 43 59 15 29
67 24 55 26 70	35 58 31 65 63	79 24 68 66 86	76 46 33 42 22	26 65 59 08 02
60 58 44 73 77	07 50 03 79 92	45 13 42 65 29	26 76 08 36 37	41 32 64 43 44
53 85 34 13 77	36 06 69 48 50	58 83 87 38 59	49 36 47 33 31	96 24 04 36 42
24 63 73 87 36	74 38 48 93 42	52 62 30 79 92	12 36 91 86 01	03 74 28 38 73
83 08 01 24 51	38 99 22 28 15	07 75 95 17 77	(97) 37 72 75 85	51 97 23 78 67
16 44 42 43 34	36 15 19 90 73	27 49 37 09 39	85 13 03 25 52	54 84 65 47 59
60 79 01 81 57	57 17 86 57 62	11 16 17 85 76	45 81 95 29 79	65 13 00 48 60
94 01 54 68 74	32 44 44 82 77	59 82 09 61 63	64 65 42 58 43	41 14 54 28 20
74 10 88 82 22	88 57 07 40 15	25 70 49 10 35	01 75 51 47 50	48 96 83 86 03
62 88 08 78 73	95 16 05 92 21	22 30 49 03 14	72 87 71 73 34	39 28 30 41 49
11 74 81 21 02	80 58 04 18 67	17 71 05 96 21	06 55 40 78 50	73 95 07 95 52
17 94 40 56 00	60 47 80 33 43	25 85 25 89 05	57 21 63 96 18	49 85 69 93 26
66 06 74 27 92	95 04 35 26 80	46 78 05 64 87	09 97 15 94 81	37 00 62 21 86
54 24 49 10 30	45 54 77 08 18	59 84 99 61 69	61 45 92 16 47	87 41 71 71 98
30 94 55 75 89	31 73 25 72 60	47 67 00 76 54	46 37 62 53 66	94 74 64 95 80
69 17 03 74 03	86 99 59 03 07	94 30 47 18 03	26 82 50 55 11	12 45 99 13 14
08 34 58 89 75	35 84 18 57 71	08 10 55 99 87	87 11 22 14 76	14 71 37 11 81
27 76 74 35 84	85 30 18 89 77	29 49 06 97 14	73 03 54 12 07	74 69 90 93 10
13 02 51 43 38	54 06 61 52 43	47 72 46 67 33	47 43 14 39 05	31 04 85 66 99
80 21 73 62 92	98 52 52 43 35	24 43 22 48 96	43 27 75 88 74	11 46 61 60 82
10 87 56 20 04	90 39 16 11 05	57 41 10 63 68	53 85 63 07 43	08 67 08 47 41
54 12 75 73 26	26 62 91 90 87	24 47 28 87 79	30 54 02 78 86	61 73 27 54 54
33 71 34 80 07	93 58 47 28 69	51 92 66 47 21	58 30 32 98 22	93 17 49 39 72
85 27 48 68 93	11 30 32 92 70	28 83 43 41 37	73 51 59 04 00	71 14 84 36 43
84 13 38 96 40	44 03 55 21 66	73 85 27 00 91	61 22 26 05 61	62 32 71 84 23
56 73 21 62 34	17 39 59 61 31	10 12 39 16 22	85 49 65 75 60	81 60 41 88 80
65 13 85 68 06	87 64 88 52 61	34 31 36 58 61	45 87 52 10 69	85 64 44 72 77
38 00 10 21 76	81 71 91 17 11	71 60 29 29 37	74 21 96 40 49	65 58 44 96 98
37 40 29 63 97	01 30 47 75 86	56 27 11 00 86	47 32 46 26 05	40 03 03 74 38
97 12 54 03 48	87 08 33 14 17	21 81 53 92 50	75 23 76 20 47	15 50 12 95 78
21 82 64 11 34	47 14 33 40 72	64 63 88 59 02	49 13 90 64 41	03 85 65 45 52
73 13 54 27 42	95 71 90 90 35	85 79 47 42 96	08 78 98 81 56	64 69 11 92 02
07 63 87 79 29	03 06 11 80 72	96 20 74 41 56	23 82 19 95 38	04 71 36 69 94
60 52 88 34 41	07 95 41 98 14	59 17 52 06 95	05 53 35 21 39	61 21 20 64 55
83 59 63 56 55	06 95 89 29 83	05 12 80 97 19	77 43 35 37 83	92 30 15 04 98
10 85 06 27 46	99 59 91 05 07	13 49 90 63 19	53 07 57 18 39	06 41 01 93 62
39 82 09 89 52	43 62 26 31 47	64 42 18 08 14	43 80 00 93 51	31 02 47 31 67
59 58 00 64 78	75 56 97 88 00	88 83 55 44 86	23 76 80 61 56	04 11 10 84 08
38 50 80 73 41	23 79 34 87 63	90 82 29 70 22	17 71 90 42 07	95 95 44 99 53
30 69 27 06 68	94 68 81 61 27	56 19 68 00 91	82 06 76 34 00	05 46 26 92 00
65 44 39 56 59	18 28 82 74 37	49 63 22 40 41	08 33 76 56 76	96 29 99 08 36
27 26 75 02 64	13 19 27 22 94	07 47 74 46 06	17 98 54 89 11	97 34 13 03 58

Source: Paul G. Hoel, *Elementary Statistics*, 4th ed. Copyright © 1960, 1966, 1971, 1976 by John Wiley & Sons, Inc. Reprinted by permission.

The X axis describes the percent of the times we would be "incorrect" in taking a random sample of a certain size. The Y-axis describes the degree of accuracy we could obtain. Thus, if we wanted to be incorrect in our estimate of a population 5 percent of the time (correct 95 percent of the time) with a degree of accuracy of ± 4 percent, we would need a sample size of 600. In other words, if we randomly sampled from a population with a parameter of 50 percent, with a sample size of 600, 95 percent of the time we would obtain a research sample statistic between 46 and 54 percent (50 percent ±4 percent).

To illustrate how a table of random numbers is used, let us suppose that we have 100 elements in some population we want to know about. Assume further that we have decided that 10 subjects would be an adequate sample size. A simple random sample could be drawn if we could number each person in our population from 00 to 99. Once this was done we could consult a table of random numbers similar to the one presented in Table 15.4. To use the table we would pick an arbitrary starting spot. In this example our arbitrary spot is the 97 that is circled in Table 15.4. Starting from this point we could go up, down, left, or right to choose elements for our sample. We shall go down in the column directly under 97. Starting with the person who was numbered as "97," the other nine subjects chosen for our sample would be subjects number 85, 45, 64, 01, 72, 06, 57, 09, and 61. These ten subjects would constitute a simple random sample of ten subjects taken from a population of 100 subjects. Other procedures and tables could be employed in a similar manner depending on the size of the population and the size of the sample needed. When very large samples or populations are involved, computers are often used to make the process faster.

Systematic samples

Systematic sampling is a simple procedure which approximates obtaining a simple random sample. To do this type of sampling it is again necessary to enumerate the population, that is, to have a list of the elements of the population. Once a listing of the desired population is obtained, sample size must be determined. The first step in selecting a systematic sample is to divide the number of elements in the population by the desired sample size. Using a sample size of 10 out of a population of 100 elements as an illustration, we would divide 100 by 10 resulting in a quotient of 10. The result of the division indicates that every 10th element on the list of our population will be selected for our sample. A *systematic sample* selects every *n*th element from a listing of the population. In a strict statistical sense this is not equivalent to a simple random sample. In a practical sense it is close enough so that most researchers treat system-

Ex: draw every 10th card in student files, Bias?

436

atic samples the same as simple random samples. This type of sampling is often used when there is some available listing of potential subjects. For example, systematic samples are often taken from phone books, student rosters, city directories, and so on. Utilizing such lists for systematic sampling often has the effect of defining the population of a research study. Many lists that are available either underrepresent or overrepresent certain types of people. For example, if we were to use the telephone book in Peoria to select a systematic sample, the research population would not be all the citizens of Peoria, but those people in the Peoria area who have a listed telephone number. Those citizens without a telephone number would be underrepresented if we wanted to use this list as the population of Peoria.

Stratified samples

Simple random sampling or systematic sampling does not guarantee that specific subparts of a population will be selected. If there is an important reason for making certain that a sample has every subpart of the population represented, a stratified sample may be helpful. For example, if we would like to survey a city concerning political attitudes of citizens we might want to stratify our sample in terms of political party affiliation. This means that prior to selecting a sample (usually by a simple random sampling procedure) we would separate (stratify) our research population according to political party. Democrats would be one subpart (stratum) of the population. Republicans, Independents, American Independents, Socialists, Communists, and so on, would be in other strata from which samples are drawn. The number of elements chosen from each strata of the population could be proportional to the number of elements in the subpart. The number could also be disproportionate to the number in the population. Disproportionate sampling is often done to guarantee that enough subjects are selected to do statistical procedures. For example, since there are very few registered Communists in the United States, if we wanted to have more than a few in our sample it might be necessary to disproportionately select them. If simple random sampling is done from each stratum, the sample would be a probabilistic one.

Cluster samples

Surveys are very often conducted over a large geographic area such as the United States. Whenever a very large area is of interest to researchers or whenever geographical location is seen as being important in a study, cluster sampling might be utilized. Cluster sampling is somewhat similar to stratified sampling. The exception is that instead of using characteristics of the subjects to separate the population into subparts, geographic location is used. When studying a very large metropolitan area such as New York, three or four states might be involved. To help organize sampling procedures we might split the area to be investigated into areas such as census tracts or borroughs and towns. Such geographic subparts are called *clusters*. Sampling would be done from each cluster by some selecting procedures. If simple random sampling was done from each cluster the resulting sample would again be a probability sample.

Purposive samples

The purpose of all samples is to generalize to populations. The term purposive sample denotes a sample procedure which cannot easily result in a probabilistic sample.

Quota samples

Whenever a researcher desires to have a certain number of elements that have some characteristic in a sample, quota sampling could be used. In quota sampling the researcher sets some criteria levels (either number or proportion) for various types of elements. For example, a researcher may decide that for some reason a sample is needed where 50 of the subjects are male students majoring in engineering and 50 of the subjects are female students majoring in home economics. The researcher would then find any student of each type until the quota of 50 each is reached. No attention would be paid to how the students are selected.

Availability samples

The most typical type of nonprobability sample used in research is the availability sample. An *availability sample* is one where elements are sampled on the basis that they are easily accessible to the researcher. Available samples may be students in a researcher's class, paid volunteers from the community, passersby on a street corner, shoppers in a plaza, and so on.

You may get the idea from this discussion that since the problem of generalization is so important, researchers would be ill advised to utilize anything but a probability sample. In one sense this is true. However, in the real world researchers often have to make difficult choices. Sometimes researchers may be put in the position that they have to use a nonprobability sample or not do the research. Many valuable research findings have been the product of studies conducted with nonprobability samples. The major problem with nonprobability samples is that there is no formal procedure for generalizing results.

4. SAMPLING AND OTHER RESEARCH DESIGNS

Experiments

As we said in Chapter 9, the ideal way to design an experiment is to use random selection in combination with random assignment to experimental groups. Theoretically any of the above sampling procedures could be used to select subjects. However, the vast majority of experiments involving human subjects are conducted on availability samples. There are very few experiments which utilize simple random sampling and even fewer with stratified or cluster samples. Quota samples are used with some frequency by virtue of using matching to arrive at equivalent groups instead of random assignment. In such cases it is the structure of the experimental groups which determine the sample characteristics instead of the other way around. This is not usually considered to be a quota sample in the usual sense of the term.

Unobtrusive studies

As described in Chapter 12, unobtrusive measures include content analysis, documents and archival research, erosion measures, and the examination of other products left by human activity. In most of these cases there are very specific populations studied wherein sampling is not particularly necessary. However, when a general research population is identified, the researcher using unobtrusive measures may use any of the types of sampling we have discussed. The problem for the researcher is that sampling is dependent on the availability of something unobtrusive to observe. This limits the researcher in the selection of a sample. The difficulty is so great that purposive sampling is very often necessary in such designs.

Participant observation

Almost without exception studies using participant observation utilize an availability sample. Because of the time and energy required to conduct participant observation there are usually a very small number of situations (groups, organizations, etc.) examined. The group or setting must be selected so that the researcher has access to it. Thus factors other than statistical generalizability may be dominant in the selection of a sample. Although researchers doing participant observations are just as concerned with generalizing their results as other researchers, the studies usually conducted with this method rely more upon the power of the in-depth information obtained than upon the sampling plan.

Simulation

In game simulation the question of sampling comes down to who is doing the gaming. If a game involving world politics were the focus of the simulation perhaps the best sample to generalize to the real world would be a sample of world leaders. Since this would probably not be possible, the researcher often relies on an available sample of subjects. Game simulations are often used to study the process of human activity rather than to come to specific conclusions. That is, they are often designed to sensitize the researcher, the participants, or the audience to some social phenomena.

On the other hand, computer simulation is often employed to study hypothetical or contrived populations. Because of the power of the computer populations may be explored by simulation without the necessity of sampling. Where sampling is necessary the number of elements involved is still usually so large that generalizing presents few problems. The more important problem for the simulator is to select which characteristics of the population are to be considered in the simulation. Since not all characteristics can be included, the investigator must decide on which characteristics to select. Although this might seem like taking a sample of characteristics, this selection process is not considered a part of sampling. Such decision should be made on the basis of the theoretical importance of variables or on their usefulness in past research.

In summary, any sampling procedure can be used in conjunction with any research design. In practice, surveys use the widest variety of sampling procedures. The major distinction between different types of samples is whether or not they are probability samples. Probability samples have the advantage that they can be compared to known sampling distributions of various statistics. This aids the researcher in deciding whether or not to generalize the sample findings to the research population. Without the aid of statistical inference, the question of generalization is very problematic.

The choice of which sampling procedure to employ is made after considering many factors. The nature of the problem under study, adequacy of fundings, availability of field staff, and so on, must be examined. Each of the various types of sampling has its advantages and disadvantages which may serve to guide the researcher in the choice of sampling procedures.

5. ADVANTAGES AND DISADVANTAGES OF VARIOUS SAMPLES

Table 15.5 briefly describes the advantages and disadvantages of each of the samples described above. Remember, these are only part

TABLE 15.5
Advantages and disadvantages of various types of samples

Type of sampling	Advantages	Disadvantages
Simple random	Do not need to know much about the elements in the population Can use statistical inference to help deciding about generalizing Offers the easiest chance of obtaining a representative sample	Must be able to enumerate the elements of the population May not be as sophisticated as other designs so that conclusions might be limited
Systematic	Easiest to do Approximates a simple random sample and has some features of a stratified sample if the listing is ordered on some property	Must have a list of the population The list may limit the scope of the research population
Stratified	Can make certain that particular type of elements are included Comparisons can be made with other populations	Requires that you know something about the population prior to sampling Definition of strata may be faulty and introduce error More costly and time consuming
Cluster	Lowest cost if population is geographically dispersed Requires enumerating only part of the population	Must be able to assign each element to a particular cluster Need relatively large sample size
Purposive	Reduces cost of selecting sample May be most appropriate for research of certain types May increase ability to generalize to certain types of elements	Cannot use statistical inference May be the most biased Must know a great deal about research topic

of the basis on which the type of sample is selected for a particular study.

The problem of generalization is important and it is one of the major places in the research process where we can go wrong. Replication is one way that confidence can be gained in research results. If similar findings are discovered in many different types of samples at various points in time, we tend to have more confidence that the observed results are not a product of unrepresentative samples. Despite the fact that we do not need large sample sizes to use statistical inference, there seems to be increased confidence in research results obtained from very large samples. Finally, we tend to have more faith in results that have been obtained from probability samples because probability sampling produces the best chance of obtaining a representative sample from a population.

6. SUMMARY

One of the major goals of research is to determine the parameters of research populations. Since it is often not possible to observe all of the elements in a population, sampling becomes necessary. Sample statistics must be relied upon to infer population parameters. Any one research sample may not be representative of the research population, no matter which procedure is used. Sampling procedures which provide representative samples in the long run, however, are called bias free. When bias free sampling procedures are used, sampling distributions of any statistic can be computed. These distributions contain the proportion of times each value of a statistic will be calculated (in the long run) from a population with a particular parameter. A research sample statistic can be compared to a sampling distribution to determine the probability of obtaining such a statistic from the given type of population. A decision must then be made about generalization. Whatever the decision, it might be wrong. Replication is the major way we gain confidence in results obtained from research samples.

Samples often used for surveys include: simple random, systematic, stratified, cluster, and purposive. The important distinction for samples is whether they are probability or nonprobability samples. Purposive samples are the only type that are not usually probability samples. While any sampling procedure can be used with any research design, there are some common practices. By and large, designs other than surveys seldom use probability samples. While this may be necessary because of specialized purposes, it does limit our ability to use formal rules of statistical inference. The advantages and disadvantages of each technique must be weighed when designing or critiquing a particular research study.

1. Find a large number (preferably 30 or more) of identical objects of which you may have of two different colors (like the yellow and green marbles in the chapter). You could use paper, marbles, candy, buttons, beans, and so on. Place an equal number of each color in a box or bag. Mix well.

   a. Take 10 samples of four, replacing the sample before drawing another sample.

   Compare your percentage distribution with the sampling distribution in Table 15.2. If your distribution is different, why might this be so?

   b. Suppose you were to take 50 additional samples of four and construct a new distribution. What would you expect?

   c. Suppose for each sample you had flipped a coin four times instead of taking objects from a bag or box. What should a sampling distribution of the percentage of heads look like?

2. a. Using your same bag or box, suppose you had taken samples of size 10 rather than 4. How would your sampling distribution change?

   b. Take a series of 20 samples of size 10 and record your percentage distribution. Was your estimate in exercise 2(a) correct?

3. What would be the most frequent score in your sampling distribution if there were 75 percent of one color and 25 percent of the other?

4. For each of the following situations recommend a type of sample which would be advantageous to employ and state why.

   a. An experiment on how noise affects concentration.

   b. A preliminary investigation to see if the instructions are clear on an upcoming pilot study questionnaire.

   c. A content analysis of a children's television program.

1. If you were to reconstruct your study in terms of the sampling considerations introduced in this chapter, describe the nature of the sampling design you would employ for each project you have undertaken.

2. For those projects in which you would have selected a probability sample, describe what lists of populations you have available to you (e.g., student directory or city directory). Assess how adequate you feel these lists to be (e.g., can you stratify on desired variables? Are the lists complete?).

BABBIE, E. *Survey Research Methods.* Belmont, Calif.: Wadsworth, 1973.

BLALOCK, H. *Social Statistics,* 2d ed. New York: McGraw-Hill, 1972.

CHEIN, I. "An Introduction to Sampling. In Selltiz, C. *et al. Research Methods in Social Relations.* New York: Holt, Rinehart and Winston, 1959.

KISH, L. *Survey Sampling.* New York: Wiley, 1965.

SLONIM, M. *Sampling.* New York: Simon and Schuster, 1960.

CHAPTER 16
FORMAL TESTS OF THE EXISTENCE
OF A RELATIONSHIP

After studying this chapter, students should be able to:

1. Explain the necessity of testing for the existence of a relationship.

2. Describe and interpret sampling distributions.

3. Describe and explain the role of a comparison population in formal tests of significance.

4. Describe the alternatives and the impact of these alternatives in the decisions of inference.

5. Explain what is meant by the uncertainty principle.

6. Describe, explain, and interpret the logic of statistical inference using both standard language and the special terminology of inference, including terms like general hypothesis, research hypothesis, statistical hypothesis, null hypothesis, Type I error, and Type II error.

7. Calculate and interpret chi-square tests of significance for percentage table analyses.

8. Understand uses of t, Z, and F in tests of significance when measures of association are used.

Chi square Special statistic of inference which operates in such a way that a comparison is made between the data table that has been produced from a research sample and one that has similar marginals but contains no relationship.

Comparison frequency table Table constructed which utilizes expected frequencies.

Comparison population A population from which a sampling distribution has been drawn for a formal test of statistical inference.

Degrees of freedom A number calculated on the basis of the number of cells in a percentage table which allows one to select the correct sampling distribution from a comparison population.

Expected frequencies Frequencies that are expected to appear in a percentage table similar to the observed table but where there is no relationship between variables.

General hypothesis A general statement about some phenomena.

Generalization The process of assuming that a relationship found to exist in the data from a research sample would also exist in the (potentially available) data of the research population from which the units of the sample have been drawn.

Level of statistical significance The probability of making a Type I error when rejecting a null hypothesis.

Null hypothesis Usually a statement that there is no relationship between variables within the comparison population in formal tests of significance. (Sometimes a statement about a specified strength of a relationship or a prediction about a single parameter.)

Observed frequencies Frequencies that are observed in a percentage table constructed from data collected in a research sample.

Parameter A characteristic or description of a population of units.

Research hypothesis A statement about the nature of a relationship between variables which can potentially be measured and tested.

Sampling distribution A list of all the possible statistics that might be calculated from a particular sized probability sample along with the probability that each value would be calculated from such a series of samples over the long run.

Statistical hypothesis A description of the research hypothesis in statistical terms which is expected to be true in the data from the research sample.

Type I error The possibility of making an error in the long run when rejecting a null hypothesis.

Type II error The possibility of making an error in the long run when failing to reject a null hypothesis.

Uncertainty principle The everpresent possibility of making an error in the decision of inference.

1. TESTING FOR THE EXISTENCE OF A RELATIONSHIP

The idea of testing for the existence of a relationship was introduced in Chapter 15. You will recall that the problem of the existence of a relationship comes up when data have been collected on a research sample rather than on a research population. Assuming that no errors have been made in the research, if data have been collected for a sample of units rather than the population, the question of generalization can be raised. Generalization refers to the process of assuming that a relationship *found to exist in data from a research sample* would also "exist" in the data potentially available in the research population. When we raise the question of the existence of a relationship it is in this sense. We are assuming that the research procedures are sound and have been carried out correctly. Therefore any conclusion reached about a relationship in the data from a sample is considered correct. Since we want to know about the population, not just the sample, we need to know whether the statistic we have found in the sample data accurately describes some parameter (i.e., a relationship in the population). This question must be raised because any one sample statistic can be different than the value of the population parameter. This is a potential problem whenever any research design utilizing a sample is employed. Almost all research in the behavioral and social sciences and education is conducted using some type of sample rather than a population. This would include surveys and experiments as well as most other research designs discussed in Chapter 12.

The decision about whether or not to generalize sample results to the units of the population may be made on many bases. They may be made on the basis of intuition, fraud, experience, or an assessment that the sample is representative according to some set of characteristics of the units. In order to use any of the *formal* tests of the existence of a relationship that are presently available, the data in question would have to come from a probability sample. In addition, the statistic would have to have a known sampling distribution.

2. REVIEW OF SAMPLING DISTRIBUTIONS

As was discussed in Chapter 15, a sampling distribution consists of a list of all the possible statistics that *might* be calculated (observed) from a particular sized probability sample. These values are accompanied by the proportion (probability) of times that each value would be calculated over a very large number of same size samples (*in the long run*). In other words, it is a probability distribution of all possible values of a statistic which has been constructed from a very large number of same sized probability (random) samples. This "calculation" is not necessarily actually done by hand, but is often constructed using the mathematical theory of probability.

The statistic in a sampling distribution might be a percentage (as in the example of Chapter 15), a mean, a measure of association, or some special calculation. Some sampling distributions used in formal tests of existence are made up of special calculations and some are more standard statistics. The particular sampling distribution used depends on what type of analysis the researcher wants to use and the sample size being employed in the research. In addition, the values of a sampling distribution depend on the characteristics of the population used to construct the distribution. The population from which the sampling distribution was drawn will be referred to here as the *comparison population*. The statistic which has the highest probability in the sampling distribution is the value of the statistic which would have been calculated in the comparison population. In other words, the statistic with the highest probability in any sampling distribution has the same value as the parameter of the comparison population.

Before detailing how to use a sampling distribution in the decisions of statistical inference, we give an example of constructing a sampling distribution using the mean number of employees in a population of small industries. The statistic in this illustration is a descriptive one instead of a relational one. Table 16.1 shows the value of this variable for eight companies that make up our comparison population, along with the value of the parameter for this population.

The parameter in this comparison population is equal to 27 workers. It can be interpreted that in this comparison population of industries the average number of workers is 27. Suppose we wanted to study some population of small industries. We could compare a

TABLE 16.1
Comparison population for constructing a sampling distribution

Factory	Number of workers
A	10
B	16
C	26
D	30
E	8
F	50
G	44
H	32
Total	216

Parameter = the mean number of workers = $\frac{216}{8}$ = 27 *research sample statistic* against a sampling distribution of our *comparison* population. If we use a sample size of 3, a sampling distribution from the comparison population could be calculated using a sample size of 3. Table 16.2 shows the first step in calculating a sampling distribution from our comparison population.

This table contains a list of all of the possible samples of three industries from the *comparison* population. The number of workers in each of the samples is added together and then divided by 3 to obtain the mean number of workers in each sample. We can see that some of the sample statistics are quite different than the population parameter of 27. The sample statistics range from a low of 11 in the A, B, E sample to a high of 42 in the F, G, H sample. If random sampling is used, there is an equal probability of each of the samples in the list being selected at any one point in time. An exact

TABLE 16.2
All possible samples of size 3 from the comparison population

Sample Industries	Number of Workers	Mean	Sample Industries	Number of Workers	Mean
A, B, C	$10 + 16 + 26 = 52$	17	B, D, G	$16 + 30 + 44 = 90$	30
A, B, D	$10 + 16 + 30 = 56$	19	B, D, H	$16 + 30 + 32 = 78$	26
A, B, E	$10 + 16 + 8 = 34$	11	B, E, F	$16 + 8 + 50 = 74$	25
A, B, F	$10 + 16 + 50 = 76$	25	B, E, G	$16 + 8 + 44 = 68$	23
A, B, G	$10 + 16 + 44 = 70$	23	B, E, H	$16 + 8 + 32 = 56$	19
A, B, H	$10 + 16 + 32 = 58$	19	B, F, G	$16 + 50 + 44 = 110$	37
A, C, D	$10 + 26 + 30 = 66$	22	B, F, H	$16 + 50 + 32 = 98$	33
A, C, E	$10 + 26 + 8 = 44$	15	B, G, H	$16 + 44 + 32 = 92$	31
A, C, F	$10 + 26 + 50 = 86$	29	C, D, E	$26 + 30 + 8 = 64$	21
A, C, G	$10 + 26 + 44 = 80$	27	C, D, R	$26 + 30 + 50 = 106$	35
A, C, H	$10 + 26 + 32 = 68$	23	C, D, G	$26 + 30 + 44 = 100$	33
A, D, E	$10 + 30 + 8 = 48$	16	C, D, H	$26 + 30 + 32 = 88$	30
A, D, F	$10 + 30 + 50 = 90$	30	C, E, F	$26 + 8 + 50 = 84$	28
A, D, G	$10 + 30 + 44 = 84$	28	C, E, G	$26 + 8 + 44 = 78$	26
A, D, H	$10 + 30 + 32 = 72$	24	C, E, H	$26 + 8 + 32 = 66$	22
A, E, F	$10 + 8 + 50 = 68$	23	C, F, G	$26 + 50 + 44 = 120$	40
A, E, G	$10 + 8 + 44 = 62$	21	C, F, H	$26 + 50 + 32 = 108$	36
A, E, H	$10 + 8 + 32 = 50$	17	C, G, H	$26 + 44 + 32 = 102$	34
A, F, G	$10 + 50 + 44 = 104$	35	D, E, F	$30 + 8 + 50 = 88$	30
A, F, H	$10 + 50 + 32 = 92$	31	D, E, G	$30 + 8 + 44 = 82$	27
A, G, H	$10 + 44 + 32 = 86$	29	D, E, H	$30 + 8 + 32 = 70$	23
B, C, D	$16 + 26 + 30 = 72$	24	D, F, G	$30 + 50 + 44 = 124$	41
B, C, E	$16 + 26 + 8 = 50$	17	D, F, H	$30 + 50 + 32 = 112$	37
B, C, F	$16 + 26 + 50 = 92$	31	D, G, H	$30 + 44 + 32 = 106$	36
B, C, G	$16 + 26 + 44 = 86$	29	E, F, G	$8 + 50 + 44 = 102$	34
B, C, H	$16 + 26 + 32 = 74$	25	E, F, H	$8 + 50 + 32 = 90$	30
B, D, E	$16 + 30 + 8 = 54$	18	E, G, H	$8 + 44 + 32 = 84$	28
B, D, F	$16 + 30 + 50 = 96$	32	F, G, H	$50 + 44 + 32 = 126$	42

sampling distribution could be constructed by taking a very large number (theoretically, an infinite number) of random selections from the list and computing the proportion of times each value is obtained. However, for this illustration we can approximate a *comparison sampling distribution*. Table 16.3 shows how a comparison sampling distribution could be constructed using the statistics from Table 16.2. The number of samples in each category are determined and then the percentage distribution is computed. The sampling distribution follows directly from the percentage distribution by changing the percentages into decimals and calling them probabilities.

Before moving to a detailed discussion of the decisions of statistical inference, we can show how to use the sampling distribution in Table 16.3. Suppose we were doing a research study about the average number of workers in factories around our neighborhood. We would like to know about the average number of workers in factories within our community. Let us say there are three factories that we could look at. (Assume this is a random sample of the factories in our community.) Finding the average number of employees results in a mean = 13 workers. Comparing this mean of 13 to the sampling distribution shows a probability of .0357 (for the 11–15 category). This means that if the average number of workers in our

TABLE 16.3

Constructing a comparison sampling distribution

Mean number of workers	Number of samples	Percentage
41–45	2	$2/56 \times 100 = 3.57\%$
36–40	6	$6/56 \times 100 = 10.71\%$
31–35	9	$9/56 \times 100 = 16.07\%$
26–30	15	$15/56 \times 100 = 26.79\%$
21–25	14	$14/56 \times 100 = 25.00\%$
16–20	8	$8/56 \times 100 = 14.29\%$
11–15	2	$2/57 \times 100 = 3.57\%$
	56	99.99%

Sampling distribution of means

Mean	p
41–45	.0357
36–40	.1071
31–35	.1607
26–30	.2679
21–25	.2500
16–20	.1429
11–15	.0357
	.9999

community (the research population) is really 27, we would get an average of 13 (from the research sample) only 3.57 percent of the time just by chance. The odds are that the average number of workers in factories of our community is not 27. We would probably decide that our community is different from one in which the average number of workers is 27. Until we get more information we would use 13 as the average number of workers in factories in our community. We would also know that in doing so, there is a .0357 chance that the average is really 27.

Although the formal tests we will be exploring in this chapter do not construct their sampling distributions exactly the same way we did in the illustration, the principle in the same. In all tests some statistic from a *research* sample is compared to a *sampling distribution* of that statistic from some *comparison* population. After this comparison is made, the researcher must make a decision about the existence of a relationship in the research population (or the magnitude of some parameter). The researcher must decide whether or not to generalize the results obtained in the *research sample* to the *research population*. It is important to recognize that the researcher is making the decision. The decision is not made by the test itself. Judgment is always involved, as is the possibility of making an error in that decision.

3. THE DECISIONS OF STATISTICAL INFERENCE

In formal tests of statistical inference there is no way to make a direct decision about whether to generalize research sample findings to the research population because we usually do not "know" the value of the research population parameter. Instead, a comparison is made between a test statistic from the research sample and a sampling distribution constructed from the comparison population with a specified parameter. The decision that must be made on the basis of probability is whether or not the value of the research sample statistic most likely comes from a population similar to the comparison population. If the decision is that it probably *does,* then you "infer" that the research population is like the comparison population. When the inference is made that the research population *is* like the comparison population, you use the defined parameter of the comparison population as the value for the research population. If the decision is that it probably *does not,* then you "infer" that the research population is *not* like the comparison population. When the inference is made that the research population is *not* like the comparison population, the only guide you have to the value of the parameter in the research population is the statistic from the research sample. Therefore the conclusions reached in the research sample are used to describe the research population by additionally "inferring" that the research sample statistic accurately reflects the research population parameter. That is, you would further infer that the research sample statistic is approximately equal to the parameter of the research population. Figure 16.1 displays this chain of reasoning in graphic form.

Because we are dealing with probabilities instead of certainties,

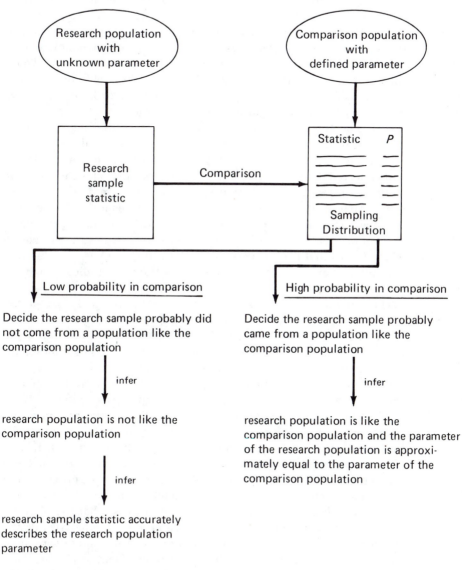

FIGURE 16.1
The decisions of statistical inference

there is always the possibility that the decision we make is a wrong decision. This idea is sometimes referred to as the *uncertainty principle*. If the probability in the comparison is low, the inference is made that the research population is not like the comparison population. This decision could be wrong. As a matter of fact, the magnitude of the probability is the "odds" that the decision is a wrong one. The magnitude of the probability is the chance of obtaining the value of the research sample statistic from the comparison population. Therefore it is the probability that this decision is a wrong one in the long run.

If the probability in the comparison is high, the inference is made that the research population is like the comparison population. This decision might also be wrong. Even though the probability of being the same is great, there is a smaller probability that they are not similar. The important thing to note is that there is always some probability that this type of decision is in error.

In any one decision about inference we have either made an error in the decision or we have not. Unfortunately the only way to tell for sure is to find the parameter of the research population. If we had collected data on the research population, the whole exercise of statistical inference would be unnecessary and would not make any sense. Therefore we never know for sure if in this one case we have made an error. We can only make a statement about the probability of error of this *type* of decision in the long run. This situation is one of the forces that lead to a stress on replicating studies. For this reason, replication may be particularly important in studies which involve sampling.

The remaining consideration in this testing process is how to define the parameter of the comparison population, the population from which the sample distribution is constructed. In order to make sense out of defining the comparison population, we need to remember some of the discussion in the first part of this text. The key factor is that science is a continual process of eliminating possible alternative explanations. A theory or hypothesis supported by observation (data) is tentatively accepted as the accurate explanation of the phenomena. The tentative nature of science can be viewed as explanations or theories waiting to be eliminated. In this vein the comparison population is defined in such a way that the emphasis is on the negative. In most formal tests of significance the comparison population is typically defined as one in which there is *no relationship* between variables. It is defined so that the distribution of the dependent variable is the same for all categories of the independent variable. When the parameter of the comparison population is defined in this way, a high probability (obtained in the comparison of the research sample statistic to the sampling distribution from the comparison population) means that there is probably no relationship between variables in the research population. On the other hand, a low probability, which results in inferring that the research population is *not* like the comparison population, means that any description of a relationship in the research sample is probably accurate for the research population. Therefore results in the research sample can be generalized to the research population.

The usual motif in research is that a study is attempting to find data that support a hypothesis about a relationship between variables. Most research is devised in such a way that the researchers believe they will find relationships. Therefore most researchers would not like to infer that their research sample comes from a population where there is no relationship between variables. Because of this, researchers have a vested interest in inferring that the research population is not like the comparison population.

The whole process of inference and the description of it is rather "wordy." In order to communicate the same types of information in an easier manner, researchers have developed a set of terminology to use in formal tests of statistical inference. These terms, reflected in Figure 16.2, will simplify communication once they are learned and it is this set of terminology which is used in research publications.

The process begins with a general idea about some phenomena. For example, a researcher may have a feeling that there is some relationship between pornography and sexual deviance. This general idea is sometimes called a *general hypothesis* (H_g). General hypotheses tend not to be very specific and/or detailed. In order to conduct research, the general idea must be translated into a hypothesis about variables which could potentially be measured and tested. This hypothesis is called the research hypothesis (H_1) and is often a statement about the nature of a relationship between variables. In our example the research might hypothesize that viewing pornographic materials will lead to an increase in sex crime. From this research hypothesis a statistical hypothesis could be derived. A statistical hypothesis (H_s) is derived from the research hypothesis and translates the research hypothesis into statistical terms. Using the pornography example, one statistical hypothesis could be that the bivariate percentage table between the prevalence of pornography in society and the rate of sex crimes will show a direct relationship. In other words, studying a sample of countries or communities should result in a positive relationship between pornography and sex crimes. It is usually suggested that the research and statistical hypotheses should be stated prior to the conduct of the research. This puts the investigator's prejudices "up front" and allows the consumers of the research to know the intentions of the research.

Comparing of the research sample statistic with the sampling distribution of the comparison population is essentially comparing the

456

H_s to the null hypothesis (H_o). The null hypothesis states that there is no relationship between variables. (This is a characteristic of the comparison population by definition.) The only decision in formal tests of significance concern the null hypothesis. It is called the

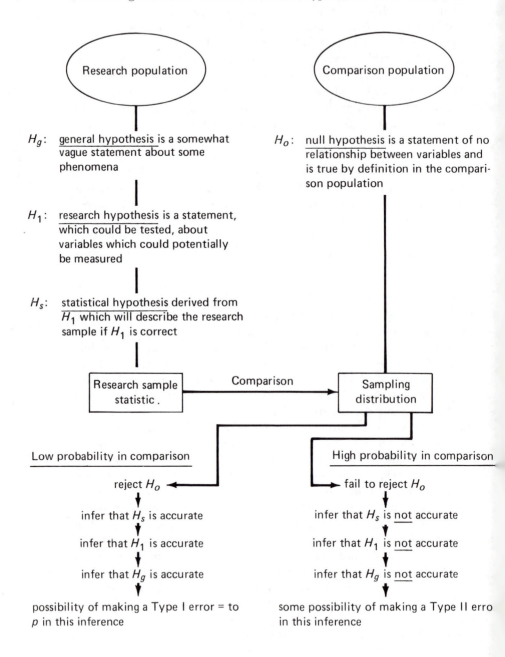

FIGURE 16.2
Terminology for formal tests of significance

null to communicate the idea of *no* relationship. The researcher must decide to reject the null hypothesis or fail to reject H_o. The terminology of "failing to reject" rather than saying that you "accept" the null hypothesis stresses the tentative nature of the decision. If the decision is to reject the null hypothesis, there is some probability of making an error. This type of possible error is called a Type I error.

If the decision is to fail to reject the null hypothesis, there is some probability of making an error. This type of possible error is called a Type II error.

Inferences about the statistical hypothesis, research hypothesis, and general hypothesis follow from the decision about the null hypothesis. The null hypothesis in our pornography-sex crime illustration would probably be that the percentage cross-tab will show no relationship. This would be true in the comparison population. Sometimes the null hypothesis is not that the association is zero, but that it is either positive or negative. In these cases, slight modifications in the above process are necessary. These modifications are beyond the scope of this text.

4. TESTS WHEN USING PERCENTAGE ANALYSIS

The most popular test of statistical significance for percentage table analysis is called the chi-square test (χ^2). Chi-square makes a comparison between a table that has been produced from a research sample and one that has similar marginals (row totals, column totals, and table total) but contains no relationship. The logic of this test is consistent with the foregoing discussion of inference.

As an illustration, we shall use a table analyzing the relationship between two ordinal variables. The independent variable is a measure of the prevalence of pornography in a community. It is operationalized by determining whether there are pornographic movies in the community. The dependent variable is the sex crime rate of the community arranged into three categories. Table 16.4 contains the data to be used for the illustration. The frequency table is given on the left and the percentage table on the right. The frequency table is needed in order to conduct a chi-square test of statistical significance. The percentage table is needed to determine the form and strength of the relationship.

Notice that the relationship in this sample data is direct but the strength is not too strong. However, before describing the relationship we must determine if it exists. Remember, we are assuming the data on the table are good data. The existence we are talking about is for this research population. In order to make that decision, a comparison must be made to a sampling distribution constructed from a comparison population where there is no relationship.

TABLE 16.4
Sample data for chi-square illustration

FREQUENCY TABLE

Presence of pornographic
movie theaters

		No	Yes	
Sex crime rate	H	6	6	12
	M	10	25	35
	L	9	9	18
		25	40	65

PERCENTAGE TABLE

Presence of pornographic
movie theaters

		No	Yes
Sex crime rate	H	24%	15.0%
	M	40%	62.5%
	L	36%	22.5%
		100%	100%

Defining the comparison population

By definition, the comparison population is one in which there is no relationship. We need to construct the comparison population in such a way that a meaningful comparison with our sample data can be made. We do not want to compare apples with oranges. In order to make a meaningful comparison, we will use the frequencies that were observed in the research sample as a basis to describe the comparison population. The frequencies that we observed in the research sample are denoted by the symbol f_o. We would like to compare these frequencies with those that we would expect to find in a similar table where there is no relationship. One way to have no relationship in a percentage table is to have the distribution of the dependent variable the same for every category of the independent variable. We use this fact to construct a comparison table. The comparison table has frequencies which we would expect if there were no relationships. We label those frequencies f_e. Table 16.5 shows how a comparison table is constructed for the data in Table 16.4. The first step is to calculate a percentage distribution from the Y frequencies that compose the Y marginals. It is this distribution of Y that will be used to calculate the appropriate expected frequencies for all the columns of X. To do this we take the total frequencies in each column and multiply them by all the percentages in the Y marginal distribution. This will result in a set of frequencies that can be put into an expected comparison frequency table. Notice that the marginals of such a table are exactly the same as the observed table for the research sample data in Table 16.4. To show that such a table has no relationship within it, the expected percentage table is also provided in Table 16.5. Note that the percentage distributions

TABLE 16.5
Constructing an expected comparison table

Y MARGINAL DISTRIBUTION

Y	Frequency distribution	Percentage distribution	f_e for No category of X	f_e for YES category of X
H	12	$\frac{12}{65}$ X 100 = 18.5%	18.5% X 25 = 4.6	18.5% X 40 = 7.4
M	35	$\frac{35}{65}$ X 100 = 53.8%	53.8% X 25 = 13.4	53.8% X 40 = 21.5
L	18	$\frac{18}{65}$ X 100 = 27.7%	27.7% X 25 = 6.9	27.7% X 40 = 11.1
	65	100%	24.9[a]	40.0

EXPECTED COMPARISON TABLE

Expected frequencies:[b]

presence of pornographic movie theaters

Sex crime rate	No	Yes	
H	4.6	7.4	12
M	13.4	21.5	35
L	6.9	11.1	18
	24.9	40	65

Expected percentages:

presence of pornographic movie theaters

Sex crime rate	No	Yes
H	18.5%	18.5%
M	53.8%	53.8%
L	27.7%	27.8%[b]
	100%	100.1%[b]

[a] This is a result of rounding.

[b] Formally, a correction factor may be used if any cell frequency is small.

are the same in all columns which means there is no relationship between the variables. This expected frequency table can now be compared to the observed table since it has no relationship in it and yet the marginals are identical. This comparison will be in the form of calculating a chi-square.

Chi-square: a calculation of difference

The major part of the calculation of chi-square is the determination of the difference between the observed frequencies and the expected frequencies, that is, the frequencies actually observed in the research sample and those expected in a similar table that has no relationship. In order to do away with plus and minus signs, each difference is squared. To get an idea of the relative size of the difference, the squared difference is divided by the expected frequency. This last step is necessary since a difference of, say, 20 is a relatively large difference if the expected frequency is 10, but it is relatively small if the expected frequency is, say, 545,678. By doing this calculation for each cell of the table and then adding them up, we will get a measure of how different the observed table is from the comparison (expected) table. (See Table 16.6)

TABLE 16.6
Calculating chi-square

$f_o{}^a$	$f_e{}^b$	$f_o - f_e$	$(f_o - f_e)^2$	$(f_o - f_e)^2/f_e$
6	4.6	1.4	1.96	$1.96/4.6 \ = .426$
10	13.4	−3.4	11.56	$11.56/13.4 = .863$
9	6.9	2.1	4.41	$4.41/6.9 \ = .639$
6	7.4	−1.4	1.96	$1.96/7.4 \ = .265$
25	21.5	3.5	12.25	$12.25/21.5 = .570$
9	11.1	−2.1	4.41	$4.41/11.1 = .397$
				Chi–square $= 3.160$

Formula for chi–square: $\chi^2 = \Sigma \dfrac{(f_o - f_e)^2}{f_e}$

[a] Data from Table 16.4.
[b] Data from Table 16.5.

Once chi-square has been calculated, we need its sampling distribution to be able to determine the probability of getting our observed frequencies from a population where there is no relationship.

Understanding and using a chi-square table

As was pointed out in the previous examples of sampling distributions, a different distribution would be calculated depending on sample size. The analogous situation for percentage table analysis is that a different sampling distribution of the same statistic would be calculated depending on how many cells a table has. In order to find the right chi-square sampling distribution, it is necessary to calculate a number called the degrees of freedom.

Degrees of freedom is a number calculated on the basis of the number of cells in a percentage table. It allows one to select the correct sampling distribution from a comparison population for use in statistical inference. Degrees of freedom is sometimes abbreviated as df and is calculated by subtracting one from the number of rows in a table and multiplying that number by the number obtained by subtracting one from the number of columns in the table. The formula for such a computation would be df $= (r-1)(c-1)$ where r equals the number of rows and c equals the number of columns. In our illustration $r = 3$ and $c = 2$. Therefore df is $(3-1)(2-1) = 2$. There are 2 degrees of freedom in a table with six cells.

In order to make the decision of inference we would need to have a sampling distribution of chi-square from a comparison population where there is no relationship. That sampling distribution would have to have 2 degrees of freedom.

Table 16.7 shows portions of several chi-square sampling distributions. Each of the rows in this table is a part of a sampling distribution. The df numbers at the left indicate the size table for the distribution. To the right of these df numbers are various values of chi square which would be calculated from a comparison population with no relationship between variables. The probabilities at the top of the table are the proportion of times, in the long run, that such values (or higher; see the section on one- and two-tailed tests) would be calculated from such a comparison population. Notice that not all of the possible values of chi-square are included in any of the various sampling distributions. This is merely to save space. By only including some of the various values in each sampling distribution, 30 different sampling distributions can be represented in the space taken by Table 16.7.

Making the comparison

The next step is to compare the value of chi-square we calculated from the research sample (3.160) to the sampling distribution from the comparison population which has 2 degrees of freedom. To make this comparison we find the df of 2 on the left-hand side of Table 16.7. Once this has been located, all the numbers to the right are values of chi square in that sampling distribution. An easy way to make the comparison is to find the value in the sampling distribution that is closest to 3.160. Upon inspection of the table it appears that 3.219 is closest to the value calculated from the research sample. The probability at the top of the column in which 3.219 appears is .20. In other words, a chi-square value of 3.219 occurs about 20 percent of the time just by chance out of a comparison population in which there is no relationship.

The decision of inference

Now that we know that a value of chi-square equal to 3.160 will be calculated from a population in which there is no relationship between variables about 20 percent of the time in the long run, just by

TABLE 16.7
Partial sampling distributions of chi-square with various degrees of freedom

			Probabilities			
df	.99	.98	.95	.90	.80	.70
1	.000157	.000628	.00393	.0158	.0642	.148
2	.0201	.0404	.103	.211	.446	.713
3	.115	.185	.352	.584	1.005	1.424
4	.297	.429	.711	1.064	1.649	2.195
5	.554	.752	1.145	1.610	2.343	3.000
6	.872	1.134	1.635	2.204	3.070	3.828
7	1.239	1.564	2.167	2.833	3.822	4.671
8	1.646	2.032	2.733	3.490	4.594	5.527
9	2.088	2.532	3.325	4.168	5.380	6.393
10	2.558	3.059	3.940	4.865	6.179	7.267
11	3.053	3.609	4.575	5.578	6.989	8.148
12	3.571	4.178	5.226	6.304	7.807	9.034
13	4.107	4.765	5.892	7.042	8.634	9.926
14	4.660	5.368	6.571	7.790	9.467	10.821
15	5.229	5.985	7.261	8.547	10.307	11.721
16	5.812	6.614	7.962	9.312	11.152	12.624
17	6.408	7.255	8.672	10.085	12.002	13.531
18	7.015	7.906	9.390	10.865	12.857	14.440
19	7.633	8.567	10.117	11.651	13.716	15.352
20	8.260	9.237	10.851	12.443	14.578	16.266
21	8.897	9.915	11.591	13.240	15.445	17.182
22	9.542	10.600	12.338	14.041	16.314	18.101
23	10.196	11.293	13.091	14.848	17.187	19.021
24	10.865	11.992	13.848	15.659	18.062	19.943
25	11.524	12.679	14.611	16.473	18.940	20.867
26	12.198	13.409	15.379	17.292	19.820	21.792
27	12.879	14.125	16.151	18.114	20.703	22.719
28	13.565	14.847	16.928	18.939	21.588	23.647
29	14.256	15.574	17.708	19.766	22.475	24.577
30	14.953	16.306	18.493	20.599	23.364	25.508

chance, a decision can be made. There are two options in the decision of inference. The first is to conclude that the research sample is likely drawn from a population like the comparison population. The second option is to conclude that the research sample is *not* likely drawn from a population like the comparison population.

If we think that a 20 percent chance is fairly high, then we would conclude that our research sample *is* from a population like the comparison population. If we take this option, there is a certain probability of making a Type II error in doing so. If we think that a 20 percent chance is fairly low, then we would conclude that our research sample *is not* from a population like the comparison popu-

TABLE 16.7 (continued)

			Probabilities				
.50	.30	.20	.10	.05	.02	.01	.001
.455	1.074	1.642	2.706	3.841	5.412	6.635	10.827
1.386	2.408	3.219	4.605	5.991	7.824	9.210	13.815
2.366	3.665	4.624	6.251	7.815	9.837	11.345	16.268
3.357	4.878	5.989	7.779	9.488	11.668	13.277	18.465
4.351	6.064	7.289	9.236	11.070	13.388	15.086	20.517
5.348	7.231	8,558	10.645	12.592	15.033	16.812	22.457
6.346	8,383	9.803	12.017	14.067	16.622	18.475	24.322
7.344	9.524	11.030	13.362	15.507	18.168	20.090	26.125
8.343	10.656	12.242	14.684	16.919	19.679	21.666	27.877
9.342	11.781	13.442	15.987	18.307	21.161	23.209	29.588
10.341	12.899	14.631	17.275	19.675	22.618	24.725	31.264
11.340	14.011	15.812	18.549	21.026	24.054	26.217	32.909
12.340	15.119	16.985	19.812	22.362	25.472	27.688	34.528
13.339	16.222	18.151	21.064	23.685	26.873	29.141	36.123
14.339	17.322	19.311	22.307	24.996	28.259	30.578	37.697
15.338	18,418	20.465	23.542	26.296	29.633	32.000	39.252
16.338	19.511	21.615	24.769	27.587	30.995	33.409	40.790
17.338	20.601	22.760	25.989	28.869	32.346	34.805	42.312
18.338	21.689	23.900	27.204	30.144	33.687	36.191	43.820
19.337	22.775	25.038	28.412	31.410	35.020	37.566	45.315
20.337	23.858	26.171	29.615	32.671	36.343	38.932	46.797
21.337	24.939	27.301	30.813	33.924	37.659	40.289	48.268
22.337	26.018	28.429	32.007	35.172	38.968	41.636	49.728
23.337	27.096	29.553	33.196	36.415	40.270	42.980	51.179
24.337	28.172	30.675	34.382	37.652	41.566	44.314	52.620
25.336	29.246	31.795	35.563	38.885	42.856	45.642	54.052
26.336	30.319	32.912	36.741	40.113	44.140	46.963	55.476
27.336	31.391	34.027	37.916	41.337	45.419	48.278	56.893
28.336	32.461	35.139	39.087	42.557	46.693	49.588	58.302
29.336	33.530	36.250	40.256	43,773	47.962	50.892	59.703

Source: Table 16.7 is taken from Table IV of Fisher and Yates, *Statistical Tables for Biological, Agricultural and Medical Research,* published by Longman Group Ltd., London (previously published by Oliver and Boyd, Edinburgh), and by permission of the authors and publishers.

lation. If this is the option chosen, there is a possibility of making a Type I error. The probability of making such an error in the long run is equal to .20.

The norms of research are that a probability of .20 is too high to infer that a relationship exists. Most researchers would like no higher than a 5 percent chance of making a Type I error in inferring that a relationship exists in the research population. Therefore it is likely that researchers would decide not to generalize the results in the research sample to the research population. In so doing they would realize that there is some probability that they have made a Type II error. Most scientists are more comfortable with the possibility of making an error by not inferring a relationship that really exists than they are inferring that a relationship exists in the research population when it really does not. Therefore, even though we can describe a relationship in the research sample data in Table 16.4, it would not be appropriate to do so because the decision of statistical inference would likely be that there is no relationship in the research population. The relationship shown in the sample data is considered to be an accident of probability and not a true reflection of the research population.

One-tailed and two-tailed tests

Most sampling distribution tables are constructed so that the probabilities in them refer to the probability of obtaining a given value of the statistic (in our example 3.160) plus the probabilities associated with all statistics higher than that particular one. In other words, the probability of obtaining a chi-square equal to *or greater* than 3.219 (with 2 df) is .20 in our example. In this way each probability is a sum of smaller probabilities and represents one end or "tail" of the sampling distribution. Because of this, sometimes inference tests are referred to as *one-tailed* or *two-tailed* tests. In a one-tailed test the researcher predicts that the research sample statistic will be similar to a value in one tail or end of the appropriate sampling distribution. If the researcher does not really know where to predict the value, the test will likely be a two-tailed test. In such a test the research sample value is expected to be in one or another of the tails (ends) of the appropriate sampling distribution. In both cases the researcher expects the probability to be low so that the null hypothesis can be rejected and the research sample results generalized to the research population. The difference between these two types of tests is somewhat esoteric and when the terms are encountered in research they can usually be ignored for most purposes.

Terminology

The terminology introduced in the earlier part of this chapter can be used to summarize this example of a formal test of statistical significance. The general idea of the illustration, sometimes called the general hypothesis, is that pornography will lead to or cause sexual deviance. This general hypothesis is translated into a research hypothesis: a direct relationship exists between the presence of pornography in a community and the level of sex-related crime. This is translated into a statistical hypothesis that a percentage table of the presence of pornographic movies and the sex crime rate will show a direct relationship. The null hypothesis is that such a percentage table will show no relationship. Using a chi-square test of statistical significance showed computations which resulted in failing to reject the null hypothesis. Therefore we infer that the statistical hypothesis is in error, the research hypothesis is not confirmed, and these data give no support to the general hypothesis. Of course all of these conclusions might be in error and the type of error that might be made in the long run is called a Type II error. The relationship in the research sample data is said to be *not statistically significant.*

The hope of this research was to be able to reject the null hypothesis and support the general hypothesis. If the probabilities were such that that could have been done, then the relationship in the research sample would be said to be *statistically significant at the _____ level.* The blank would be filled in with the probability found in the formal test of significance. However, in our example, even though a relationship existed in the research sample data, it did not generalize to the research population. Therefore the relationship does not exist and any description of the percentage table is meaningless.

5. TESTS WHEN USING MEASURES OF ASSOCIATION

It is common to find statistical hypotheses that say we expect to find a certain kind of association. For example, we might hypothesize that a positive r will be found between two variables. The most common statistics used to test the significance of relationships when using measures of association are t, Z, and F. We will not go into the computation of these statistics, but each has certain assumptions that are required of the data and each is well known in statistical analysis. When reading research articles that utilize these tests you will usually find the value of the statistic along with the level of statistical significance of the research sample data.

For example, if r were being used to analyze a relationship, it would be possible to calculate a Z to test for the statistical significance of such a relationship. If the probability of the calculated Z were high, the r would not be statistically significant. If the probability of the calculated Z were low, the relationship would be statistically significant at that level of probability.

There are additional ways to arrive at statistical significance but the basic logic is the same. The important thing to consider is that any one research sample may not reflect the research population accurately, even if selected properly and even if no other mistakes have been made. Formal tests of significance confront this issue when probability samples are used. Although the procedures do not allow researchers to arrive at positive conclusions, they do allow any decisions about generalization to be associated with the level of risk in making such decisions in the long run. It is felt that a known level of risk, even if in the long run, will increase the likelihood of making wise decisions regarding the generalization of research sample results to the units of the research population.

6. LEVELS OF SIGNIFICANCE: USEFUL OR MEANINGLESS

One of the characteristics of the mathematics involved in formal tests of statistical significance is that the larger the sample size (number of units involved), the easier it is to get a low probability (say .05) and to reject the null hypothesis. If the sample size is even moderate, it is very easy to obtain a statistically significant relationship at the .05 level, or even at the .01 or .001 levels. (This simply means that if you generalize your sample findings to the research population, the chances of making a Type I error in doing so, over the long run, is very small, 5, 1, or .1 percent, respectively.) Because of this and the fact that most social research involves relatively large samples, it is common for researchers to find their relationships to be statistically significant.

In addition to these phenomena, each test involves certain assumptions about the quality of the data in question. One of these assumptions is that data are from a probability sample. There are other more technical assumptions which we have not mentioned in this text that are even more difficult to meet. Many data have difficulty meeting the strict requirements of many of the formal tests of significance. There is much disagreement in the field about how much error is introduced into the analysis of inference when certain of these assumptions are not met. Some statisticians believe that even small violations of any of the necessary assumptions invalidates the procedures. Others believe that the formal tests are still useful if the assumptions are not flagrantly violated. Our view is that replication should provide adequate protection from making a serious error in research conclusions. With replication, errors in one test of significance may not be that crucial.

In any event, many researchers do not completely check out all of the necessary assumptions of formal tests of significance. Also, most samples are large enough so that even a minute relationship will be statistically significant. The question posed in this section is whether these two conditions result in formal tests of significance being nothing more than ritual. In one way we believe that many formal tests of significance are nothing more than ritual and provide no real information about the data. In another way we believe that even if the tests are ritual, they at least provide a set of procedures for determining the existence of a relationship. We believe there is too much focus on statistical significance and more attention should be paid to the nature of the relationship discovered. We further believe that it is important to separate the four aspects of the nature of a relationship in exploring a relationship – existence, form, extent, and precision. By clearly separating each of these aspects and following through on each of them, the most complete picture of data can be obtained.

It is also important to understand that the conclusions about one of the aspects of the nature of a relation have no necessary bearing on the other aspects. Of particular importance in this chapter is that once the existence of a relationship is established, that tells us nothing about the form, extent, or precision (strength in the case of percentage analysis). Each of these aspects must be described independently if the most accurate description of the relationship is to be given. Of course even after the technical description of the relationship has been determined, it is necessary, desirable, and proper to evaluate the importance of the data. The importance of the described relationship will be determined by values, orientations, prejudices, and external events, as well as the customs of the times. The level of statistical significance has nothing to do with the usefulness or value of conclusions reached in the search for relationships.

7. SUMMARY

Whenever research is conducted on samples, the question of generalization must be addressed. Statistical inference is a set of procedures designed to help us make the decision about generalizing research sample results to research populations. There is no way we can be certain about generalization unless we actually make observations in the research population. By definition we have not done this. The key to statistical inference is the comparison of a sample statistic to a sampling distribution of that statistic. The sampling distribution is computed from the comparison population. The probability associated with the research sample statistic is the focus of inference decisions. If the probability of obtaining such a statistic from the comparison population is high, we decide that our research population is like the comparison population. If the probability of obtaining such a statistic from the comparison population is low, we decide that our research population is not like the comparison population. From these decisions we infer that our research population has the same parameter as the one defined in the comparison population, or we infer that the research sample accurately reflects the parameter of our research population. In either case we might be wrong.

If our analysis deals with percentage tables, the most common way to conduct tests of statistical significance is to use chi square. If our analysis used measures of association, t, F, or Z tests are used. We want to find out whether we can trust our research sample results or whether it is likely that they are accidents of probability. No matter which test is used we must make this decision based on the odds. One way to think of tests of significance is that they are tests to see if the relationships found in research samples really "exist," that is, do they probably exist in the research population. If the probabilities are on our side, we have found the goal of our search for relationships.

1. a. How many degrees of freedom are in a 3×2 table? 3×3? 3×4?
   b. Examine Table 16.7. With 4 degrees of freedom (df) what are the chi-square values associated with the probability values of .80, .30, and .05?
   c. Explain what each value means.
   d. Do the chi-square values increase or decrease as the probabilities decrease? Therefore the larger the x^2, the _____ the probability value.

2. Using a 3×5 table, a student obtained a chi-square of 14.36. The level of significance was .05. How many degrees of freedom are in this table? Should the student fail to reject or reject the null hypothesis? Why? What kind of an error is the student trying to avoid?

3. a.

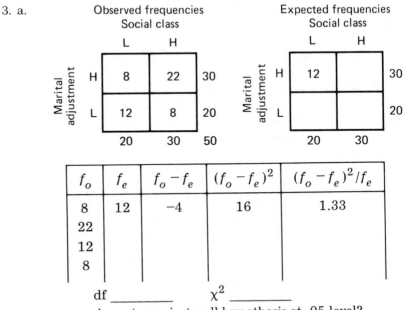

		Observed frequencies Social class			
		L	H		
Marital adjustment	H	8	22	30	
	L	12	8	20	
		20	30	50	

		Expected frequencies Social class		
		L	H	
Marital adjustment	H	12		30
	L			20
		20	30	

f_o	f_e	$f_o - f_e$	$(f_o - f_e)^2$	$(f_o - f_e)^2 / f_e$
8	12	−4	16	1.33
22				
12				
8				

df _____ x^2 _____

Accept or reject null hypothesis at .05 level?

(b)

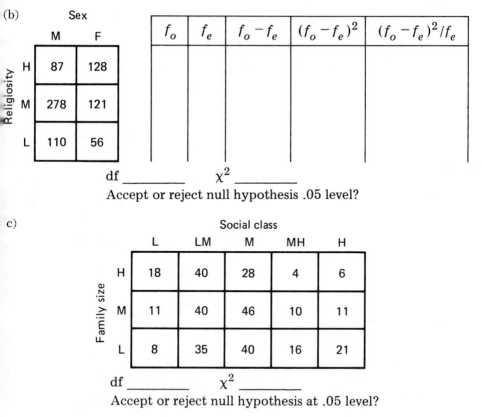

	Sex		f_o	f_e	$f_o - f_e$	$(f_o - f_e)^2$	$(f_o - f_e)^2 / f_e$
	M	F					
H	87	128					
M	278	121					
L	110	56					

Religiosity

df _____ χ^2 _____

Accept or reject null hypothesis .05 level?

c)

Social class

Family size		L	LM	M	MH	H
	H	18	40	28	4	6
	M	11	40	46	10	11
	L	8	35	40	16	21

df _____ χ^2 _____

Accept or reject null hypothesis at .05 level?

4. Assume the tables in Chapter 4, Exercise 2 and Chapter 13, Exercise 2, are from samples. Establish a level of significance. Calculate χ^2. Evaluate the null hypothesis and make a statistical inference.

5. On 25 slips of paper each write low Y, low X; low Y, high X; high Y, low X; and high Y, high X. This gives you a 2 × 2 table with 100 observations of 25 in each cell. The percent distribution is 50 percent in each cell. (The χ^2 equals zero.) Let this be your comparison population. Shuffle your slips of paper and place them in a large bag and mix well in order to randomize. Work in groups and select 25 samples of 20 cases each. Compute the χ^2 for each sample. Make a percentage polygon for the 25 χ^2 scores. Compare the shape of this distribution to the sampling distribution you created in Chapter 15.

6. Explain the logic of statistical inference. Include at least all the following terms: sampling distribution, comparison population, general hypothesis, research hypothesis, statistical hypothesis, null hypothesis, Type I error, Type II error, level of significance.

7. Place Type I error and Type II error into the following table:

	Fail to reject the null hypothesis	Reject the null hypothesis
Actually no relationship in the population		
Actually there is a relationship in the population		

8. What is the connection between the nature of a relationship and statistical significance?

PROJECT

Pretend that all the data you have collected were collected with probability sampling.

1. Complete tests of statistical inference for all bivariate data you have analyzed.

2. You can also use chi-square for multivariate tables. To do so, one option is simply to do a separate chi-square test for each table.

3. Controlling produces smaller numbers in each table. Since chi-square is affected by the size of the table, chi-squares in controlled tables may not be significant simply because of sample size. If there is not a complicated relationship, a single chi-square can be computed for both control tables. This is called a pooled chi-square because the chi-squares from each control table are combined or pooled. To do this, add each table's chi-square value and each table's degrees of freedom.

REFERENCES

BABBIE, E. *The Practice of Social Research.* Belmont, Calif. Wadsworth, 1975.

BLALOCK, H., JR. *Social Statistics,* 2d ed. New York: McGraw-Hill, 1972.

MUELLER, J., SCHUESSLER, K., AND COSTNER, H. *Statistical Reasoning in Sociology,* 2d ed. Boston: Houghton Mifflin, 1970.

SIMON, J. *Basic Research Methods in Social Science.* New York: Random House, 1969.

VI FINISHING TOUCHES

CHAPTER 17
READING AND EVALUATING
RESEARCH PUBLICATIONS

After studying this chapter, students should be able to:

1. List some assumptions that are made about research articles because of the procedures and problems associated with journal publications.

2. Prepare an outline of a research article based on the master outline provided.

3. Write a critique of a research article based on the outline prepared from the master outline.

Critique An evaluation or appraisal of published research.

Draft A manuscript that is written for review by others, not necessarily the final version.

Limitation Some research or analysis procedure or technique that is less desirable than the ideal but that may or may not be the best possible for the situation.

Rejection rate Proportion of manuscript submissions that are rejected.

1. EVALUATING RESEARCH PUBLICATIONS

Before a report of research gets into publication a review process typically takes place. For research articles published in journals (periodicals), the usual procedure is for an author to submit a draft of the article to the editor of the publication. If, after an initial superficial screening, the article appears to be appropriate for the particular journal, the editor will send it to several reviewers. These reviewers are very often faculty members at universities who are known to be knowledgeable in the area to which the article pertains. These reviewers provide the editor with a written evaluation of the article along with their recommendation as to whether or not the editor should publish the article. It is quite common for these reviewers to suggest possible modifications of the article in order to have it meet the standards for publication. The editor must then make a decision about what to tell the author. If the article receives a totally good evaluation from the reviewers, it will very likely be published (perhaps after some revisions). If the editor receives mixed reviews, the author might be asked to do a major revision of the article and to resubmit it for publication. Sometimes, if the reviews are very poor, or if the periodical has too many submitted articles, or if the editor does not feel the article fits in with editorial policy, the author is told that the article has been rejected. Rejection rates vary depending on the particular publication. A rejection rate of over 50 percent is not uncommon. Although some of these rejected research reports eventually get published, this process of review has many implications for the readers of most professional journals.

One major implication is that a number of "experts" have reviewed the work before it gets into print. This means that in their opinion the work was sound enough and well written enough to get into print. This procedure does not guarantee that those articles published are excellent. However, because of the competition for space in most journals, it does probably mean that the articles finally published are among the best received for review. One of the conditions which makes some journals more prestigious than others deals with the level of competition among authors to get their work published. The most prestigious journals are those that have the highest levels of competition for space. Some people think that with increased competition for space, the quality of those articles finally published increases.

There are many critics of the review procedures of some journals. The most cynical of these critics argue that the whole enterprise is a political one in which personal contacts and the prestige of the institutions with which authors are affiliated are the major determinant of which research gets published. Another critical comment very often heard is that anything can get published if it is submitted often enough and to enough different publications. This argument is made largely because there has been such an increase in the number of publications in the past few years. Critics feel that many of these publications do not have very high standards.

We do not really know which situation is closer to the truth. We do know that from time to time articles get published which have such severe limitations that we have questioned whether they should have been published at all. We suspect that other scientists would disagree with our evaluation. The implication from this is that consumers of research journals cannot simply rely on the fact that a study has been published as evidence that the article has merit. Each piece of published material must be evaluated independently. That is, the consumer cannot merely read the abstract or conclusions of an article and completely trust the statements made there. As students, you should now have enough skill, knowledge, and expertise to critically evaluate most research articles. Some statistics will not be familiar to you, but even in these cases a general understanding of multivariate models and the idea of measures of association will provide you with enough background for a sound evaluation.

The typical structure for a research article is that the body of the article is preceded by a brief abstract. The abstract is a summary of the content of the article. It usually emphasizes what the problem or hypotheses were and what the findings are. The body of most articles includes: (1) problem statement and/or statement of hypotheses, (2) review of relevant literature, (3) research methods employed, (4) findings, (5) conclusions, and (6) implications. These sections are very often labeled for ease of reading, but even when they are not this is the usual progression followed. We have found that if students note the title of various sections in an article or remember the general format, it is easier to keep track of what the author(s) is (are) saying. One of the realities of reading research articles is that they are not always written as clearly and as straightforward as might be possible. Therefore, any aids to reading an article are potentially helpful.

Another point which must be stressed is that the tables and figures in an article must be examined. The temptation for most of us is to read around the tables and assume that the author has adequately interpreted them. This is not a very good practice and we strongly urge you to make a point of reading and independently interpreting each table. There are two reasons for this. The first is that sometimes authors do not interpret tables in the same way that you would and your interpretation might be better. The second is that very often only one point is made about a table in the text of an article or only one aspect of the table is emphasized. By examining each table it is often possible to gain more information about the subject than by merely reading the text. This additional information might lead you to view the findings of the article differently or it may suggest alternative interpretations for the data. On rare occasions data in a table that are not reported in the text of an article may directly contradict the data reported. More often, unreported aspects of a table may lead the reader to infer different implications of the study than does the author.

Because there is such competition for the space available in journals, the editors want authors to write articles in as brief a fashion as possible. Because of this it is customary to give authors the benefit of the doubt in terms of certain kinds of omissions. For example, if a standardized test is used in a study, all of the information about such a test may not be given in an article if it can easily be found elsewhere. Definitions of terms are not always provided if the term should be familiar to those reading the journal. You must remember that these journals are mainly for professionals. Therefore readers are expected to be somewhat knowledgeable about the subject matter. This should not discourage you from reading journals, particularly in the social/behavioral sciences, humanities, and education. In these fields most of the terms are somewhat familiar, and with the help of one of the specialized dictionaries that are available for most disciplines, a beginning student should not have too many problems. If you do come across a statistic, term, or phrase you cannot interpret, do not hesitate to ask your instructor. Most instructors would be pleased that you show that much interest in a research article.

In addition to giving the author the benefit of the doubt about certain kinds of omissions, it is assumed that the research has been correctly done and ethically reported. Unless there is some particular reason to question a study, it is assumed that the data are honest and have not been tampered with, the analysis was done correctly without any mechanical errors, the statistics have been correctly calculated, and the author has no information that would contradict or detract from the content of the article. Although there may be exceptions, it is our belief that most researchers are sincere, honest people who adhere to high standards in reporting research. For this reason we seldom question the assumptions mentioned above.

FIGURE 17.1

Master outline for writing a critique of a research article

TITLE OF ARTICLE
Author(s)
Name of Journal, Volume No., Year, Pages

I. General Concerns for Problem Statement

    1. What is the problem or what is the general issue at stake?

II. Conceptualization

    1. What are the major concepts?

    2. How clear are the conceptual definitions?

III. Hypotheses and Theory

    1. Are there clearly stated hypotheses? If yes, what? If not, are they implied?

    2. Is the form, extent, and precision of expected relationships made explicit?

    3. Are the hypotheses designed to add to knowledge? Do they utilize previous science?

    4. Are any of the hypotheses tautological, true by definition, or composed of overlapping concepts?

    5. Is the temporal order between concepts well established?

    6. Does the review of literature allow for meaningful interpretation of results?

IV. Operationalization and Measurement

    1. Is the transition from concepts to indicators adequately explained?

    2. Is the reliability and validity of indicators discussed? If yes, how adequately? If no, does this present a major problem?

    3. Are the indicators and/or manipulations specified and adequately defended?

    4. Are the cutting points and categories reasonable?

V. Design

    1. What is the nature of the research design?

    2. Are the strengths and weaknesses of the design acknowledged?

    3. Could the design have been easily modified to improve the study? If yes, how?

    4. What are the problems of the design in terms of confounding influences and in terms of generalization?

    5. Is the research population clearly defined?

    6. Is the population appropriate for the question and/or hypotheses?

    7. Is the type of sample specified?

    8. Is the sample adequate for the kinds of questions and/or hypotheses the study attempted to investigate? Why? Why not?

VI. Data Gathering and Analysis

    1. Are the data appropriate for the study?

    2. Do the scatterplots, percentage tables, or other statistics reflect the questions asked in the article?

    3. How well are the problems of statistical inference covered?

    4. How clearly are the three characteristics of a relationship

(form, extent, and precision) described where appropriate?

5. Does the analysis appropriately reflect the control variable(s)?
6. Are the control variables properly located in the research design?
7. Are there obvious control variables which should have been included in order to fully understand the main relationship(s)? If yes, what are they?
8. Are the conclusions consistent with the tables and/or figures and statistics presented?
9. Are there alternative conclusions that are consistent with the analysis?

VII. Overall Comments

1. What is your overall impression of the adequacy of the study for exploring the general issue or problem raised by the research?
2. What is your evaluation of the balance between the limitations (weaknesses) of the research and its importance and contribution?

2. PROCEDURES FOR CRITIQUING A RESEARCH ARTICLE

A critique is an evaluation or appraisal of an article. In a critique there is a tendency to be critical and to find fault but it has become custom to appraise the good points of an article as well as the negative points; however the good points typically receive less emphasis. A critique is not a summary of an article and the writer of a critique need not make a point of summarizing every point. In the process of raising questions and making criticisms, the content of the article will become clear to the reader. A critique is basically the end product of asking a series of questions about the research process and providing answers to those questions.

The result of this process is very often a series of negative statements about the article—things that could have been done better or procedures that could have been improved. All research has limitations. That's just the nature of things. Therefore a piece of research cannot be set aside just because it has limitations. If that were done, there would be no research articles. Since this is a reality with which we must live, an evaluation has to be made about the balance between the limitations of a study and the contribution or value of a study. There are probably very few published articles that have so many limitations that the study is totally without merit. However, it is not that unusual to find articles with so many limitations and problems that one questions how certain one can be about the correctness of the conclusions. Unfortunately there are no rules for determining at what point the limitations become so severe that conclusions are questioned. This final decision is a matter of judgment that people must make for themselves. However, in a critique the writer must defend the choice that has been made.

We suggest a three phase procedure for preparing a critique. The first phase is to carefully read the article in question and to take a set of notes as the article is read. The second phase is to complete an outline of the critique based on the notes that have been taken. The third phase is to translate the outline into a narrative critique. The final product should be a well-written series of paragraphs utilizing complete sentences and correct grammar. Figure 17.1 provides our master outline for preparing critiques. By using this format, writing a critique becomes somewhat simplified.

3. ILLUSTRATION OF WRITING A CRITIQUE

In this section we shall go through the three phases of preparing a critique. A real article has been selected from one of the leading sociological journals. A set of notes taken by one of the authors of this text the first time he read the article appears below; the master outline for this article has been completed from these notes. Finally, a narrative critique generated from that outline is presented. It can serve as a model for the product that might be expected from a student at the level of this text. The article selected is comparable in difficulty to many research articles. There are many that would have been simpler, but we believe this article has the degree of difficulty which provides the most meaningful example for writing a critique.

Sample article

The Impact of Sesame Street on Readiness *

Judith Haber Minton

Department of Psychology
Marymount Manhattan College

This study investigated the effects of the first season of Sesame Street on readiness in kindergarten children. Metropolitan Readiness Test (MRT) scores of children from one school district, who had attended kindergarten in the two years prior to the first broadcast season, were compared with the scores of children who had attended kindergarten in 1970, the year of the first season of Sesame Street. In each comparison total MRT scores and the six subtest scores were analyzed separately. There was a significant difference found in favor of the 1970 group on the Alphabet Subtest. There were no significant differences in favor of this group found on any of the other subtests nor on the total test. No significant interaction was found between age and exposure to Sesame Street. A significant interaction effect in favor of the 1970 boys was found on the Alphabet Subtest. The scores of children from an advantaged community were found to be significantly higher on the Alphabet Subtest in 1970 than the Alphabet Subtest scores of similar advantaged groups from previous years. The scores of the kindergarten children of 1970 from the summer Head Start program were not significantly different, on any of the subtests nor on the total test, than the scores of the summer Head Start groups from previous years.

In November 1969 *Sesame Street* began its first broadcast season. The script and format implemented techniques directed toward the instruction of specific educational goals, selected by the staff of the Children's Television Workshop and the many psychologists, sociologists, and educators who served as consultants. It was an initial attempt to teach preschool children, through the medium of broadcast television, in order to learn whether the achievement of these goals was within the potential of television (Reeves, 1970). The medium which trained the young for the frontiers of consumption — to tell the difference between

*This research was originally prepared as a doctoral dissertation at Fordham University. It was accepted in May, 1972. Harry B. Gilbert, Ph.D., was the faculty advisor.

Sociology of Education 1975, Vol. 48 (Spring): 141-151

Pepsi-Cola and Coca-Cola (Riesman, 1961) — was appointed to instruct the young in attainments relevant to academic goals. Universal acclaim accompanied this first season. *Sesame Street* succeeded remarkably in capturing the attention of its preschool audience. One agency, Educational Testing Service, was given the task of assessing the impact of *Sesame Street* on three to five year old children, the target age group. New instruments, determined by the specific content, objectives and goals of the show, were developed and used for that evaluation (Educational Testing Service, 1969).

Because of its innovative nature and mass appeal, *Sesame Street* provided a natural opportunity to research media potential for children. Essentially, a new era had been ushered in for both young children and television. It was entirely possible and probable that many cognitive and personality variables, whether precisely targeted in the original objectives or not, had been affected in the viewers. If television was capable of creating mass population changes, *Sesame Street* provided an opportunity to investigate this capability. There already existed previously standardized measures for young children. By detecting changes in these test scores, some of the effects of *Sesame Street*, whether intended or incidental, could be ascertained.

The Metropolitan Readiness Test (MRT) has been a standardized test for the assessment of readiness skills of beginning school children for many years. A readiness score on the MRT consists of a total of scores from six separate subtests, namely, Word Meaning, Listening, Matching, Alphabet, Numbers, and Copying. As stated in the manual (Hildreth et al., 1969), the subtests include the following:

1. Word Meaning, a 16-item picture vocabulary test.
2. Listening, a 16-item test of ability to comprehend phrases and sentences instead of individual words.
3. Matching, a 14-item test of visual perception involving the recognition of similarities.
4. Alphabet, a 16-item test of ability to recognize lower-case letters of the alphabet.
5. Numbers, a 26-item test of number knowledge.
6. Copying, a 14-item test which measures a combination of visual perception and motor control.

The general instructional goals to which the content of *Sesame Street* was directed were similar to the skills needed for the development of readiness as defined by the authors of the MRT. Among the skills thought necessary for readiness are: comprehension and use of oral language, visual perception and discrimination, richness of verbal concepts, capacity to infer and reason, knowledge of numerical and quantitative relationships (Hildreth, et al., 1969). These attainments both resembled and widened the stated goals of *Sesame Street*, which extended into the categories of symbolic representation, cognitive processes, and understanding of the physical and social environment. Because of the general similarities of the goals of *Sesame Street* and the skills comprising readiness, the present research was conducted on the effects of *Sesame Street*, specifically to determine changes in readiness. The research was concerned with children who were in kindergarten during the first broadcast season. It investigated not only the effects of *Sesame Street* on readiness for a general population but also the relationship of specific variables to these effects. The variables with which this research was concerned were: (1) age, (2) sex, (3) socioeconomic class. For comparison by age, the children were divided into groups of three-month intervals according to their age in May of their kindergarten year. (May is the month during which the MRT was given.) The categorization into socioeconomic class separated "advantaged" and "disadvantaged" children.

Scores on the MRT (Form A) were available for the kindergarten class of 1970, the group which had been exposed to *Sesame Street*, as well as the kindergarten classes of the prior years. The design, therefore, which presented a feasible means for this investigation was a "simulated before-after design" (Kerlinger, 1964). Fox (1969) referred to this design as an evaluative experiment. This design is utilized when there are no data for the group prior to the experimental treatment. Experimental comparison is made on the basis of previous data available from presumably similar groups. Not only were the total groups analyzed for a study of effects on a general population but, because of the quasi-experimental nature of the main design, more precisely matched subgroups were specifically selected for investigation. This was done to allow the elimination of alternative hypotheses arising from the non-random (by year) assignment into groups. A comparison was made between the MRT scores of children in the 1970 kindergarten classes who had had siblings attend kindergarten within three years prior to their own kindergarten entrance (between 1967 and 1969), and the MRT scores of their siblings. This increased the internal validity of the study by eliminating possible biases which may have occurred due to the differential selection, by year, of samples in the main research design. In order to separate systematic variance arising from sibling order (older versus younger sibling), scores of the 1969 kindergarten children who had had siblings attend kindergarten during the three years prior to their entrance (1966 to 1968) were compared to the scores of these siblings. Also included within the study were subsamples of children who entered parochial school from the kindergarten. This represented another attempt to eliminate possible extraneous factors, such as differing family and ethnic variables arising from the quasi-experimental nature of the main design, which, if present, would contaminate the conclusions. If all the findings from these samples proved consistent, more definitive conclusions about the effects of *Sesame Street* on a general population could be reached.

Method

MRT scores of children who had attended kindergarten in 1970, the year of *Sesame Street's* first season, were compared to MRT scores of children who had attended kindergarten in 1968 and 1969. One school district with a heterogeneous population was selected to provide sample groups for the study. This school district encompassed one large urban community and three smaller outside communities. Each year approximately 500 kindergarten children had been enrolled in one school which housed all the kindergarten classes in the district. Children from the entire district were randomly assigned into classes. The parochial school in the area has no kindergarten, so children who go on into parochial school attend kindergarten in the public school. The racial composition of the area consists of a white majority, a small segment of whom are Spanish-speaking, and a black minority. White children come from homes representing a complete continuum from affluence to poverty. The large majority of white children can be characterized as growing up in "advantaged" homes. Although the public assistance population includes both white and black families, the black children of the community can be characterized as nearly all growing up in circumstances labelled "disadvantaged." In the years of this study, the ethnic composition of the total groups was as follows:

		Race		
	N	White	Black	Spanish-speaking
1968	482	431	51	18
1969	495	434	61	9
1970	524	436	88	25

The children who, prior to kindergarten entrance, had attended the summer Head Start program were randomly placed into classes. In both 1968 and 1970 slightly more than half of the children from this program were black. In 1969 more than half were white. Entrance into this program is automatic for welfare. Maximum family income requirement is based on subsistence level for the area, about $4000 a year for a family of four. One community in the district was easily categorized as an advantaged community in terms of income and parental occupation. For the purpose of this research, children from that particular community were considered "advantaged" and children from the summer

Head Start program were considered "disadvantaged," although there were many other advantaged and disadvantaged children attending the kindergarten classes. The parochial school in the community is a Catholic parochial school. All parochial school children in the research samples were white. These children were drawn largely from working-class, middle-income families but all socioeconomic levels were represented.

A questionnaire was constructed in order to ascertain the amount of *Sesame Street* viewed by the 1970 kindergarten classes. In May 1970 children were individually taken out of their classroom by an interviewer and brought into a separate room in the school. Each child was shown a group picture of the *Sesame Street* characters and asked various open-ended questions, i.e. "Where have you seen these people?", "What are their names?", "How often have you watched the show?". The responses, when assessed by group, gave general rather than precise measures of exposure and viewing habits. A few children, who were absent at the time or refused to leave their classroom, were not administered the questionnaire.

MRT scores were analyzed by year, utilizing the 1968, 1969, and 1970 scores for total group and specific subsample assessments. The sibling study was conducted simultaneously. Single and Double Classification Analysis of Variance were the statistical methods used throughout.

Findings

Exposure data revealed that *Sesame Street* was viewed a great deal by children in the 1970 kindergarten classes. Responses for the total group are presented in Table 1. Total group responses by sex are presented in Table 2. Observation reveals that boys and girls reported similar viewing habits. Specific subgroup responses are presented in Table 3. Advantaged children reported that they watched more and, also, they correctly identified more *Sesame Street* characters, than did Head Start children.

Comparison of MRT scores of the total groups revealed a significant difference in favor of the 1970 group on the Alphabet Subtest. There were no significant differences in favor of the 1970 group found on any of the other subtests nor on the total test. Table 4 presents the means and standard deviations for the Alphabet Subtest and total MRT score[1] for the total groups.

Similar results were found on the sibling analyses. A significant difference in favor of the 1970 kindergarten children was found only on the Alphabet Subtest. Table 5 presents the

---

[1] Statistics for other subtests proved too lengthy to include.

TABLE 1

Distribution of Responses
Exposure to *Sesame Street:* Total Group*

Frequency of Viewing *Sesame Street*	N	%
Everyday	266	54
Sometimes	212	43
Never	13	3

Character Identification (grouped by amount of viewing):

Number of characters
identified correctly   Children who responded:
(out of 6 presented):

	Everyday		Sometimes		Never	
	N	%	N	%	N	%
6	94	35	58	27	2	15
5	23	9	33	15	2	15
4	28	11	23	11	0	0
3	32	12	29	14	2	15
2	32	12	27	13	2	15
1	29	10	20	10	0	0
0	2	11	22	10	5	40

*Total N = 491 (33 children were not interviewed)

means and standard deviations for the sibling groups on the Alphabet Subtest and total MRT Score.

Parochial school results were similar to both the total group and sibling analyses. A significant rise in 1970 was found only on the Alphabet Subtest. Table 6 presents the analyses of the Alphabet Subtest and total test scores.

The results of the first three analyses justify the conclusion that there was a general rise in Alphabet Subtest scores in 1970. This was first evidenced in the total group analysis and then

TABLE 2

Distribution of Responses
Exposure to *Sesame Street:* Total Group by Sex

Frequency of viewing *Sesame Street*	Boys (Total N = 250)		Girls (Total N = 241)	
	N	%	N	%
Everyday	133	53	132	55
Sometimes	113	45	100	41
Never	4	2	9	4

TABLE 3

Distribution of Responses
Exposure to *Sesame Street:* Specific Subgroups

Frequency of viewing *Sesame Street*	Parochial School (Total N = 83)		Advantaged Children (Total N = 33)		Head Start Children (Total N = 94)	
	N	%	N	%	N	%
Everyday	40	48	22	67	53	56
Sometimes	40	48	10	30	39	42
Never	3	3	1	3	2	2
Number of characters identified correctly						
6	28	34	19	58	6	7
5	12	14	3	9	8	8
4	8	10	3	9	9	10
3	10	12	3	9	14	15
2	11	13	3	9	21	22
1	9	11	2	6	16	17
0	5	6	0	0	20	21

TABLE 4
Alphabet Subtest and Total MRT Score Means and Standard
Deviations for the Total Groups.

Year	N	Alphabet Subtest Means	SD	Total MRT Score Means	SD
1968	482	9.00	4.39	61.36	16.36
1969	495	8.49	4.31	60.44	16.58
1970	524	10.45	4.63	62.08	18.50
		$(F = 26.52, p < .001)$		$(F = 1.15)$	

TABLE 5

Alphabet Subtest and Total MRT Score Means and Standard
Deviations for the Sibling Groups

Group	N	Alphabet Subtest Means	SD	Total MRT Score Means	SD
1969	132	8.63	4.10	62.38	15.43
1969 siblings	132	8.27	4.49	58.08	17.13
1970	122	10.42	4.48	62.81	18.09
1970 siblings	122	8.00	4.14	58.77	16.13
		(Year X sibling $F = 7.19, p < .01$)		(Year X sibling $F = .01$)	

TABLE 6
Parochial School Children

		Alphabet Subtest		Total MRT Score	
Year	N	Means	SD	Means	SD
1968	68	9.30	3.96	63.82	13.46
1969	84	8.88	3.78	64.17	12.21
1970	87	11.32	3.96	66.50	16.14
		(F = 9.28, p<.001)		(F = .86)	

supported in the sibling and parochial school analyses. The improvement in Alphabet Subtest scores can be considered attributable to instruction via television from *Sesame Street*. No other effect appeared either on the total test or any other subtest. Upon examination, scores for other subtests and for the total test were not found to be significantly different from those of previous years.

No significant interaction was found between age and exposure to *Sesame Street*. When the scores were grouped by sex, a significant interaction effect in favor of boys was found in 1970 on the Alphabet Subtest. In groups separated socioeconomically, the means of children from the advantaged community were found to be significantly higher on the Alphabet Subtest than the means from prior years. The means of kindergarten children of 1970 from the summer Head Start program were not significantly different, on any of the subtests nor on the total test, from the means of summer Head Start groups of previous years.

Table 7 presents the means and standard deviations for the Alphabet Subtest and the total MRT score for the total groups separated by sex. Table 8 presents the means and standard deviations of advantaged community children. Table 9 presents these statistics for the Head Start children. Maximum score on the Alphabet Subtest is 16. The Standard Deviation for 1970 advantaged community children, reported in Table 8, was found to be significantly smaller than the standard deviation of previous years (F max = 2.3, p < .01) suggesting a ceiling effect. In examining the actual data, it was found that more than one-quarter of advantaged community children scored at the maximum possible score. It can be concluded that exposure to *Sesame Street* had improved Alphabet Subtest scores for advantaged children.

Conclusions about the effects on the Alphabet Subtest, according to sex, are less positive. An interaction effect in 1970 was found in favor of the boys but if adjusted to accord with the

TABLE 7

Alphabet Subtest and Total MRT Means and Standard Deviations
for the Total Groups Separated by Sex

Year	Alphabet Subtest						Total MRT Score					
	Boys			Girls			Boys			Girls		
	N	Means	SD	Means	SD	N	Means	SD	N	N	Means	SD
1968	245	8.33	4.44	9.69	4.23	237	59.79	17.14	245	237	62.98	15.34
1969	258	7.96	4.29	9.07	4.25	237	59.18	16.60	258	237	61.82	16.46
1970	267	10.55	4.55	10.55	4.70	257	62.55	18.45	267	257	61.59	18.54

(Year X Sex F = 4.46, p<.05)   (Year X Sex F = 2.13)

489

TABLE 8

Advantaged Community Children

Year	N	Alphabet Subtest		Total MRT Score	
		Means	SD	Means	SD
1968	37	11.13	4.27	69.94	12.44
1969	36	10.38	3.80	70.41	13.10
1970	34	13.58	2.80	76.05	12.02
		(F = 6.90, p<.01)		(F = 2.49)	

number of statistical analyses performed in the research, an $F = 4.46$ becomes nonsignificant.

No effects of *Sesame Street* on the MRT were detected for Head Start children. Definitive conclusions about the effects of *Sesame Street* on any particular skills or the general readiness of disadvantaged children should await further research. One plausible explanation, arising from this research, was that disadvantaged children viewed *Sesame Street* less than advantaged children.

Implications

Sesame Street did not appear to improve total readiness nor particular skills involved in the separate subtests, aside from the Alphabet Subtest. By the rise in Alphabet Subtest scores for kindergarten children, *Sesame Street* did prove itself a capable teacher of letter recognition. (Letter recognition is the only performance required on the Alphabet Subtest.) Improvement in letter recognition did not appear to aid children on the Matching Subtest which requires, for many of the items, matching of groups of letters of the alphabet.

Other findings for the Alphabet Subtest are suggestive. *Sesame Street* appeared to be differentially effective according to

TABLE 9

Head Start Children

Year	N	Alphabet Subtest		Total MRT Score	
		Means	SD	Means	SD
1968	70	6.40	3.38	46.04	14.82
1969	85	6.43	3.98	51.41	16.11
1970	99	6.95	4.32	48.06	16.35
		(F = .55)		(F = 2.27)	

sex and socioeconomic class. Ball and Bogatz (1970), after evaluating the first year of *Sesame Street*, had hypothesized that television can reduce the educational gap separating advantaged and disadvantaged children before they enter first grade. The results reported herein do not confirm those expectations. Tentatively it may be stated that on the MRT, although the gap between the sexes appeared to close, it appeared to widen between social class.

More research and exploration is needed to understand both the effects of television and the interaction of these effects with particular variables. Communication theory has emphasized the individuality of effects from exposure to mass media (Klapper, 1960). This study also suggests a lack of uniformity of effect from exposure to *Sesame Street*. This demonstrates that the study of mass media effects, if it is to be meaningful, must not only focus on effects but also on individual variables which may be critically related to these effects.

References

Ball, S. and G. Bogatz.
    1970   A summary of the major findings in "The first year of *Sesame Street*: an evaluation." Princeton: Educational Testing Service.
Educational Testing Service.
    1969   Evaluating Sesame Street: A Proposal for the Children's Television Workshop, Princeton, N.J.
Fox, D.
    1969   The Research Process in Education, New York: Holt Rinehart.
Hildreth, G., Griffiths, N. and N. McGauvran.
    1964   Manual of directions, Metropolitan Readiness Test (Forms A & B). New York: Harcourt, Brace.
Kerlinger, F.
    1964   Foundations of Behavioral Research. New York: Harcourt, Brace.
Klapper, J.
    1960   The Effects of Mass Communication. Glencoe: Free Press.
Reeves, B.
    1970   The first year of *Sesame Street*: the formative research. New York: Children's Television Workshop.

492

Notes on sample article

The previous article should be read before examining the notes presented below. As an exercise you might try taking a set of notes as you read the article. You can compare your notes to the example notes. They should not differ too much. In order to facilitate following the article with the notes, the page or section of the article on which the note has been made appears in parentheses at the left of the notes.

Page or section	Notes
(abstract)	• study about the effect of first season of *Sesame Street* (SS)
	• sample was kindergarten (k) kids from one school district
	• Metropolitan Readiness Test (MRT) used as dependent variable
	• '68 and '69 kids (w/o SS) compared to '70 kids (w/SS)
	• total MRT and six subtests analyzed separately
	• kids differed only on the Alphabet Subtest (AS)
	• no interaction between age and exposure to SS
	• sex matters, in favor of boys
	• advantaged kids gained more than disadvantaged
(142)	• general ? = can TV have an effect on people?
	• assertion = goals of SS similar to those tested by MRT (seems o.k.)
(143)	• control variables = age, sex, socioeconomic status (SES)
	• age categorized in 3 month intervals as of May year entered k
	• MRT given in May also
	• SES dichotomized (two categories), no reason or technique given
	• design = simulated before-after design, an evaluative experiment with simulated control group being '68 and '69 k kids
	• no random assignment (by year)
	• only kids who had siblings in k from '68–'69 were used and those kids were compared only to their siblings
	• assertion = this procedure increased internal validity by reducing possible bias due to differential selection by year

- scores on MRT of '69 kids who had siblings in k from '66–'68 were compared (doesn't say how this comparison was used)
- additional variable was whether kids entered parochial school after k

(144)
- assertion = parochial school proxy variable for family and ethnic variables

(Method)
- '70, '69, & '68 k kids from one school district used
- one school used for all k classes, kids randomly assigned to rooms
- community of district: white majority
                         small Spanish speaking segment
                         black minority
                         mostly advantaged kids but full range of SES
                         most all blacks disadvantaged
- racial distribution of '68–'70 kids given for information
- kids for one richer community in district were labeled "advantaged" (no evidence)

(145)
- kids from Head Start program labeled "disadvantaged" (no evidence)
- all parochial kids white
- open-ended questions about amount of SS viewed were individually, privately asked of all respondents, no coding information given

(Findings)
(Table 1)
- viewing habits of kids given, 54% every day, 43% sometimes
- number of SS characters identified varies w/amount of viewing, distributions pretty spread out

(Table 2)
- viewing habits by sex, no difference

(Table 3)
- advantaged kids watched more than Head Start kids and they watched more than parochial kids

(Table 4)
- means on MRT of groups compared, they differed only for AS (no other data given) statistical inference test used the F test

(Table 5)
- when '70 kids had younger siblings they scored higher on AS, F test used; when '69 kids had siblings they did not score higher (F used)

(Table 6)
- for parochial subgroup of kids: '70 kids were higher than '68 or '69 kids only on the AS (F test used)

494

(146)	• conclusion = general rise in '70 AS of MRT (o.k. from Table 4, 10.45 compared to 8.49 & 9.00, maximum = 16)
(148)	• claim = because of sibling & parochial kids analysis, improvement can be attributed to *SS* viewing (? this)
(Table 7)	• more of an increase for '70 boys than '70 girls, only on AS (girls actually decreased on total MRT score)
(Table 8)	• only for kids labeled "advantaged": significant increase for '70 kids on AS only (F test used)
(Table 9)	• only for kids from Head Start: no significant difference for '70 kids (F test used)
(148)	• note: advantaged kids already scoring high on AS in '68 & '69; call this a ceiling effect, i.e., can't get any higher than 16
(148)	• conclusion = *SS* has an effect on advantaged kids on AS
(148–9)	• conclusion about controlling for sex is unclear
(150)	• conclusion = no effect of *SS* for Head Start kids, note—maybe this is because they watched it less***
(Implications)	
(150)	• *SS* seemed to be able to increase letter recognition
(151)	• increase seems to depend on sex and SES
(151)	• gap between advantaged & disadvantaged was widened instead of decreased by *SS*
(151)	• call for more research on effects of mass media

Outline for sample critique

The notes in the previous section will be used to answer the questions in the master outline provided in Figure 17.1. The following outline corresponds to that master for the sample article.

I.   General Concerns or Problems Statement:
   1. The general issue is whether television can have an impact on a population. The specific example for this research is whether *Sesame Street* has had an impact on the cognitive functioning of children getting ready for school.
II. Conceptualization:
   1. The independent variable is the presence of *Sesame Street* on television. The dependent variable is performance on the Metropolitan Readiness Test (MRT). Control variables are age, sex, and SES. Two other variables were also considered: whether subjects had older siblings who just completed kin-

dergarten and whether or not they later enrolled in a parochial school.

2. The independent variable was clearly defined as an event.
The information provided on the MRT was limited. It appeared that this was a well-established standardized test to
measure cognitive skills. There was no conceptual definition
of "readiness." Age and sex needed no conceptual definition.
SES is such a well-established concept that no definition
seemed needed. The existence of siblings and whether kids
went on to parochial school were events which were clear.

III. Hypotheses and Theory:

1. There were no stated hypotheses, but it was clear that the ex-
pectation was that *Sesame Street* would help kids get ready
for kindergarten.

2. No expectations about any relationships were given.

3. The research seemed to stand alone, but the general question
is important and particularly the question about *Sesame
Street* because it was designed to have an impact on kids.

4. There was no problem with hypotheses because none
existed. The concepts were distinct.

5. The temporal order of events and variables seemed obvious
except for the concept of readiness. However, this is more a
problem of design than temporal order.

6. There was no review of literature and there really was no
theory or framework into which to place the findings.

IV. Operationalization and Measurement:

1. Explication of indicators presented no problems for many of
the variables. However, so little information was given on
the MRT that we have to accept that this test is appropriate
for readiness.

It seemed unusual to use enrollment in Head Start and residence in a community as a measure of SES. It seems this
could have been better. Finally, the claim that whether or
not kids eventually went to a parochial school could be used
as an indicator of family and ethnic variables seems totally
unfounded.

2. Reliability and validity are never discussed. This does not
seem to present any major problem with the exception of the
MRT. If this is a widely used standardized measure, then it
seems that at least reliability measures should be available.

3. Specification of indicators was clear.

4. Two problems with categories exist. The first has to do with
supposedly representing the SES extremes with the indicators used. Perhaps even more important is how the researchers decided about the amount of time that kids

watched *Sesame Street*. While the procedure of interviews seemed fine, more information about coding and categorization is needed.

V. Design:

1. The design is called an evaluative experiment by the researcher and it is a quasiexperimental design where the experimental group is measured only with a posttest and the stimulated control group is measured at a previous time. Apparently this previous measure is assumed to be the posttest for the "control" group. It also seems that it is assumed that both groups would have been equivalent if they had been given a pretest.

2. Although the strengths and weaknesses were not explicitly mentioned, the research did try to account for some of the problems. They did compare kids who had older siblings to try to show that this was not the cause of any change in readiness. The techniques used for this comparison were not very clear.

3. Since the students were measured on the degree to which they watched *Sesame Street*, it seems that a simple analysis would have been done to see if those kids who watched more often were more ready for school. As it was, only the total group of 1970 kids was compared to the total group of 1969 and 1968 kids, without controlling for how much the 1970 kids watched *Sesame Street*. It seems unrealistic to analyze the effects of a television show if the kids did not watch it. Only about half of the kids watched it a great deal by the researcher's measurement.

4. The design is not experimental so there could be any number of confounding influences. Perhaps the most serious potential problem is sample selection; it is a nonprobability sample. There is no way to use formal tests of significance to make the decision about generalization to other students. There was very little information provided about the children that would enable one to generalize the findings to other similar children by any other technique.

5. The research population is not defined, but it seems clear that it was meant to be all prekindergarten children.

6. If that was the population, it seems appropriate to the question.

7. The type of sample was clearly given as an availablity or purposive sample. It was one school district somewhere with no information given as to why this particular district was used.

8. Although the sample may have been appropriate, it would be desirable to know more about the characteristics of the children.

VI. Data Gathering and Analysis:

1. The data are generally appropriate, but it seems the analysis should have used a different measure of SES and then examined all of the children using this other measure as a control variable. In addition, it does not seem appropriate to use the attendance at a parochial school for the purpose of "controlling" for a student's family and ethnic background.

2. The tables seem generally appropriate except that there was no analysis using the amount of viewing as an independent or as a control variable. In addition, tests of significance using F are not appropriate since the sample was not a random one.

3. Formal tests of inference were conducted but they are not legitimate for purposes of generalization due to the type of sample.

4. Only differences between the average score on the MRT were used to demonstrate relationships. This is fine, but since the F tests do not seem appropriate, there does not seem to be any guidelines for determining when a difference really exists. Even accepting the use of F as a decision tool, only the existence of a relationship was discussed. The other characteristics of relationships were not even mentioned.

5. Control variables are handled appropriately.

6. The control variables are appropriately placed in the analysis with the exception of amount of viewing time.

7. As we stated before, it seems the amount of viewing should have been a variable in the analysis instead of just being given for information.

8. There are no apparent errors in the interpretation of the tables.

9. The variation in the average standardized test scores in one school district from year to year may have many causes. In the total group the difference between the average score in 1970 and 1968 was only .72 points. Even on the alphabet subtest the difference for the same years was only 1.45. To claim that this difference is real and not a result of sampling or some other variable seems very tenuous. The conclusion about the effect of sex is uncertain, and any conclusion about SES seems tenuous because of the way that SES was operationalized. This seems particularly important since the author claims that the gap between the advantaged and disadvantaged may have been widened by *Sesame Street*. This type of charge is very serious and perhaps should not be made on such evidence.

VII. Overall Comments:

1. The question is very important, but the way the study was

designed and analyzed seems to be inadequate. With minor alterations the analysis would have made much more sense, and with a better measure of SES a more sound conclusion could have been reached. The parochial variable seems out of place. In addition, a clearer distinction should have been made between the mass media having a general societal effect versus the effect of a program on individual viewers. These two separate questions were not clearly separated either in theory or in analysis.

2. In balance, it seemed like the researcher had some interesting data that could have been handled in a much more productive fashion. The major limitations were in how the data were handled as opposed to any severe overall problem. The question is surely important and the information given is important, but it seems that the manner of analysis makes it almost impossible to clearly interpret the relationship between viewing television and cognitive functioning. The data were there and some important control variables existed, but the analysis did not allow us to see how the major independent variable and the control variables fit together in any particular multivariate model.

Sample critique

Using these notes, a narrative critique must now be prepared. It is not necessary to include in the critique every point from the outline. It is important to provide the major points and conclusions.

Critique of
"The Impact of *Sesame Street* on Readiness"
by Judith Haber Minton

in *Sociology of Education*, 48, No. 2, 1975, 141–151

The general issue of whether the mass media can have an impact on people's cognitive functioning is explored. Kindergarten children are examined in one school district to see if the first year of *Sesame Street* increased their readiness for school. Readiness was measured with the Metropolitan Readiness Test (MRT) and age, sex, and SES were controlled. In addition, separate analyses were done on children who previously had siblings in kindergarten and children who later entered the parochial school system. There were no stated hypotheses, nor was there any review of the literature which allowed for integrating the findings of this study with previous research. Some minor problems of measurement are worth noting. Not all children were categorized for the SES variable. Rather, those children who had been in Head Start were labeled disadvantaged, while those coming from one of the better neighborhoods in the district were labeled advantaged. In addition, there was insufficient information provided about how children were assigned to different categories of how often they viewed *Sesame Street*.

The design of the study was an "evaluative experiment" in which kindergarten children prior to *Sesame Street* were used as the quasicontrol group. In this type of design, viewing *Sesame Street* would have been the experimental variable. Because not all children viewed with the same regularity, it would seem that a quasi-multiple X design could have been used, but the author chose to treat all the children who were in kindergarten the first year of *Sesame Street* as being in one "experimental" group. This procedure did not seem to make much sense since a measure of viewing habits was available. The purpose of providing a separate analysis for children who had older siblings in kindergarten the year before *Sesame Street* seemed unimportant for the research, as did the analysis for whether or not the children went on to parochial school after kindergarten. Because the sample was a nonprobability one, no formal tests of significance were appropriate for purposes of generalization of results. However, the author chose to use significance tests to decide whether a difference in readiness existed between the different kindergarten children before and after *Sesame Street*. No mention was made about the importance of the amount of difference in readiness.

Using tests of significance as a decision tool resulted in claiming an increase in readiness as a result of *Sesame Street* for the total group of children only in the Alphabet Subtest (AS) of the MRT. The AS is one of six subtests in the MRT and is determined by letter recognition. The average increase in this subtest was equal to 1.45 letters. Controlling for sex was inconclusive according to the author but the boys seemed to be favored. Controlling for SES showed that the advantaged children increased in readiness (only on the AS) while the disadvantaged children did not. This widened the gap between these SES extremes. The manner in which this analysis was done seems questionable. Coming to such a potentially important conclusion on the basis of these data seems unwise.

The major problem with this research was the design utilized for the analysis. Rather than treating the whole kindergarten class of 1970 as one quasiexperimental group, it would have been desirable to separate the students into groups depending on how often they viewed *Sesame Street*. It does not make much sense to claim the program did not have an impact for those students who did not watch it. Indeed all of the conclusions reached in the article could have been due to different viewing habits. Because of this, no conclusion about the control variables is warranted. If the author wished to make a comment on the general impact of a societal event such as a television program, the approach of the research should have been different. This research could provide some valuable information about the impact of *Sesame Street* on individual children by modifying the type of analysis conducted.

4. A NOTE ON STYLE

The master outline provided in this chapter is offered only as a guide. There are many other potentially useful outlines, depending on the purpose of the critique. In addition, every article is a little different. The suggested outline might not fit all articles. The important thing is that the writer of a critique must be aware of all the elements that make for sound research, and this knowledge must be put to use in evaluating the worth of a particular study. The impersonal writing style is most often preferred when writing a critique. This means that words like I, you, and we should be avoided. The critique is usually written as though a detached third party was evaluating a study and anonymously reporting it to a group.

Each person will likely see different things in an article which seem important. Thus there is probably no such thing as the "best" critique. Although objectivity is important in evaluating particular procedures and practices, subjective evaluation will partially determine what aspects of the research are focused on, and stressed in, a critique. This will vary depending on the training, interests, and values of the writer, the purpose of the critique, and the nature of the study.

5. SUMMARY

All research has limitations and shortcomings. The task for the critical consumer of research results is to strike a balance between the limits of a study and the value of the findings. Each phase of the research can be examined and evaluated. Design, sampling, measurement, and analysis should be appraised with a critical eye. Conclusions should be examined to see if they flow from the data. The data should be creatively appraised to see if alternative conclusions could also be drawn from the same data. Finally, the consumer must make some sense out of how a particular study fits in with the rest of the literature on a particular topic. Hopefully, the writer will adequately review the relevant literature and attempt to integrate the research with previous science. Nevertheless it is the consumer who must ultimately put each study in the appropriate framework within the search for relationships.

1. Select one of the articles you examined in Chapter 3, Exercise 5; in Chapter 5, Exercise 4; or one assigned by your instructor. Critique the article according to the outline in this chapter.

2. Based on what you have learned in this course and on your experience with Exercise 1, do you feel that the outline is adequate? If not, what other questions would you raise?

1. Critique each project you have done according to the master outline in this chapter.
2. Are there criticisms you would make that are not in the outline?

MINTON, J. The Impact of Sesame Street on Readiness." *Sociology of Education*, 48, Spring 1975, 141–151.

CHAPTER 18
THE NEVER-ENDING PROCESS

OBJECTIVES

After studying this chapter, students should be able to:

1. Discuss the various components of the search for relationships, including hypotheses, propositions, theories, laws, and principles.

2. Discuss the role of luck, imagination, and hard work in the research process.

Academic disciplines   Various subjects and/or departments in a college or university, such as sociology, political science, economics, history, and so on.

Hypotheses   Specific statements about the nature of a relationship between variables which are tested through the use of operational definitions.

Laws or principles   Theories about which we have a great deal of confidence and which are no longer actively questioned.

Mature disciplines   Disciplines that have well-established principles and laws.

Propositions   Statements about the nature of relationships between concepts.

Serendipitous finding   Accidental or unanticipated research findings.

Theories   Sets of interrelated propositions and/or hypotheses.

Young disciplines   Disciplines that have relatively few principles or laws.

1. WHAT'S IT ALL ABOUT?

At times it may appear that the social sciences produce an almost endless supply of studies which have limited scope and questionable applicability to everyday life and the problems of mankind. Individuals may from time to time get "lost" in the morass of doing research, obtaining funding, and trying to get research results published. However, if the time were taken to reflect upon the whole business some overall sense could be made of it all. Once students become able to critique research reports and to apply some of the knowledge presented in this text it is easy to lose sight of what it's all about.

All academic disciplines which propose to adhere to the principles of the scientific method are attempting to achieve the same goal. By using scientific procedures they are searching for relationships between variables. Our choice for the title of this book stems from this reality. Although all disciplines are searching for relationships, some are more advanced and sophisticated than others. Sophistication in science is judged by how certain people are about the relationships which are thought to exist and the complexity of the phenomena being explained by these relationships.

Certainty about relationships progresses through several stages ranging from very uncertain to very certain. One element of the scientific belief is that every fact, no matter how certain, is always open to question. The uncertainty principle of science holds that any conclusion about a relationship can be questioned if new scientific information warrants it.

For practical purposes people become more certain about relationships between variables as the number of research studies demonstrating the relationship increases. Replication is the basic tool science uses to gain confidence in the existence of a particular relationship. The original idea about any relationship might come from scientists involved in a particular discipline or they may come from the general culture. These original ideas may stem from common sense, intuition, or some general observation. For example, the relationship between two masses that we call gravity resulted from people observing that objects always fall to the ground. From such general notions about relationships it is often possible to develop testable hypotheses.

Hypotheses are more specific about the nature of a relationship between variables because operational definitions of variables must be provided so that a scientific test can be conducted. At some point in time a sufficient number of different tests of hypotheses using different indicators have been conducted that scientists have enough confidence to feel that the various indicators used in these tests have represented the concepts they were supposed to represent. At this point a proposition exists. A proposition is a statement about the nature of a relationship between concepts. A proposition is often a more abstract version of an hypotheses.

When more than one hypothesis and/or proposition concerning the same phenomena exists it may be possible to combine them in some interrelated fashion. If they can be combined, it might be possible to explain more complex phenomena than if taken separately. When it is possible to combine them in this way the result is a theory. Theories are interrelated sets of propositions and/or hypotheses. When theories have had sufficient documentation so that each part of the theory is very certain, the final goal of scientific disciplines has been reached. When scientists become very confident about theories they are said to be "laws" or "principles." For all practical purposes, scientific laws are theories which people no longer actively question.

Figure 18.1 shows the relationship between the different components in the search for relationships. Notice that the more concrete elements are used to "build" the more abstract components. This is illustrative of the "building block" notion of science. In addition, the amount of evidence necessary to say that each component has been documented and demonstrated is related in the same fashion. That is, it takes more documentation (proof) to be confident that a law or principle is accurate than it does to be confident that a hypothesis is correct. Of course even if one has a great deal of confidence in any element of the search for relationship, that confidence is always open to question with the introduction of new scientific evidence.

There are no rules which determine at what point enough hypoth-

FIGURE 18.1
Components in the search for relationships

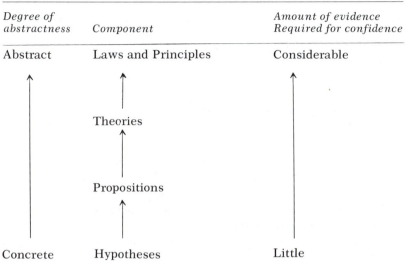

Degree of abstractness	Component	Amount of evidence Required for confidence
Abstract	Laws and Principles	Considerable
	Theories	
	Propositions	
Concrete	Hypotheses	Little

eses have been tested so that a proposition can be claimed. Nor are there any procedures for determining at what point a theory "becomes" a law. These seem to be a matter of consensus which develops over time. It is probably safe to say that the longer a discipline (such as chemistry, psychology, nursing, etc) has been actively engaged in science, the more laws can be claimed. Although time is not the only variable, it seems to be a crucial one. The search for relationships is ultimately the search for laws and principles. Each discipline's development can be traced through the various stages described above. A mature discipline will have well-established principles and laws, while a young discipline will have relatively few laws or principles. However, both the mature and young disciplines will have new ideas, intuitions, and hypotheses that are currently being developed and worked on.

Individual disposition and personality are important determinants of how comfortable one is with disciplines at various stages of development. Some may see involvement in young disciplines as a waste of their time which will probably not "pay off." Others may see the same kind of involvement as providing the ultimate type of challenge to their intellect and imagination. Some may approach mature disciplines with enthusiasm because of the solid base of principles available. Others may see the more mature disciplines as being dull because they have already discovered so many laws and principles. There is room for all different perspectives and orientations in the various disciplines using scientific methods. For each person dedicated to contributing to knowledge, the answer to "What is it all about?" may be a little different. For every consumer of research results, the basic answer is that as disciplines demonstrate laws and principles, the world becomes less of a mystery, and a sense of mastery is obtained. It is a never-ending process because there is always more to be known. The supply of unknowns and uncertainty seem endless at this point in time, particularly in the behavioral/social sciences and education.

2. LUCK, IMAGINATION, AND HARD WORK

With all of the stress that we have put on exactness, precision, and carefulness in the research process, it may appear that only very perfect people could be good scientists. This of course is not true. Doing science is a very human enterprise. Luck, imagination, and plain old hard work are sometimes more important than the most careful planning and training.

Luck plays a role in many ways. It may be more or less luck that a particular sample of respondents send back questionnaires that have been mailed to them. It may be luck that an investigator hits it off with the head of a group in which participant observation is proposed. Even the findings of a particular research project may be a matter of luck. In fact, there is even a term for conclusions that are unanticipated and that have not been planned for. They are called *serendipitous findings*. Some of the most crucial scientific discoveries have been accidental, or serendipitous findings. Although there is no substitute for planning and sound research designs, luck is a most valuable asset, if you can get it.

Imagination is perhaps the major characteristic that separates really effective scientists and "run-of-the-mill" scientists. Although it may be possible to teach and learn imagination and ingenuity, it seems clear that they are not taught in most schools or colleges. However, the capacity to conceptualize reality in unique ways, to see things a little differently, to have more insight, to have a fresh approach, and to be truly creative are traits that are indeed valuable to the scientist. We think that, for most people, imagination increases with experience. It is largely a matter of going beyond the things that are taught to us and incorporating our unique personality and experiences together with the insights and imagination of those who have gone before us. There is a cliche that goes, "there's nothing new under the sun," but while that may be true, there are many different ways to look at the same old thing, and these differences make all the difference in the world.

Perhaps the place where imagination is most crucial to researchers is in the interplay between theory and research. We have not made a clear separation of the importance of theory, methodology, or statistics in this text because we feel any clear distinction is not a real one. To truly understand the search for relationships, theory, methods, and analysis must be viewed as an integrated whole. This is not always easy. It is not always easy to determine which hypothesis should be tested to most adequately support a particular theoretical viewpoint. It is not necessarily a straightforward decision about which analysis would be most effective for a particular set of data. Even more difficult is the job of taking various bits and pieces of research and making some theoretical sense out of them. In many cases there is one hypothesis here and another proposition there that supposedly are concerned with that same phenomena. They may appear to be so distinct that it is difficult to see how they fit together. Often results from some studies seem to contradict results from other research. The ability to rise above individual pieces of research and to "see" how they can be combined into useful and accurate theories is a very valuable ability.

Even with luck and imagination, hard work plays an important role in the life of most researchers. There are two features of the scientific method that dictate this. The first is the cumulative nature of science, and the second is the stress on replication. In order to carry on a truly cumulative science, it is necessary for researchers to know what previous science has produced. For most disciplines this means that a vast body of literature must be approached and mastered with some degree of excellence. Previous science must be integrated and understood so that present science can be used to build future knowledge. Replication dictates that studies must be conducted many times in many different places under many different circumstances. The search for relationships is indeed a never-ending process.

INDEX

516